THE

Revolutiona

IN THE

Hackensack Valley

THE
Revolutionary War
IN THE
Hackensack Valley

The Jersey Dutch and
the Neutral Ground, 1775–1783

Adrian C. Leiby

Rutgers University Press

NEW BRUNSWICK, NEW JERSEY

Second printing, revised edition, 1992. This reprint is supported by a grant from the New Jersey Historical Commission.

Library of Congress Catalog Card Number: 60-15807
ISBN 0-8135-0898-3 (pbk)

Map, pages x and 1, copyright © 1976 Bergen County
Board of Chosen Freeholders
Permission to reproduce it is gratefully acknowledged

The staffs of the William L. Clements Library of the University of Michigan, the New York Public Library, the Library of Congress, the Huntington Library, the Colonial Williamsburg Research Center, the New-York, New Jersey, Pennsylvania and Massachusetts Historical Societies, the Libraries of Union College, Rutgers University and Princeton University have been most patient in helping me to gather the small items that make up local history. In fact, everyone to whom I have turned has been helpful. Interested friends, particularly members of the Bergen County Historical Round Table, have suggested material, have helped with my research and the collection and preparation of illustrations; several have been kind enough to review drafts. My sister, Catherine Marchbank, has been particularly helpful. My wife has worked for years on every aspect of the book. I am deeply grateful to all of them.

ADRIAN C. LEIBY

Preface

Overshadowed on two sides by her great and historically minded neighbors, New Jersey, though aptly called the cockpit of the Revolution, has seemed to Jerseymen to have had little notice of its place in that dramatic war, and what notice it has had has centered largely upon the Battle of Trenton and the short campaign that preceded and followed it, with perhaps some further notice of the Battle of Monmouth. The student of the war will know the names of John Witherspoon, Elias Boudinot and the Rev. James Caldwell, and the role that the men of middle Jersey played in the war, and perhaps something of the Jersey Quakers of the country to the south.

New Jersey north of Newark also had a dramatic part in the Revolution.

Its people were Jersey Dutch, cut off in many ways from their English countrymen in the rest of the colony. These men, only recently come to full estate in British colonial politics and more comfortable talking plain Dutch than the language of the royal capital at Perth Amboy, spent the months before Lexington, like their English neighbors, in quarreling among themselves over the Intolerable Acts and the other issues of the day, never, we may be sure, realizing that it was to be the Jersey Dutch farmer, not the New Englander or the Virginia planter, who would find himself surrounded by contending armies when war came.

The British moved the theater of war from New England to New York in the summer of 1776. Thereafter Bergen County Dutchmen lived in the dread neutral ground, forced, as few other colonists were ever forced, to make a final choice between loyalty to American principles and loyalty to the British crown. It will not be surprising to see that their posture in the earlier religious wars largely affected their decisions.

The actual invasion of New Jersey came through the Jersey Dutch country, where General Howe had laid careful plans for the help of Tory Dutchmen. His pilots and guides on the invasion were Jersey Dutchmen and he raised a regiment of Tories in Bergen County to support his conquest of New Jersey. The patriots of Bergen County, overwhelmed by British power and Tory neighbors, kept up a stiff-necked resistance in a seemingly lost cause during the early weeks of British occupation, and when the fortunes of war drove the British back to their bastion on Manhattan Island, settled down to a five-year war of neighbors in the neutral ground.

The patriot militiaman farmed during the day and did sentinel duty at night, never knowing when Van Buskirk's Greencoats would raid his farm and carry him and his sons off to Sugar House Prison, never knowing whose home and barns had next been marked for the torch. British spies and Highland gang leaders used the Dutch countryside as a highroad to the thin American lines; American scouting parties and raiders occupied the Dutch villages in their turn. British foraging expeditions of thousands of men too often reaped the harvests that Bergen County farmers had sown, for the American forces in the Hudson Highlands were seldom able to help their friends between the lines. Indeed, more than once the Americans were forced to strip Bergen County farms for their own existence, and many a Jersey Dutchman who had risked his life for years in the patriot militia found that to a foraging Continental he was but another damned Tory.

Since neither the British nor the Americans were ever willing to risk a general engagement in the country between the Highlands and New York City, no great battle was fought there, but there were a dozen minor engagements. The Continental ferries at Dobbs Ferry and Kings Ferry put the northern part of the Hackensack valley on the main military routes from New England to the south; and the American army spent much of the war there. André's trial and execution at Tappan was one dramatic episode in the country between the two armies. James Moody and other British irregulars and spies made it their special province.

The source materials are many: Sir Henry Clinton's headquarters papers, the correspondence to and from General Washington, the papers of Generals Wayne, Heath, McDougall, Lamb, George Clinton, the papers of Dirck Romeyn—the Princeton graduate who served as minister of the two principal Dutch Reformed churches in the Hackensack valley during the war and then went on to found Union College; the letters of William Livingston, a few scattered letters of John Fell, member of the Continental Congress, the pension applications of Revolutionary War soldiers, André's journal and the journals of other British officers, to mention the principal sources. The Amsterdam correspondence of the Dutch Reformed churches gives many details of the religious war in the Hackensack valley, the excellent Dutch church records show the religious affiliations of the contending parties, and a number of polemical religious pamphlets confirm the story of the intimate connection between the Whig-Tory conflict and the conflict of the Dutch Reformed religious factions.

That the story of the Bergen County Dutchman in the war has not been told in any detail is itself a matter of interest, one that again touches on the Dutch Reformed church conflicts of a century and a half ago. The Hackensack valley patriot, embittered by hatred of his old neighbors among the Tories, found it hard to join his more enlightened (and less injured) fellow countrymen in forgiving and forgetting Toryism. In good part because of past Tory conflicts, the Dutchmen who made up the backbone of the patriot forces in Bergen County finally seceded from the Dutch Reformed church, cutting themselves off from even that connection with their old enemies.

Never adept at publicizing themselves, the earnest patriots of the Hackensack valley drew themselves in from their neighbors more and more as Tories were brought into the councils of church and state, content to tell their children and their children's children of the heroic days of 1776 and to let their enemies paint themselves as they wished. The last generation that heard these things from their fathers has now almost passed away; the story of patriot Bergen County Dutchmen and their neighbors in Orange County must now be got from dry books and records that tell the story only to those who knew its outlines before they began their search.

ADRIAN C. LEIBY

June, 1961
Bergenfield, New Jersey

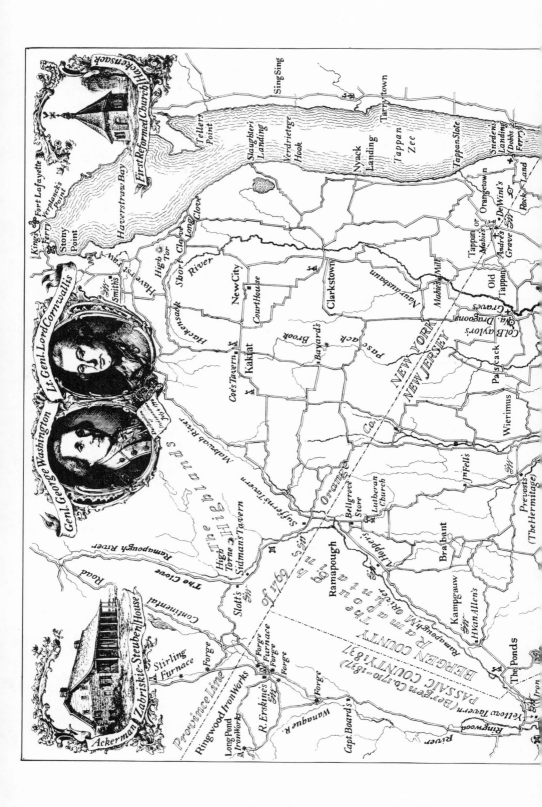

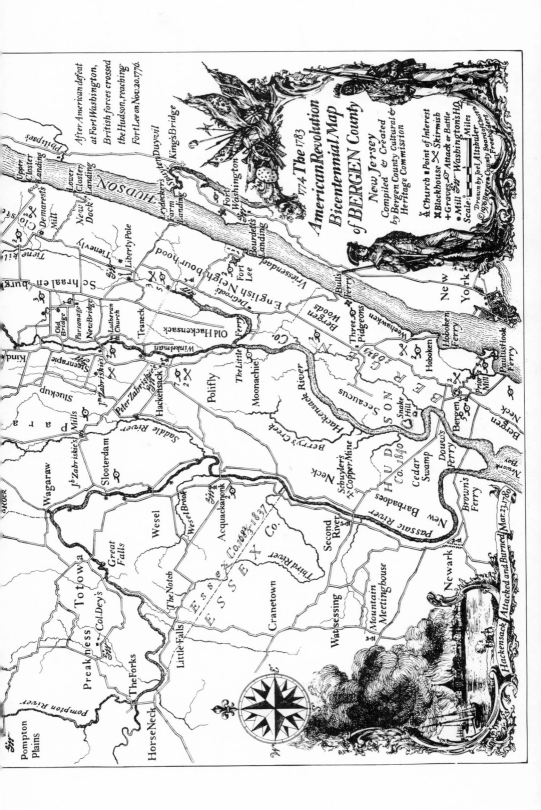

1774 The 1783

American Revolution
Bicentennial Map
of BERGEN County

New Jersey
Compiled & Created
by Bergen County Cultural &
Heritage Commission

⚜ Church ▪ Point of Interest
✗ Blockhouse ⚔ Skirmish
✝ Graves ⚔ Attack or Battle
✳ Mill ⚜ Washington's H.Q.
Scale: |————| Miles

Drawn by Joel Altshuler
©1976 Bergen County Board of Chosen Freeholders

After American defeat
at Fort Washington,
British forces crossed
the Hudson, reaching
Fort Lee on Nov. 20, 1776.

HUDSON

Philipse's
Upper Closter Landing
Clo ste
Demarest's Mill
Lower Closter Landing
New Closter Dock Landing
Tiene Kill
Tienevly
Liberty Pole
Schraalenburg
Dydecker's Snyten Duyvil Farm
King's Bridge
Fort Washington

Fort Lee

Bourdett's Landing

"Vriessendael"

English Neighbourhood

"Dericks Ferry"

Old Hackensack

Bergen Woods

Three Pidgeons

Weehawken

Bull's Ferry

Hoboken Ferry

New York

Paulus Hook Ferry

Prior's Mill

Hoboken

Parsonage
Old Bridge
New Bridge
Lutheran Church
Teaneck
Winkelman

Sherrerape's
Kind
Slaughr
Jm Zabriskie's
Peter Zabriskie's
Hackensack

The Little Ferry

Polifly

Moonachie

Hackensack River

Berry's Creek

Secaucus

Snake Hill

Bergen

HUDSON Co. 1840

Cedar Swamp

Dow's Ferry

Brown's Ferry

Bergen Neck

Newour Bay

P a r a

Saddle River

Jb Zabriskie's Mills

Wagaraw

Slooterdam

Wesel

Wesel Brook

Acquackanonk

Schuyler's Copper Mine

New Barbadoes Neck

Second River

Passaic River

Newark

Essex Co. 1682-1837

ESSEX Co.

Third River

Craneton

Wat-sessing

Mountain Meetinghouse

Totowa

Great Falls

Col. Dey's

The Notch

Little Falls

Preakness

The Forks

Horse Neck

Pompton River
Pompton Plains

Hackensack Attacked and Burned Mar. 23, 1780

THE
Revolutionary War
IN THE
Hackensack Valley

THE rocky heights of Jersey, wrote Washington Irving, "spring up like everlasting walls, reaching from the waves into the heavens . . . fashioned, if traditions may be believed, in times long past, by the mighty spirit Manetho, to protect his favorite abodes from the unhallowed eyes of mortals." Sheer rock cliffs, often three hundred or more feet in height, they make a western wall for the majestic Hudson from a point just above Hoboken to the boundary between New York and New Jersey, meeting there the first of the Hudson Highlands whose rugged mountains dominate the river for miles to the north, mountains which, in colonial times, made the country immediately to the west of the Hudson almost impassable to travelers.

Behind the Palisades, in the Hackensack valley between the Hudson and the mountains to the north and west, Dutch colonists found a country far closer to their hearts than stony Manhattan, a country whose fertile land and tidewater streams had drawn Dutch planters from the earliest days. By the 1770's the prosperity of this country was a byword in British America. Admiring colonists of every province agreed that Dutch New Jersey was the very garden spot of America and that hard-working Jersey Dutchmen and their good vrouws had made it so. "The towns," wrote one pleased traveler, "are inhabited chiefly by Dutch people. The churches and dwelling houses are built mostly of rough stone, one story high. There is a peculiar neatness in the appearance of their dwellings, having an airy piazza, supported by pillars in front and their kitchens connected at the ends in the form of wings. The land is remarkably level, the soil fertile and being generally advantageously cultivated, the people appear to enjoy ease and happy competence. The furniture in their houses is of the most ordinary kind, and such as might be supposed to accord with the fashions of the day of Queen Anne. They despise the superfluities of life and are ambitious to appear always neat and cleanly, and never to complain of an empty purse." [1]

When the Revolution came, New York City was to be, for all but the first year of war, the chief citadel of the British invader. In the mountains to the north and west there were to be thousands of armed Continentals, waiting and maneuvering for a chance to drive the hated redcoats into the sea. On Manhattan, Britain was to gather the largest army it had ever assembled in America, an army that lashed out at the surrounding rebel forces when it could, now and then striking out somewhere else in an effort to draw the American forces from the protecting mountains, but never forgetting that New York City was the great target and prize of the Continental army and that the Hudson Highlands were its base.

As a result the country between the armies became the dread neutral ground, a neutral ground which, save for those earnest Jersey Dutch patriots who would not let danger drive them from their homes, was to be far too perilous for any but desperate men, hungry for vengeance, gold or glory.

This is chiefly the story of that neutral ground and the Jersey Dutchmen who lived there during the long years of war. It treats, like an earlier story of New Netherlands, "of times long past, over which the twilight of uncertainty has already thrown its shadows and the night of forgetfulness is about to descend forever," almost, like that story, "trembling on the lips of narrative old age, and day by day dropping piecemeal into the tomb."

It treats for the most part of the valley of the Hackensack, a river that rises near High Tor, on the very edge of the Hudson Highlands, from which it flows down through New York and New Jersey, never more than a few miles west of the Palisades of the Hudson, and finally empties into Newark Bay, perhaps thirty-five miles from its source. The Hackensack valley was small, as valleys went in the colonies, a mere country vale compared with the mighty valleys of the Connecticut, the Hudson, the Delaware, and the Potomac; but Continental troops from all the colonies were to know it well before Yorktown and peace.

Its principal town was Hackensack, or New Barbadoes,[2] the county

---

[1] Thacher 156. For abbreviations see Key to Short Titles preceding Index.
[2] The country between the lower Hackensack and Passaic Rivers was called New Barbadoes by its early patentees, John Berry and others, some of whom had been born on the Island of Barbados. "Hackensack" originally referred only to the country between the Hudson and the Hackensack Rivers.

seat of Bergen County, about five miles west of the Hudson and perhaps ten miles north of the Paulus Hook ferry, a short afternoon's journey from the center of New York City.

A traveler to Hackensack in the 1770's would board the ferry in New York at the foot of Cortlandt Street at about noon. There "boats properly constructed, as well for the conveniency of passengers, as for the carrying over of horses and carriages . . . constantly [plied] from one shore to the other, the distance between the two places being about three-quarters of a mile." [3] Paulus Hook, the landing on the west shore, was an island surrounded by tidal lowlands, connected with the mainland by a long causeway. Though more than a mile distant from the nearest village, Paulus Hook boasted a tavern, Verdine Ellsworth's, and a racetrack which had been established there in 1754 by the New Jersey proprietor of the ferry, Cornelius Van Vorst.[4]

Van Vorst's substantial farmhouse stood along the highway a short distance inland. A man of considerable means, known as "Fatty" in the town of Bergen, he was full of fun and practical jokes, though the establishment of the ferry against the opposition of powerful interests testified to his determination, and he frequently represented the township of Bergen in the county government at Hackensack.[5]

Once landed at Paulus Hook, the traveler boarded one of the several stages which made the trip to Hackensack, perhaps Verdine Ellsworth's own "new caravan," whose horses, he advertised, were "very quiet and caravan new," or perhaps the Flying Machine of Andrew Van Buskirk, who announced that he had furnished himself with "four good horses and a very commodious machine for the better accommodation of passengers," or perhaps the stage of Isaac Vanderbeek, who prided himself upon a "new Wagon, very genteely furnished, sufficient to convey fourteen or fifteen passengers with comfort," or perhaps that of Peter Demarest, whose wagon was "new and well fitted, with curtains," and whose horses, he said, were "in excellent heart." Ownership of the stages changed from time to time. The driver might also have been John Berdan, Samuel Demarest, or Adam Boyd. Certainly the traveling public did not suffer from lack of competition between stagedrivers; on the contrary, from time to time the competition became extremely acrimonious. The fare to Hackensack was 2 shillings 6 pence per passenger.[6]

The stages left Ellsworth's tavern at two in the afternoon, arriving

3   24 NJA 389. In this, and in most other quotations, spelling, capitalization and punctuation have been modernized. See also Winfield, Hudson County, 242, etc.
4   Winfield, Hudson County, 433; 26 NJA 463; 27 NJA 233; 28 NJA 527.
5   Winfield, Hudson County, 433; MJFBC 41 and passim.
6   26 NJA 274, 339; 31 NJA 127, 216; 28 NJA 461, 507; 26 NJA 289; 31 NJA 133, 173; 28 NJA 150, 475.

The Van Vorst homestead near Paulus Hook ferry.
Winfield, Hudson County.

at Campbell's Tavern or Watson's Tavern at Hackensack in the late afternoon, and then going on to the New Bridge, about a mile to the north, after a half-hour stop in the center of the village.[7]

The road from Paulus Hook to Hackensack passed first over the causeway to the mainland, then ran about two miles to the northwest, over the hill that made the backbone of the Bergen Neck peninsula, until it reached the edge of the great salt meadows, where it met the road running due north from Bergen. A short distance beyond the junction, the stages stopped briefly to refresh the travelers at the celebrated Three Pidgeons Inn, then proceeded north along the edge of the meadows to lower English Neighborhood, where the road to Hackensack turned due west toward the Little Ferry over the Hackensack River, the north and south road continuing on to Liberty Pole, Tenafly, Closter and Tappan.

The country along the road from the Three Pidgeons Inn to the junction of the Little Ferry road was rocky and heavily wooded. North and west of the junction the road, as one writer described it, ran for "forty miles through a fine, level country, thick-settled, the whole way one small town."[8] It is hard to believe that the colonies had any more

[7] See 31 NJA 133, 173, 216; 26 NJA 274.
[8] 28 NJA 70, 71. The writer was defending the road from the aspersions of "one Mr. A. Z., who would give us to understand that he thinks he is one Big John, of great consequence in the world, and that he can regulate the world to his own mind; if so we have reason to fear a blow from his awful hand." Mr. A. Z. had called

attractive and prosperous farms than those which lined the road on both sides as it went through the rolling country of the Hackensack valley. The farm at the junction of Hackensack River and Overpeck Creek, occupied by Captain Josiah Banks, the ferryman at Little Ferry, was an example:

> . . . a pleasant and well-situated farm or plantation on Hackensack River and Overpeck Creek . . . containing . . . five-hundred acres, by much the greatest part is a valuable meadow; about eighty acres cleared, which produces timothy grass and clover and bears good crops of rye, Indian corn, oats and other grain; on the other part of the meadow may be cut two hundred tons of good fresh grass. All the produce of the farm may be transported to New York, Hackensack or elsewhere. The boats from Hackensack daily pass by. It affords excellent pasture in the spring and summer seasons, and is very commodious for raising of cattle. There is on it a good house, kitchen and barn, placed so advantageously on an eminence as to command a view of the whole farm.[9]

As the road continued to the west of the river, one farm joined another until the traveler reached the green in the village of Hackensack, three miles above the Little Ferry.

The village green, facing the road on the east, made a charming picture of Jersey Dutch tranquillity and prosperity: on the north side at the far end stood the sandstone Dutch church with its short white steeple and brass Dutch weathercock. Next to it was the small stone courthouse of Bergen County. Nearby was Archibald Campbell's inn and the frame house formerly occupied by Daniel Isaac Brown, clerk of court and surrogate.[10] At the head of the green, on the north side, stood the Zabriskie mansion, a large building of dressed stone with walls three feet thick, built in 1751 by Judge Peter Zabriskie and finished in fine paneling and Dutch tiled fireplaces.[11] On the opposite side of the green was a three-acre plot owned by Samuel Benson Leydecker, "the whole surrounded by a very handsome pole fence." Facing the post road on the west was a large stone house, not yet fully completed, and behind it a new grist mill on a very pretty small brook, which had been sufficiently deepened down to the river so that boats of as much as eight tons' burden could come up to the side of the mill. A small house faced the green. Leydecker

---

the road "crooked [and] unfrequented"; the writer found it "nearer by several miles on the west side than on the east . . . a much livelier road, which everyone will confirm that ever rid both roads."

9   28 NJA 456.
10   NJHC 82; 28 NJA 405.
11   Bailey 333.

described the property, with some pride, as "universally allowed to be the finest place for the bigness" in or near Hackensack.[12]

Just beyond the green was the new academy building,[13] where students from far and near were brought from elementary subjects to courses so advanced that the College of New Jersey at Princeton had been granting degrees to some of its graduates without further study.[14]

The village proper continued for perhaps a mile north along the post road, with large and small houses and tradesmen's places of business interspersed. One of the houses was the residence of John Romeyn, about three quarters of a mile north of the church and courthouse. The Romeyn property contained about forty-four acres. "Part is, and in one season most may be made, the best of English mowing ground; on said farm is a dwelling house, five rooms on a floor, with a large orchard of about two hundred trees of the best of apples and other fruit, etc. Its natural situation is supposed to exceed any in those parts and would be very agreeable for a retired life or advantageous for trade of any sort, having a spacious, clean, bold shore, the only one for near six miles on the west side of Hackensack River, a good grist mill adjoining along said river and the two main country roads meeting near the premises." [15]

The houses in the village and elsewhere in the Hackensack valley were chiefly one-story sandstone structures, capped, in the case of the older houses and the older wings of new houses, by a high-peaked roof with curved, overhanging eaves and, in the case of the newer houses, by a low gambrel roof, of heavy wood shingles, made of two slopes, the top slope short and fairly flat and the lower slope long and less flat, running out to a heavy overhanging porch roof. The Dutch doors were equally distinctive, massively built and strengthened on the inside by a second set of boards, usually divided in the center, the upper half opening separately. The rooms on the lower floor were often finished in the most careful cabinetwork, generally in a sturdy, neat style that Jersey Dutchmen had brought to perfection.[16] The red barns behind the houses were

[12]   27 NJA 24. Another Samuel Benson Leydecker property is described at 26 NJA 49.
[13]   See 25 NJA 347; 28 NJA 151. The academy building is pictured in Koehler, Three Hundred Years.
[14]   Solomon Froeligh, Stephen Goetschius, and John M. Goetschius were three who appear to have received degrees from the College of New Jersey immediately upon their graduation from the Hackensack Academy. 29 NJA 53, 498. Stephen Goetschius biography, Banner of Truth, Vol. 5, p. 212, Aug. 1, 1870.
[15]   28 NJA 195. The property evidently lay on the river just south of Terhune's Mills, modern Anderson Street, Hackensack.
[16]   Bailey 20, etc. Early Dutch Houses in New Jersey, G. G. Wendehock, The White Pine Series, Vol. XI, No. 3.

large and seldom empty, and the fat, well-fed Dutch horses and the heavy Dutch farm wagons were a byword in the colonies.

Looking down on the village from the hill about a half mile to the west, it was easy to agree that Hackensack was one of the pleasantest places in the middle colonies, its thirty or more houses stretched out along the meandering stream and clean salt meadow for a mile or so and, in the distance, the high hills bounding the Hudson.

"The inhabitants . . . ," a British officer said of the Jersey Dutch country after the war had started, "are chiefly the posterity of the first settlers . . . who were Dutch, and they seem to retain their principles, industry, frugality and assiduous perseverance in the means of striving." "Before the war," he went on, "they must have been in an affluent and happy state, especially their farmers." [17]

The men and women who had made the Bergen County countryside the admiration of its neighbors spoke Jersey Dutch most of the time and English when they had to, just as many New Yorkers then did. They listened to Dutch sermons on Sunday and gave their children Dutch names, and the women and children wore clothes having more than a hint of Holland in their style. Certainly no one could have confused the Dutch country in and around Hackensack with the English settlements in middle Jersey or the Pennsylvania German settlements in the neighboring province to the south. Yet the good people of the Hackensack valley, proud as they were of their Dutch foundations, had perhaps abandoned the ways of the Old World more fully than any of the other colonists in British America, for the men and women of the Dutch settlements of New York and New Jersey, after a hundred years of British rule, had long since lost even their emotional ties with Holland without wholly taking up Britain as a model and guide for their pattern of living. Seen in the perspective of two centuries, Dutch New Jersey was a marvelous example of the New World casting off the ways of the Old; [18] at the time it seemed principally to show how bright hopes and hard work could transform a wilderness.

To a casual question, a resident of Hackensack would have given the casual answer that he was Holland Dutch. Pressed for details, many would have added, with some pride, that their own first American ancestors were not Dutch, but French or Scotch or Walloon or German or English or Polish. The Jersey Dutchman of pure Holland Dutch stock was rare if not nonexistent in Bergen County; indeed he was seldom found elsewhere in New York or New Jersey.

In the case of the Hackensack valley, almost all of its people were

[17]   2 Anburey 160.
[18]   See e.g. Wertenbaker, Middle Colonies, 29, etc.

descended from men and women who had come to America a century or more before. As a result, most of them, whatever their names, were related by blood or marriage to almost everyone else among their neighbors, to the point, in fact, where a common name no longer indicated close family ties. Indeed, as elsewhere, many families who bore the same name had been at variance over one thing or another for decades. In Tappan almost everyone was either a Blauvelt or a Haring or related to the Blauvelts or the Harings. In nearby Schraalenburgh everyone, whatever his name, seemed to be related to the Demarest family. The families in the village of Hackensack could not be so narrowly marked, but its people too were closely tied together by family connections. Among the names most frequently encountered in the central part of the county were Ackerman, Banta, Berdan, Berry, Blauvelt, Bogert, Brinkerhoff, Brouwer, Christie, Cole, Dey, DeBaun, DeGroot, Demarest, Doremus, Durie, Earl, Haring, Hopper, Kipp, Kuyper, Leydecker, Lozier, Paulison, Peek, Post, Prevost, Ryerson, Romeyn, Terhune, Van Blarcom, Van Buskirk, Vanderbeek, Van Giesen, Van Houten, Van Horn, Van Norden, Van Saun, Van Voorhees, Van Winkle, Varick, Vreeland, Westervelt, Wortendyke, and Zabriskie.[19]

If one had been asked to name the leading citizen of Hackensack just before the Revolution, several men would have come to mind, but perhaps the one who came closest to such a distinction was Peter Zabriskie, who occupied the fine house at the northwest corner of the village green. His father was John Zabriskie, Sr., the merchant of New Bridge.[20]

[19] Hackensack Church Records. In an effort to avoid confusion, Dutch names, which were often spelled differently, have been regularized: thus "Herring," though entirely correct, has been made "Haring"; "Romine" has been made "Romeyn," etc. Few of the sources are consistent as to the name of any single man and it would be difficult if not impossible to be sure what spelling the person himself used, if indeed that was always the same. The celebrated Abraham Van Buskirk dropped the "Van" from his name either before or when he joined the British, though others continued to call him Van Buskirk.

[20] The first Zabriskie had come to America from Poland by way of Holland in 1662, apparently a member of the Protestant branch of the distinguished Polish family of Sobieska. No better example of the complicated national background of Hackensack valley Dutchmen could be found than Peter Zabriskie. His mother was Margariete Durie, whose ancestors were French Huguenots who had settled in the Hackensack valley in the 1670's. His wife was Martina Varick, a member of one of the most distinguished families in Dutch New York and New Jersey, a lady whose great-grandfather, Rudolf Varick, had come to America from Germany as a minister of the Dutch Reformed Church and had found great difficulty in adjusting to the unrestrained ways of America. See MRC 870; ERNY passim. One of Zabriskie's grandmothers, a Vanderlinde, was of Dutch stock and his aunts and uncles included Terhunes, Mabies, and Hoppers, all of them distinguished Dutch families of the county. GHHB 49; Bailey 333; Zabriskie Genealogy No. 319. Among his wife's relatives were some of the

Zabriskie had served many times as one of the justices of Bergen County and before that as a member of its Board of Chosen Freeholders,[21] and often handled important matters for the Board of Proprietors of the Eastern Division of New Jersey.[22]

His father's store and docks at New Bridge were among the most impressive in the province. He and his father and his brother John, compeers of the Jersey ironmasters and of the men on the Governor's council, rightly saw themselves at the very forefront of the great things that were happening in the middle colonies in the 1770's.[23] Like the majority of the leaders of Dutch New Jersey, Zabriskie was a deeply religious man. He served often as a deacon or an elder in the Dutch Reformed Church of his brother-in-law, Domine Goetschius, and was a zealous adherent of that church during many bitter church controversies.[24] In 1771 he had been a leading figure in the conferences that led to the celebrated reunification of the American Dutch Reformed Church, conferences which incidentally had brought peace to the church as a whole but none to the warring churches of the Hackensack valley.[25] He was a founder and trustee of Queens College, another storm center of Dutch church controversy.[26] Wealthy, of strong convictions in both religion and politics, he was to have a prominent place in Bergen County's activities during the Revolutionary War.

When war came, patriots from other colonies, at first repelled by his hard "Dutch" name, soon vied with each other to show their respect; when the war was over Tories who had hated him for his politics were only too happy to praise his high character.[27]

Peter Zabriskie was not alone in these virtues. The Jersey Dutch country bred many such men; indeed, all the American colonies bred more than their share: steadfast men, often unknown beyond the small circles of their own communities, who bore much of the heat and burden of the next decade of war. It was well that it did; as it turned out, the Hackensack valley and the colonies were to have need of many Peter Zabriskies.

---

wealthy Dey family and others of local fame. Her brother, John Varick, was a prominent merchant of the county and her nephew, young Richard Varick, was now reading law in the office of one of New York City's leading attorneys.
21 MJFBC passim.
22 III Mins. Board of Proprietors 399, 401.
23 NJA passim.
24 ERNY 3549, 3617, 3627, 3635, 3690, 3693, 4086, 4211, 4212, 4243, 4246.
25 ERNY 4210, 4212, 4243, 4246.
26 25 NJA 343, 344, 345.
27 See e.g. LYT NYPL "William Bayard."

2

★

I T W A S Peter Zabriskie who took the lead when the first meeting was called in Bergen County to join in pushing forward plans for a Continental Congress; and Zabriskie acted as chairman when the meeting convened in the courthouse in Hackensack on Saturday, June 25, 1774.[1]

The people of New Jersey had been called "the most Easie and Happy People of any Collony in North America." [2] To a stranger set down in Bergen County on that June day in 1774, Hackensack must have seemed the very picture of tranquillity. The good vrouws of the town, in their copious skirts and white aprons, had scrubbed its stoops until the light-blue paint fairly shone against the red sandstone walls of its houses. The green of the leaves of early summer and the blue of the June sky set off the white steeple of the church on the green, its brass weathercock bravely facing every breeze, the church below seemingly Dutch Calvinism cast in stone. The pungent salt meadows to the east of the green ended at the deep little tidal river a quarter of a mile away, where a pettiauger, her sails flapping idly, lay at the new dock at the foot of the village street.

No Hackensack valley Dutchman would have been deceived by this tranquil scene, however, once he had observed the number of farm wagons at the hitching posts in front of the courthouse, and the tense and solemn Dutch farmers, black-coated in their Sunday best, crowded outside the courthouse door on that Saturday afternoon. Nor would any

[1]   29 NJA 411.
[2]   L. H. Gipson, Coming of the Revolution (New York 1954) 134.

stranger whose curiosity moved him to look in at the courthouse meeting ever again accept the picture, sometimes credited even then, of placid Dutchmen content to whiff their pipes and leave politics to their English neighbors.

The meeting named Theunis Dey, John Demarest, Peter Zabriskie, Cornelius Van Vorst, and John Zabriskie, Jr., to meet at New Brunswick to elect delegates to the Continental Congress,[3] and adopted a set of resolutions on the issues of the day.

This meeting [the resolutions read] being deeply affected with the calamitous condition of the inhabitants of Boston, and considering the alarming tendency of the acts of the British Parliament for the purpose of raising revenue in America, resolves that this meeting thinks it their greatest happiness to live under the government of the illustrious house of Hanover and that they will steadfastly and uniformly bear true and faithful allegiance to His Majesty, King George III, in the enjoyment of their constitutional rights and privileges, that they conceive it to be their privilege to be taxed only by their own consent, and that they will heartily unite with others in the colony to elect delegates to attend a general congress from the several provinces of America to try to determine upon some effectual emendment for obtaining a repeal of the acts of Parliament, which appear to the meeting so evidently calculated to destroy that mutual harmony and dependence between Great Britain and her colonies, which are the basis and support of both.[4]

Most of the good people of Bergen County supported the resolutions. There were others, small in number but large in determination, who would sign no resolutions and join in no votes against Parliament or the Tory ministry, who said in plain Dutch that they did not belong to Massachusetts Bay and did not care what went on there; who had no use for the Sons of Liberty who ruled the New York streets or for their friends in the Hackensack valley. New Jersey was to hear more of them.

The delegates were among the leading citizens of the county. The rankest Tory would not have dared to call them revolutionaries: Van Vorst was the proprietor of the Paulus Hook ferry; Theunis Dey was a large landholder of Preakness, west of the Passaic River, owner of an elegant Georgian plantation house and numerous slaves, and known and respected far beyond the boundaries of New Jersey;[5] John Demarest,

3   29 NJA 411.
4   29 NJA 411.
5   Preakness Church History; Bailey 504. He was also associated with the coetus group of the Dutch Reformed Church in the controversial founding of Queens College. ERNY 4086.

conservative in politics, had represented the county in the Provincial Assembly for many years; [6] Peter Zabriskie has been mentioned; and John Zabriskie, Jr., his brother, who had taken over the store and landings at New Bridge upon his father's death, was fast becoming as prominent among merchants as his distinguished father had been. Even men who doubted the wisdom of the resolutions and of any continental congress could agree that Bergen County's participation was in the hands of solid citizens. Perhaps a few ardent Whigs could have wished, privately, for a somewhat less conservative group, but they had carried the day in approving a patriot congress and they were in no mood to complain about the delegates. Patriots had every reason to congratulate themselves upon their afternoon's work when the meeting hall finally emptied and the last countryman went home that Saturday afternoon.

[6] Demarest Genealogy 40, 41. In this rare instance the scholarly Demarest Genealogy appears to be wrong. John Demarest, No. 63, a coetus adherent, was not the John Demarest who served in the Assembly, where he had opposed the coetus church charter, the assemblyman probably being the conferentie adherent, No. 87.

The problem of identical names greatly complicates any effort to be specific about individuals in Dutch New Jersey. There may well have been a half dozen John Demarests in the Hackensack valley just before the Revolution. There were at least four adult David Demarests in Hackensack Precinct alone, four or more Wiert Bantas in and around Hackensack, four or more Johannes Blauvelts in Tappan, and three or more Abraham Mabies in Tappan. The task is somewhat simplified by excellent Dutch church records and by several carefully prepared genealogies, notably the Banta, Blauvelt, Demarest and Westervelt family histories.

An additional help is the fact that the middle name or middle initial of a Jersey Dutchman almost always indicated the name of his father. When the Dutch settled New Netherlands they were still using the archaic patronymic naming system, by which a child had no surname, but took, besides his baptismal name, the first name of his father, generally with the addition of *sen, s, z,* or *zoon,* meaning son, say Martin Paulisen—Martin, son of Paulus. He might add, say, "Van Norden" (from Norden), or "Brouwer" (brewer) or "Ten Eyck" ("at the oak") after his name in a legal paper if necessary to distinguish himself from some other possible Martin Paulisen. Children were almost never named after their fathers, but very often after their paternal grandfather; the names Paulus Martinsen and Martin Paulisen alternated generation after generation in the Hackensack Church Records.

When surnames came into common use, some Dutchmen took the current patronymic as the family name (Adriance, Jansen, Garretson, Cornelison, Paulison, Ryerson, Lefferts); some took the name of their occupations (Bleeker [bleacher], Kuyper [cooper]); some took the name of their home town or a nearby landmark (Van Buskirk, Van Antwerp, Van Horn, Van Riper, Vanderbeek [of the brook], Vanderberg [of the hill], Opdyck [on the dyke]); some took a more arbitrary name (Blauvelt [blue field], Wyckoff [parish court]).

At the time of the Revolution, though baptized with only a first name, most Jersey Dutchmen (whether or not originally Dutch) used the patronymic as a second name (e.g., Cornelius Abraham Haring), frequently reflected as a middle initial (Peter S. Demarest; Wiert C. Banta). There were exceptions. Samuel Benson Leydecker's mother was a Benson, not his father; the Goetschius family gave children good Swiss middle names. See HBP 46.

★

Mark well these Bergen County Dutchmen, with their hard names and Jersey Dutch accents, as they climb into their wagons and make their way home from the courthouse meeting. Before three years have passed, many who spoke at that meeting in defense of the London ministry are to be defending the same ministry with force and arms; some will exile themselves from America forever because of their attachment to Toryism. Sad to say, some who loudly supported the cause of liberty will also take up arms in support of British rule. There is a British colonel-to-be among these Dutchmen, who will burn and sack more than one American town; there are British spies who will mean the death of hundreds of patriot soldiers; there are territorial soldiers who will spread death and destruction among hundreds of patriot neighbors. There are others, too, men who are to be impoverished and die in British prisons rather than submit to British oppression; Continental officers; American revolutionary leaders and patriot soldiers to whom generations yet unborn owe eternal gratitude.

Few who attended the meeting that day saw that the end of such debate was war; none, we may hope, had any premonition of the shadow which that war was to cast over the fertile and prosperous lands along the peaceful Hackensack.

3

THE next twelve months brought the American colonies from meetings and protests to war. Nearby New York City seethed with conflict, and the Hackensack valley, though in no such turmoil, could not escape the troubles of the times; indeed Dutch tempers were as short along the Hackensack as they were in New York City, and Dutchmen there were soon abusing each other in language every whit as violent as that of their city cousins. The Hackensack valley had a long history of conflict and hard language; in many ways the quarrel with Britain merely added new fuel to old fires.

Bergen County had for years named to office a fairly small group of political figures whose names were familiar to all. Lawrence Van Buskirk, John Demarest, Reynier Van Giesen, Jacobus Peek, and Jacob Titsort, to name some of them, were men who had been elected to county office year after year for two decades.[1] They were by no means universally admired and respected,[2] but if there was any organized opposition to them it had only infrequently succeeded. During the last few years, Peter Zabriskie also had been named to county office,[3] though he was probably personally at variance with Demarest, Van Giesen, Peek and Titsort, and perhaps with Van Buskirk as well.[4] The name of John Fell also had

[1] MJFBC, passim.
[2] Their position in the church wars, if nothing else, would have raised a host of opponents. Cf. ERNY 3689 and passim.
[3] MJFBC, passim.
[4] See ERNY 3632, 3689, 3693 and passim.

appeared in county affairs from time to time in more recent years, as had the names of Roelif Westervelt, Thomas Moore, and Abraham Montagna.[5]

All these men were of good family background, well known in the county, and most of them and their families were to play an active part in the Revolution.

Lawrence Van Buskirk, for example, who later turned strongly to the Tory side of the war, was descended from men who had been prominent in public affairs since the first days of New Netherlands.[6] Van Buskirk was getting on in years in 1774, and two of his sons, Andrew and Abraham, were coming into prominence. Andrew had operated a tavern at New Bridge, and owned and drove one of the stages to the New York ferries.[7] Abraham practiced surgery from his home in Teaneck, and also from time to time, when Andrew was otherwise employed, drove the family Flying Machine to Paulus Hook.[8]

A well-to-do farmer who lived on the River Road in Teaneck, Lawrence Van Buskirk had been active in politics for most of his life, and he and his family were leaders of the Lutheran church there.[9] Since the two small Lutheran groups in the county included a number of somewhat recent immigrants,[10] who were perhaps more inclined to follow a political leader than were the well-established members of the Dutch Reformed Church, Van Buskirk's Lutheran connections may have helped him politically. There can be no doubt that many of the Lutheran people adopted his Toryism when the war started.

The great Lutheran minister, Henry Melchoir Muhlenberg, made it no secret that he thought a political career had cooled the religious zeal of Van Buskirk's father. "A little temporal good fortune," Muhlenberg wrote, "association with unbelieving gentlefolk . . . and his inexperience in the practical side of spiritual things, all worked together and almost extinguished the spark of religion implanted in him. He had not attended divine service for several years and had grown very cold." [11] Some of the small cynicism of the father may have passed on to Lawrence Van Buskirk and his sons; they certainly were unmoved by revolutionary fervor when war came.

Reynier Van Giesen, another of the group who often held county

5 MJFBC, passim.
6 Winfield, Hudson County, 487, etc.; ERNY 2381, 2930, 3078.
7 26 NJA 274, 339; 28 NJA 461, 507; 31 NJA 216.
8 31 NJA 127; LYT NYPL.
9 Cf. 1 Muhlenberg 284; NJFBC, passim.
10 Lutheran Church Records, HSYB 1907; Muhlenberg, passim.
11 1 Muhlenberg 284.

office, was, like Van Buskirk, well to do and well connected and getting on in years. He died before the Revolution started.[12]

John Demarest, forty-four years old in 1774, had often been one of the justices of Bergen County and had recently been elected to several terms in the Provincial Assembly.[13] His great-grandfather was the Huguenot David Demarest, founder, a hundred years before, of the celebrated French settlement on the Hackensack River several miles northeast of Hackensack.[14] John Demarest had been active in political affairs for a long time, and doubtless felt more at ease in the company of well-connected Englishmen in the royal government at Perth Amboy than among his French and Dutch neighbors of Old Bridge. Unlike many Demarests, John Demarest, too, became a Tory when war came to New Jersey.

Jacobus Peek was a farmer of Schraalenburgh, where he and his wife had been among the founders of the Dutch Reformed church in 1723.[15] He died in 1775, leaving four grown sons, Johannes, Jacobus, Samuel, and David,[16] three of whom were to become well known for their Toryism as the next few years went by.

In the county elections of 1774, Lawrence Van Buskirk, Peter Zabriskie, Roelif Westervelt, Thomas Moore, and Abraham Montagna were named justices [17] and Theunis Dey and John Demarest were elected representatives in the Provincial Assembly.[18]

It would be hard to draw any conclusions about revolutionary sentiment in Bergen County from the elections. Dey, Moore, Westervelt, and Zabriskie were Whigs, although one of the most vociferous of the local patriots thought Dey and Moore lacked something of Whig zeal.[19] Demarest and Van Buskirk, though probably regarded as Whigs at the time, later became Tories, as, apparently, did Montagna.

In truth, Whig and Tory political lines had probably not yet hardened in the county. New York and New Jersey vacillated between opposition to the Intolerable Acts and opposition to the extremists of the

---

[12]   His first ancestor in America was Reynier Van Giesen, still remembered after a century for his forty-three years of service as voorleser of the Bergen church. HSYB 1914, 1915; GHHB 242.
[13]   Demarest Genealogy Nos. 63, 87. It is believed that the biographical material under No. 63 is in fact applicable to No. 87.
[14]   Demarest Genealogy, pp. 13, 445. The so-called French Patent, a tract about two miles wide, lay between the Hackensack and the Hudson, from New Bridge northward.
[15]   Schraalenburgh Church Records.
[16]   34 NJA 385.
[17]   MJFBC 124.
[18]   MPC 63.
[19]   Draft letter, Robert Morris to Philadelphia, Morris Papers RUL.

Liberty party; in New Jersey, Governor William Franklin would sometimes seem to have the support of the Assembly; at other times he and his royal authority would be completely ignored. All Americans were loud in their allegiance to King George, Tories because of their attachment to royalty, Whigs because they believed the King was at heart a Whig, imposed upon by a Tory ministry.

On March 14, 1775, a month before Lexington, Thomas Moore presided at a meeting of his neighbors of Hackensack Precinct, called to show "their loyalty to their King and love to their country," the thirty-seven men present resolving:

1. That we are and will continue to be loyal subjects to his Majesty King George, and that we will venture our lives and fortunes to support the dignity of his Crown.
2. That we disavow all riotous mobs whatsoever.
3. That by humbly petitioning the throne is the only salutary means we can think of to remove our present grievances.
4. That we have not, nor (for the future) will not, be concerned in any case whatsoever, with any unconstitutional measures.
5. That we will support his Majesty's civil officers in all their lawful proceedings.[20]

When the Hackensack Precinct resolutions reached the royal government at Perth Amboy, Governor Franklin had every reason to congratulate himself that the good people of that prosperous section of Bergen County wanted no part in the agitations of the Liberty party and that the London ministry had a true friend in Thomas Moore; after the resolutions it is easy to excuse the Whig leader who dismissed Justice Moore as a very weak man and many of his neighbors as Tories. The resolutions certainly had more than a hint of Toryism.

Both Whig and Tory were to be proved profoundly wrong: the ways of Jersey Dutchmen are not always easy to understand. Within five years Thomas Moore was to die in a British prison for his patriotism,[21] and many of his thirty-seven neighbors were to become patriot heroes. In the spring of 1775 political judgments were hard to make in Bergen County.

There was, however, one conflict in the county in which sharp lines were drawn, and it was not political: virtually everyone in the Hackensack valley had long since taken sides in a factional war in the Dutch Reformed church, a war so bitter that few of the people on one side

[20] MPC 98.
[21] LYT NYPL "Thomas Blakeney."

would have anything to do with those on the other. Outsiders who saw the prosperity of New Netherlands assumed that the Dutch were irreligious. "You will find his home and his farm to be the neatest in the country," one French traveler wrote, "and you will judge by his wagon and fat horses that he thinks more of the affairs of this world than those of the next." [22] Good husbandmen Dutchmen were, and neat, but nothing could be more profoundly wrong than to think them indifferent to the next world: great religious issues had kept Dutchmen at swords' points for twenty years before the Revolution; many a prosperous Jersey Dutchman spent much of his time in prayerful concern over his spiritual condition.[23] Throughout all of Dutch New York and New Jersey, virtually every Dutch church had been broken apart by conflict. A dissident group of ministers calling itself the "conferentie" was at the bottom of the trouble; it had set up separate churches at Hackensack and Schraalenburgh out of enmity for John Henry Goetschius; it had set up an irregular church at Tappan in an effort to destroy Goetschius' friend and former student, Samuel Ver Bryck; it had taken over bodily the Dutch churches at English Neighborhood and Paramus.

The majority of the Dutch Reformed ministers and people in America opposed the conferentie. They came to be known as the "coetus" party; it has been said that it could well have been called the American party, for the opposing conferentie often appeared to be moved by violent hatred for all things American. When war came, most of the conferentie party, in the Hackensack valley at least, became Tories; the coetus party mostly Whigs.[24]

The conferentie sometimes represented its battle as one to preserve the authority of Amsterdam and the ways of the fathers in the American Dutch church: whatever the pretenses, its real objective was to oppose the great religious revival that had swept the colonies in the thirty years before the Revolution, the revival that has come to be called the "Great Awakening."

The coetus-conferentie conflict was by no means confined to the

[22] Crévecoeur 50.
[23] The Rev. Henry M. Muhlenberg found among the Dutch Reformed in the Hackensack valley perhaps the most spiritual people he had seen in the colonies. 1 Muhlenberg 298, 305, 306. See also ERNY, passim.
[24] The conferentie-coetus controversy is described at length in every history of the American Dutch Reformed Church. See MRC; Demarest, Reformed Church in America.

Wertenbaker, Middle Colonies, and Maxson show the conflict in the perspective of other colonial issues. Local church histories give many colorful details, particularly Messler, Memorial Sermons; Cole, Tappan Church; and Demarest, Lamentation over Solomon Froeligh. The source materials are in ERNY.

Hackensack valley, but nowhere else in New Netherlands was it so bitter and divisive, nowhere else so long continued.[25]

"Houses of worship were locked by one part of the congregation against the other, tumults on the Lord's Day at the doors of the churches were frequent, preachers were sometimes assaulted in the pulpit and public worship either disturbed or terminated by violence." In these attacks the conferentie were almost always the aggressors, but, as might be expected, their attacks were often met by a furious zeal which itself did little honor to the Christian name.

The Hackensack and Schraalenburgh churches came to have two preachers, John Henry Goetschius, of the coetus congregation, and Warmoldus Kuypers, of the conferentie congregation. When Domine Goetschius preached at Schraalenburgh, the coetus party at Hackensack traveled to Schraalenburgh to hear him and the conferentie people at Schraalenburgh went to Hackensack to hear Warmoldus Kuypers; on the next Sunday, when Goetschius preached at Hackensack, the travel was reversed. Neither faction spoke to the other as the two passed on the road.[26] Jersey Dutch families who were set at odds in that day have hardly been reconciled since; for a hundred and fifty years after the Revolution the opposing parties in Bergen County viewed each other with suspicion and distrust.

Many of the older Dutch Reformed ministers of the conferentie party

25   Romeyn, Hackensack Church; Taylor, Bergen Classis; Paramus Classis History. In the Hackensack valley there is the somewhat curious situation that many of the local church histories have been written from the conferentie viewpoint, because the chief coetus congregations, those at Hackensack and Schraalenburgh, and many coetus sympathizers among the members of the Paramus and English Neighborhood churches, seceded from the Dutch Reformed Church in 1822 to establish the True Reformed Dutch Church, leaving in Bergen County a heritage of bitterness which lasted for a century. As a result, the authors, in some degree the successors to the conferentie, were faced with the difficulty of condemning the conferentie in principle and praising its churches and works in practice.

Taylor, Bergen Classis, written by the son-in-law of the pastor of the former conferentie North Schraalenburgh church, is an example, in which the conflict is described in terms that make it hard to tell that the North Church was the conferentie church and the South Church the coetus. Gordon and Brinkerhoff are little more than partisan attacks on the True Reformed Church, more remarkable for their anger than their facts. Demarest, Lamentation over Solomon Froeligh, is a partisan statement of the seceders' position. Cole, the author of the History of the Reformed Church of Tappan, though no seceder, wrote with strong coetus sympathies, as did Messler, Memorial Sermons.

The descendants of Bergen County patriots have borne the name "seceders" proudly for well over a hundred years.

26   Taylor, Bergen Classis, 180, etc. ". . . although the people were intermarried, families were divided among themselves—the husband against his wife—parents against the children. Many indignities were heaped upon one another." Ibid. 183; ERNY, passim.

seemed perfectly content with their comfortable positions of dignity in a church that demanded no religious fervor; the newer Dutch Reformed ministers—the coetus party—, stirred by the Great Awakening, saw their conferentie enemies as whited sepulchres, dead to religion.

The older ministers had for years striven to transfer control of the American church from Amsterdam to their own hands, but they came to see that any transfer of power to America would put control into the hands of their coetus enemies. Unembarrassed by inconsistency, they thereupon became violent advocates of foreign ordination and control. This position of convenience was soon raised to one of principle, and over the years the conferentie has come to be known for no other.

Coetus preachers and their congregations had little against Amsterdam; what they opposed was a religion that seemed to them to end with church attendance and decent public conduct. The conferentie congregations, for their part, earnest churchpeople by most standards, felt that the coetus party was trying to rob Dutchmen of their religion by talk of new birth and prayer meetings, and stopped at nothing to destroy them.

Domine John Henry Goetschius and his mentor, Theodorus J. Frelinghuysen of New Brunswick, were the principal prophets of the Great Awakening among the Dutch, and after Frelinghuysen's death Goetschius became the chief target for the slanders and blows of the conferentie.[27]

Goetschius died in 1774 at the Schraalenburgh parsonage.[28] Short of stature and short of temper,[29] the dynamic Swiss-born pastor left no man unmoved. He had been the principal founder of Queens College.[30] He had taught theology to virtually every Dutch Reformed minister ordained in America at the time of his death,[31] and his former students, almost to a man, considered him the greatest preacher in the American Dutch church. To the conferentie, who saw him as the very root cause of their troubles, his name was anathema. He and Frelinghuysen, both men of great zeal and little consideration for their opponents, were not backward in controversy, and if the conflict itself was the evil, and not the rights and wrongs of the case, they bore their full share of guilt: nonetheless they set the Dutch Reformed church upon a path of piety and earnestness which put generations in their debt, a path which departed greatly from the ways of the self-satisfied, institutional Dutch Reformed church which they found here. As a result, in a very real sense the church they led ceased to be a Dutch national church and became

27 ERNY, passim.
28 31 NJA 63.
29 Romeyn, Hackensack Church, 55, 60; MRC 489; ERNY, passim.
30 ERNY 4085, 4086; 25 NJA 343, 344, 345; Wertenbaker, Middle Colonies, 97.
31 See biographies of contemporary ministers, MRC.

an American church.[32] Certainly it can be said of Goetschius in the Hackensack valley, as it was said of Frelinghuysen along the Raritan, that his churches showed the fruits of his work for more than a century after his death.[33]

The Great Awakening was and is a controversial subject, though careful students of the period now see it as an important and constructive force in molding American character. It moved rich and poor alike, the educated and the uneducated, the worldly and the otherworldly. Every charitable, educational, and progressive movement in America was stimulated by it: "An impartial study of the period . . . free from partisan and denominational bias, leads to . . . [the] . . . conclusion . . . that thousands were given by the Great Awakening a new view of life's values, and from this view were derived new energies and new sympathies which gave direction not only to the subsequent career of these thousands but to the development of the whole American people. It was more than wave on wave of excitement; it was a transforming process in the nation's life. . . . There is an intimate connection between the American Revolution and the intercolonial religious ferment which preceded it. . . . The fear of invasion by the English government of their religious liberties were evidences of a spiritual union of the colonies which was prophetic of national union. . . . The denominations, like the Presbyterian and the Baptist, which were built up by the revival, took almost unanimously the patriot side. It was their meetinghouses that were burned as nests of rebellion and their pastors that were hunted as instigators of treason." [34] In a sense the Great Awakening among the Dutch Reformed was an even clearer prologue to independence, for independence from Amsterdam, forced by Amsterdam's misguided support of the conferentie, had made independence from foreign rule a cardinal tenet of Goetschius and his friends years before the Revolution.

It was not mere chance, then, that made the reborn and revitalized churches of Hackensack, Schraalenburgh, and Tappan centers of patriotism when war came to the Hackensack valley, nor chance that made their conferentie opponents the willing props of Toryism. Indeed, there were Dutchmen who believed that John Henry Goetschius, in his grave under the Schraalenburgh pulpit, had done as much for the American revolutionary cause as many a Continental officer who marched past that little church during the next decade of war.

With the outbreak of fighting at Lexington and Concord in April,

32 See e.g. Wertenbaker, Middle Colonies, 100.
33 See Messler, Memorial Sermons, 29, 30.
34 Maxson, 139, 149, 150.

1775, the Revolution in America had begun. Before the end of the afternoon service in the church on the green on Sunday, April 23, 1775, everyone in the village of Hackensack had heard the news of the Battle of Lexington, and, for the moment at least, patriot, neutral, and Tory seemed united, the spectacle of redcoats shooting American farmers having convinced all but the most obdurate that American arms must answer ministerial arrogance. Every traveler from New York brought word that the leaders of the Sons of Liberty had virtually taken over the city, seizing public muskets, powder and shot, closing the customhouse, and driving many open friends of government to flight. Scores of Tories joined the throngs shouting against the ministry and threatening its representatives.[35]

If patriotic Jerseymen had doubts about the new-found ardor of some of their neighbors, they kept them to themselves. During the next few weeks Bergen County seemed all but unanimous in its opposition to government. A standing Committee of Correspondence was set up in emulation of the committees of other provinces, cocked military hats were on every head, militiamen drilled on every green. "The people . . . ," Robert Erskine wrote to his London proprietors, "are sincerely in earnest everywhere. I have been applied to for gunpowder by the principal people of the County of Bergen . . . where they, who till now hardly thought anything of the matter, are forming into regular disciplined bodies as fast as possible, which is the only business attended to at present anywhere." [36] Dutchmen at Hackensack who had hardly spoken to each other for years now found themselves marching side by side in the shadow of the church over which they had fought so bitterly. Many men of the Hackensack Precinct across the river who had but recently assured his Majesty's civil officers that they would support them in every way now shouldered their muskets with neighbors who had as loudly proclaimed their hatred of such fawning servility toward those in power. True, there were Dutchmen who made no pretense that Lexington had altered their Tory views, but they were few and far be-

[35] See e.g. Wertenbaker, Father Knickerbocker, 53 etc.
[36] Heusser, The Forgotten General, 92. Thirty-six years old on his arrival here in 1771, Robert Erskine was the son of a prominent Scotch minister and a graduate of the University of Edinburgh. He had been sent over as the new manager for the London Company's iron mines and furnaces at Long Pond, Charlottenburg and Ringwood, in the hope that he would bring some solid business sense to a project that showed the soaring imagination and great engineering skill of Peter Hasenclever but no profit whatever for the £100,000 that had been invested in the enterprise. Though his sponsors were among the most prominent men at the British royal court, the young ironmaster of the Jersey Highlands soon showed himself a zealous Whig. In course of time he became surveyor general of the Continental army. Heusser, The Forgotten General. 1960 BHSP83.

tween in Bergen County and scarce enough even in New York City. When the fighting started many thoughtful Americans in the middle colonies were convinced that at last King George must drop his tolerance of Lord North and put a stop to his tyrannical government; and there were many others who said and believed that even if King George did not, the same American farmers who had humbled the French and won Canada for their monarch would force the end of the ministry by driving the ministerial troops off the continent. Each day that passed proved how wrong they were: British troops seized Boston and made it ready for siege; the talk was of British reinforcements, not British withdrawal.

The men chosen for the Bergen County Committee of Correspondence on May 12, 1775, apparently did not include any who held pronounced Tory views, but there were among them some who had certainly never been regarded as fiery Whigs. The members of the committee were John Fell, Esq., Theunis Dey, Esq., Thomas Brown, Esq., Peter Zabriskie, Esq., John Demarest, Esq., Mr. Samuel Berry, Mr. Cornelius Van Vorst, Mr. Isaac Noble, Mr. Arent J. Schuyler, Mr. Jacob Terhune, Dr. Abraham Van Buskirk, John Van Buskirk, Esq., Mr. Gabriel Ogden, Mr. Joost Zabriskie, and Mr. Gabriel Van Norden.[37] The patriot temper of the committee as a whole, however, could not be doubted when it chose John Fell as chairman. Fell was the former senior member of the merchant firm of John Fell and Company of New York, who had several armed merchant vessels plying the seas as early as 1759. He had retired and moved to Bergen County before 1769, establishing a country estate which he called Petersfield, after his young son, on the road north of the Paramus church.[38] Wealthy as he was, the committee chose the dour Fell for his patriot zeal and ability, not for his social position. He was later to serve New Jersey with distinction in the Continental Congress.[39] Despite important connections with the royal government, there was no firmer Whig in the province of New Jersey than John Fell.

When the justices and freeholders met on May 10, 1775, they directed Peter Zabriskie and Isaac Vanderbeek to see to the cleaning of guns belonging to the county and authorized payment of 1s 6d to John Bant,

[37]   MPC 115.
[38]   1 NJA (2) 54, n. He was born in New York City on Feb. 5, 1721. Congressional Biography, "John Fell."
[39]   1 NJA (2) 54, n. He served in Congress from 1778 to 1780 and as a member of the State Council in 1782 and 1783. He later moved to Coldenham, N.Y. Congressional Biography, "John Fell."

BEING fully convinced that the Prefervation of the Rights and Privileges of the Britifh Colonies in America, now depends on the firm Union of their Inhabitants, in a vigo-rous Profecution of the Meafures neceffary tor their Safety; and dreading a State of Anarchy and Confufion, which will neceffarily attend the prefent Struggle for our Liberty, unlefs the proper Steps are taken to preferve Regularity and Unanimity among us :---We the Freeholders and Inhabitants of the County of Bergen, being greatly alarmed at the avowed Defign of the Britifh Miniftry, and the Acts of Parliament for raifing a Revenue in America, independent of the Provincial Affemblies, and being extremely fhocked and grieved at the unhappy Confequences which have attended the Attempts to enforce the late unconftitutional Acts of the Britifh Legiflature, DO refolve, that we will not fubmit to thofe Acts of Parliament which impofe Taxes on us without our confent, and deprive us of our Conftitu-tional Rights and Privileges ; and therefore do affociate under the Ties of Honor, and Love to our Country, that we will abide by and endeavour to carry into Execution, all Conftitutional Meafures whatfoever, which may be advifed by the Continental Congrefs, and recommended by the Provincial Convention, for the Purpofe of preferving our Conftitution and oppofing the feveral oppreffive Acts of Parliament, until a Reconciliation on Conftitutional Principles (which we moft ardently defire) may be effected between Great-Britain and the American Colonies : And that we will in all Things follow the Advice of the County Committee for the Purpofe aforefaid, and for the Prefervation of Peace and good Order, and the Safety of Indi-viduals and Security of private Property.
May 12, 1775.

ALZOO wy ten vollen overtuygd zyn, dat de Behoudenis van de Regt en ... vilegien der Brittifche Colonien in America, thans afhangt van de volkomene eendragt van derfelver Jnwoonders, in het kragtdadig voortfetten van die maatregulen welke tot derzelver behoud noodzaakelyk zyn, en vreezende voor een Staat van Anarchie .. verwarring, welke de tegenfwoordige ftryd voor onze Vryheid bazig zoude moeten flepen, ten zy behoor-lyke maatregulen genomen werden ter bewaring van goede ordre en eendragt onder ons : Soo is het, dat wy, de Freeholders of Eygenerfden en Jnwoonders van de County Bergen, grootelyks aangedaan zynde over het opzettelyk oogmerk van het Brittifch Minifterie en de Acten des Parlaments, om in America een Schatting te heffen, onaf hangelyk van de Provinciale Affemblies, en zynde ten uyterften ontroerd en bedroeft over de ongelukkige gevolgen, welke reeds uyt de pogingen om de laafte met de Conftitutie ftrydende Actens van het Brittifch Parlament ter uytvoer te brengen, zyn voort gevloeyt; vaftelyk voornemen, dat wy ons zelven niet zullen onderwerpen aan die Actens van het Parlament, welke ons zonder onze toeftemming met Schattingen beswaren, en ons van onze Conftitutionele Voorregten en Privi-legien beroowen, en daarom ons zelven onder de banden van Eer en liefde tot ons Vaderland verbinden, dat wy ons zullen gedragen aan en ter uytvoering tragten te brengen, alle Conftitu-tionele maatregulen hoe ook genaamt, welke door het Continentale Congres zullen worden aangeraden en door de Provintiale Conventie nader gerecommandeert, met oogmerk om onze Conftitutie te bewaren, de onderfcheydene onderdrukkende Actens van het Parlament tegen-teftaan, tot dat een verzoeningop Conftitutionele grond beginzelen (welke wy ten vurigften wenfchen) tuffchen Groot-Brittannien en de Americaanfche Colonien mag worden te weeg gebragt : Als mede dat wy in alle zaaken, de raad van onze County Committee zullen opvolgen ten voorfchreven eynde, en ter bewaring van goede order en ter beveiliging van elk perfoon in't byzonder en Verzekering van ieders eygendom.
May 12de, 1775.

The Bergen County patriot resolutions adopted May 12, 1775, were circu-lated in the county in both Dutch and English.
Courtesy of Rutgers University Library.

the armorer, for each one cleaned. Seventy-nine stand of arms were sold for Continental use.[40]

Like the other counties of the province, Bergen County proceeded at once after Lexington to try to put its militia on a solid footing. The war was in faraway Massachusetts, but if the London government was ever to be brought to its senses even Jerseymen would have to show their

[40] MJFBC 125, 128, 129.

willingness to fight. Indeed in the middle counties of New Jersey troops were already enlisting for the Jersey Line of the Continental army.[41]

However, even Whigs could not stop their workaday affairs. Petti-augers, two-masted flat-bottomed schoonerlike vessels, much favored by the Dutch, each capable of carrying ten or twelve tons of cargo,[42] sailed up and down the Hackensack on every tide, carrying country prod-uce to New York and merchandise back to the farms and mines of northern New Jersey;[43] the stages between Hackensack and Paulus Hook were busier than ever. Indeed one Jersey Dutchman and his wealthy patron, William Bayard, felt the prospects for travel between New York City and northern New Jersey so good that they opened a new ferry at Hoboken on May 1, 1775:

Cornelius Haring begs leave to present his most respectful compliments to the public and to inform them that he intends, on Monday the 1st of May next, to open the new established ferry from the remarkable, pleasant and convenient situated place of William Bayard, Esquire, at the Kings Arms Inn, from which place all gentlemen travellers and others, who have occasion to cross that ferry, will be accommodated with the best of boats of every kind, suitable to the winds, weather and tides, to convey them from thence to the New Market near the new corporation pier, at the North River, opposite Vesey Street in New York. [Haring went on to praise the Kings Arms Inn as] a most elegant and convenient house, where travellers [will be] provided with lodging, eatables and liquors of the best kind, and particular attention will be given to the clean feeding and doing strict justice to all travellers' horses. The elegance of the situation, as well as its affording many

41 Robert Erskine had evidently enlisted a company of soldiers for the Jersey Line from the workers at the ironworks, and outfitted them at his own expense. Heusser, The Forgotten General, 110. Few Jersey Dutchmen in the Hackensack valley enlisted in the Continental army, and of the few who did, most enlisted late in the war, e.g., Frederick Blauvelt (who described himself as a common laborer), Harman Blauvelt (a weaver) and his brother, Abraham Blauvelt, enlisted in the New Jersey Line in 1780. Peter Lozier joined Lee's Legion in the same year. See affidavits of Frederick Blauvelt, Pension Records, W24700; Harman Blauvelt, Pension Records, S959; and Peter Lozier, Pension Records, S42886. John Hopper was commissioned as an ensign in the 2nd Regiment of New Jersey Line on July 19, 1781, and "was in the battle at Yorktown when Cornwallis surrendered to the American Army." Affidavit of John Hopper, Pension Records S34409. George Van Buskirk, of Closter, was in the New Jersey Line in 1776. Affidavit of George Van Buskirk, Pension Records S42601. Perhaps most Jersey Dutchmen were too well settled and prosperous to be professional soldiers; perhaps they were not sufficiently exercised about the war when it began. As it turned out, they may well have been more useful as militiamen in the neutral ground than they would have been in the regular army.
42 W. J. Lane, From Indian Trail to Iron Horse (Princeton 1939), 8.
43 See e.g. 28 NJA 456; 26 NJA 49.

amusements, such as fishing and fowling, added to these, its being stocked with the greatest variety of the best English fruits, will make it an agreeable place for the entertainment of large companies, having besides a number of convenient rooms, one of fifty feet in length, by which means (as he will have the best cooks, particularly for the dressing of turtle, and every other dish fit to be set before either gentlemen or ladies), he hopes to be honored with their company, assuring them there will be nothing wanting on his part to make it convenient and agreeable, as well to entitle him to the honor of their countenance as custom.[44]

The boats, the advertisement added, were to be distinguished by the name "The Hobook Ferry" painted on the stern.

The good people of Hackensack could hardly have failed to be pleased at this new evidence of their commercial importance, and Abraham Van Buskirk quickly announced that "the Flying Machine that used to ply between Hackensack and Paulus Hook, will for the sake of a better and shorter road, begin on Saturday, the 13th day of May and henceforth continue to drive from Hackensack to Hobuck." [45]

May 17, 1775, was observed as a day of fasting and prayer by the congregations of all the Reformed Protestant Dutch churches in New York and New Jersey.[46]

Meanwhile New Jersey was going through an amazing transition, changing from a royal government to a revolutionary government without the firing of a gun.[47] To the utter distress of the Tories, the province soon found the Governor and Council shorn of power and the lawful Provincial Assembly superseded by the rebel Provincial Congress. The Bergen County Committee of Correspondence had named John Fell, John Demarest, Hendrik Kuyper, Dr. Abraham Van Buskirk, and Edo Marcellus to be deputies to represent the county at the Provincial Congress to be held at Trenton on May 23, 1775.[48] When it convened it proceeded to take over most of the functions of government, prohibiting exports to parts of Canada, proposing patriot associations, establishing numerous militia companies and appointing their officers, levying

---

[44] 31 NJA 124. There were not less than three Cornelius Harings active in Bergen County during the Revolution. Two were Tories, and one or more were active in the patriot government. MCSNJ; Damages by British NJSL; MJFBC; HBP 69, 70. The ferryman took the patriot side. See 4 Carleton Papers 73 (7644).

[45] 31 NJA 127. In the same issue of the Gazette, Robert Erskine was able to inform the holders of notes issued by the Ringwood, Long Pond and Charlottenburg ironworks that their notes "would be received in payment for bar iron at the market price at the works or the landings at Haverstraw, Hackensack or Aquackanonk, or in New York." 31 NJA 130.

[46] 31 NJA 132.

[47] MPC, passim.

[48] 31 NJA 138.

taxes, and generally acting as though the royal government of New Jersey did not exist.[49] Among the militia officers it appointed were Richard Dey, the son of Theunis Dey, and John Mauritius Goetschius, son of the late John Henry Goetschius, both of whom were named majors of militia companies intended for service in New York City.[50] The particular companies were probably never formed, but Dey and Goetschius served in the New Jersey militia with great distinction when war actually came to the middle colonies.

The first chief militia officers of the county, chosen, in the manner of the day, more for their standing in the community than for any presumed military merit, were Theunis Dey, of Preakness, colonel; John Zabriskie, Jr., of New Bridge, lieutenant colonel; Cornelius Van Vorst, of Bergen, lieutenant colonel; Peter Fell, of Paramus, lieutenant colonel; Richard Dey, of Preakness, captain, 1st major; John Mauritius Goetschius, of Schraalenburgh, captain, 2nd major; George Ryerson, adjutant; and Abraham Van Buskirk, of Teaneck, surgeon.[51] The lesser officers included many other distinguished names of the county. Some of these men were to see years of hard service in the patriot cause; others were to face more patriot muskets than they fired.

With war an actuality, patriots had every reason to be concerned about the self-styled moderates among Bergen County's Committee of Safety and to congratulate themselves that they had at least been able to elect enough men of their own views so that the steadfast John Fell was chairman of the committee and Peter Zabriskie one of its leading figures. When new elections were called to be held September 21, 1775,[52] however, patriot leaders who knew the sentiment of the county were much concerned lest they lose their narrow margin of control. They had been elected in the great burst of patriot sentiment after Lexington. Might not an election now add enough lukewarm patriots to the committee so that all their activities would be frustrated?

In recent months one of the most active men in the moderate party had been Daniel Isaac Brown, a lawyer of Hackensack. Brown was not a Jersey Dutchman, having been born and raised on Long Island and in Newark, where his father was an Anglican clergyman.[53] Brown had lived and had his law office in a small house facing the village green but

49 MPC, passim.
50 MPC 484.
51 HBP 71; MPC, passim.
52 MPC 186.
53 LYT NYPL "Daniel I. Brown"; Jones, Loyalists, "Daniel I. Browne; Isaac Browne." This is one of the few instances in which the historian William Nelson appears to be in error. Cf. 1 NJA (2) 57n.

had recently moved into a larger house. Though his practice was not extensive, he was well enough connected to be named clerk of court and surrogate and from time to time he was hired by the county to prosecute a criminal, his most celebrated case of that kind having been the prosecution of the slave of Hendrik Christian Zabriskie for the murder of Nicholas Toers, a case for which the county paid him £3.[54] He had been active in watering down the patriot resolutions in 1774 [55] and since that time had become the open enemy of avowed Whigs in the county and the ally of their political opponents. Both Tories and Whigs considered him a trimmer. John Francis Ryerson, an outspoken Tory, who perhaps was prejudiced by what he considered Brown's moderate views, said after the war that Brown's practice as a lawyer "was not so great as some others and that he was not so clever in speaking," that "he was much employed in giving advice which tended to promote suits which often proved unsuccessful, but produced fees for himself." [56] Whigs detested him. Being exempt as a lawyer from militia duty and careful not to go so far as to excite patriot violence, by the fall of 1775 he seemed to be devoting almost all of his time to promoting the interests of the London ministry in Bergen County,[57] while still claiming to be as much a friend of American liberties as any patriot.

Brown and his friends played shrewdly upon the fears of many conservative Dutchmen that the Hackensack valley faced the danger of lawless mobs if its patriot leaders were given power; they worked hard to take advantage of the political sentiment for the county's long-time political figures; and they never neglected a word where it would do the most good to keep alive the twenty-year-old hatred of the conservative conferentie church people for their coetus enemies.[58] No one could be sure their efforts were in vain.

When John Fell rose to the rostrum to call the meeting to order in the courthouse on election day, Thursday, September 21, 1775, he knew that New York City had recently seen self-styled moderate men, exactly like Daniel Isaac Brown, take over the reins of power, and that the same thing could easily happen in Hackensack. When the meeting got under way, it was soon evident that it was not a question whether a few lukewarm men would be added to the committee but whether any known patriot could be elected. When the votes were counted, the results could

---

[54] LYT NYPL, "Daniel I. Brown"; MJFBC 97.   [55] LYT NYPL. A copy of a set of resolutions is in NJHSL.   [56] After the war Brown said his practice was worth £500 per annum, a fine income indeed for a country lawyer. Apparently he owned a large amount of real and personal property. He tried to hire Richard Varick after the war to collect his debts. Frazer 543; LYT NYPL, "Daniel I. Brown."   [57] LYT NYPL, "Daniel I. Brown."   [58] Draft letter Robert Morris, Morris Papers RUL.

hardly have been worse: John Fell, Peter Zabriskie, and every other patriot of standing on the committee were defeated. The moderates swept the election, naming as the Bergen County Committee of Observation and Correspondence, "with full power as well to superintend and direct the necessary business of said county, as to carry into execution the resolutions and orders of the Continental Provincial Congress": Thomas Brown, Esq., John Jacobus Van Buskirk, Esq., Daniel Smith, Esq., Michael Moore, Albert Zabriskie, Jacob Quackenbush, Arent Schuyler, Gabriel Van Norden, Daniel Isaac Brown, Garrabrant Van Houten, Hendrick Doremus, David Board, Garret Garretse, Cornelius Lozier, Johannes J. Ackerman, John Van Buskirk, Esq., Isaac Blanch, and David Duryea,[59] and naming as Bergen's representatives to the Provincial Congress: John Demarest, Esq., Dr. Abraham Van Buskirk, and Jacobus Post.[60]

When the Committee of Correspondence met and chose Daniel Isaac Brown as its president,[61] no one who knew the county had any doubt how the committee proposed to carry into execution the resolutions and orders of the Continental Congress. If the cynical, second-rate lawyer Brown and his friends were the men that Bergen County chose to entrust with its patriot government, Bergen County Whigs had every reason to be disgusted and disheartened. If patriots had known the full truth they would have been desperate indeed: Brown, while pretending to be a patriot who differed with others only as to means, was in fact acting under express instructions from the British warships in New York Bay.[62] Three months after the Battle of Bunker Hill, and at a time when the county's militia was actually in arms building fortifications at Elizabethtown and Amboy against a threatened British invasion,[63] the voters of Bergen County, wittingly for some, unwittingly for many, had handed over the patriot cause to its enemies.

The Provincial Congress which convened in Trenton on January 31, 1776, included many patriot leaders whose names have come down through the years for their warm support of the cause of America: Abraham Clark, William Winds, William Dehart, Hendrick Fisher, William Maxwell, William Paterson, and Lewis Ogden, to name but a few. Probably to the surprise of many Whigs, Bergen County's Demarest, Post, and Van Buskirk voted with the patriot majority on most of the meas-

59   1 NJA (2) 55, 56. Some of the committeemen were patriotic enough: David Board, for instance, later served in the patriotic county government (MJFBC); the majority clearly were Tories.
60   1 NJA (2) 55.
61   1 NJA (2) 57.
62   LYT NYPL "Daniel I. Brown."
63   Affidavits of Samuel Vervalen, Pension Records, S29203, and Abraham Vanderbeek, Pension Records, S1130.

ures before the Congress; [64] indeed, on February 17, 1776, Van Buskirk confounded those who suspected his patriotism by accepting a commission from the Provincial Congress for active service as surgeon for the regiment of foot militia in the county of Bergen.[65]

But if the lukewarm Provincial Congressmen from the county were willing to co-operate with zealous patriots at Trenton, Brown and his friends at Hackensack certainly were not. The leaders of the County Committee found it less and less necessary as time passed to make any pretense whatever of zeal for the American cause. When Pennsylvania troops on their way to Albany applied for provisions, the committee gave them a thousand excuses but not one bushel of grain, despite the threats of the Continental officers and the indignation of local Whigs.[66] One of Brown's schemes was for the County Committee to ask the Provincial Congress for blank commissions which they could fill up themselves. Whigs had no illusions that any patriot would find his name on any such document if the request was granted. "It gives the minds of many besides your petitioners great uneasiness," the Committee of Observation and Correspondence of Hackensack Precinct wrote in the spring of 1776, ". . . we think the safety of the common cause depends upon our officers being hearty in the cause of American freedom." [67]

There were others in the county who were prepared to go much further than this mild complaint in denouncing the moderate party. One of the most outspoken was Robert Morris, the county's leading lawyer. Destined to be the first chief justice of the state of New Jersey and one of the first judges of its federal court,[68] Morris had been a leader in Bergen County's Whig councils, though he had not stood for public office. He was thirty-one years old at the outset of the war, the natural son and heir of Robert Hunter Morris, one-time governor of the province of New Jersey, and the grandson of another royal governor of the province. He and his family were large landowners, who were close to the

---

[64] MPC, passim.
[65] MPC 375.
[66] Draft letter Robert Morris, Morris Papers RUL.
[67] Committee to Provincial Congress, "Provincial Congress," NJHSL. The signers were: Thomas Moore, Chairman, Joost Zabriskie, Garret Leydecker, John Demarest, Albert H. Banta, David Banta, Samuel Couenhoven and Samuel Demarest. They proposed James Stagg, James Christie, David Demarest, Daniel Westervelt, John Brinkerhoff, Samuel Moore, Joost Lozier and John Westervelt as officers, many of whom later served the patriot cause with distinction. Garret Leydecker, cousin of the conferentie minister, for example, was "a prominent and influential man, possessed of large landed estates, who became a captain in the Revolutionary war and subsequently a member of the legislature." HBP 277. His descendants to the fifth generation were active in the coetus branch of the Reformed church. Idem.
[68] 3 NJA (2) 446 n. The certificate of appointment is in Morris Papers RUL.

councils of the New Jersey proprietors.[69] He had quickly come to represent many people of means in Bergen County in the few years that he
had practiced at Hackensack.[70] "The County lies," Morris wrote to a
friend in Philadelphia, "under the direction of men who in their hearts
are our secret enemies and oppose the measures taken by the Continent,
and do no one thing in their capacity as a Committee but what fear com-
pels and they secretly disapprove."

"We [are]," he went on, "represented by and under the direction of
those [who will] do nothing more than is absolutely necessary to preserve them from the [resentm]ent of the neighboring counties and colonies. Judge you, sir, what a damp [these men] throw upon those among
us who are heartily disposed to favor the cause [of our] country. I . . .
fear for the consequences."

"Men have been suffered publicly to avow and support [sentiments]
daringly inimical to America . . . both in and out of Committee, and
even in the pulpit," Morris complained. "[Others] who have not talents
for public declamation, or so much art to use them, have done perhaps
as much or more mischief in a less public way. [These] men are suffered
and no notice taken of them." [71]

Morris, who could have heard the same Tory preaching in his own
Anglican church in Perth Amboy,[72] did not identify the Dutch Tory
preacher, but it is not hard to guess who he was. Despite the Tory views
of many members of the conferentie church at Hackensack, it was hardly
likely that their pastor had voiced any daringly inimical sentiments, for
the Rev. Warmoldus Kuypers was, to all appearances, the very embodi-
ment of a neutral. A corpulent Dutchman directly out of *Knickerbocker's History of New York*, not half as ardent in the church wars as
his congregations, he seems to have been indifferent to the political fires
that burned around him at the outset of war. It was said of Nicholas
Vedder, the great man of Rip Van Winkle's legendary village, "that
though he was rarely heard to speak, his adherents perfectly understood
him, for as he sat in the shade of the large tree in front of his inn, when
anything was read or related that displeased him, he was observed to
smoke his pipe vehemently and to send forth short, frequent and angry
puffs, but when pleased, he would inhale the smoke slowly and tran-

69   See 3 NJA (2) 446 n.; McCormick, Experiment in Independence, passim; Morris
Papers RUL. If the cynical Thomas Jones is to be believed, his father "had no
religion." Jones, New York During the Revolution, 223.
70   His name appears frequently as a witness to important wills in the NJA abstracts.
See Erskine Papers NJHSL.
71   Draft letter Robert Morris, Morris Papers RUL. The bracketed matter supplies
missing data in the partially torn copy.
72   DAB "Robert Morris."

quilly, and emit in light and placid clouds." The more one reads of Warmoldus Kuypers the more one observes his kinship to Vedder. Though the Revolution raged around him for years, and though his own sympathies were with the London government, so far as one can learn today Kuypers never expressed any views on it. Born in Holland and first emigrating to Curaçao,[73] he had been brought to the Hackensack valley by men who refused to sit under the evangelical preaching of Goetschius, and he suited the preaching tastes of his new congregations perfectly, expounding upon his texts in perfectly formal sermons that never put them in danger of unseemly religious zeal. "In person, he was quite large and corpulent and wore a wig. He preached in Dutch; he is said to have been a man of high classical attainments. . . . It is said that his method of tea-taking . . . was to sit at the table after the rest were through the meal and quietly alternate a sip of tea with a whiff from his pipe. . . . When some of his congregation tried to involve him too deeply in the church wars, it was his habit to say, 'Trouble I hate. The temporalities of the church I wish to leave to others.' " [74]

Surely it was not Warmoldus Kuypers who was preaching violent Tory politics. Nor was it Benjamin Van der Linde, the conferentie preacher at Paramus, for he was moved more by personal animosity to Goet-schius [75] than by any strong views, religious or political. The man to whom Morris referred was Garret Leydecker, of the English Neighbor-hood Dutch Reformed church. (Why the place was called English Neighborhood is something of a mystery. At the time of the Revolution it was as thoroughly Dutch as Schraalenburgh or Tappan; probably some of its first settlers were English.) In any case, the Dutch Reformed church, the only church in the community, had in its pulpit a man whose Tory sentiments were no product of recent events. Son of Richard Ley-decker and Maritie Benson, and a brother of the once-wealthy but now unfortunately bankrupt Samuel Benson Leydecker, Domine Leydecker was forty-seven years old in 1776, with a handsome, aristocratic face, somewhat lost in the rotundity of double chins, and notable for the small steel spectacles which adorned it. He was slightly crippled, and had always been somewhat frail. He had studied at the College of New Jersey, that nursery of the Great Awakening, graduating in 1755. After graduation he commenced his theological studies under John Henry Goetschius and was apparently a zealous adherent of the coetus party.

[73] MRC 560.
[74] Romeyn, Hackensack Church, 76, 77. Onderdonk, Jamaica Church History, 88, 89, volunteers the curious observation that Kuyper's son, whose politics were remembered for seventy-five years, would have been a tory if he had acted during Revolutionary times. Another son was an open Tory. 4 Carleton Papers 102 (1772).
[75] ERNY 3627, 3628, 3689 and passim.

The Reverend Garret Leydecker,
1729–1794.
Historical Magazine of the Protestant Episcopal Church,
December, 1944.

Something happened during those studies, for he and Goetschius soon parted, and Leydecker finished his work under Goetschius' enemy, the Rev. John Ritzema, the most reactionary minister of the entire conferentie. Leydecker went on to become the only native Dutch Reformed minister who was ever ordained by the conferentie party. He had come to the English Neighborhood church as its first pastor in 1767.[76] His and his congregation's position in the church wars exactly suited their political views: no minister of the Church of England was firmer in his defense of London, no Anglican congregation received such preaching with more satisfaction. Contemptuous of Whig opinion, he had taken into his home as a refugee from New York the hated Tory mayor, David Mathews, a charming, articulate man whose political and personal morals offended even his Tory supporters. Leydecker's pulpit rang with prayers for the King and government, and Morris was not the only Whig who wished that he could be punished for it.

In good time he was, for when the war was over Leydecker paid for his Toryism by exile.[77] Meanwhile Whigs could no nothing but fume at him.

Indeed, irritating as it was to have Toryism preached by a Jersey Dutchman under the name of Dutch Calvinism, patriots did not deceive themselves that Garret Leydecker was an important enemy; there were men in his congregation, and all too many others in the county, who, patriots had every reason to believe, were doing far more than preach Toryism.

The election for which Robert Morris had such high hopes was held

---

[76] Historical Magazine of the Protestant Episcopal Church, December, 1944. MRC 586; LYT NYPL "Garret Leydecker." The Samuel Benson Leydecker property was advertised at a sheriff's sale in 27 NJA 527.
[77] "Under the severe gripe of penury and want," he wrote later. LYT NYPL "Garret Leydecker."

on the fourth Monday in May, 1776. It should have given Morris pause to know that Bergen County had cast one of the two deciding votes in favor of dissolving the existing Provincial Congress and holding the new election, and this despite Whig claims that the earlier election, under which Demarest, Post, and Van Buskirk held their seats, was irregular.[78] Indeed, Robert Morris, brilliant as he was and right as he was about the conduct of Bergen County's lukewarm committeemen, lacked that sense of public and private sentiment that is so important to any politician. Full of the self-confidence of an outsider in all matters Dutch, he credited Tory planning too much and fundamental differences too little for the political situation. "The former religious and political parties of the county," he wrote, "are artfully managed and kept up by the leaders of the Tories, so as to give them a large majority in the middle of the county." [79] He could hardly have been expected, as a stranger to the Dutch religious wars, to see that more than artful management was involved in that division; that Tappan's conferentie congregation and others far beyond the reach of Bergen County Tories had taken exactly the same position. Like many a bystander to religious conflicts, he found it hard to understand that those ideas too have consequences. Morris feared for the Committee of Safety in Franklin and Harrington and thought that all but two of the Committee of Safety in Hackensack Precinct were Tories and that "one of them, Justice [Thomas] Moore, was a very weak man." [80] Morris did not know Jersey Dutchmen. Many who prided themselves on their dignity and soft words were stubborn beyond belief when they wanted to be: Moore was no weakling. He was not weak-willed when he took the trouble to pass by the Rev. Garret Leydecker to take his children miles away to Hackensack or Schraalen-burgh to be baptized by Domine Goetschius; he was to prove himself strong-willed indeed before the end of the war. Nor were his fellow committeemen Tories because they talked little; or others Tories because they had Tory family connections. Dey was as thoroughly committed to the patriot cause as Morris himself; if Jersey Dutchmen were to be judged by their family connections, no one could stand.

Morris was soon proved wrong, too, in his optimism about the elections: when the fourth Monday of May came, the voters were more emphatic than ever in rejecting Whig leadership, this time with the added indignity of naming Daniel Isaac Brown himself to be a delegate to the Provincial Congress. The other successful candidates were John

[78] MPC 388, 391.
[79] Draft letter Robert Morris, Morris Papers RUL.
[80] Draft letter, op. cit. He also suggested that Richard Dey, of Preakness, was burdened with Tory connections.

Demarest, Isaac Post, and two others from the ranks of the Tories, Jacob Quackenbush and John Van Buskirk.[81]

The most charitably minded Whig must by now have found it hard to believe that any large part of the voters were being deceived by Brown's pretense of moderation; if they were, they were surely being trapped by a snare set in their own sight.

It was an open secret in the spring of 1776 that the British meant to move the theater of war to New York City as quickly as the troops which evacuated Boston could regroup and new troopships could be made ready abroad. Every letter from London told the same story; every Tory in New York knew that he had but to wait a few months for the arrival of the British army.

The reasons were plain to all. Sir Henry Clinton put them very well after the war: "New England and the colonies to the south are entirely separated from each other by the River Hudson, which falls into the sea at New York, after forming a broad, navigable communication for one hundred and seventy miles between that city and Albany. . . . The possession of [that river] would [secure] to Great Britain a barrier between the southern and eastern colonies which would have most effectually divided the strength of the inimical states, by depriving those to the southwest of all assistance from the populous and hardy eastern provinces, unless by a difficult, circuitous inland intercourse through the mountains, for as long as a British army held the passes of that noble river and her cruisers swept their coasts, the colonists would have found it almost impossible to have joined or fed their respective quotas of troops." [82]

The people of Bergen and Orange counties saw this as clearly as anyone. They could hardly be expected to see what the campaign for the strategic Hudson was to mean to the men and women who lived in the angle between the river and the Hudson Highlands.

In the spring of 1776 New York City was rapidly being garrisoned by the main Continental army under the command of General Washington.

The British royal government had fled to the safety of the British warships a year before, but for a long time, until the Continental army drove them off, the ships were anchored within pistol shot of the Whitehall steps, where British and American sentries could exchange insults and intercourse with the city was easy. They now moved to an anchorage in the center of the river, where the communication was far quicker

81 MPC 445.
82 Clinton, American Rebellion, 11.

and easier to the Hackensack valley than to hostile Manhattan, and Bergen County soon became the ships' main source of both provisions and intelligence, and the little towns of Hackensack, New Bridge, and Tappan hives of enemy activity. British agents went about almost openly offering five guineas bounty and two hundred acres of land for each man, one hundred acres for his wife and fifty for each child, to any recruit who would enlist in King George's service,[83] and patriots suspected with cause that large numbers of young men of the neighborhood had gone aboard the warships to accept.

James Mason, "one of the workmen of Mr. Erskine, who had some time ago been discharged at the Ringwood Furnaces," was one of them. His story was probably not unlike that of many others who were lured by the five guineas and two hundred acres. He came down from the Jersey hills, went in to New York City, waited there in hiding for days in a tavern frequented by Tories, probably the Sergeant's Arms or Corbie's Tavern, and was finally taken aboard a warship. When he got aboard and enlisted, he was told that he would not be openly put into service but was to go back to his home and await further orders. "The new men," he explained when arrested, "were to assist the King's troops when they came; they were not to go on board because they could do more good on shore, and besides they were on short allowances on the ships, and crowded." [84]

In the Hackensack valley neighbor eyed neighbor suspiciously. No Whig who heard hoofbeats on the King's Highway or Queen Anne Road in the dead of night but saw in his mind's eye an enemy of twenty years on some errand of strife for the British warships; no Jersey Dutch Tory who saw the plight of New York's refugees but knew what lay in store for him if violent Liberty men ever seized the reins of power in the county.

During the past two years the Hackensack valley north of the New York-New Jersey line had seen much the same course of events. The little Dutch town of Tappan, or Orangetown, at the edge of the Highlands, the county seat of Orange County, was much less a commercial center than Hackensack and, though but twelve miles away, was much closer to the open frontier, but the same political and religious controversies that were dividing Dutch New Jersey divided its people.

In 1774, when the courthouse at the edge of the village green burned down, Whigs were sure it was Tory arson directed at the patriot deputy sheriff, Ebenezer Wood, who lived there.[85] Under the leadership of men like John Haring, Whigs circulated patriot associations which proved little about any but known Tories, for they alone refused to sign; patriots formed militia companies and sent off delegates to New York's Committee of Safety, John Haring, in fact, having been its president for a time.[86]

As the months passed after Lexington, self-styled moderates like Joshua Hett Smith, Thomas Outwater, and Dr. Sherwood were able, as their fellow moderates in Bergen County had been, largely to take over the patriot government.[87]

Orange County Dutchmen had much the same troubles as their neighbors to the south in trying to shape farmers into patriot militiamen, and not all of the troubles came from politics. Abraham Lent had been colonel and Johannes David Blauvelt lieutenant colonel of the Orangetown militia for many years under the royal government, and in December, 1775, when the patriot militia was put on a formal basis, they took the same posts, with Johannes Joseph Blauvelt, major; Jacobus de Clark, adjutant; Isaac Perry, quartermaster; and Johannes Jacobus Blauvelt, Isaac Smith, and Johannes Bell, captains.[88]

In March, 1776, Captain Johannes Jacobus Blauvelt and Lieutenant Jacobus Smith, with a party of thirty-five minutemen, and Captain Gilbert Cooper, with a company of local militia, marched to Nyack landing, boarded boats and sailed downriver to New York, where they were engaged for over two months in fortifying a place called Bunker's Hill, returning to lower Orange County in July.[89] During the last months of the year the same company was busy fortifying Tellers Point. Their colonel, Abraham Lent, however, resigned, apparently because of the difficulty of getting Dutchmen to leave their homes for such militia duty.[90] "Colonel Lent was with me the evening before last and appeared to be much out of humor on account of the late behavior of part of his regiment," John Haring wrote to the Provincial Committee of Safety on March 28, 1776. "He says that his orders have been treated with contempt and himself hindered by those from whom he expected assistance.

85 Cole, Tappan Church, 63.
86 Cole, Rockland County, 31.
87 Leake, Lamb, 377; 1 Force (5) 1385, 1386. The deputies to the New York Provincial Congress which convened July 9, 1776, were Colonel William Allison, Mr. Little, John Haring, David Pye and Mr. Outwater. Allison, Pye and Haring, at least, were firm patriots.
88 Cole, Rockland County, 31.
89 Affidavit of Rynard Hopper, Pension Records, S1022. See affidavit of Garret Serven, Pension Records, S1022. Bunker's Hill was a sod redoubt near the present intersection of Grand and Centre streets. Bliven, Battle for Manhattan (New York, 1955), 54, 55.
90 Cole, Rockland County, 33.

The Colonel has for a number of years last past been a militia officer and I believe we never had one who was more punctual in obeying and performing the orders of his superiors, and he consequently expected that those under his command should also obey him, but by experience he finds that he cannot get the orders of Congress . . . properly expedited and he is apprehensive that if he continues in office he will be censured by his superiors as well as blamed by his inferiors." [91] Haring laid the difficulties to the fact that the Orangetown regiment was "chiefly composed of such as know but little of the English language, and nothing of military affairs, wherefore, I must impute their backwardness and delays to ignorance and ill-founded jealousies of being imposed upon by their commanders and not to disaffection." Lent had been elected a member of the Orange County Committee of Correspondence in 1774, at the outset of the quarrel with London.[92] "I am fearful," Haring added, "that Lent's resignation will be followed by others, but I shall do all in my power to prevent it." [93]

"I have thought proper to resign my said commission," Lent wrote, ". . . choosing rather to serve as a private than to command people who are prejudiced against me." [94] Some of Lent's enemies in Tappan wondered whether there was not more to his resignation than annoyance at militiamen who knew but little of the English language and were prejudiced against him, but everyone agreed that he had worked under great difficulties. Indeed there were those who thought that both Lent and Haring were glossing over the situation. On June 30, 1776, the Provincial Congress noted that "a majority of the men who comprise the company of militia now or lately commanded by Captain [Arie] Blauvelt are notoriously disaffected." (Colonel Hay was directed "immediately to apprehend seven of the most refractory men of said company, and also to seize and take all the arms belonging to the disaffected men in said company . . . [and] . . . send the seven men and arms" to New York City.) [95]

Like Hackensack and Schraalenburgh, Tappan's troubles were complicated by a decade or more of bitter war in the Dutch Reformed church.[96] Since in Tappan almost everyone seemed to be a Haring or a

[91]   Cole, Rockland County, 32, 33.
[92]   Cole, Rockland County, 27.
[93]   Cole, Rockland County, 33. Lent was succeeded by Johannes D. Blauvelt. 1 Force (5) 1503. Major Hendrick Ver Bryck also resigned his commission, which he had received on July 17, 1776, for reasons of health. See 1 GC 321; 1 Force (5) 1413.
[94]   Cole, Rockland County, 33. At about the same time Captain Isaac P. Smith "became disaffected and would not serve any more." See affidavit of Cornelius Blauvelt, Pension Records, S22650.
[95]   Cole, Rockland County, 34. Blauvelt Genealogy No. 503.
[96]   Cole, Tappan Church, passim; ERNY, passim.

Blauvelt or related to them, the church war was perhaps even more violent than at Hackensack. Hardly a family lived there that was not divided against itself: Cornelius Abraham Haring was one of the founders of the irregular conferentie church, John Haring a pillar of Ver Bryck's coetus congregation; Theunis Blauvelt was a member of the irregular church, Johannes Jacobus Blauvelt an elder of the Ver Bryck church. Smiths were on both sides of the controversy, as were deClarks, Coles, Mabies, Underdonks, Bogerts, and Demarests, and all the other local people.

The fact that Dutchmen on both sides of the provincial line were engaged in the same religious conflicts hinted the truth plainly enough: there was more to the conferentie-coetus battle than a stubborn clash of wills between angry men. Though each side saw the conflict in simple terms of the wickedness of the other, great political and religious issues that had divided men for centuries were at stake, issues that are by no means resolved two hundred years later.

4

T<small>H E</small> summer of 1776 brought the war to New York and New Jersey.
On June 29, 1776, David Baulding, a blacksmith, went into New York
from Bergen County to tell Philip Livingston and John Jay, of the
New York Committee on Conspiracies, that the German settlement at
Ramapo kept up a treasonable correspondence with the British man-of-
war, that he, Baulding, was told on June 17 that Lawrence, Thomas and
Abraham Van Buskirk and a schoolmaster were going on board the
British man-of-war, but that something prevented all but the schoolmaster, who, he verily believed, did go. Baulding went on to say that on
his way to the city he had stopped for a toddy at the Three Pidgeons
tavern at Bergen Woods, where Francis Stevens, a patron who took him
for a Tory, told him that fifty sail of British ships were near Sandy Hook
and a hundred more to come. The tavernkeeper Earl added, in the
solemn way of bartenders before and since, "That news came from on
board the man-of-war this week."[1] Governor Tryon's people on board
H.M.S. *The Dutchess of Gordon* had not misinformed their Jersey Dutch
friends. The British were poised for invasion.

June 29, 1776, the day Baulding told his story, was a Saturday. On
Sunday, Monday, and Tuesday British ships kept moving into the
harbor, until more than one hundred sail were collected inside Sandy
Hook, most of them transports, their decks filled with redcoats, who

[1]   The schoolmaster was undoubtedly Robert Timpany, a Scotch-Irishman who kept
a school a few miles from Hackensack. He had never hidden his British sympathies.
Abraham Van Buskirk, on the other hand, had accepted a commission in the patriot
militia as recently as four months before, and it is quite possible that he was still
regarded as a patriot. There can be no doubt of the truth of Baulding's story.

proceeded to disembark and move into encampments on Staten Island.

Confident as Tories may have been that the armed might of Britain would soon answer colonial impudence, the reality exceeded all expectations: William Howe and his brother Admiral Lord Howe, it was clear, had brought to New York a force fully able to put down the rebellion, and at once. Local Tories who had stood silently by while Whigs set up revolutionary Committees of Safety now saw no reason not to protest; refugees from New York in the Hackensack valley, who saw the day of deliverance at hand, made ready to return to New York City in triumph, waiting only for General Howe to drive out the posturing rebels who had occupied their homes. William Bayard, the owner of the Hoboken ferry, once a somewhat lukewarm member of several patriot committees but for the past fourteen weeks a Tory refugee in the Hackensack valley, had been suspected of recruiting for the British in and around Kakiat, where he had a small farm, and he was now at English Neighborhood. Whigs had long assumed that Bayard was more than a mere refugee of convenience and few were surprised when they learned that Bayard's son was now aboard Howe's ship, the *Eagle*.[2] Some, indeed, would have added the Anglican pastor, the Rev. Charles Inglis, to the refugees in English Neighborhood who were under suspicion.[3] Inglis, who was certain that Presbyterian ministers had started the war,[4] had preached destruction of rebels for years, but Whigs were probably wrong if they thought he was plotting action against them. Frederick Rhinelander, a New York liquor dealer, and Benjamin Huggett, the owner of a New York china shop, were, on the other hand, two Tories in English Neighborhood whose activities had become so notorious that General Washington himself asked the New Jersey authorities to apprehend them: "There are some also, of very dangerous characters, who I am informed are lurking in the neighbourhood of Hackensack and what they call the English Neighborhood; . . . [their arrest] is now become the more necessary, as from the intelligence I have this day received, there is the greatest reason to believe, that the enemy intend to begin their operations in a very few days, and that with a very powerful force."[5]

Less than two weeks after the fleet arrived two British ships made a move which brought Bergen County and lower Orange County somewhat closer to the reality of war. At three o'clock in the afternoon on July 12, the *Phoenix*, a 24-gun frigate, and the *Rose*, carrying 28 guns,

2 LYT NYPL "William Bayard."
3 LYT NYPL "William Bayard."
4 Serle Diary 115.
5 5 GW 388.

cut out from the fleet, got under sail, and headed up the Hudson. The American batteries on Red Hook, Governor's Island, lower Manhattan, and Paulus Hook opened fire at the two vessels with every gun, but they sailed past almost unscathed and proceeded upriver, first to a point opposite Nyack and then to Haverstraw Bay.[6]

Panic seized the inhabitants of New York as the ships passed, though it soon became clear that they had no purpose in going upriver but to anchor in Haverstraw Bay. There they lay for weeks, openly contemptuous of American artillerymen, inviting every disloyal American in lower Orange County to attach himself to the British cause and giving the good people of Nyack and Haverstraw their first taste of musket and cannon fire,[7] as small boats from the ships sought, generally without success, to provision them by raids on shore. Their one successful raid, patriots claimed, was the burning and plundering of the home of poor, half-blind Jacob Halstead, who lived in an isolated place under Dunderburg Mountain: "Captain Wallace headed the party that committed this robbery. His share of the plunder was a handkerchief full of salad and a pig so very poor that a crow would scarcely deign to eat it. The house stood single under a mountain and we thought the poverty of the owner would be sufficient protection." [8]

The ships of course intensified Tory activity between Haverstraw Bay and New York City. It was not long before every Jersey Dutch patriot on the west side of the river knew that the man who had gone down to New York to pilot the boats upriver was Robert Sneden, one of the five sons of the widow Sneden, who lived between the Palisades and the river at Sneden's Landing, a little pocket of tillable land opposite Dobbs Ferry, and kept the ferry there.[9] He and some of his brothers were among the few who had refused to sign the Orange County patriot association in July, 1775. The trade of ferryman, like that of stagedriver, innkeeper or miller, does not seem to predispose man to great causes, a fact in which the cynic may see proof that daily dealings with men do not lead to the love of man. The Snedens were ferrymen and, whether their calling had anything to do with it or not, Orange County patriots

---

6 1 Force (5) 258, 330, 374, 452.
7 "The regiment of this county," John Coe wrote from Haverstraw on July 13, "is now and has been under arms all night, occasioned by the appearance of several ships of war of the ministerial fleet now lying in Tappan Bay." I Force (5) 374, 375, 452, 580.
8 1 Force (5) 544, 545. Halstead had, he said, "one blind eye, occasioned by an indisposition in the head . . . sees badly with the other; is forty-one years old and has nine children, one of whom is a soldier in Captain Blauvelt's company." He lost, besides his house, nine of his hogs and his poor furniture. 1 Force (5) 1490. See also 1 Force (5) 546, 580.
9 1 Force (5) 648.

believed that all but one of them were carrying on a treasonable correspondence with America's enemies on the British ships of war, taking advantage, the Committee of Safety said, "of the great opportunity afforded them in the privilege they have by keeping ferry," and accusing them of being "inveterate enemies of the common states of America." The Committee of Safety ordered the Snedens "not to operate their ferry, nor to employ any other person to ferry in their room." Indeed, "all persons were forewarned against having any correspondence with the above Snedens whatsoever." The Committee of Safety did at the same time, however, correct the story that John Sneden was anything other than a warm friend of the cause of America.[10]

On July 21 two deserters from the American forces at New York stole a rowboat, crossed the Hudson to a marsh near Hoboken, and started out toward the north. They slept in a Teaneck hay barrack that night; on the second morning they stopped at the tavern at New Bridge for breakfast. "The tavern was on the [east] side of the New Bridge on the west side of the road and about one-quarter of a mile or less from the bridge; a sign on a sign pole close by the east corner of the house." [11]

After they had finished their meal, the tavernkeeper asked who they were and where they were going. They showed purported discharges from the American army. When the tavernkeeper said that they were well out of it because the Americans were sure to be beat, one confidence led to another until the men admitted that they were deserters. The tavernkeeper then suggested that he knew a man in the neighborhood who was willing to pay a large sum in gold to anyone who would go aboard the *Phoenix* man-of-war with a message. Though the deserters did not give the name, it is not hard now to guess that the man in the neighborhood who wanted a messenger badly enough to pay in hard British gold was one of the Van Buskirks who lived a mile or so down the River Road.

The two men then "continued along the common road after breakfast, stopping now and then only for a drink," and arrived at Suffern's tavern in the dusk of that evening. On being asked there for his pass by the patriot tavernkeeper, one of them confidently handed over a

[10] 1 Force (5) 648. The reference to John *Snyder* is thought to be a typographical error. Dennis Sneden evidently took an active part in recruiting Tory troops. "Jacob, Isaac, Henry and Abraham [Gesner] took the opportunity to go to New York . . . in possession of the English, with some others. [They] went off with an open small pettiauger belonging to Dennis Sneden, who went also from Sneden's." The Gesners joined Bayard's Orange County Rangers, though their relatives after the war believed they had no intention of doing so when they left Sneden's Landing. Nicholas Gesner Diary, July 19, 1834, Palisades (N.Y.) Library.
[11] 1 GC 270, 271.

paper reading, "this is to Serty'Fy that John Green is Got His DisCharge from the Contententle Serves By His own Request From the Fleet Belongin to Philladelphe the Andrew Dorey Admerel Hopkins Captain Beetle." The landlord turned both men over to the American authorities. When questioned, Green told an elaborate story about service with General Braddock in the French and Indian War, enlistment on board the row galleys at Philadelphia, discharge from the navy, enlistment in the New York Continental forces, discharge and plans to go to the Sterling Iron Works. Peter Buckstaff, the other deserter, said simply that he had left the army to go home.[12]

Both men solemnly assured the Americans that they had rejected the British gold offered them at New Bridge, but they were nevertheless sent in for spies. Nothing seems to have been done to apprehend the tavernkeeper or the disloyal man in the neighborhood. John Green later received thirty-nine lashes for desertion, and a subsequent thirty-nine lashes for breaking jail.[13]

On August 2 six Tories who had been aboard the warships in Haverstraw Bay were arrested in the Bergen Woods near Bull's Ferry.[14]

By this time many Hackensack valley Dutchmen of doubtful sympathies had almost disappeared from sight, leaving their patriot neighbors to imagine what plans were being concocted on the British warships for their destruction. With the British fleet at hand and British soldiers but twenty miles away, the Hackensack valley had begun to take on the character it was to hold throughout the long years of war, a meeting place for spies, deserters, and all the shadowy characters that hoped to profit in such a place; hardly the countryside whose smiling fields had charmed visitors a few years before; hardly, in fact, a countryside to charm anyone.

Washington concentrated his troops on Manhattan, Long Island, and those points in New Jersey directly opposite Staten Island, the New Jersey posts being manned by New Jersey and Pennsylvania troops, including Captain Board's Bergen County militia company, who were stationed on Bergen Neck on the east side of Newark Bay.[15] Optimistic patriots regarded them as a strong shield for the country to the north

12 1 GC 247, 270, etc.
13 5 GW 376, 462.
14 1 Force (5) 1484. The names are not Dutch; they probably were residents of Westchester. "Some of them . . . are in indigent circumstances, and have large families." Idem.
15 Affidavit of Abraham D. Banta, Pension Records, S6575; affidavit of Samuel Demarest, Pension Records, S15081. See 1 Force (5) 337. "Many of the Jersey militia are gone to the Kills and Bergen Point. They are the best militia and with better arms and accoutrements than any other militia I have ever seen." 1 Force (5) 257, 452.

and west. "Our men," Peter Elting wrote to Richard Varick, "are in high spirits and ready to meet them at any hour. The town swarms with people. I doubt not but our army consists of at least twenty thousand men, and the country about us very willing to lend us their assistance." [16] Elting would have been shaken to know that Washington himself was almost desperate about the situation. The passage of the *Phoenix* and the *Rose* proved what little dependence could be placed upon his forts, and the panic of the people of New York under the bombardment of those two vessels, not to speak of the conduct of his soldiers, gave him little cause to hope for a spirited defense of the city when the British chose to move.

On August 22, 1776, General Howe opened the attack. The British forces landed on Long Island and marched rapidly inland, driving the Americans before them in headlong flight and capturing two American generals, Stirling and Sullivan. The Battle of Long Island was soon over and the strategic places of Kings County in the hands of the British. Patriots who had wished for a British attack now deplored the city's weakness, with that quick shift from optimism to panic that seemed to characterize the people of New York. "The town appears to me," wrote Peter Elting, who had been saying the exact opposite a month before, "to be in a bad state of defense. It seems the greatest dependence is made on the musketry." [17]

He was right in thinking poorly of musketry as a block to British Regulars. September 15 saw the Americans easily driven from lower Manhattan; a little later the strong point of Paulus Hook across the river and the town of Bergen were evacuated by the American forces without a battle.[18] The capture of New York and the occupation of Paulus Hook and Bergen Neck made it obvious to the most optimistic patriot that the Hackensack valley was in great danger. "We are now left the open frontier," Elting wrote from Hackensack on September 23, "only a few troops along the banks of the meadows. This together with the many disaffected persons about this place occasions many citizens to leave it. Mrs. Elting has pressed me hard this day to move her and child and some of my most valuable effects to Kingston." [19] Mr. Elting was quite right in seeing the Hackensack valley as an open frontier, and Mrs. Elting was also not mistaken in thinking it wise to move to the north.

Disloyal Dutchmen became bolder by the hour. Lukewarm patriots

16 NYAR 99, 100.
17 NYAR 105.
18 Serle Diary 112, 114, 119.
19 Schoonmaker, History of Kingston, 239.

now shunned the company of men like John Fell, Roelif Westervelt, and Peter Zabriskie. Indeed, if John Zabriskie's reports of the refusal of Bergen County Dutchmen to sell grain to the army were correct, even warmer patriots may have begun to cool: General Biddle "engaged [Lt.] Col. John Zabriskie near Hackensack to purchase about 2,000 bushels of oats, corn & rye, which he said could be got in that neighborhood . . [but] Col. Zabriskie . . . got no grain, as the inhabitants would not sell it without gold & silver." [20] It is perhaps proper to add that, things being what they were, Colonel Zabriskie was not the most zealous patriot in the county, and may have blamed his neighbors for his own backwardness.

As soon as the British were well established on Manhattan, those Tory refugees who could manage it worked their way back into the city. William Bayard, concealing himself by day and moving by night, came down through the Hackensack valley from his hiding place at Kakiat, got to Weehawken and was taken off from there to New York disguised as a servant. Anxious to confer at once with Governor Tryon on the British warships, he went down to the Whitehall steps and demanded to be rowed over and finally, "with much difficulty from his appearance," was carried on board a warship, from which he returned with a commission to lead his brigade of Orange County Rangers as lieutenant colonel.[21]

The British, prepared for the worst by Tory reports, warmly received their friends who had "escaped out of the tyranny of those insolent demagogues." "It excited one's sympathy," one Briton wrote, "to see their poor meagre faces, and to hear their complaints of being hunted for their lives like game into the woods and swamps, only because they would not renounce their allegiance to their King and affection for their country." [22] So far as Colonel Bayard was concerned, he soon lost any poor meager face he may have had, and before long was back in New York's social whirl, entertaining "large Assemblies of the Beaus & Belles of New York" at his mansion house at Greenwich.[23] The Hackensack valley, for its part, saw a new influx of refugees, patriot leaders in flight from New York and Long Island. Indeed, in the newly conquered parts of Long Island and Manhattan it was now the patriots' turn to be hunted down, and large numbers of refugees from British and Tory vengeance fled into the Hackensack valley, where patriots were doubtless equally struck by their friends' poor meager faces. One of them, Domine

[20] NJRC 11.
[21] LYT NYPL "William Bayard."
[22] Serle Diary 40.
[23] Serle Diary 186.

Solomon Froeligh of the Queens County Dutch Reformed church, a graduate of Peter Wilson's Academy and later a student of Domine Goetschius, and the husband of a popular Hackensack girl, preached at the Hackensack church on the green on the next Sunday after his arrival on II Chronicles 11:4: "Thus saith the Lord, Ye shall not go up, nor fight against your brethren," exhorting the congregation to hold together for independence. It was a powerful sermon, warmly commended by the local Whigs and patriot refugees in the congregation; Tory Dutchmen, who found the text much too pointed for their taste, caused an open disturbance before the end of the service.[24] A number of other Dutch Reformed ministers were with Froeligh.

When Hugh Gaine, the former Whig printer, defected to the British at the end of October, 1776, he told his new friends that "the people in the Jerseys, to his own knowledge, were quite tired of their democratic tyranny, and that he [believed] the people in general would embrace reconciliation but for the inflammatory declamations and instigations of their preachers." [25] Gaine underrated the independence of Calvinist congregations, but he did not underrate the enmity of Presbyterian preachers and their friends among the Dutch Reformed to the whole Tory establishment, civil and ecclesiastical.

Almost every house between Hackensack and the Highlands sheltered one or two refugees. General Washington had hoped to establish a Continental hospital in lower Orange County, but his chief medical officer, who had gone about the countryside with John Haring looking for a possible site, reported that no place could be found in Orangetown "without turning a number of distressed persons out of doors. . . . Almost every house is filled and crowded with people who fled out of the city. I cannot find in Orangetown room for one such person without discommoding someone or other. Every hovel in Orange County," he added, "is full of inhabitants from New York." [26]

The arrival of a strong British fleet, the poor showing of the American troops at the Battle of Long Island, and the evacuation of New York had, by the middle of October, 1776, shaken the faith of many, not only in Bergen and Orange counties but elsewhere in the middle colonies. The less zealous were able to say plausibly that they had supported the American cause against the British ministry but had no thought of independence and drew back from it. Some few may have had the candor to add that, so far as they could see, American arms

24 Millstone Centennial 58; Demarest, Lamentation over Solomon Froeligh.
25 Serle Diary 135.
26 1 GC 345,346.

had lost the war and further resistance was useless. The British did everything possible to encourage this view.

General Sir William Howe, a Whig himself, who probably sincerely wanted to bring the colonists back to Britain without bloodshed, offered attractive terms to American leaders who would come over to his side. Handbills attacking Congress were broadcast to American troops stationed in lower Orange County,[27] Rivington's *Gazette* began again to pour out its abuse of the American cause from New York, and neither Howe's offers nor Rivington's threats were wholly without effect. Some seemingly well-affected Dutchmen were perfectly explicit in their opposition to independence: Colonel A. Hawks Hay reported to the New York Committee of Safety that most of his men "refused to attend the service, though repeatedly summoned." Some of them complained that the last troops "had been drawn off from the immediate defense of their wives, children and property . . . contrary to their expectations." Others declared that if they left their farms their families would starve, "and would therefore as leave die by the sword as by famine. A third set, and the most numerous, declare that the Congress have rejected all overtures for a reconciliation inconsistent with independency; that all they desire is peace, liberty and safety and if they can procure that, they are contented." [28]

A few weeks later Colonel Hay repeated much the same thing to General Greene at Fort Lee, in complaining that his militiamen refused to do duty. "They say that General Howe has promised them peace, liberty and safety and that is all they want." "What," Greene asked Washington with more than a hint of despair, "is to be done with them? This spirit and temper should be checked in its infancy." [29]

Greene could suggest nothing better than to send fifty Continentals from Fort Lee and threaten to put the militiamen into service at the fort if they did not comply with Hay's orders.

Hay was somewhat inclined to pessimism and may have been too easily discouraged, for many Orange County militiamen were determined patriots, but he was not wrong in believing that many of his neighbors were impressed by British promises and British power.

The fort to which Greene threatened to take the militiamen had by this time come to be one of the principal military works in the country. About the middle of July, 1776, General Washington had determined to lay out a fort on the heights of the Palisades, directly opposite Fort

27   3 Force (5) 498.
28   2 Force (5) 1066, 1067.
29   3 Force (5) 523.

Washington, and had personally supervised some of its beginnings.[30] Originally named Fort Constitution, it was renamed Fort Lee on October 19, 1776, after General Charles Lee's victory at Charleston.

The site was almost a natural fortification. A clove in the Palisades, where a farm road from English Neighborhood twisted its way from the heights down to a river landing, left a high promontory standing out from the Palisades, inaccessible from three sides because of precipitous rocks, which fell off hundreds of feet to the river on one side and far enough on the other to discourage any assault. Ten acres were cleared, partly on this promontory and partly on the high land to the west, all rocky and heavily wooded wasteland on the farm of Peter Bourdet,[31] whose farmhouse and cultivated land lay to the west, along the road to Bergen.

At the northern entrance to the promontory an abatis of felled and pointed trees was built. Within this protected eminence heavy gun emplacements commanded the Hudson River below. To the west a square bastioned earthwork was built, and surrounding this, log huts for thousands of soldiers.[32] Lieutenant Joseph Hodgkins of the Massachusetts Line wrote from the fort on September 30, 1776, that he was then "on the Jersey hills, where we have been ever since the 20th of this month and I hope we shall stay here this campaign as I have been at the trouble of building a log house with a stone chimney. I got it fit to live in three days ago, before which I had not lodged on anything but the ground since we left Long Island." [33] (He was shortly moved back across the Hudson to join the other New England troops there.)

The garrison at the fort varied from a few hundred to more than two thousand,[34] and it was commanded by the celebrated General Nathanael Greene,[35] who, it is believed, made his headquarters at one of the

30 Henderson, Shadow on the River, 9, citing Hall, Fort Lee, 171, and Fitzpatrick, General Washington's Accounts of Expenses 1775–1783, 34.
31 Damages by Americans, NJSL, Hackensack Precinct, "Bourdet."
32 Henderson, 1960 BHSP 17, etc.; Hall, Fort Lee, passim. 160 men, with a field officer, three captains, six subalterns, six sergeants, six corporals and six drums and fifes had been sent on August 6, 1776, to relieve an existing party at Burdett's Ferry, at the foot of the Palisades, below the site of Fort Lee; and Colonel Hitchcock's regiment relieved the detachment under the General Orders of Aug. 12, 1776. 1 Force (5) 1139. By Aug. 20, 1776, the General Return of the Army in New Jersey under command of General Hugh Mercer showed about 2,300 of the Pennsylvania Flying Corps at Fort Lee. Henderson, Shadow on the River, 21, citing Hall, Fort Lee, 109.
33 Glorious Cause 223.
34 Henderson, Shadow on the River, 23, citing General Orders of the American Army.
35 See Thayer, Greene, 111, etc. Many Bergen County militiamen were in and around Fort Lee at the time, among them those under Captains Post, Romeyn, Stagg and Van Houten, "making the fort . . . , doing guard duty and other services . . .

commodious Dutch farmhouses in the English Neighborhood to the west.

The soldiers at the fort quickly destroyed Bourdet's fences and crops. He had, he complained, "125 acres in good fence and not one left . . . three acres of corn on the field destroyed . . . four acres of flax and oats, very good destroyed." [36]

The artillery at the fort, like others of the day, was not accurate enough to block up the river, but it was perfectly able to prevent the British from using their naval forces to any advantage against the Amer-

Forcing the Hudson River Passage, October 1776.
Sketch after Dominic Serres. E. Tone, 1962.

icans north of the city. Several of the guns at Fort Lee were able to reach any part of the river; indeed, when the British later seized Fort Washington they were able to drop shells into the captured fort, well above the water. At eight o'clock in the morning of October 9, two British warships, the *Phoenix* and the *Roebuck*, sailed upstream despite the fort's heavy cannonading, without damage, so far as the Americans

and assisting in dealing out provisions." Pension Records, Affidavits of Abraham Vreeland (W20525), Abraham D. Banta (S6575), Abraham H. Garrison (W857) and Daniel G. Smith (S3942).

[36] Damages by Americans, NJSL, Hackensack Precinct, "Bourdet." The Jersey Dutch fences, like their houses and barns, were sturdily built. An officer in the French army wrote: "The fences there are arranged like the fence rails in France; there are ordinarily five of them, one on top of the other. . . ." Von Closen Journal 109.

[37] Henderson, **Shadow on the River**, 15, 16, 17.

could see, although in fact there had been a good number of casualties aboard.[37] After a time the two ships returned to lower New York Bay.

On October 27, 1776, at seven in the morning, two other British frigates moved up and anchored directly between Fort Washington and Fort Lee. This action proved too bold, and the ships were soon driven off by artillery fire from the forts.[38]

British deserters spoke of the last move as part of a plan of General Howe to visit the Jerseys,[39] but the general view was that the attempt was so dangerous and so long delayed that it could scarcely still be planned.[40]

In point of fact, whether or not the British had any immediate plan to move into Jersey, they were not anxious to keep Washington from withdrawing across the Hudson to the west side, and their ships had placed themselves in the Hudson because General Howe had received reports that the Americans "were very busy . . . in transporting cannon, baggage, etc., across the North River to the Jersey shore." The British did not underestimate the strength of the post there.

Washington was at White Plains with the main force of the Continental army. With him was at least one company of Hackensack valley troops, Captain James Smith's company of Orange County militia, in the left wing under command of General Putnam. In one sharp battle this company withstood a hot fire from the British for more than an hour before they were forced to retreat to their entrenchments in White Plains. "When engaged in said battle," John P. Blauvelt of Orangetown wrote later, "one of my neighbors, a soldier, Abraham Onderdonk, was killed by a cannon ball from the enemy separating his head from his shoulders, two besides of our men fell within a few feet of me." [41]

38 2 Force (5) 1266.
39 See 6 GW 261.
40 3 Force (5) 630.
41 Affidavit of John P. Blauvelt, Pension Records, W20728.

5

E VERY military rule dictated the end of Howe's campaign with the beginning of winter, but Washington's spies and British deserters were at one in saying that Howe had no choice but to move into Jersey, if only to obtain the wood on which the city's inhabitants depended to keep from freezing. Accordingly, when General Howe pulled back his forces facing the American positions in Westchester, Washington had to decide whether Howe had given up his campaign for the winter or planned to continue it with an attack on northern New Jersey. He correctly guessed that Howe was going to attack. "I think it highly probable and almost certain that [Howe] will make a descent with part of his troops into Jersey," he wrote, "and as soon as I am satisfied that the present maneuver is real and not a feint, I shall use every means in my power to forward part of our force to counteract his designs." [1]

Washington's first step was to urge Governor William Livingston, at Trenton, to clear northern New Jersey of anything useful to an army. "The article of forage is of great importance to them," he wrote; "not a blade should remain for their use." [2] Having been tempted to burn New York rather than let it become the winter headquarters for the British, he had nevertheless permitted others to dissuade him from that course: he now hoped to avoid the same mistake in New Jersey.[3] To

[1]   6 GW 249.
[2]   6 GW 255.
[3]   Governor Livingston, always impatient with slow minds, listened to a committee of the Assembly debate the matter for two days, but assured Washington that whatever they decided, patriots would approve anything the military did under "so evident a stamp of necessity." 3 Force (5) 617, 618.

General Nathanael Greene, at Fort Lee, Washington sent an express directing him "to impress speedily and forcibly" upon New Jersey farmers the importance of destroying or removing their forage and grain.[4] On the next day he sent another express, authorizing Greene to order the evacuation of Fort Washington on the New York shore, if necessary to save the garrison. He should have ordered, not authorized, the evacuation of the fort.[5]

Washington's order repeated his directions to strip the Jersey countryside: "As the enemy have drawn great relief from the forage and provisions they have found in the country, and which our tenderness spared, you will do well to prevent their receiving any fresh supplies, by destroying it if the inhabitants will not drive off their stock, and remove the hay, grain, etc., in time. Experience has shown that a contrary conduct is not of the least advantage to the poor inhabitants, from whom all their effects of every kind are taken without distinction and without satisfaction." [6]

Jersey Dutchmen were to need another winter to learn that lesson, and, unfortunately, so was General Greene. That foundryman-turned-general—mindful of the furor that would follow if he started to seize patriots' property while Howe sat quietly in New York, apparently planning nothing but a comfortable winter season at headquarters—affected to misunderstand Washington's plain directions: "If the enemy crosses the river I shall follow your Excellency's advice respecting the cattle and forage." He added philosophically that "these measures, however cruel in appearance, were ever maxims of war in defence of a country." [7] When the British actually crossed the river, General Greene was to find himself moved by quite a different maxim of war, the precept that he who runs away lives to fight another day. The redcoats, when they got to the Hackensack valley, found it a rich storehouse of food and fuel for their army.

Greene went on to report that he had tried to stop the almost open communication between Bergen County and British New York by ordering "all the boats stove in from Burdett's Ferry to Hobuck and from Powley's Ferry to Bergen Point. There is a vile generation here as well as with you," he added.[8]

4   6 GW 254. The Essex County Committee ordered appropriate action; it is doubtful if the Bergen County authorities did anything. 3 Force (5) 629.
5   6 GW 257, 258. Greene's reasons for not evacuating the post are in his letter to Washington of Nov. 9, 1776. 3 Force (5) 618, 619. He correctly observed that Fort Lee was of importance only in conjunction with Fort Washington; he was wholly mistaken on the main issue.
6   6 GW 257, 258.
7   2 Greene Greene 265.
8   3 Force (5) 523; 2 Greene Greene 258, 259.

On November 7 there was a flurry of excitement on the west side of the river. General Greene had loaded several pettiaugers with flour destined for the main army and had attempted to run them up the river past the British ships, which immediately put out several barges, two tenders, and a row-galley to seize the American boats. "Our people," Greene reported, "ran the pettiaugers ashore and landed and defended them," the British attempting to land several times without success.[9]

For several days the main British army lay at Dobbs Ferry, opposite Sneden's Landing, as if poised for an attack on the west shore,[10] but after a time they moved off to the south, seemingly having given up the plan.[11]

Sunday, November 10, 1776, was a warm, pleasant day; indeed the whole autumn of 1776 had seen "the finest weather for the season ever known, and such a fall as no man can recollect." [12] Domine Dirck Romeyn preached to a full church at Schraalenburgh, baptizing four children when the service was over; [13] Warmoldus Kuypers preached at Hackensack; Garret Leydecker at English Neighborhood; Domine Ver Bryck at Tappan, and Domine Van der Linde at Paramus, but it was hardly a serene Sunday. Everyone in the county knew that the heights of the Palisades were a hive of military activity; Schraalenburgh church-goers from Closter and Tenafly passed hundreds of marching troops on the County Road as they came to the morning service.[14]

Greene wrote to Washington in the course of the day: "I am taking every measure in my power to oppose the enemy's landing, if they attempt crossing the river into the Jerseys. I have about five hundred men posted at the different passes in the mountains fortifying. About five hundred more are marching from Amboy directly for Dobb's Ferry [Sneden's Landing]. . . . I have directed the Quartermaster General to have everything moved out of the enemy's way, particularly cattle, carriages, hay and grain. The flour at Dobb's Ferry is all moved from that place; and I have directed wagons to transport it to Clarke's and Orange Towns." Though he confessed that he could not believe the British would have given such a full warning if they really intended to invade New Jersey, he assured Washington that he was taking the same precautions that he would have taken if he expected an attack. "I am sure the enemy cannot land at Dobb's Ferry, it will be so hedged up by night. The flats run off a great distance; they can't get near the shore with their

9   3 Force (5) 556; 2 Greene Greene 261.
10   3 Force (5) 556, 557, 558.
11   3 Force (5) 653.
12   1 Kemble 101.
13   Schraalenburgh Church Records.
14   2 Greene Greene 266; 3 Force (5) 629.

ships. If the enemy intends to effect a landing at all, they'll attempt it at Naiac's or Haverstraw Bay."[15]

The time was to come when patriots would agree that, next to Washington, Nathanael Greene was the best general officer in the American army establishment, but he was to learn his generalship in a hard school, a school that had but begun in November, 1776; indeed, General Howe was to teach him two great lessons in strategy within the fortnight.[16]

Washington did not share Greene's view that the British threat to New Jersey was a feint; he had already begun to move troops across the Hudson.[17]

Three short days later, on Wednesday, November 13, General Washington himself was at Greene's headquarters.[18] He had crossed the river at King's Ferry, with all the Continental troops from New Jersey, Pennsylvania, Maryland, and the states to the south, and after a circuitous march of 65 miles from White Plains in very cold rainy weather, his troops encamped in and around Hackensack.[19] Washington and his staff established their own headquarters at Peter Zabriskie's house on the village green.[20]

As Washington reviewed his situation, it was bad but far from desperate. He had been forced into a quick withdrawal from New York City, but that was not unexpected. He still had a large army in being and the first blasts of winter would send Howe into winter quarters and give the Americans another season to enlist a larger one. At Fort Lee, four miles due east of Hackensack, General Greene held a strong position, with the sheer wall of the Palisades of the Hudson making an almost impassable precipice for ten miles to the south and twenty or more miles to the north. He commanded over 2,400 troops on the west

[15] 2 Greene Greene 266; 3 Force (5) 629, 630. "In Jersey, across the river from Dobbs Ferry," a Hessian officer wrote, "the enemy had a small camp, which high shrubs prevented us from seeing entirely, and in front of which, behind an embankment, they had posted an 18 pounder, which fired on a frigate and two transports that lay at anchor close to our shore." Baurmeister 67.

[16] Greene was protecting every crossing but the one the British planned to use. 3 Force (5) 630.

[17] Twelve hundred men under General Lord Stirling crossed at King's Ferry to Haverstraw on Saturday, Nov. 9; 2700 under Hand and Beall crossed on Sunday morning. 3 Force (5) 634.

[18] 6 GW 279.

[19] 6 GW 279.

[20] "I hastened over on this side with about five thousand men by a roundabout march (which we were obliged to take on account of the shipping opposing the passage at all the lower ferries) of near sixty-five miles." 6 GW 244. The Zabriskie mansion, in a much altered condition, stood on the green at Hackensack until the middle of the twentieth century, when it was torn down. Its loss is a grave reflection on the people of New Jersey. See Bailey 333 and 1 Westervelt, Bergen County, 106, for the early history of the house.

The Hackensack Green.
Historical Collections of the State of New Jersey, 1845.

side of the river.[21] Directly opposite Fort Lee was Fort Washington, where Colonel Robert Magaw had an additional 1,200 of Greene's troops,[22] and Washington had another large force with him in and near Hackensack.[23] He had left General Heath at Peekskill with 3,000 men,[24] and General Charles Lee commanded 7,500 in Westchester. The British would doubtless move, but their road would not be an easy one.

Almost before General Washington had settled himself at the Zabriskie mansion, the British movement began. Late in the afternoon of

[21] Greene's official return for Nov. 14 showed 2,667 rank and file fit for duty, of which 508 (under Colonel Durkee and Major Clarke) were at Sneden's Landing (Dobbs Ferry); 145 were detached to Bergen(town), Hoboken. Bull's Ferry, Hackensack and Clinton Point, opposite Spuyten Duyvil; 1,510 were detached to New York island (Fort Washington). There were more troops at Fort Lee when it was attacked a few days later, Washington having on Nov. 16 "stopped General Beall's and General Heard's Brigades [at the fort] to preserve the post and stores here, which with other troops I hope we shall be able to effect." 6 GW 287. A return dated the day before shows 4682 rank and file under Greene's command in New Jersey. Greene Papers Transcripts HL. The accuracy of the returns is questionable.
[22] Heard commanded about 800 rank and file (3 Force [5] 501, 502); Beall probably about the same number. The other troops at Fort Lee were "what remains of General Ewing's brigade." Washington to President of Congress, Nov. 19, 1776. 6 GW 293.
[23] Washington believed that his own force numbered 5,000. It was probably much less. 4 Freeman 241.
[24] Of these, 400 under Colonel Huntington were posted west of the Hudson at Sidman's Bridge, on the Ramapo River, at the south end of Smith's Clove, the historic pass from the Jersey Dutch country through the Hudson Highlands. 3 Force (5) 664.

November 15 the crowd of village idlers and boys on the green opposite Washington's headquarters saw a Continental horseman gallop up and rush into the house, and a moment later Washington and three or four of his aides rode off rapidly toward Fort Lee. The express had brought word that Fort Washington was threatened by advancing British troops.[25]

It took perhaps an hour for Washington to ferry across the Hackensack and ride up the steep western slope of the Palisades; by the time he reached Fort Lee the last slanting rays of the November sun had disappeared, and General Greene and General Putnam had already crossed the Hudson to help Colonel Magaw put the threatened fort in a state of defense. General Mercer and the other officers who were left at Fort Lee earnestly repeated Greene's assurances that the fort could hold out for a month. Now that the test had come, Washington could only hope that Greene had the military acumen to justify the self-confidence which had placed so large a part of his small army—1,200 men, as Washington supposed—at hazard in a single engagement. When several hours passed without word from the other side of the river, Washington finally decided to end the pointless discussion at Fort Lee and go over to Fort Washington, where he could see at first hand what was being done. He took one or two of his staff and went quickly down the rocky ravine that led to the river, boarded a boat and started across. Before the little craft had reached the middle of the stream they met the returning Greene and Putnam, who told Washington that "the troops were in high spirits, and would make a good defense." Thus assured, it being late at night, he returned to the Jersey shore.[26]

At ten o'clock the next morning the actual attack began, a tragic drama which was soon over. The garrison, Washington now learned to his dismay, was not 1,200 men, but over twice that number, Greene having sent about 1,500 more troops across the river as a last-minute reinforcement. The defenders were quickly driven from their outposts, the unseasoned troops retreating in panic to the protection of the fort after a brief exchange of fire. As Washington, Greene, Putnam, and Mercer watched from the other shore, Hessian troops occupied the outer redoubts and poured in on the overcrowded defenders of the main fort a fire so hot that a quick surrender was inevitable. All firing from the fort stopped almost at once. Seeing this, Washington sent two daring volunteers to Magaw with word that an attempt would be made under cover of darkness to bring off the garrison if he could only hold out till

[25] 4 Freeman 241; 3 Force (5) 699, 700.
[26] 6 GW 286.

evening, but they soon returned with word that the post was already surrendered.[27]

Washington sat down at once to the heartbreaking task of preparing a dispatch to Congress, then rode wearily back to Hackensack with the weight of disaster on his shoulders, cursing his folly for listening to the empty words of incompetent subordinates and bitter at Congress for setting up so worthless a military establishment. Publicly Washington made no excuses, but as he and his young friend and aide, Colonel Joseph Reed, made their way back to headquarters, he poured out his anger that "the post had been held contrary to his wishes and opinion," observing sharply that America would never have an army as long as the states persisted in creating officers who were "not fit to be shoeblacks" merely because they were friends of this or that member of Congress.[28] Washington had a deserved reputation for round talk when he was angry; the ferryman at Little Ferry may well have heard enough Virginia oaths in one short crossing to match years of experience with Jersey Dutch teamsters.

With two to three thousand of his best troops lost in one footless gesture, Washington had no choice but to move most of his small force from Bergen County to the south. His aides reported that they would be posted "along from Newark to Amboy, as places easy of communication with each other, and through which the enemy must pass if Philadelphia or any place southward is their aim. Troops will be left at the passes leading from the North River into Jersey and New York, to prevent supplies from going to the enemy." [29] Washington reported to Congress on November 19 that he intended to place his forces even farther south, in and around New Brunswick.[30] Fort Lee was to be abandoned: "always considered as only necessary in conjunction with [the fort on] the east side of the river, to preserve the communication across and to prevent the enemy from a free navigation, [it] has become of no importance by the loss of the other, or not so material as to employ a force for its defense." [31]

Hackensack valley patriots put the best face they could on the Fort Washington defeat, accepting the optimistic reports of the American junior officers about a spirited defense, but it was not long before everyone in and around Hackensack knew as well as Washington that the

[27] 6 GW 286, 287.
[28] 6 GW 242, 246. Howe "had supposed all along that the Americans would abandon the fort." Baurmeister 69.
[29] 3 Force (5) 740.
[30] 6 GW 294.
[31] 6 GW 293.

loss of the fort was a new disgrace to American arms, which could not stand many more.

Disheartened as Washington was at the needless loss of the Fort Washington garrison and concerned as he was over the poor prospects for defending the west side of the Hudson, he was at least spared one piece of intelligence that could only have deepened his gloom: while he was at the Zabriskie mansion planning American defenses, many of his neighbors were busily plotting his destruction. For the first time in the war the British had been able to set up a well-organized force of Tory troops in a territory they were about to invade. Though Washington's staff knew that there were Tories in Jersey, as elsewhere, many of them must have found it hard to accept the warnings of Peter Zabriskie and his friends as anything more than the exaggerations of nervous countrymen. It would have given them pause to know—and even local Whigs would have found it hard to credit the full truth—that there were Dutchmen who lived within a few minutes' walk of headquarters who had just received secret commissions in the British territorial army, and dozens of others who had secretly enlisted in the British service, some of them men who had once pretended a considerable attachment to American principles. Abraham Van Buskirk, son of Lawrence Van Buskirk, one-time stagedriver, farmer, doctor, member of the Provincial Congress and surgeon of patriot militia, who had always been able to oppose patriot measures by a highly patriotic argument, had been made a lieutenant colonel of the King's Volunteers; Daniel Isaac Brown, lawyer, court clerk, surrogate, and member of the Provincial Congress, the moderate patriot who had been too much the professional man to join the American militia, now found himself commissioned a major of the same regiment of Volunteers. How many Tory recruits they had assembled only time would tell. Edward Earl, William Van Allen and others also held commissions, awaiting only the British move into Bergen County for an open avowal.[32] They had not long to wait. Four more days saw the actual invasion of the country west of the Hudson.

Fort Washington fell on Monday, November 16, 1776. Washington spent the next three days at Hackensack and at General Greene's headquarters at the English Neighborhood, planning the painful withdrawal forced upon him by that disaster. With thousands of his best troops captured at Fort Washington, the British would hardly close their campaign with a single victory; there was every reason to expect

[32] The dates of the commissions are in MSS. British Army List 1781, HC Papers CL.

them to cross the Hudson and attack him in New Jersey.[33] Washington saw that his first task was to withdraw the large body of troops from their exposed position at Fort Lee. Before they could be pulled back, however, the stores at the fort would have to be removed—no small task, for Fort Lee had become an important supply depot in the few months of its existence—and under his orders General Greene started to move them to Bound Brook, Springfield, Princeton, and Acquackanonk Bridge, "places that will not be subject to sudden danger in case the enemy should pass the river." [34]

"I am sending off the stores as fast as I can get wagons," Greene reported on the 18th. "I have sent three expresses to Newark for boats, but can get no return of what boats we may expect from that place. The stores here are large, and the transportation by land will be almost endless. The powder and fixed ammunition I have sent off first by land, as it is an article too valuable to trust upon the water." [35]

Washington planned to draw back the main body of his troops to New Brunswick and the intermediate posts as soon as the stores were removed from the fort, "to guard against the designs of the enemy and to prevent their making an irruption, or foraging with detached parties." The Hudson River landings were to be covered only with enough troops to prevent civilian traffic with the enemy, since his force was far too weak to garrison both the river defenses and the land route across Jersey. "If the enemy should make a push in this quarter," he told the President of Congress, "the only troops that there will be to oppose them will be Hand's, Hazlet's, the [five greatly reduced] regiments from Virginia" and "the troops belonging to the Flying Corps under Generals Heard and Beal, with what remains of General Ewing's Brigade . . . now at Fort Lee." [36] He hoped to add militiamen from middle Jersey when he reached New Brunswick. The enlistments of the few troops he had were almost expired.

When he finally found a moment to himself, on the 19th, he sat down at Hackensack headquarters and emptied his heart to his brother Augustine: "It is impossible for me in the compass of a letter to give you any idea of our situation, of my difficulties, and the constant perplexities and mortifications I constantly meet with. . . . I am wearied almost to death with the retrograde motions of things, and I solemnly protest that a pecuniary reward of £20,000 a year would not induce me

[33] 6 GW 293.
[34] 6 GW 293. Local wagoners were pressed into service to speed the move; Albert Banta, for instance, later sought compensation for "eight days riding with a two horse wagon" during the withdrawal. Damages by Americans, NJSL, 53.
[35] 1 Greene Greene 277.
[36] 6 GW 293.

to undergo what I do. . . . God grant you all health and happiness; nothing in this world would contribute so much to mine as to be once more fixed among you in the peaceable enjoyment of my own vine and fig tree." [37]

The only thing that had favored Washington's recent activities was the generally fine, warm weather, and that now ended.[38] When he and his aides woke on the 20th they looked out at a sodden Hackensack green and a cold, gray rain; the worst possible weather for moving military stores, weather that would soon turn the Jersey roads into seas of red mud. Breakfast over, Washington decided to take advantage of the rain and turn to military correspondence, and he and his aides, Colonels Harrison and Grayson, started two long letters to General Heath and General Schuyler.[39]

At ten o'clock (he noted the hour particularly) Colonel Harrison cut off the letter to Schuyler: "This minute an express from Orange Town advises that some of the enemy have landed below Dobb's Ferry. A smart firing is also heard below Fort Lee, towards Bergen. It is probable the immediate object they have in view is to shut in such of our troops and stores as lay between Hackensack and Hudson's River. I trust they will be disappointed. They seem determined to push matters, and the weather is most favorable for 'em." [40]

Harrison was mistaken about an attack from the south, but his intelligence about the landing near Dobbs Ferry was all too accurate. "Their advanced party is said to be within five or six miles of this place. . . His Excellency has gone over since the advice came." [41]

Washington went at once to Greene's headquarters in English Neighborhood. If the word he received there was correct, the British had now committed their principal forces to the west of the Hudson. He accordingly decided to move some of the troops he had been holding in Westchester across the river: General Charles Lee's division to cross at Kings Ferry and Generals Heath, Lord Stirling and Stephen to hold themselves in readiness to follow. Greene was busy evacuating the Fort Lee garrison; it looked as if most of the men could be brought off safely if the British

[37] 6 GW 242, etc.
[38] 1 Kemble 101. 3 Force (5) 1071. See HBP 52.
[39] 3 Force (5) 779, 780.
[40] 3 Force (5) 780. Cornwallis reported that it was a countryman who alerted Greene (3 Force [5] 925). Paine's account said that it was an American officer on patrol, the one perhaps inclined to discredit, the other to defend, American vigilance. Glyn Journal, PUL, which appears to parallel closely Cornwallis' official orders and reports, also speaks of the countryman. See 1 NJA (2) 314, 315.
[41] 3 Force (5) 780.

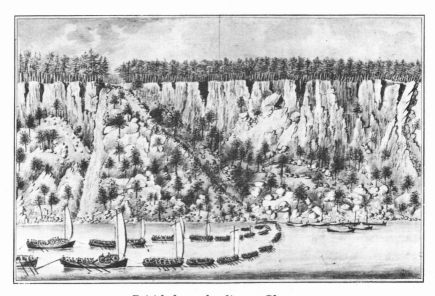

British forces landing at Closter.
Stokes Collection, New York Public Library. Thomas Davies, circa 1776.

did not move too fast. Washington then rode back in the rain with his aide, Colonel William Grayson, to the crossroads at Liberty Pole, where they parted, Washington placing himself at the junction of the north-and-south road and the road to New Bridge, the point where the first British attack would probably fall, Grayson continuing on to head-quarters at Hackensack to get the necessary orders off to Westchester.[42]

At that hour, about eleven o'clock in the morning, a British advance party had reached a point two miles north of Liberty Pole, but the road from Fort Lee to New Bridge was still in American hands:

His Excellency had directed me to write to you and acquaint you with the late movements of the enemy. They landed this morning between Dobb's Ferry and Fort Lee, as it is imagined at a place called Closter Dock, nearly opposite to Philips's house, and (as the General has been informed) in great numbers, and an advanced party of them have proceeded as far as a hill two miles above the Liberty Pole, about a mile and a half above General Greene's quarters, where I left his Excellency. The road from thence to the bridge above Hackensack, as well as the bridge, is open for our troops to retreat; and from present appearances, it is expected that they may be got off without the loss of many of them. What their object is cannot at present

[42] 3 Force (5) 780. Grayson's letter, quoted below, would seem to indicate that Greene's headquarters were a mile and a half south of Liberty Pole—probably at the Moore or Bourdet farmhouse at the junction of the road to the fort and the main road—not at Fort Lee itself.

be clearly ascertained; but it is imagined the getting possession of Fort Lee is one part of their design; however, it is possible, and perhaps probable, they may have other and more capital views.[43]

The British had planned their attack on New Jersey carefully. Twenty flatboats had been sent up along the east bank of the Hudson under cover of darkness on the 15th. Since this was the day before Fort Washington was attacked, Howe evidently assumed that that post would not long impede his move into New Jersey. "About 30 flatboats went up the North River last night as far as Kingsbridge," Captain Mackenzie wrote on that date.[44] These were placed at King's Bridge, on Spuyten Duyvil Creek, to await further orders. At nine o'clock on the night before the attack, several thousand British troops struck their tents and marched, under the orders of Lord Cornwallis, to the Phillipse house on the east shore of the Hudson and were there embarked on the flatboats which had been moved up during the night, taking advantage of the complete absence of patrols at the Closter Dock Landing to cross the river at that point.[45] "At daybreak [on the 20th]," one of the junior officers wrote later, "the first division disembarked on the Jersey shore, having a very perpendicular bank of rock [two hundred] feet high to ascend, the path to the summit very broken. This was beyond the usual landing place and considered as inaccessible for any body of troops. As soon as the boats could return the second division embarked at Phillipse's farm and the whole corps made good their landing without any opposition; Lord Cornwallis immediately formed his corps into two columns, the right consisting of the Light Infantry, Chasseurs and Brigade of Guards; the left of the British Reserve." [46] Howe's official dispatch to Lord Germain dated November 30 listed the troops as "the First and Second Battalions of Light Infantry; two Companies of Chasseurs; two Battalions of British and two ditto of Hessian Grenadiers; two Battalions of Guards; Thirty-third and Forty-second Regiments." [47] Another officer placed the hour of their landing at about nine in the morning.[48] One hundred Tory troops without arms and two engineers, with twelve carpenters and three guides, were with the invading troops.[49]

[43] 3 Force (5) 780.   [44] 1 Mackenzie 104. 3 Force (5) gives the 18th as the date.   [45] 3 Force (5) 818; Robertson 112; HC Papers CL; 1 NJA (2) 315 n; 1 Kemble 411 lists the forces that were put under Cornwallis' command for the movement. Baurmeister 71 also has some details, not entirely consistent with Kemble. Serle Diary 144.   [46] Glyn Journal PUL. See also 3 Force (5) 925; 1 NJA (2) 314, 315.   [47] 1 NJA (2) 314, 315 n.   [48] Robertson Diary 112.   [49] 1 Kemble 411. See Robertson Diary 112. The choice of the undefended Closter Dock Landing was a brilliant stroke by the British: Major General Greene was convinced that every landing place was so well guarded that no British crossing was possible; Washington himself had been on the ground for days without suggesting a

The timing of the British and American movements was critical. Cornwallis had completed his landing at about nine o'clock in the morning. Word of the landing reached Washington at Hackensack at about ten o'clock. Fort Lee was only about ten or eleven miles distant from the British landing place by the nearest route, but the first half mile of that route, from the landing to the heights of the Palisades, was up a sheer precipice, over a twisting path too narrow for the carriages of light cannon, and the last half mile of the route, from Bourdet's house on the English Neighborhood Road to the fort itself, went up a narrow farm road almost as steep. Washington's headquarters at Hackensack was perhaps six miles from the fort. The route of the advancing British troops met the route of the retreating Americans at Liberty Pole Tavern, three and one-half miles from Fort Lee and six or seven miles from Closter Dock Landing. Washington's problem was to keep the road through Liberty Pole to New Bridge open for an American retreat; Cornwallis' problem, had he seen the picture clearly, was to move enough of his men forward to cut off the American retreat at Liberty Pole.

The vanguard of the British troops did not reach Liberty Pole until the whole American garrison had passed that point. The soldiers and sailors had been obliged to drag their cannon up the rocky Closter Dock Road to the top of the Palisades by sheer manpower; time had been lost there in forming the army for the march to the south; two miles from the landing the army had been obliged to halt to wait for the cannon to come up.[50] The Americans, for their part, wasted no time in forming into companies or marching in military array; they evacuated the fort and moved down the Palisades through Liberty Pole and over to New Bridge and a junction with the main army without standing upon any order or ceremony, with every advantage to themselves, so far as speed was concerned.

different defense of the river crossings. Indeed Closter Dock Landing was by no means an obvious place for a landing. Even after Cornwallis had used it, Major General Anthony Wayne reconnoitered Closter Dock Landing for General Washington in 1780 and concluded that it was completely unsuitable for any large military operation: "It was formerly made use of by the inhabitants in the vicinity and rendered practicable for a sled and two horses from the edge of the mountain to the water, one-half mile of which is too steep and narrow to admit of a common carriage, the descent being on an average one foot in five." The area at the bottom of the mountain, Wayne added, was far too small for handling supplies satisfactorily (Wayne to Washington, Oct. 19, 1780, Wayne Papers HSP). The evidence clearly establishes that the landing was at Lower Closter Landing (Huyler's). HBP 282; NYHS Map Coll., Erskine Map 26, part 3, 1778 (Watkins). All three Bergen County histories agree on Lower Closter Landing. [50] Glyn Journal PUL; 1 NJA (2) 314, 315; Robertson Diary 112.

There was, of course, no thought of an American defense of Fort Lee. It had been decided days before to abandon it; the troops were there to get off stores, not to try to beat off an attack. The British should have seen as clearly as Washington that the fort was indefensible and had to be abandoned, and it is hard today to understand Cornwallis' strategy. His failure to push an advance force to Liberty Pole and cut off the American line of retreat was doubtless based on the assumption that the Americans would defend Fort Lee as they had defended Fort Washington, not a shrewd assumption but an understandable one. But by the time the British reached Liberty Pole they knew very well that the Americans had passed the same point shortly before; they nevertheless chose deliberately to take the abandoned fort and not to pursue its retreating garrison. As they saw their situation, they had come to capture the fort and were doing so. British Regulars did not scramble after a frightened and disorganized rabble, they marched in formation to the

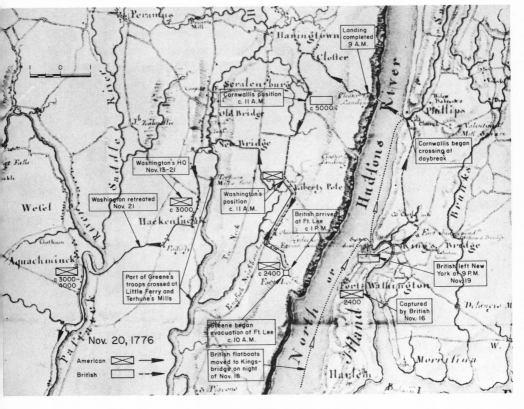

Attack on Fort Lee, November 20, 1776.
E. Tone, 1962.

roll of drums; no provincial who saw that force would ever again doubt Britain's power to deal with rebels.

Indeed, so far as that was concerned, the British had every right to march proudly through Closter and Tenafly, Liberty Pole and English Neighborhood. They had completed one of the most difficult of military operations, an amphibious landing on (as they supposed) a heavily defended shore; they had found and used the one unguarded landing place on the west side of the river; they had formed their troops after landing with no opposition; they had transported cannon up a seemingly impassable precipice two hundred feet high; they were about to occupy one of the most celebrated of American forts by sheer threat of their power. If they moved somewhat ponderously, who was to say that they did not move with effect? Certainly not the Americans, fleeing headlong down the road to New Bridge.

The first of the British troops reached the fort about one o'clock in the afternoon. They found its blockhouse and redoubts empty, and blankets and provisions, even artillery, scattered about where the retreating troops had left them. Three hundred tents were standing, the breakfast kettles were boiling over the fires and the woods nearby were filled with American stragglers, who were quickly gathered up to be sent across the Hudson to prison.[51] ". . . It had been evacuated by the rebels so precipitately that the pots were left absolutely boiling on the fire and the tables spread for dinner of some of their officers. In the fort they found but twelve men, who were all dead drunk. There were forty or fifty pieces of cannon found loaded, with two large iron sea mortars and one brass one with a vast quantity of ammunition, provisions and stores, with all their tents standing." [52]

The American retreat had been almost completely disorganized. One Briton claimed that a group of wagoners wearing red coats but without

[51] "Such was the confusion of the enemy that not only all their tents were standing, their meat at the fire, but all their sick fell into our hands; had not a countryman early in the morning apprised them of our landing the whole might have been prisoners." Glyn Journal PUL. 1 NJA (2) 314, 315. Greene went back two hours after the evacuation to try to round up stragglers who had "skulked out of the way for fear of fighting." 3 Force (5) 1071. "Several gentlemen from Hackensack" arrived at Elizabethtown on Nov. 21 with word that there had been a second large landing at Hoboken, but that report was mistaken. 1873 NYHS Cols. 404. If a letter of General Knox to his wife is correctly dated, the loss of Fort Lee was not known at White Plains on the 22nd. It was probably written on the 20th: "The enemy have landed part of their force on the other side with intent as we suppose of transacting the same affairs at Fort Lee that they executed at Ft. Washington, but I hope that they will be prevented. We shall endeavor to get them in a hobble." Knox to Mrs. Knox, Nov. 22, 1776, Knox Papers MHS.
[52] Rawdon [?] to Auchmuty, Nov. 25, 1776, quoted in Commager and Morris 496.

arms had driven off a whole American company.[53] As the British marched along "they found the roads thick strewed with muskets, knapsacks, etc. The number of cattle taken in the Hackensack meadows, which had been driven from Pennsylvania and some parts of the Jerseys for the use of the rebel army, is truly astounding, and amount to many thousands." [54] Scattered along the road to Hackensack, where the troops had left them in flight, were eight pieces of heavy artillery on traveling carriages and four pieces of light artillery which the retreating army had first hoped to carry off and then abandoned.[55]

To the west of the fort Cornwallis, heavy of figure and awkward of gait, stood with his staff and his guides at the brow of the precipitous hill looking out over twenty miles of Dutch farmlands, laid out like a map below him. At his left, with the gray, cold rain clouds scudding overhead, was the wide sweep of the Hackensack marshes, stretching from the base of the hill to the southwest as far as the eye could see, cut by the winding Hackensack River, whose branch, the Overpeck, made another marsh a mile west of the fort and three or four miles to the north. He could see, through the rain, a low ridge of land—the set-

[53] 1 Jones, New York During the Revolution, 124; 3 Force (5) 925. General Vaughan improved on this by reporting that "the consternation of the rebels was so great that the very camp women that followed [his] regiment took them prisoners." 44 MHSP 105. Patriots, as usual, tried to minimize the defeat. The report was that the British force was 14,000; Washington's about 6,000; that Washington, "disgusted at the Congress for not increasing his army," blamed the authorities for his sad plight, that he had drawn out "his whole army from Fort Lee resolved to give the Regulars battle till he discovered them to be more than double his number." Smith Journal NYPL; 3 Force (5) 1058.

[54] Rawdon [?] to Auchmuty, Nov. 25, 1776, quoted in 1 Commager and Morris 496. The same writer added that "His Lordship pressed forward as quick as he could toward Hackensack New Bridge, but the people belonging to the fort had the heels of him. However on the road he met with three or four thousand fresh lads coming from Newark to assist in garrisoning the forts. To these gentry the troops distributed a couple of rounds and sent them ascampering." Ibid. No other evidence suggests such a troop movement: the dash to New Bridge, the patriot gentry, the couple of rounds and the scampering soldiers were all doubtless added for a flourish. Another British officer reported that it was the sight of the Regulars that had driven off the Americans. "On the appearance of our troops, the rebels fled like scared rabbits, and in a few moments after we reached the hill near their entrenchments, not a rascal of them could be seen. They have left some poor pork, a few greasy proclamations and some of that scoundrel Common Sense man's letters, which we can read at our leisure, now that we have got one of the 'impregnable redoubts' of Mr. Washington's to quarter in. . . . We intend to push on after the long faces in a few days." 1 Moore 350. See 3 Force (5) 856, 925. They would have been well advised to push harder.
[55] 3 Force (5) 1058.

tlements of Old Hackensack, Teaneck, and Schraalenburgh—running parallel to Overpeck Creek. Between that and the next ridge, his guides told him, the Hackensack River flowed. To the west he could barely make out the white steeple of the church on the green of Hackensack, and his guides agreed that the nearest bridge over the river was two miles above the church; doubtless Greene's routed forces had already retreated across it. To the north and west, out of sight in the gray haze, were the foothills of the mountains, the First Mountain, the Ramapos, and the Hudson Highlands. One could almost see, in the mind's eye, the whole of America from these conquered heights.

Major General James Grant, surveying the country to the west, must have smiled to think how often he had assured his Tory colleagues in the House of Commons that he could march from one end of the continent to the other with five thousand men.[56] The retreating Americans had fallen away from Fort Lee at the mere approach of the army; it was hard to imagine any force in the rolling farmlands stretched out before him that could make him withdraw his boast. Fate was indeed to march five thousand Regulars from one end of the continent to the other within the year, but the scornful General Grant was not destined to ride at their head. They were, in point of fact, to be Burgoyne's surrendered army, under American guard; there were yet thorns and snares in the invader's path which could not be seen from the heights of the Palisades.[57]

On the 21st Sir William Howe himself was rowed across the Hudson to view the site of Fort Lee and to congratulate its captors; his orders for the next day "desired officially to return his thanks to Lieutenant General Earl Cornwallis, Major General Vaughan, Brigadier General Matthews, Colonel Donop and the officers and soldiers under his Lordship's command for the meritorious services performed by them on the 20th, accomplished with infinite fatigue to the troops."[58] No one on the British side failed to see that the Regulars might easily have captured the Fort Lee garrison as well as the fort: "Had not the enemy been apprised of my moving toward them by a countryman," Cornwallis complained, "I would have surrounded the two thousand men in the fort, who escaped in the utmost confusion."[59] If "the situation of this ground [had] been perfectly known with regard to Overpeck Creek," wrote another officer, "the most of the rebels might have been inter-

[56] See e.g. Alexander, Lord Stirling, 162 n. Grant's words had incensed many Americans.
[57] Grant spent the next few days foraging in the nearby country. LYT NYPL "James Van Buren."
[58] 1 Kemble 413.   [59] 3 Force (5) 925.

cepted in their retreat." [60] These were, however, the words of men over-whelmed with their own success, not disappointed men. They had every reason to be pleased with their day's work, and they were.

Most of the American soldiers had pushed northwest toward Liberty Pole and the New Bridge. Some in desperation had gone toward Little Ferry and crossed there and some others had waded into the water and marshes on the east side of the river opposite Terhune's Mill in Hacken-sack and were taken over in small boats.[61]

Washington returned to the Zabriskie mansion that night, after a cold, sodden day of disaster; a day that began with panic-stricken flight from Fort Lee and ended with thousands of rain-soaked officers and men huddled together on the west bank of the Hackensack without tents or coats or the least protection from the winter's cold; worse, it was a day of disaster that could have been avoided if there had been wagons and boats to speed the withdrawal of stores from Fort Lee or if there had been a defense force at Closter Landing. Washington could hardly fail to think of such things, but he was no man to think long of them. His answer to mistakes and misfortunes was to redouble his efforts. He had saved most of Greene's troops by his day's work, and he and his officers took what comfort they could from that.

The next day Washington described the events of the 20th in sober but not desperate terms; indeed, some might have thought them hardly desperate enough: "After the unfortunate loss of Fort Washington, it was determined to evacuate Fort Lee, in a great measure as it was in a manner useless in obstructing the passage of the North River without the assistance of Fort Washington. The ammunition and some other stores were accordingly removed, but before we could effect our pur-pose, the enemy landed yesterday morning in very considerable numbers about six miles above the fort. Their intent evidently was to form a line across from the place of their landing to Hackensack Bridge and thereby hem in the whole garrison between the North and Hackensack Rivers. However, we were lucky enough to gain the Bridge before them, by which means we saved all of our men, but were obliged to leave some hundred barrels of flour, most of our cannon and a considerable parcel of tents and baggage." [62]

60 Robertson Diary 113.
61 3 Force (5) 1291.
62 6 GW 301, 302. When Tom Paine came to write his *American Crisis* a few weeks later, he too viewed the events at Fort Lee and New Bridge in terms of British frustration, hinting that the British had been too prudent to risk a fight for New Bridge: "Our first object was to secure the bridge over the Hackensack which lay up the river between the enemy and us about six miles from us and about three from

Washington had been lucky indeed, for Cornwallis' pilots and guides, some of them,[63] had lived within a stone's throw of the New Bridge all of their lives and needed no one to tell them of the strategic importance of that river crossing. Patriotic Jersey Dutchmen probably assumed that the Tories who guided the invaders were so overweening and self-confident that they had not thought it necessary to cut off Greene's line of retreat; the Tories, for their part, like as not spent the day in damning the self-confident British officers for not listening to their pleas that the New Bridge was the key to the peninsula between the Hackensack and the Hudson.

Whatever the grand strategy, and whether the British or the Americans were right in thinking that they had come off best in all of the marching and countermarching on the 20th, the day was certainly black beyond description for Hackensack valley patriots. Some of them must have seen, when Fort Washington was lost, that more disasters would follow; none could have imagined the American army's collapsing in panic before their very doorsteps. To all appearances the tragic drama was over, the end of the dream of a new Zion on these western shores; the end, not in a great Armageddon, but in sodden troops marching silently through the rain-swept darkness of a Jersey Dutch village street.

"It was about dusk when the head of the troops entered Hackensack," one of them wrote later. "The night was dark, cold and rainy, but I had a fair view of Greene's troops from the light of the windows as they passed on our side of the street. They marched two abreast, looked ragged, some without a shoe to their feet and most of them wrapped in their blankets." [64]

On men like these, wet, cold and ragged, wrapped in their blankets, defeated on every field since Howe's arrival in America and now retreating ingloriously before a cruel invader, rested the only hope of the American cause; that night patriots who had spent the day doing the little they could, heartsick to see their country going down under overwhelming odds, must, many of them, have prayed tearfully, and tears

---

them. General Washington marched at the head of the troops toward the bridge, which place I expected we should have a brush for, however, they did not choose to dispute it with us and the greatest part of our troops went over the bridge." See 3 Force (5) 1291. Paine and Washington to the contrary, Freeman is almost certainly right in saying that "there is nothing to indicate the British contemplated a race for the bridge" or any other supposed bridge over the Hackensack. (4 Freeman 258 n.) Fort Lee was apparently the whole object of the first day's operations.
[63]   Abraham Van Buskirk, for example. LYT NYPL. See also 1 GC 510.
[64]   Romeyn, Hackensack Church, 26.

Vanderbeek House, Hackensack, built 1716.
Rus Anderson, 1962.

did not come easily to the eyes of Dutchmen whose forefathers had bled and died to keep the Spanish terror from their homes. It would have been catastrophe enough if it were the British army that was overwhelming them, but by now even the dullest Jersey Dutchmen knew that they were losing the war as much to embittered Tory neighbors as to foreign tyranny. The disaffected, the cynical scoffers at American arms and American ideals, men who had pushed the tolerance of their patriot neighbors to the breaking point with their mocking, now could hardly wait for the feeble American army to fall apart.

The next day, the 21st, the countryside was a hive of activity.

Colonel Peter T. Curtenius, son of a former Dutch Reformed minister at Hackensack and Schraalenburgh, now commissary general of the Continental army, spent the day trying to conceal Continental property that the army could not take on its retreat. He took two large barrels of goods to Mr. John Varick's store and asked Mrs. Varick to conceal a hundred soldiers' shirts in the Varick house; he got Guilliam Varick, the gunmaker, to bury some gun parts and sent thirty-five hundred pounds of lead and bullets to Henry Bogert at Steenrapie, above the New Bridge.[65]

Rumors and counterrumors spread through the country all day: The Americans had saved all their ordnance from Fort Lee and were retiring to make a stand at New Bridge; the man who piloted the British from

[65]   1 GC 541, 542, 543.

Closter Landing to Fort Lee was John Acker of English Neighbor-hood; [66] General Charles Lee with ten thousand fresh Continentals was almost at hand. There were hundreds of stories; almost none of them true.

This day, which had been coming closer for years, the day when America's friends and America's enemies must stand and be counted, had rushed down on the Hackensack valley at express speed. Militia and militia officers, sunshine patriots by the score, deserted the American cause overnight: hundreds of Jersey Dutchmen who had hitherto called themselves moderate liberty men now claimed firmer allegiance to King George than any open Tory. Doubtless there were some who had once considered themselves Whigs who did the same. But there were other Jersey Dutchmen who made the hard decision to hold to their principles and take the consequences. Let no man say their decision was vain; only the ignorant and cynical will scoff at these stiff-necked men, facing thousands of British Regulars even then pouring down on them from the heights of the Palisades; men too stubborn to admit that the rebellion was over, too trusting to think that Providence would abandon so just a cause: the cynical were to prove the fools, not they.

Washington was still in his quarters on the green on the morning of the 21st and had with him his staff, his life guard, a company of foot, a regiment of cavalry, and some soldiers from the rear of the army.[67] Before he left Hackensack he rode down to the dock beyond the church and courthouse.[68] Looking across the deep, narrow little tidewater stream, he could see a season's campaign lost and few hopes for any other. He had expected that hunger would hamper the British; hence-forth hunger was to be the enemy, not the ally, of America. The rich farms east of the river, he knew, were already being stripped to feed Howe's huge army.[69] To the knavish General Charles Lee, who refused to obey orders and send his troops to aid Washington because he claimed to be protecting the fine fertile country of upper Westchester, Washington wrote sharply that further defense of Westchester was

---

[66] Acker was said to have been with the British, 1 GC 510; many other more im-portant Jersey Dutchmen were there too. LYT NYPL.
[67] HBP 52; Westervelt, Bergen County, 106.
[68] Romeyn, Hackensack Church, 27.
[69] Cornwallis hoped to keep the soldiers from stripping the county. "As the in-habitants . . . are in general well affected to government, Earl Cornwallis expects the commanding officers . . . will exert themselves to prevent plundering amongst the troops. A distribution of fresh provisions will be made as a gratuity to the fatigue they have undergone." Glyn Journal PUL.

foolish, for the British "now . . . have one much more so and more contiguous." [70]

Washington was about to abandon more Hackensack valley farms to British foraging. He could not risk being trapped between the Hackensack and Passaic rivers with his whole army, and there was nothing to do but retreat further:

Our present situation between the Hackinsack and Passaic Rivers being exactly similar to our late one [between the Hudson and Hackensack], and our force here by no means adequate to an opposition that will promise the smallest probability of success, we are taking measures to retire over the waters of the latter, when the best disposition will be formed that circumstances will admit of.[71]

He returned to the door of Archibald Campbell's tavern, called for some wine and water, then rode off toward Acquackanonk Bridge to direct the retreat.[72]

Albert Zabriskie asked the general as he left Hackensack where the army planned to go. Washington, local tradition has it, leaned over on his horse and whispered, "Can you keep a secret?" When Zabriskie firmly assured the general that he could, Washington said, "I can too," and rode off.[73] The rear guard joined Washington in the evening of the 21st.[74]

---

[70] 6 GW 297, 298, 299. Washington sent the message off, as he sent off other messages to the north, by Cornelius Cooper, 52-year-old farmer and tanner, who had come down from his tanhouse and 70-acre farm at Kinderkamack to offer his help to the army. Bailey 282; Schraalenburgh Church Records; 4 Freeman 260, 263. Cooper had been immediately pressed into service by Washington's aides to undertake the risky business of crossing the Hudson at Sneden's Landing with Washington's dispatches for Lee, Colonel Reed giving Cooper a private letter, and doubtless also a good deal of verbal ammunition, to hurry that complacent officer to the aid of the main army. Unfortunately Cooper's messages had no effect whatever on Lee, who sent him back with word that there was no means of crossing at Sneden's Landing and that the crossing at King's Ferry was too slow to be of use, very probably also telling him, as he told everyone else, that Washington's predicament was his own fault. See 1 Reed 254, 255.

[71] 6 GW 296.

[72] 1 Westervelt, Bergen County, 106; HBP 52.

[73] The story is told wherever Washington went.

[74] Rain poured down on Nov. 22 and 23. 4 Freeman 261. "'Tis next to impossible to give a true account of our situation," Colonel Samuel B. Webb wrote from Newark on the 24th: "I can only say that no lads ever showed greater activity in retreating than we since we left you. Our soldiers are the best fellows in the world at this business. Fatal necessity has obliged us to give up to the enemy much of a fine country, well-wooded, watered and stock'd; not only that, but our cannon, mortars, ordnance stores, etc. are mostly gone. Our whole body did not amount to 2,000 at the time the enemy landed in the Jerseys, of consequence we had it not in our

The regular postrider with dispatches from the north—desperately awaited by Washington—fell into the hands of the enemy, whether through carelessness or by design Washington could not say. The rider, the son of Andrew Van Buskirk, was reported to have "been kept in chat" by a refugee, Dr. McLean of New York, "while the enemy came up." Local patriots who knew that branch of the Van Buskirk family were in less doubt than Washington over the affair; when Andrew was taken up for Tory activity a year later, the loss of the mails was but one of the items laid to his charge.[75]

With Washington's forced withdrawal, Hackensack was now abandoned to the British and Hessians, and, as it turned out, to the Tories.

---

power to make a stand, till we arrived at this place, where we have collected our force and are not only ready, but willing to meet the lads in blue and red as soon as they think proper." 1 Webb 172.

[75] Washington, in no mood for further misfortunes, called his conduct "negligent and infamous" (6 GW 306); others reported that Van Buskirk was "apprised of his danger and took no care to avoid it." NJRC 93. The report that reached Colonel Huntington at Ramapo was that it was Cornelius Cooper who had fallen into the hands of the British on his return from Westchester, but this was mistaken. Heath Papers MHS. See 3 Force (5) 833.

S<small>OME</small> of the British crossed the Hackensack the next day, November 22.[1] "About noon the British took possession of Hackensack," a resident wrote later, "and in the afternoon the church green was covered with Hessians, a horrid frightful sight with their whiskers, brass caps and kettles or brass drums." [2]

As the hours passed the streets of Hackensack began to fill with Americans who had come in to the village to join the invaders. Hundreds of young men, secretly enlisted during the past few months, now came forward to proclaim their loyalty to Bergen County's Tory leaders, and to King George. As they gathered in the village to be mustered in, to

[1] Glyn Journal PUL.
[2] Romeyn, Hackensack Church, 27. The Hessians, for their part, were perfectly delighted with New Netherlands. "The prosperity of the inhabitants, whose forbears were all Dutch, must have been very great indeed," one Hessian general wrote on his first sight of the Dutch countryside on Long Island. "Everywhere one sees real quality and abundance. One sees nothing useless or old, certainly nothing dilapidated. . . . The houses are beautiful and are furnished in better taste than any we are accustomed to in Germany. At the same time everything is so clean and neat that no description can do it justice. The women are generally beautiful and delicately brought up. They dress becomingly according to the latest European fashions, wearing Indian calicoes, white cotton goods and silk crepes. There is not a single housewife who does not have an elegant coach and pair. They drive and ride with only a negro on horseback for an escort. Near the dwellings are the cabins of the negroes, their slaves, who cultivate the fertile land, herd the cattle, and do all the rough housework." Baurmeister 45. He exaggerated the wealth of the Dutch farmers around New York and the ease of the hard-working Dutch vrouws; he did not overstate the admiration of British and Hessian alike for the Dutch countryside.

receive their arms and their new green uniforms, many patriots must have observed that, for a cause that prided itself no less on its social distinction than on its loyalty to the King, its friends had certainly collected an undistinguished body of men to fight for their monarch. Three out of four of the enlisted men were (Scotch) Irish, probably from the iron trade, or Germans from the Ramapo settlement.[3] The officers were Jersey Dutch, of established families, and some of the men, but there was good reason to think that most of the others, and perhaps some of the Jersey Dutch, were moved as much by the five guineas bounty as by zeal for the Tory cause. It would have been unfair to call the recruits, as one writer called a like body of Tory troops in the south, "the idle, the desperate and the vindictive," but many of them were men with little stake in Jersey Dutch society. Perhaps it would have been too much to expect more of professional soldiers of the day, Whig or Tory.

Abraham Van Buskirk, Daniel Isaac Brown, Peter Rutan, Robert Timpany, William Van Allen, James Servanier, Edward Earl, Joost Earl and others, the new officers of the 4th Battalion of New Jersey Volunteers, moved briskly about on their new errands, conferring with the British officers, ordering their troops about, and generally making the most of the British triumph and their part in it.[4]

Robert Timpany, the 34-year-old Hackensack schoolteacher, had been born in Ireland and educated at the University of Glasgow. He had not waited for the British to invade New Jersey to enter their service, and

[3] Of four muster rolls of Bergen County's 4th New Jersey Battalion of territorial troops (muster rolls of troops under Captain Samuel Ryerson, Captain Peter Rutan and Captain William Van Allen, from the Department of Canadian History, New Brunswick Museum, St. John, N.B., and the Call Roll of Major Timpany, Nov. 20, 1777, HC Papers CL), only about six out of twenty-eight; fourteen out of forty-eight; fifteen out of forty-six and eight out of forty, respectively, appear to have been Jersey Dutchmen. Other muster rolls, in the Public Archives of Canada, Vols. 1851–1866, show that Colonel Van Buskirk's own company, Major Philip Van Cortland's company and Captain Jacob Van Buskirk's company had no greater percentages of Jersey Dutchmen. See also 1 GC 483. The county's patriot militiamen were almost entirely Jersey Dutch. HBP 71, 72.

It is hard to say what the Tory recruits thought of each other when they met on the Hackensack green that November day. A Sussex County Tory, writing in London after the war, described his own seventy recruits as they had then come to see themselves: "All honest men, of the fairest and most respectable characters . . . in general, men of some property; and, without a single exception, men of principle." Moody Narrative, 10, 11, 12, 13, 14.

[4] LYT NYPL; Fraser, passim; see MSS. British Army List 1781, HC Papers CL; Sabine, passim. Heath Papers MHS, Dec. 20, 1776, gives the homes of Greencoat officers: Colonel Van Buskirk, New Bridge; Brown, Timpany, Van Allen, Hackensack; Rutan, Captain Van Buskirk, Marsh, Servanier, Babcock, Wheeler, Ramapo; Dobbs, Saddle River; Philip Young, Naurashan.

now held a commission as major in the New Jersey Volunteers.[5] Joseph and Samuel Ryerson, like Timpany, officers in the 4th Regiment of Tory troops, were busy with the sixty or more men they had enlisted in and around Totowa and Saddle River township, west of the Passaic.[6]

Joseph Barton, the one-time patriot leader of Sussex County, was there in a lieutenant colonel's uniform, with a large contingent of Tory youths from the Jersey mountains, who boasted of hundreds more to come,[7] and James Servanier, who had been made a lieutenant, had brought nearly fifty men down with him from the northern part of the county.[8] It was common talk that the reason Abraham Van Buskirk had been honored with a lieutenant colonel's commission was that he had enlisted over a hundred men, largely in the German colony at Ramapo, though he now made it no secret that he had also rendered many more services to the British than merely enlisting Greencoat troops; indeed, he boasted openly that he had stood for a seat in the Provincial Congress only "at the desire of Governor Tryon" and that he had "remained in New Jersey until the British came there, but held a correspondence with Governor Tryon, Lord Percy and with General Campbell and had been into Paulus Hook before the British landed in New Jersey." British officials themselves added that Van Buskirk had been "very active in intelligence and in assisting Loyalists to join the British army before he himself joined." [9]

Van Buskirk had been moving more and more to an open espousal of the British cause since the Declaration of Independence, and had resigned from the Provincial Congress rather than sign the oath of abjuration, but he had been able to say plausibly that his differences with other patriots arose over independence. Now that pretense, too, was gone; if there were any moderate patriots left in Hackensack to chide themselves for believing Van Buskirk's talk about American liberties during the elections, they now had the belated opportunity to do so; men like Peter Zabriskie and John Fell had always known that he was a brazen liar.

Van Buskirk and the other Greencoats were not the only Jersey

[5] 2 Sabine 356; MSS. British Army List 1781, HC Papers CL, gives the date of his commission as Nov. 18, 1776; see also Call Roll of Major Timpany, Nov. 20, 1777, HC Papers CL. [6] 2 Sabine 250; LYT NYPL. [7] 1 Sabine 214; Fraser 599, 600. Barton, who lived about eight miles from the court house at Newton had extensive holdings of small farms and woodland in western New Jersey. [8] 2 Sabine 274; Fraser 299; LYT NYPL. The weaver James McCullough, of Hackensack, an old soldier of the French and Indian Wars, went off to Fort Lee to show his loyalty to King George. LYT NYPL "James McCullough." [9] A very full account is given in LYT NYPL "Abraham Van Buskirk." See also Fraser 562; 1 Sabine 277; 2 Sabine 376.

Dutchmen who moved about Hackensack in jubilation: Gabriel Van Norden, the late committeeman, told everyone that he had been working with Van Buskirk for months, that he was finding food and lodging for large numbers of the new troops, that he too could have had a commission for the asking; [10] Andrew Van Buskirk was already busy helping the Regulars to take patriots into custody; [11] Christian Pulisfelt, Robert Wanamaker, James Van Emburgh and Adaniah Van Emburgh, Laurence Van Horn, Edward Earl, Joost Earl, Abraham Vanderbeek, John Post, John Van Buskirk, Mathew Benson, John Baker, Nicolas Peterson, Christian Peterson and dozens of others were also busy on the King's business, all congratulating each other upon the destruction of the Continental army.[12]

Daniel Isaac Brown, resplendent in the uniform of a territorial major, now told one and all that he had gone on board *The Dutchess of Gordon* and asked Governor Tryon's advice before standing for office in the patriot government the year before, and had acted as a committeeman and member of the Provincial Congress only in the King's interest.[13]

Nine months before, Robert Morris had written airily, after explaining to a Whig friend that he did not then want to call in the military to intervene against men like Brown and Van Buskirk: "[If we] should be called out to oppose an invasion I am fairly resolved I will not leave certain men behind [who, I am] convinced, would take advantage of an unfortunate occurrence and arm [the enemies of] the country, and I am not alone." Wherever he and his friends were in hiding that day, Morris had ample time to reflect on his fine resolutions.[14]

[10]   Van Norden was born Oct. 27, 1737, the son of John A. Van Norden and Theodosia Earle. The Earle family included many Tories. Van Norden Genealogy; Fraser 561; 2 Sabine 379.
[11]   It would be wrong to conclude that all Van Buskirks were Tories from the prominence of Van Buskirk in Tory councils. There were Van Buskirk patriots who suffered greatly from British and Tory action. See e.g. 3 NJA (2) 359, 370. As in the case of other families, father and son and brother and brother often took opposite sides of the war. Lawrence Van Buskirk of Orange County (a cousin, not the father of Abraham) was one who claimed, when he sought British indemnity after the war, that he had lost a farm worth £1,800 by a rebel brother's action. Lawrence and his three sons held commissions in Colonel Bayard's Tory corps. "Before the war," he asserted, "his father James had made a will giving lands to the value of £600 to claimant, on which he laid out £1,200. His younger brother James was a violent rebel and assured their father that unless he gave him a deed to all his lands they would be seized by the Americans. In consequence he did give him a deed of gift" and Lawrence lost the property. Fraser 665.
[12]   LYT NYPL; Sabine, Fraser, passim.
[13]   LYT NYPL; Fraser 541. Brown's commission dated from Nov. 17, 1776. MSS Army List 1781, HC Papers CL.
[14]   Draft letter Robert Morris, Morris Papers RUL.

★

With every allowance for the difficulties of moving an eighteenth-century army, the British invasion of New Jersey proceeded at a most leisurely pace. Delighted with their easy triumph, the army spent the night of the 20th at Fort Lee, taking advantage of the abandoned American tents and blockhouse; [15] they set up headquarters at English Neighborhood on the 21st,[16] where, twenty-four hours after it should have been done if the British had really been concerned about the bridge, Cornwallis ordered "the 2nd Battalion of Light Infantry, the 2nd Battalion of Grenadiers, with one company of Chasseurs, to be in readiness to march at nine this morning under the command of Major General Vaughan . . . to secure the New Bridge on the Hackensack River from being destroyed by the enemy in their precipitate retreat." [17] That night the people of Hackensack could see their fires about a hundred yards apart gleaming brilliantly in the blackness of the night, from a point some distance below the town for more than a mile up the river toward New Bridge. On the 22nd and 23rd nothing was done except to move some troops over to occupy the town of Hackensack, although Cornwallis had evidently already made up his mind to pursue the retreating American army; on the 25th the main British force crossed the river at nine in the morning and "laid on [their] arms all night on the heights beyond Hackensack, having passed the Bergen meadows." [18] It was November 26 before they forded the Passaic, where the bridge, unlike the New Bridge, had been destroyed; [19] more days passed as the Americans abandoned Newark, New Brunswick and Trenton, and the British moved on to occupy them.

The British advance left Bergen County guarded by its local Tories;

[15]   Glyn Journal PUL.
[16]   Glyn Journal PUL; 1 Kemble 101.
[17]   Glyn Journal PUL.
[18]   Glyn Journal PUL. There were some additional British and Hessian movements through Hackensack for a few days. On Nov. 25, the 4th Brigade encamped at New Bridge and the 2nd Brigade at English Neighborhood, then moved to the south. Baurmeister 72. On Nov. 28 General von Mirbach's brigade, under the command of Colonel Johann Gottleib Rall, crossed the Hudson at Fort Lee and camped at English Neighborhood without tents, moving to Hackensack the next day, and then marched toward Staten Island before joining the British on their march southward. A month later, after the Battle of Trenton, patriots of Hackensack were to have reason to remember the colonel more particularly. Baurmeister 72, 73, 74.
[19]   Glyn Journal PUL.

Whigs had now lost even the small protection of British army discipline.[20]

To most British officials, as to many Americans, the war now seemed over. Sir William Howe was no man to deny himself warm quarters in New York to chase ragged countrymen farther into the winter wilderness of America. He had already marched to the Delaware when he had intended at most to go to the Raritan, and he readily concluded that no further winter campaign was necessary; the Continentals might freeze or starve, he cared little which. There seemed nothing for the British to do but to wait for the rebellion to collapse of its own accord, though some of Howe's more cautious officers added that there might still be a spring campaign against New England.[21]

Victory seemingly assured, the British offered free pardon to those who had taken up arms against their king, provided they subscribed an oath of allegiance, and Americans who took the oath were given protections which required British, Hessian, and Tories not to molest them.[22]

Howe's generous terms were intended to bring in all but the most obdurate rebels, and in the conquered province of New Jersey, at least, he was not disappointed. Nearly three thousand Jerseymen took the oath, many of them in the Hackensack valley. Probably most of them were fainthearted patriots, if they were patriots at all, but many had been among the most active supporters of the American cause, including Samuel Tucker, the one-time president of the Provincial Congress and Richard Stockton, one of the signers of the Declaration of Independence. "People join them almost in captain's companies to take the oath of allegiance," Col. Huntington wrote five days after the loss of Fort Lee.[23]

Howe's action, and the ready American response, distressed Whig and Tory alike; Whigs, understandably, to see how shallow were the pretenses of patriotism of hundreds of their friends; Tories, for their part, to see so many of their enemies going off scot free just as they were being reduced to submission; indeed, one official who himself felt that Americans could be governed only by fear reported that the proclama-

---

[20] Dr. John Morgan informed General Charles Lee, as Lee passed through the Highlands on his way to join Washington, that he had "seen a very intelligent person at Suffern's who . . . says that there are not more than a thousand Hessians and Waldeckers at Hackensack and none of the British troops, the enemy having pushed on to Newark and Elizabethtown." 1872 NYHS 327.

[21] 3 Force (5) 1316, 1317, 1318; Clinton, American Rebellion, 55.

[22] 3 Force (5) 927; Lundin 159.

[23] Lundin 159, 160, 161; Ebenezer Huntington to Jabez Huntington, Nov. 23, 1776. Huntington Papers HL.

tion "violently offends all those who have suffered for their attachment to government." [24] Patriots took what comfort they could from Governor William Livingston's observation that the oaths of allegiance had at least the advantage that they enabled patriots "to distinguish their friends from their enemies, to discriminate the persevering patriot from the temporizing politician"; actually they were clear proof that the American cause had almost collapsed, and unfortunately the defection of some Jerseymen did not stop with taking one of Lord Howe's protections. Many an American whose prudence exceeded his principles, who had run with the hares while patriots controlled New Jersey, now joined the hounds in attacking his former friends, often making up in ferocity for the time he had lost since Lexington.[25]

In the war of neighbors which ensued, none exceeded in venom the conflicts between Jersey Dutchmen of the Hackensack valley.

Colonel Ebenezer Huntington, a Continental officer near Suffern's Tavern, wrote on November 24: "By the best information the greatest part of the people [of Bergen County] are friendly to the British and will do them all the service in their power. If I had men to spare I would send a strong body to inspect their conduct." Some of the people in Huntington's own immediate neighborhood were brazen enough to try to recruit Tory troops out of his regiment of Connecticut Line. He "had six men taken up by the guards for trying to inveigle a soldier by giving him money." [26]

"Bergen County," he added a day later, "is to raise a regiment to join the British Army. . . . One Buscart or some such hard name is appointed colonel and . . . they have given a specimen of their valor by shooting a Whig, one Zabriskie." [27] Jersey Dutch patriots he found

24 Serle Diary 155.
25 Lundin 159, 160, 161.
26 3 Force (5) 833. Huntington overestimated the Tories, but there were far too many for patriot comfort. He was not alone in his views. See Smith Journal, NYPL, Dec. 5, 1776. See also 3 Force (5) 931. Some have suggested that Tories greatly outnumbered Whigs in Bergen County. One French officer, whose European background deceived him, was told that the Dutch "were as attached to England as the Orange family." Von Closen Journal 238. The close votes in the elections of 1775 and 1776, the relative numbers of coetus (Whig) and conferentie (Tory) church people, and the relative numbers of Tory troops and patriot militiamen, indeed almost all of the evidence, is to the contrary, except the complaints of patriots who were strangers to the Jersey Dutch country, men who deplored even a strong minority of Tories. Between one third and one half of the people of the Hackensack valley appear to have been Tories and Tory-minded neutrals, no more. Daniel Coe, precinct committeeman for Kakiat and Orange County south of the mountain, estimated that one third of the two hundred eighty men comprising the militia of his precinct were "disaffected to the cause." 3 Force (5) 1095. Cf. R. M. Keesey, Loyalism in Bergen County. 18 William and Mary Quarterly 558 (1961).
27 3 Force (5) 840, 841.

almost as troublesome: "Every man, and I was going to say every woman, within a large circle of this place who stand for Whigs, and for ought I know are really such, are continually distressing me from their fears and apprehensions of the enemy and Tories. They are confident the latter have so much knowledge of the country as to guide a body of troops anywhere among the mountains. Their anxiety has gone far towards intimidating some of my own troops." [28] A number of Tories in his neighborhood had gone over to the British, "telling persons they meet on the road that they intend to conduct the [British] up to Colonel Huntington and surround him and his party." [29]

If the peppery little colonel had known his new neighbors better he would not have passed off patriots' fears and apprehensions lightly, nor, in point of fact, would he have laughed at Dutch Tories, for time was to show that Bergen County's Tory regiment, however hard the name of its colonel, was one of the most daring and effective units in the whole British army establishment.

On the day after Hackensack was occupied, the British troops, with their newly found Jersey Dutch Tory friends, descended on the parsonage of Domine Romeyn at Schraalenburgh, which stood on the south side of the road, east of the church, facing the Long Swamp Brook. Heartsick patriots who knew that the domine's house was being sacked as much because he was an enemy of the conferentie as because he was a Whig, watched the soldiers, their women, the officers' servants, the Negro workers and the shouting and cheering Dutch Tories while they emptied the barns of their hay and grain, drove off the domine's milk cows, and carried away his furniture and his clothes, one of the greedy thieves even ripping the brass locks from the doors. In the course of an afternoon the once comfortable home became an empty shell, its windows and doors broken and everything in it gone.[30] Dirck Romeyn had accepted the call to the united churches of Hackensack and Schraalenburgh in April, 1776, and had moved into the parsonage at Schraalenburgh only seven months earlier. Thirty-two years old, a graduate of Princeton and a student of John Henry Goetschius, Romeyn had been born and reared in Hackensack. He was a zealous partisan of the coetus party of the Dutch Reformed church and an even more zealous partisan of American political liberties. Reserved, self-confident, of aristo-

[28] Idem.
[29] 3 Force (5) 842.
[30] Romeyn Papers UCL; HBP 78, 79; Damages by the British, NJSL, Hackensack Precinct, 172.

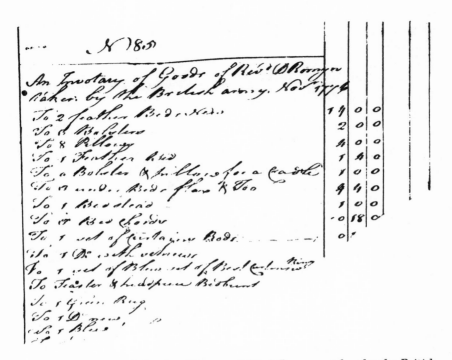

Part of "Inventory of Goods of Reverend Dirck Romeyn, taken by the British Army Nov. 1776."

New Jersey State Library

cratic temperament, many had observed how much he resembled the illustrious George Washington in appearance; as the long years of war went on, many others were to observe how much he resembled the determined Commander in Chief in character. His decision to serve the Hackensack valley churches having been made after the British had determined to move the seat of the war to New York City, he regarded his work there as providential, and he insisted upon carrying it on despite calls from more prosperous churches in perfectly safe places, and despite the urging of friends in high military office that he remove himself from the neutral ground. He lost most of his property on that rainy Saturday afternoon, the savings of years. He and his family fortunately had been visiting neighbors at the time of the raid. When he returned to find his home ruined, he set off to the north to take his wife, who was dangerously ill, and his eight-year-old daughter, to the home of his brother-in-law, Colonel Lewis DuBois, at New Paltz, seventy miles away.[31]

On the same day, November 23, the British and their followers

31 MRC 683; MSS, biography of Romeyn UCL; Romeyn Papers UCL; see also 24 NJA 637 n.

stripped the home of Romeyn's elder, William Christie, on the Schraalenburgh Road a mile and a half north of the Schraalenburgh church.

Another pillar of the Romeyn church, Garret Leydecker, who lived in English Neighborhood near Liberty Pole, had suffered almost as severely, for the British had encamped on or near his farm for days, tearing down and burning four thousand panels of four- and five-rail fence and stripping his home of everything movable.[32] Indeed, no known patriot escaped: to name a few, Jacob Wortendyke, Thomas Blanch, Thomas Campbell, Johannes Terhune, David S. Demarest, Albert Terhune, Abraham Brouwer, John Mauritius Goetschius, Abraham DeVoe, Theunis Blauvelt, John Demarest and Wiert Banta.[33] Others lost much or little, as they had much or little. No patriot home was too poor for British and Tories to plunder; and, unless Bergen County Tories were more fortunate than other Tories in the state, few of their own houses escaped some damage from British and Hessian soldiers. A British official reported that one prominent New York Tory had called upon him, "and was very warm upon the subject of our army's plundering," adding, by way of explanation, "Some of them have plundered him." [34]

Samuel and Jacobus Peek lived in Harrington or the northern part of Schraalenburgh.[35] Samuel had been an officer of the Bergen County patriot militia up to the time of the incursion of the British forces into New Jersey.[36] Samuel was forty years old; Jacobus, thirty-eight.[37] Moderately well to do, they were sons of the late Jacobus Peek of Schraalenburgh, who had often been honored by being named to the Board of Justices who headed the county government.[38] If the good people of Schraalenburgh had been asked, they would have said that the principal thing that marked the Peeks from others in the neighborhood was their father's intemperate partisanship for the conferentie group in the Dutch Reformed church and his determination to keep alive the

[32] Damages by the British, NJSL, Hackensack Precinct; HBP 79. Leydecker was a cousin of the Tory minister at the English Neighborhood church.
[33] The last three were namesakes of celebrated Tories. All of them lost heavily. Damages by the British, NJSL; HBP 78, 79 and passim.
[34] Lundin 172, etc. Serle 175. The widow of the Tory, Roelif Vanderlinde, for example, submitted a claim for £304 for British depredations during the war. Damages by British, NJSL, New Barbadoes Precinct, 58.
[35] Erskine Maps NYHS.
[36] 1 GC 554.
[37] Schraalenburgh Church Records.
[38] MJFBC 37, 46, 53–67, 71, 75, 77, 161.

schism which he had helped to start years before.[39] When the war came, some at least of their old church enemies must have confessed to themselves that they had been overharsh in judging the younger Peeks, for Samuel at least was quite willing to join in patriot activities.

True, no one would have called the Peeks warm patriots before the British invasion and no one was in the least surprised to know that the British did not arrest them when they went about the countryside seizing every patriot leader they could lay their hands on. Knowing the Peeks' antipathy for Domine Romeyn, it would not have been remarkable to find them in the throng that watched the British and Tories wreck the Dutch parsonage, more jovial than outraged when friends shouted at them to join the frolic.

To sensible, practical men it was obvious that the rebellion was over in the Hackensack valley and that it would soon be over everywhere. The great body of the conferentie people had long since given up any pretense of sympathy for the ranting Whigs, most of whom in any case had now been lodged in jail if they had not fled, and Samuel and Jacobus Peek were no men to make fools of themselves out of zeal for a lost cause. It was not long before they were leaders among the Tory foragers, or long before their younger brother David, a tanner in Schraalenburgh, took an officer's commission in the Greencoat service.[40]

On the Saturday two weeks after the first British invasion, the Peeks and their new-found friends, having exhausted the possibilities of plunder in the neighborhood of Schraalenburgh, collected a force of Tories, British soldiers, and camp followers and marched up Schraalenburgh Road in the rain to attack the patriot farmers at Tappan, eight miles to the north. Armed with whatever weapons they could find, afoot and on horseback, they set off.[41] Samuel and Jacobus Peek were in the fore-

---

39 Schraalenburgh Church Records; ERNY 3624, 3632. The Schraalenburgh records, like the Hackensack records, in fact include the marriage, baptismal and membership records of two wholly separated churches, the patriot coetus church of Domine Goetschius and Domine Romeyn and the Tory-conferentie church of Domine Kuypers and his predecessors. The two records must be separated to trace the religious affiliations of the people of the Hackensack valley. The principal key to separation is that the baptismal records beginning at page 220 of the Schraalenburgh Church Records are the records of the Tory-conferentie church; the baptismal records from page 134 to 220 being the coetus records for the period. The Tappan coetus and conferentie records are separated. When related to genealogies, these records give a reasonably clear picture of the church connections of large numbers of Hackensack valley people. It has not been possible to separate coetus and conferentie sympathizers at Paramus and Ponds.

40 3 Force (5) 1174; 2 GC 625. Peek's Negro slave, captured by the American forces at Tappan early in December, had been employed as a Tory spy. 3 Force (5) 1109.

41 3 Force (5) 1139.

front, disarming patriots, seizing what they could, and generally making themselves as useful as possible in the enterprise.[42] They were well known in Tappan, two of their brothers-in-law being Johannes David Blauvelt and Cornelius Smith. Blauvelt was lieutenant colonel of the Orangetown militia.[43]

Colonel William Malcolm, the officer commanding the New York State troops at Tappan, who finally drove off the marauders, sneered at the raid: "A notable exploit," he called it, "of cutting down a Liberty Pole at Tappan, making a prisoner of the father of one of my lieutenants and stealing a horse and two oxen." [44] The raiders did not feel their raid was futile, nor did patriots at Schraalenburgh or Hackensack make light of the affair, then or later. Embittered Whigs who saw that band of ruffians and turncoats gather and march off toward Tappan with the British soldiers never forgot their helpless anger at the brutality of a raid whose only purpose was to let the raiders show their new-found friends how willing they were to hurt their old neighbors. Actually, Colonel Malcolm himself took the raid more seriously than his report would have indicated. Warned of the attack, he had first taken a strong position in a clove in the hills back of Tappan, with artillery pieces in the road, flanked by troops, discovering too late that it was not a military move at all.[45]

The Peeks were not alone, or even the most prominent, in helping the invaders to find and arrest patriots and plunder their property. Gabriel Van Norden, of Steenrapie, who had been a member of the Bergen County Committee of Safety, was perhaps the most active man, not in a Greencoat uniform, among the Tories.[46] Andrew Van Buskirk, brother of the new lieutenant colonel, stagedriver and father of the dispatch rider, had also shown himself, according to patriot reports, "particularly cruel to Whigs." [47] John Van Buskirk, Garret Van Giesen, Garret Demarest, Cornelius Bogert, and Abraham Van Giesen were among others who were later arrested for their Tory activities at the time.[48]

John Pearsall, Thomas Gardner, Charles Gardner, and William Day

[42] 1 GC 554.
[43] Blauvelt Genealogy Nos. 216, 255.
[44] 3 Force (5) 1139; Heath Papers MHS.
[45] 3 Force (5) 1139.
[46] Fraser 554, 561; 2 Sabine 379; Heath Papers MHS.
[47] Heath Papers MHS. It was reported to Governor Livingston, when Van Buskirk was arrested, that within the week after he had taken the oath to the state he had started to furnish provisions to the British. Hays to Livingston, July 16, 1777, Livingston Papers MHS.
[48] Livingston to Boudinot, Aug. 28, 1777, Boudinot Papers LC.

were but a few of the other active Tories.[49] There were others, too digni-
fied to plunder their neighbors, who nevertheless made it quite clear
that they were delighted that the revolution was over and the ranting
Whigs in flight or in jail: men like Peter T. Herring, of Old Tappan,
Dr. James Van Buren of Hackensack, Arent J. Schuyler, of New Barbadoes Neck, and John Demarest of Old Bridge;[50] and there were still
others, somewhat less prominent, like Michael Ryerson and John Bogert,
who, though perhaps peaceable enough, were more than outspoken in
condemning the damned rebels who had lately infested the county.[51]

British recruiting agents worked busily from Hackensack as far north
as Paramus and Ringwood; the bolder ones even recruited in Tappan
under the noses of the American army.[52] Some of the more cautious loyalists, feeling that the outlying country was not yet really safe from rebel
attack, busied themselves in shipping their furniture and effects into
New York City.[53]

Washington had left several thousand troops under General William
Heath at Peekskill. These now moved to the west of the river and took
positions in the lower New York Highlands, in a wide semicircle from
the Hudson west to the Ramapos. Heath commanded four brigades of
Connecticut and New York troops, under Generals Parsons, James
Clinton, George Clinton, and John Morin Scott, totaling over five thousand men, of whom perhaps thirty-five hundred were on hand and fit for
duty. He placed Colonel Huntington with two regiments at Sidman's
Bridge on the Ramapo, at the entrance to Smith's Clove, on November
14, and posted a brigade at the King's Ferry landing and others in and
around Haverstraw, Nyack, and Tappan. The troops of General James
Clinton were garrisoned at Forts Clinton and Montgomery. All were
under orders to commence the construction of huts for winter quarters.[54]

Colonel Malcolm, at Tappan, incensed by the Peeks' raid and other
Tory insults, wrote on December 11: "I am almost in an enemy's country, I cannot get intelligence beyond the circle of my quarters but what

[49]   Idem.
[50]   MCSNJ, passim; MCSNY 352, 353.
[51]   Heath Papers MHS.
[52]   1 GC 583. Within four days after the British invasion General John Morin
Scott reported that "thirty men were enlisted in the enemy's service" in and around
Tappan. 3 Force (5) 325.
[53]   1 GC 469, 561; Heath 91, 92.
[54]   See 6 GW 275; 3 Force (5) 833. Heath Papers MHS.

is brought by my scouts. . . . The country from Tappan [south] is all in arms. On Sunday they were called together, and had Kings arms and ammunition delivered out among them. . . . I really think my party insufficient to take post at Tappan, but our friends are so distressed thereabouts that I think it an indispensable duty to attempt supporting them. . . . I hope Monday to run over the Tory ground and scatter their gangs." [55]

On December 9, though his troops were quite unfit for duty, many being almost barefooted, he had made just such a raid, marching to the south within three miles of New Bridge, and raising, he said, "a terrible uproar among the Tories, who abandoned their houses and guard houses." Parcels, "an arch Tory [who was] with the party on Saturday . . . was not so lightfooted as his companions and got taken," along with a Negro owned by one of the Peeks.[56]

Tories, overjoyed at Washington's abandonment of Hackensack and convinced that his retreat meant an end to the war, had been little concerned by the American troops to the north. They were soon to discover that they were by no means safe merely because Cornwallis had driven Washington out of New Jersey. Malcolm's raid was a warning. On Saturday, December 14, they received more than a warning: General Heath himself, with six hundred troops, made a forced march of twelve miles from Tappan and occupied the village of Hackensack.[57] The Regulars and Greencoats gone, Tories now felt the iron hand of military power. Heath seized a large number of them and as many Tory stores as he could find, including a good deal of property on its way to New York in river boats: "We have taken about fifty of the disaffected, and about fifty or sixty muskets, the greater part of which had been taken from the Whigs, as is supposed, and stored," he reported. "At the dock we found one sloop, loaded with hay, house furniture, some spirits, &c, which we have this day unloaded. A brig, loaded, ran down the river about seven miles, and got aground. I am afraid that we shall not be able to secure the effects. A schooner, loaded with hay, furniture, &c, which had sailed from the dock, ran on the bank of the river, the wind being very fresh, and in the night overset, by which the goods were damaged, if not lost." [58]

[55]   3 Force (5) 1173, 1174. See McDougall to Heath, Dec. 9, 1776, Heath Papers MHS.
[56]   3 Force (5) 1139. Parcels was probably Abraham Persell. See 1 Carleton Papers 399 (1833). He and his brother owned a 145 acre farm in Schraalenburgh.
[57]   3 Force (5) 1234. Local patriots, Heath reported, "received us with joy, but are almost afraid to speak their sentiments." 3 Force (5) 1235.
[58]   3 Force (5) 1234, 1235.

Fifty barrels of flour, rum, and other goods were taken at the home of Colonel Abraham Van Buskirk on the River Road at Teaneck, and other stores at Major Brown's home on the Hackensack green.[59]

The patriot militiamen who helped Heath to carry off the stores would not have been pleased to know that John Zabriskie, Jr., their late lieutenant colonel, had not walked down from his house at the New Bridge to watch them merely from curiosity, but had been busy noting their officers' names on a piece of paper, which he sent off by a slave to British headquarters that night, though his action was perhaps better calculated to show a pedestrian Tory mind than to injure the militia officers.[60]

Heath was at Hackensack only one full day, Sunday, December 15, but while he was there he found proof certain that all Jersey Dutch Tories were not as quick-witted as they fancied themselves. One of the local Tory sympathizers came up to two of Heath's officers who were walking along the street. The Tory seemed overjoyed to see them, but it was not long before the Americans saw that the reason for his joy was his belief that they were British. The Yankee officers accepted his cheerful greetings, expressed their happiness at finding so zealous a friend of government and offered to introduce him to their commanding officer, an offer which the Tory enthusiastically accepted. They brought him before General Heath, explaining that he was a friend who had joined them on the street and was prepared to give most important military information. The bald-headed, corpulent Heath, who could hardly keep from laughing, showed great interest in the Tory's intelligence that a large body of rebels had collected to the north. "He was asked if in case these rebels should advance, any assistance could be afforded by the people of the town, and whether they could be depended upon? He was asked whether there was not a number in the town who were in favor of the rebels? He answered, that there was; but that they had seized and sent off the principal ones among them and that now the others dared not show themselves. The joke was thus going on when Colonel Prescott, who stood near him, holding his hat in his hand, in which there was a red cockade (at that time a mark of the dis-

[59] 3 Force (5) 1235. "Two or three companies have been raising here and in the vicinity, and field officers appointed; one Buskirk colonel. At his house we found fifty barrels of flour, a number of hogsheads of rum, &c; and at one Brown's, who is Lieutenant Colonel, about one thousand pounds of cheese, &c. One TenPenny is Major. They are all gone down to York, to have matters properly settled, get ammunition, arms &c, and were to have returned on yesterday. I believe we have luckily disconcerted them."

[60] James Stagg to Hendrick Kuyper, July 26, 1777, NJSL. "A young . . . student . . . living at Hackensack was at New York . . . and in the evening saw John Zabriskie's negro deliver the letter." Idem.

tinction of rank), the gentleman fixed his eye upon it, and his countenance immediately fell. He was then told that those whom he termed rebels were now in possession of the place, and had now received his information. He was ordered into custody." [61]

Held for seven days, "chagrined almost to death . . . spending his time, like April, in weeping and lowering," he was finally released by Heath upon punctually performing a piece of secret service allotted to him.[62]

All but eight of the Tory prisoners taken at Hackensack were released. "About sixty disaffected persons were taken up in a few hours," Col. Huntington wrote on Thursday, after the raid, "but the General finding so great a number of those people that it would take all his division to guard them we took about eight prisoners of war . . ." [63] He proceeded to forward the eight under armed guard to Fishkill to answer to the New York Committee of Safety. Gabriel Van Norden was one of them: "a great Tory and very mischievous," Heath noted.[64] Andrew Van Buskirk was another: "ditto, has been cruel toward our friends, plundering them." Thomas Gardner, "ditto, said to have been promised a commis-

[61] Heath 93.
[62] Idem. Heath's list of prisoners hints that the prisoner was either Michael Ryer[son] or John Bogert, both of whom had their names stricken from the list, as well as the notation: "disaffected—called [patriots] damned rebels." List of Prisoners, Dec. 15, 1776, Heath Papers MHS.
[63] Ebenezer Huntington to Jabez Huntington, Dec. 19, 1776. Huntington Papers H L.
[64] Van Norden, whose politics had suffered a change with the British invasion, suffered another, with his capture by the Americans. On Jan. 19, 1777, at Fishkill, he was released from American custody, "having voluntarily taken the oath of allegiance to the State of New Jersey." An American officer at Fishkill made the release possible by swearing that he had always considered Van Norden "as a friend to the American cause and hath lately heard the same character of him from several of his neighbors." MCSNY 108. The officer had heard something that had been hidden from patriots in Hackensack and Steenrapie. LYT NYPL; Fraser 561. John Pearsall and Thomas Gardner also took the oath and were discharged, and at least two of the seamen captured on the Hackensack River schooner enlisted in the Continental navy. MCSNY 73, 112. Hackensack patriots were undoubtedly much annoyed at the release of their enemies, but the releases probably were correct, whether the oaths which procured them were true or false. Heath was wrong to arrest civilians, Tories or not, between the lines when the government of New Jersey was not exercising actual jurisdiction at the place of arrest. That the Tories had been guilty of the same offense was not to the point; Tories had been guilty of many breaches of military propriety and were to be guilty of more. A few months later Gabriel Van Norden was arrested by the New Jersey civil authorities and after trial ordered imprisoned until exchanged for a patriot in British hands. MCSNJ 83, 117. At that time, however, patriots were in de facto control of Hackensack, and were exercising the normal right to require civilian compliance with their orders. Evidently Andrew Van Buskirk also was released by the New York authorities in January, 1777, probably upon a similar oath. MCSNJ 83, 117.

sion." Charles Gardner, John Pearsall, William Day, and Henry Labach were four others.[65]

On Monday morning, December 16, General Heath and General George Clinton, who had followed General Heath down Schraalenburgh Road with some of his officers and a small detachment of American light horse, retired to Paramus with the prisoners and captured stores in the face of a strong British troop movement toward Hackensack.[66]

Clinton and Heath assumed that the movement was directed at them; actually the British were only going into their long-delayed winter quarters, the quarters in fact for which Howe had originally crossed the Hudson River, a month before.

When Heath was at Hackensack he complained that patriots, though pleased with his raid, seemed utterly afraid to speak and that no information could be got from them.[67] In truth, every passing day saw a stiffening of Whig morale; every day saw more patriots determined to strike back at the British invaders and their Tory friends. No great majority before the British invasion, scattered and seemingly helpless when the American army left them to their enemies, there were stubborn men in the Hackensack valley who had no intention whatever of admitting that they were defeated.

William Christie of Schraalenburgh was one stubborn man who was not afraid to speak. Fifty-six years old, he lived with his wife, the former Catalyntie Demarest, and their twelve children, in a stone house on his 140-acre farm in the northern part of Schraalenburgh, on the road to Tappan.[68] A stranger in the Hackensack valley, seeing him driving his fat horses to the Dutch Reformed church on Sunday, with his wife by his side and their children chattering in Dutch behind them, would have been charmed with the quaint picture of Dutch virtue and prosperity. The truth was that Christie's father was Scotch and his mother and his wife were French and, like more than one Jersey Dutchman, he and his family had little more Dutch blood in their veins than Colonel Huntington of the Connecticut Line.

Mr. Christie's home had been stripped on the same day that the British wrecked the Romeyn parsonage. The fact that he was an elder in the Romeyn church may or may not have marked his house for pillage; in any case, the British took off five hogs, one horse, and all his

65 Heath Papers MHS.
66 Heath 91, 94; 1 GC 468, 469; 3 Force (5) 1261.
67 3 Force (5) 1235.
68 Christie Genealogy. List of Ratables, Hackensack Township, 1779, NJSL.

pewter dishes, china plates, basins, teapots, rugs, blankets, feather beds, bolsters, pillows and clothes, in point of fact everything in the house but the heavy furniture.[69] If Mr. Christie congratulated himself on saving his furniture, he had but to wait. Before the end of the war he would lose that too.

When his neighbor's son, who had enlisted with the Greencoats but was planning to desert, gave him the figures of British strength at New Bridge, on December 23, 1776, he immediately made his way to Tappan to pass the information on to the American army. "Early in the evening," Colonel John Hathorn wrote to headquarters, "we learned from Mr. Christie, whose character we found to be good, that there were six companies of Regulars and three of late enlisted Tories at the New Bridge." [70] Colonel Hathorn was guilty of a gross understatement: in his whole regiment there was no man of better character or firmer Whig principles than William Christie.

It is easy to believe the family tradition that when the war ended he refused judicial office because he felt he could not be fair to former Tories.[71] His son James, born in 1744, served with distinction as a militia captain throughout the war.[72]

A few days after Mr. Christie's visit, another Schraalenburgh patriot was able to give an American agent from Tappan definite word of "a man of undoubted friendship and knowledge [who was] every day in Hackensack . . . in company with the regular officers" that there were about twelve hundred British and Hessian troops and four hundred

[69]   Damages by British, Hackensack Precinct, NJSL.

[70]   3 Force (5) 1379. Mr. Christie's report was correct. The 7th Regiment of British Regulars was at New Bridge, with the local Tory troops; the 26th Regiment of Regulars was at Hackensack. 1 Kemble 426. Map from HC Papers CL, reproduced opposite page 169, Lundin. The map does not show the positions of the Tory troops, but many intelligence reports to the Americans indicate that they were also at New Bridge. See e.g., 1 GC 496, 508. Mr. Christie added that the neighbor's son "had enlisted . . . by the persuasion of his parents." 3 Force (5) 1379.

[71]   HBP 108.

[72]   Captain James Christie died July 3, 1817, at the age of 73, "very highly esteemed for his most excellent character." Banta Genealogy No. 616; HBP 107, 108. His grandson and namesake, James Christie, died in 1913 at the age of 82, perhaps even more esteemed for his character. The grandson was so bound up in the century-old Whig-Tory and coetus-conferentie controversies that he refused to attend the South Church at Bergenfield after it gave up its identity as the True Reformed Dutch Church, even though it had joined the like-minded Christian Reformed Church. James Christie was not alone in his views. Many Bergen County Dutchmen felt strongly about the Whig-Tory controversy as late as the middle of the twentieth century.

   Captain Christie, too, had a namesake in the Greencoats, a sergeant in Captain Van Allen's company. Canadian Archives, muster rolls, Aug. 31, 1778, July 14, 1780, and Nov. 27, 1781.

armed Tories in the British camp, all thoroughly acquainted with the American positions and strength.[73] Travelers along the Bergen County highways brought more information. Mrs. Zabriskie, at the Bridge, the wife of John Zabriskie, Jr., had told one such traveler that there were two thousand British troops nearby, a figure very close to the patriot estimate.[74] The John Zabriskies were by now almost open Tories; they probably told the story not to help Americans but to frighten them, but there were dozens of others in and around Hackensack who wanted only an opportunity to avenge themselves upon the invaders.

One such patriot, in point of fact, was John Zabriskie's brother Peter.[75] Fifty-five years old when the British invaded New Jersey and exposed as he was to British reprisals, Peter Zabriskie could easily have taken a position of neutrality, risking neither his life nor his fortune in the disaster which had seemingly overwhelmed the American cause. He chose instead to put himself as openly on the patriot side of the war as he had openly espoused the coetus party in the Dutch church, and when the British re-entry into Hackensack gave him a chance to strike a blow for the patriot cause he was quick to seize it.

A few days after setting up their winter quarters at Hackensack and New Bridge the British, confident of their hold on the conquered province of New Jersey and anxious to protect their Tory friends, shifted many of Van Buskirk's Provincials over to the English Neighborhood, quartering them in the farmhouses spread along the road to the east of the meadows.

Zabriskie saw at once the possibility of cutting off these detached troops, and went to General George Clinton at Ramapo with a plan to do so. On the night of December 19, about dusk, Clinton and General Parsons, with Zabriskie as pilot and guide, set off with about five hundred troops to attack the former patriot delegate and his Tory volunteers.

Detaching two hundred of their men with orders to march east of the settlement through the fields to the edge of the Bergen Woods so that they could fix guards on the roads leading to Burdett's and Bull's ferries and come in on the back of the enemy, General Clinton and General Parsons marched down through the neighborhood from the north.

[73]   1 GC 507.

[74]   3 Force (5) 1381. The boy who made the report had been taken up and arrested by the late schoolmaster of Hackensack, Major Robert Timpany. General George Clinton's estimate was closer to that of William Christie. 1 GC 216.

[75]   GHHB 49; Bailey 333; Zabriskie Genealogy No. 319. ERNY 4086. MJFBC, passim; ERNY 3549, 3617, 3627, 3635, 3690, 3693, 4086, 4211, 4212, 4243, 4246: 25 NJA 343, 344, 345; LYT NYPL "William Bayard."

"About break a Day," Clinton reported, "we surprized and took their Advanced Guard, about a Mile from Bergen Woods. At the instant we had effected this and were about advancing to attack their Main Body, One of their Horse Men rode up and notwithstanding being challenged was fired upon by one of our People; This alarmed their Party." Thus warned, the Tories fled before the detached party could wholly shut off their retreat. As Clinton said, it was nevertheless a successful

The Bearer hereof M.r Sobriski is a most Stanch Friend and has Suffered much, He was the Guide to our Detachment that went to E.' Neighbourhood and is well acquainted with all Parts of this Country, and is deserving of notice and respect —

W Heath

Certificate of General William Heath to "Mr. Sobriski," who piloted the expedition against Van Buskirk's position at English Neighborhood, December 20, 1776.

George Washington Papers, Library of Congress.

little expedition, taking twenty-three prisoners, mostly Tories from among Van Buskirk's friends enlisted at Ramapo, some muskets, a wagon, and eight horses. "It might have been much more so," he added, "had it not been so exceeding cold and the men beat out with the length of the march, which the route we took was at least twenty-eight miles." [76]

General Clinton and General Heath sent Peter Zabriskie off to Washington's headquarters with the dispatches, an honor usually reserved for the outstanding military figure in such an affair. "Mr. Zabriskie," he

[76] 1 GC 477. A list of prisoners, showing a number of Ramapo Germans, is at 1 GC 483. See also Heath 94; 3 Force (5) 1344, 1345.

added to his dispatch, "acted as guide . . . being well acquainted with this part of the country and deserving the utmost respect." [77]

William Christie and Peter Zabriskie were by no means alone in Bergen County. As the days passed after the invasion it was more and more evident that many would not bow their necks to disaster. Their God was able to deliver them from the burning fiery furnace which lay before them, and out of the King's hand, but whether he did or not, like the three men of old who faced Nebuchadnezzar, they would not bow down and serve the King and his wicked ministers. In the end they too were to be delivered from their enemies.

John Mauritius Goetschius, son of the late Dutch Reformed minister, was one. Another was Samuel P. Demarest, who lived in Closter, just under the eastern slope of the Palisades. Garret Leydecker of Liberty Pole (cousin of the Tory preacher), Henry Bogert, John Fell, Roelif Westervelt, Joost Zabriskie, Thomas Blanch, Hendrick Kuyper, Peter Wilson, William Prevost, Adam Boyd, Abraham Brouwer, and John Lozier were but a few of the others. When Admiral Lord Howe observed to an aide, three weeks after the fall of Fort Lee, "that almost all the people of sense and spirit were in the rebellion," he had just such men in mind.[78]

When strangers pointed to the large number of Dutch Tories and observed sagely, with Tom Paine, that a servile, self-interested fear was the foundation of Toryism, they would have done well to ask themselves what their own neighbors would have done if they had been on the open frontier, with comfort and safety on one side and disaster on the other. They might have observed, even more sagely, that there were no servile, self-interested or fearful men among patriots in the conquered areas of New York and New Jersey. No one was a patriot of convenience in the Hackensack valley in December 1776.

Attacks like Clinton's and Heath's helped patriot morale, but they

[77] Heath's note to Washington read: "The bearer hereof, Mr. Zabriskie, is a most staunch friend and has suffered much. He was the guide to our detachment that went to English Neighborhood and is well acquainted with all parts of this county and is deserving of notice and respect." Heath to Washington, Dec. 21, 1776, GW Papers LC. The identification of *Peter* Zabriskie is not certain. Joost Zabriskie is a possibility.

Two of the lieutenants in Captain Bell's Orange County militia added nothing to their military characters on the expedition. Ordered to march with the state troops, "the captain readily complied, when we got about six miles from this place, both his lieutenants refused to march farther, which occasioned [a] great part of the company to stay back." 1 GC 554.

[78] Serle Diary 157.

held little real hope for the patriot cause. The military situation of the army west of the Hudson was worse than desperate; it was an army, to all appearances, with less than a fortnight to stay in being. General John Morin Scott, whose brigade had been at Haverstraw for only a few days, had lost his whole force when their enlistments expired early in December, despite every effort of Scott and his officers to keep them together.[79]

General Clinton, at his headquarters at Ramapo, got word first from Colonel Allison at Tappan and then from Colonel Hathorn and Colonel Pauling that the New York militia were determined to go home at the year end despite every effort to hold them. "I am convinced," Allison wrote as the year closed, "that the militia will go home bodily before three days, the consequence of which is obvious to every man of the least discernment." [80] Colonel Hathorn added, "Words cannot express the situation that I am in here." Stationed at Closter, where he "could hear the Regulars' drums twice a day very plain," Hathorn was obliged to report that there was "pretty general determination amongst the men to go home at all events." [81] The militiamen, he said, were not disloyal, but their own hardships, "being almost barefooted and nearly naked for clothes," added to the terrible worry over their families, resulted in almost emptying some regiments. Clinton assured his colonels that he would dismiss his men and soldiers as soon as he could; but, he pleaded, "For heaven's sake, for the sake of your bleeding country, keep your men together a few days longer. Don't let them basely desert so honorable [a] cause and suffer our inveterate and cruel enemy to plunder and distress our friends." [82]

General Clinton was not indulging in rhetoric. On the night of December 27 the British and Tory forces stationed at Hackensack raided Hoppertown and Paramus, almost in sight of the American troops at Ramapo, and carried off Garret Hopper and six or seven other Whig farmers as prisoners—a foretaste of the price that Jerseymen were to pay for their patriotism in a country between the two contending armies. The time was to come all too soon when the plight of Hackensack valley patriots was taken as one of the inevitable hardships of war, a thing that nothing could be done about; but General Clinton, utterly distressed at his inability to help, thought that if General Heath would send him a few field pieces he might do something to stop it:

[79]   3 Force (5) 1029, 1030, 1040.
[80]   1 GC 499.
[81]   1 GC 503, 511.
[82]   To add to the difficulties of the Highlands army, its deputy quartermaster had deserted from Tappan with the regimental returns, giving the British full intelligence of the American numbers and situation, if they did not have it already. 1 GC 507.

A number of the enemy . . . amounting to between five and eight hundred, consisting of Regulars and Buskirk's Regiment [arrived at Hackensack],
imprisoned and otherwise insulted the few friends we left there, and soon
after came to Paramus, plundered some of the inhabitants of that place and
took the Hoppers and others of that neighborhood, who are now confined in
Hackensack jail, and have since committed many acts of cruelty on the inhabitants. I keep out large patrolling parties every night in that neighborhood for the protection of the inhabitants, but the enemy have so good
intelligence of our thoughts and every motion that it is beyond my power
to give protection to the well disposed inhabitants in any other way than by
routing the enemy from their present quarters, which I have hitherto not
had strength to attempt with a probability of success. . . . Had I only a
couple of field pieces I flatter myself I should be able to drive the [enemy]
out of this quarter of the country. I beg, therefore, my dear sir, that you
will be good enough to order Captain Bryan and Lieutenant Jackson to join
me with the two field pieces assigned to my former brigade.[83]

Heath felt obliged to refuse the request,[84] at which Clinton observed
that "in the meantime . . . the enemy [are] imprisoning, plundering
and killing the inhabitants while you refuse me the means of opposing
them." [85]

The fate of Hackensack patriots, like that of America, depended of
course not on the Highlands forces, but on General Washington, whose
broken army, beaten and driven from one end of Jersey to the other,
now waited on the west side of the Delaware for the British to continue
their drive against Philadelphia.

The British, confident that their five months' campaign had won the
war, were waiting only for the river to freeze hard enough to cross; it
did not seem worth while even to build boats to pursue their tatter-
demalion enemies. There was plenty of time, and the Continental capital was but a day's skirmish away. With the Americans falling away like
a rope of sand, the British congratulated themselves that they would eat
Christmas dinner in Philadelphia if the river froze in time; if not, they
would dine there later.

To please Jersey Tories, Sir William Howe contemptuously spread
out a thin line of British posts from Hackensack and New Bridge in
north Jersey through Paulus Hook, Newark, Elizabeth, New Brunswick,

---

[83] 1 GC 216: misdated Jan. 1, 1776.
[84] 1 GC 522, 523.
[85] 1 GC 522.

Princeton, Trenton, and finally Burlington, a hundred miles to the south: "rather too extensive a chain," Howe admitted, but one in which he was nonetheless certain that his troops would be in perfect security.[86] Considering the state of the American army, no military man in his senses would have disagreed.

At the end of the third week of December, even Washington admitted that both he and the American rebellion were almost ruined.[87] Since the British attack at Long Island he had suffered nothing but defeat: where he might have held the British, as at Hackensack, no support had been given; [88] Congress had left Philadelphia in panic for Baltimore; Washington himself advised the removal of Philadelphia property.[89]

"No man . . . ," he wrote as Christmas came on, "ever had a greater choice of difficulties and less means to extricate himself from them." [90]

Neither Washington on the Delaware nor Heath and Clinton in the Hudson Highlands were in a mood for Christmas celebrations, but for a few hours on Christmas night the Americans under General Clinton, from Closter to Ramapo, forgot the war. Orders for night scouting parties were countermanded and, as one officer noted in his journal, "The evening ensued with delightful sports, full flowing bowls and jolly souls, spirits elevated with liquor and hearts enflamed by the beauty of woman." [91]

During the same few hours in south Jersey the poor conscripts of the mercenary Prince of Hesse also forgot the war and their families three thousand miles away. Colonel Rall canceled Hessian night scouting orders, just as the Americans to the north canceled theirs, and Hessian spirits too were elevated with liquor.

The next dawn is history; the Battle of Trenton was won and America saved.

By early morning Colonel Rall was dead, his brigade was under Amer-

[86] 1 NJA (2) 367, 368.

[87] "Ten days more will put an end to the existence of our army," Washington told the President of Congress on the 20th. "The enemy are daily gathering strength from the disaffected; this strength, like a snowball by rolling, will increase, unless some means can be devised to check effectively the progress of the enemy's arms." 6 GW 401, 402, 403, 404.

[88] "If the Jerseys had given us any support, we might have made a stand at Hackensack, and after that at Brunswick, but the few militia that were in arms, disbanded themselves or slunk off . . . upon the appearance of danger . . . and left the poor remains of our army to make the best we could of it. . . . If every nerve is not strained to recruit the new army with all possible expedition, I think the game is pretty near up." 6 GW 398. Many thought the game was up, new army or not.

[89] 6 GW 439.

[90] 6 GW 398, 399.

[91] 1 GC 516.

ican guard, and British dispatch riders were spreading panic among General Howe's men from Burlington to New Bridge.

Washington's battered and frozen army, the men whom the country-man had saved at Fort Lee, the men who were lucky enough to gain the New Bridge before the British, the Continental troops who remained after the summer soldier and the sunshine patriot had fallen away, crossed the Delaware in a sleet storm on Christmas night, fell upon Trenton, and surprised and captured or killed Rall's whole force.[92]

Washington's one stroke, pitifully small by any standard, changed the whole course of the war. Less than a thousand Hessians were involved, and perhaps twenty-four hundred Americans, but the Battle of Trenton and the short campaign that followed drove the invaders out of their winter headquarters from the Delaware to the New York line; it saved Philadelphia; indeed, it saved the American cause.

Pious Jersey Dutchmen could echo the Rev. Henry Muhlenberg, when he compared the spirit that animated Washington with the spirit that smote the whole Assyrian camp in one night (II Kings 19:35). "This occurrence on the day after Christmas [shows that it is] . . . foolish impertinence for created, limited, mortal creatures to say positively or without condition 'We shall celebrate Christmas in Philadelphia.' " [93]

Had it been given to him to see the future, Muhlenberg could have added that in a very real sense the Battle of Trenton made the rest of the war a foolish British impertinence, for it can be said, and not with-out reason, that at Trenton the British dropped forever the gage of final victory in the Revolution.

---

[92] 6 GW 441; Stryker, Battles of Trenton and Princeton. The same snowstorm lasted all day Dec. 26 in the Hackensack valley, ending that night. 1 GC 516. It was "a most tempestuous day of rain, frost, wind and snow." Serle Diary 163.

[93] 2 Muhlenberg 768.

7

★

PATRIOTS, who had seen the whole Continental army fall apart while their enemies grew in power and strength, had every reason to feel that Providence, by one stroke at Trenton, had saved the American cause.[1]

Almost helpless in the hands of their enemies before Trenton, New Jersey patriots were free men less than two weeks later, for the British saw no option but to withdraw their forces from the state after Rall's disaster proved that their posts could be destroyed one by one if they kept them there.

On the afternoon of January 5 the troops at Hackensack broke camp and marched off toward New York. General Clinton was informed the next day that they "left the town with the utmost precipitation and fright in three parties, each taking different routes . . . one toward Acquackanonk, another by the ferry and the third through the English Neighborhood." [2] The British were not fleeing in fright; they simply saw that Hackensack was untenable for winter quarters. "They have disappointed me exceedingly," Clinton went on. "I am sure I could have de-

---

[1] "There was a considerable number of the people of New Jersey who took part with the British. Many took protections and others were formed into regiments and companies, a considerable number of the people of Hackensack . . . were so formed under the command of Col. Buskirk. When the Hessians were taken at Trenton, a spirit of resistance seemed to revive amongst the people, a company was then formed at Hackensack out of the inhabitants who remained true to Whig principles." Affidavit of David R. Bogert, Pension Records, W3502.
[2] 1 GC 533, 534. See 1 Kemble 434.

stroyed the whole of them had they only continued there two days longer . . . I have sent down a strong party to possess the town and secure such stores as they may have left and bring in the Tories, who are much dejected." [3] Patriots were delighted to know that the Hoppers and the other prisoners had been released before the withdrawal.[4]

What patriots probably did not see was that the very reasons why Hackensack was unsafe for the British made it equally unsafe for the Americans, and that, far from being returned to the protection of their American friends, they were now in an abandoned country between two armies. There must have been times, in the next half decade of war, when even stanch patriots wondered whether it would not have been better to be living within the British lines.

The main British army had returned to New York City, but General Howe had not given up all of the nearby country; he still retained Paulus Hook and Bergen Point, and scouting parties of as many as four hundred of Van Buskirk's and Barton's Greencoats were frequently at English Neighborhood, only a few miles across the salt marshes from the town, to protect farmers who wanted to bring country produce to the New York ferries and the woodcutters who were already busy felling trees for New York City's fuel.[5]

Thus the Hackensack valley began its role as the dread neutral ground. Both British and American forces moved into it often, seldom in such strength as to risk a major battle, but never so quietly that Jersey Dutchmen could forget they lived in a frontier open from all sides. An American officer put the situation in a very few words: "The good people of Bergen County lay greatly exposed to both internal and external enemies, and the internal enemies have a free recourse to New York, the center and head of all British activity in America." [6]

Orange County patriots were in almost equal danger. Major Johannes Jacobus Blauvelt, of the militia, reported to his superiors that in his neighborhood, "matters are come to such a height that they who are friends of the American Cause, must (for their own safety) be cautious how they speak in public," that he had no doubt that some of those "who have been active in favour of our Cause, will soon (if any opportunity offers) be carried down to New York." The communication

[3] 1 GC 534, 535.
[4] 1 GC 534, 536. Clinton was incensed that the British had had the impudence to try to exchange prisoners two days earlier, when they knew the release was imminent.
[5] 1 GC 583.
[6] Colonel Levi Pawling had his troops posted as far south as "the entrance of the English Neighborhood" and had just returned from Closter himself when he made the observation. 1 GC 677, 701, 702.

between Orangetown and New York, Blauvelt went on, being entirely open to the Tories, he had no doubt but that they made too much use of it for patriots' good; he was understandably disturbed that "the New Levies, as they are called, are frequently in our Neighborhood and too many of the Inhabitants befriend them." [7] Blauvelt was all too exact in his estimate of the future that lay before Orangetown and the country to the south. From British headquarters in New York City and the British outposts on the western shores of the Hudson, the whole Hackensack valley lay open to their recruiting agents, their spies, and their raids. The country closest to their posts, like the Bergen Neck region to the south of English Neighborhood, was already being stripped of its trees by Tory woodchoppers, fuel being so important to the British that their recruiting agents were seemingly more anxious to get woodchoppers than to enlist Greencoats, and Robert Erskine, the patriot ironmaster, was obliged to warn that if something were not done to stop his men from going over to the British, iron production in the Jersey Highlands would stop. "I am sorry to inform you," he told General Clinton, "that the greatest part of my woodcutters have gone off to the Regulars; there have been frequently emissaries among them, the last I understand was an old gray-headed man from about Hackensack." He pointed out that without wood he could not blow his furnaces. "I am glad, however, to hear that about twenty-three of them have been taken this week in Bergen Woods where they were Cutting fewel & hope it is true." [8]

Patriots in Bergen and Orange counties were also exposed to American foragers, who were little more to be trusted in the neutral ground than Britons and Hessians, many Americans being as quick to believe that anything they wanted belonged to a Tory as the redcoats had been ready to believe that everything in America was the property of the damned American rebels; both armies, as one man put it, too often divided among the soldiers what they could divide and destroyed everything else. The Rev. Henry Muhlenberg could hardly have described the situation of Jerseymen better when he quoted Joel 1:4: "That which the palmerworm hath left hath the locust eaten; and that which the locust hath left hath the cankerworm eaten; and that which the cankerworm hath left hath the caterpillar eaten." [9]

Whigs discovered the unpleasant truth about patriot plundering almost as soon as the British had evacuated Hackensack, Captain Robert Johnston of the New York Rangers being the particular offender. Stationed at Tappan, he and a scouting party were sent off toward

[7]   1 GC 734, 735.
[8]   1 GC 583.
[9]   2 Muhlenberg 772.

Schraalenburgh two days after New Year's Day, 1777, to reconnoiter the British positions, with strict instructions, his superior officer reported, "not to be dilatory in his march downwards, lest the enemy should get information of his coming before he could take some persons we wanted and from whom we expected information." After he had been gone for some time reinforcements were sent to help him. To their great surprise, these troops had hardly gone over the low hill to the south of Tappan before they discovered Johnston and his party busy in plundering. The party had scarcely got out of sight of town before they began stripping Harrington farms, entirely neglecting the business at hand.[10] Though time was to prove that Johnston was a zealous patriot, full of that energy which a good many militia officers lacked, the Tappan people were incensed by his conduct, and it took little imagination for the authorities to see that they would get no more help from the people of the neighborhood if such things continued. "I am afraid," John Haring wrote, grossly understating the case, "that Johnston's conduct will make [the inhabitants] backward in going ascouting, for they are enemies to plundering. It seems Johnston does not think himself bound to obey the orders of the Colonels stationed here." [11]

Complaints were lodged against Johnston several times. Deputy Quartermaster Kip listed a great deal of property of Schraalenburgh residents fallen into Johnston's hands: four hundred pounds of copper hoops from Anderson's store, one and a half pipes of wine, stored there by another, four wagonloads of leather from David Peek's tannery, "the property of Schaalenburgh people left for tanning," along with ten hogsheads of rum, gin and brandy, seven wagonloads of leather from Cooper's, at Kinderkamack, and several lots of furniture, clothes and linen.[12] Anderson and Peek were Tories clearly enough, Cooper was a zealous patriot.

As for the Tories, those who were left in the neutral ground were understandably terror-stricken at the situation in which they now found themselves. Even before the British left Hackensack, Heath and Clinton had been picking up men who had helped the British. "On Wednesday night last," Clinton reported on December 26, "one of my scouting

---

[10]   1 GC 523, etc. At about ten o'clock the previous night "Colonel Allison, at the head of about one hundred men, marched into Schraalenburgh, but as he found the travelling excessive bad and the weather very cold, he returned without getting any new information." 1 GC 524.
[11]   1 GC 525. "Johnston's conduct," he added, "has much displeased the inhabitants of this place." See also Damages by Americans, NJSL, passim; Livingston Papers MHS.
[12]   2 GC 625. Michael Smith lost £83 of property to Johnston and Crane at the same time. Damages by Americans, NJSL, Hackensack Precinct No. 38.

parties took Peter Quackenbush and Benjamin Babcock prisoners near the New Bridge; they had just come from the enemy and had assisted them in moving up their baggage to Hackensack; the latter was possessed of an original letter from Governor Tryon . . . and a receipt signed by Babcock to one Grant for £8 for assisting to bring in recruits to the Royal Army. . . . The prisoners I have here closely confined and will forward as soon as I can spare a guard, or hang, I ain't certain which." [13]

On December 31 Colonel Hathorn arrested "four grand and active Tories," on the evidence of David Demarest.[14] Daniel Foshee and John Lockman were two of them: "Daniel Foshee appears to be a tobacconist . . . He lives in New York, his wife and part of his family is at Tappan, he was apprehended last evening driving fat cattle to New York, he says for the use of his family, but query, his family is principally here; however, he has been here on the same errand before, under pretence of visiting his family . . . Lockman was taken with Foshee driving the cattle." [15]

John Acker of English Neighborhood, another prisoner, Hathorn said, "is proved guilty of aiding and assisting the enemy in their march from Closter to New Bridge and also assisted in taking three persons and carrying them to Fort Lee or Paulus Hook"; another, Peter Bonter, "is also charged with being unfriendly. His general character is agreeable to the charge, and he has been in the ministerial service with his wagon some time." All of them, Hathorn was convinced, were persons "injurious to the rights of America." [16]

When the British left, on January 5, Tories had every reason to be, as General Clinton described them, "much dejected and distressed," and three of the most celebrated of them did not wait for the Americans to come and arrest them. A few weeks earlier, with two thousand redcoats at their backs, Samuel and Jacobus Peek had boldly led a mob of Tories in a raid on Tappan. Now, with the Regulars driven off to New York and no one to protect them from the vengeance of the patriots

[13]   1 GC 496.
[14]   1 GC 511. There were at least four David Demarests in and around Schraalenburgh and Teaneck in 1776. See Damages by British, NJSL, Hackensack Precinct. HBP 78. Colonel Hathorn, of course, did not identify the particular David Demarest who was willing to speak when other "neighbors and acquaintances were loath to tell the truth or even say anything about them."
[15]   1 GC 510.
[16]   1 GC 510.

they had been plundering a week before, the two Peeks decided that the best course was to surrender themselves to the New York militia. On Monday, January 13, along with Johannes Jacobus Van Buskirk, they did so. "It may not be amiss to acquaint you with their behavior," John Haring wrote to General Clinton. "They were all three with the enemy when they were at Orangetown, and the Peeks were very active in disarming our friends. Samuel Peek was an officer in the militia as modeled by Congress and when danger drew nigh he refused to march when ordered. Indeed all three have shown themselves rank Tories." [17] Johannes Van Buskirk, a year before, had been elected a member of the Bergen County Committee of Observation and Correspondence, "to carry into execution the resolutions and orders of the Continental and Provincial Congresses." Six months later he had been tried for treasonable correspondence with the British troops on Staten Island, but acquitted.[18] His presence at the Tappan raid is probably a fair measure of the zeal with which he and his friends had been carrying patriot resolves into execution, and of the truth of the testimony that led to his acquittal.

The American colonel to whom the Peeks and Van Buskirk surrendered somewhat disappointed them by taking their parole and permitting them to stay with their families until called upon.[19] None of the American officials really knew what to do with men like the Peeks, General Clinton reporting that he had mentioned the problem to General Washington, who, he said, "thought it a delicate one and gave me no decisive answer." [20] They were finally turned over to the civil authorities of New Jersey.[21]

Between the depredations of their late uninvited guests, the British and Hessian soldiers, and the plundering by the Captain Johnstons of the American armies, it was amazing that the people between the lines found food and fuel to keep themselves alive during the hard 1776–77 winter; what was more than amazing was that the British had hardly left lower Bergen County before a thriving commerce sprang up between

---

[17] 1 GC 554, 555. The day was "very cold and piercing." Serle Diary 174.
[18] 1 NJA (2) 54, 55 n.
[19] 1 GC 554.
[20] 1 GC 555.
[21] See MCSNJ 83. General George Clinton, at Paramus, sent in to the New Jersey authorities Jacobus Peek, John Eckerson, John Dey, Cornelius Van Horn, Cornelius Vanderhoef and Isaac Montanye, Jr. "John Haring, Esq., will produce testimony against them." Clinton to Livingston, Jan. 23, 1777, Livingston Papers MHS.

the British garrison in New York and those Bergen County people whose loyalty to King George III or his gold exceeded their attachment to the American cause.[22] The English Neighborhood, closest to Manhattan of the Jersey Dutch farm settlements, soon became known as a place without a patriot; pettiaugers and schooners from New Barbadoes Neck plied their trade with New York as if there never was a war, and all too many farmers in the upper county, though in constant danger of patriot reprisal, decided that hard money was worth the risk and carted their produce down to the New York ferries.[23] The trade was so heavy that the British were in the habit of sending troops out to the lower English Neighborhood to guard farmers during the rest of their journey to the city.[24] The Jersey Dutchmen who carried on the trade were not the Whigs, of course; the men in the militia and the patriots in danger of British seizure were not consorting with their enemies; it was the Tory and the man of no principles who carried his produce to the British, men, most of them, who had probably already come to describe themselves as neutrals, that happy euphemism which gave a soft name to cowardice and indifference, a name which came to be anathema to patriots.[25]

Casparus Westervelt, Cornelius Banta, Derick Brinkerhoff, John Paulison, Derick Banta, Lawrence Van Horn, Martin Roelefson, and Michael Demott brought their fat cattle into the British lines for sale and wasted not a second from any patriot scruples when they were told that the condition of payment was an oath of allegiance to King George III.[26] One of them, Lawrence Van Horn, a miller in the English Neighborhood, had earlier signed the patriot associations but, as he explained later, only "to be allowed to remain quiet." [27] Westervelt was well known at Pascack for his Toryism; Cornelius Banta, Paulison, and Derick Banta had the same reputation in and around Old Hackensack,

[22] Alexander McDougall to Washington, Feb. 16, 1777; GW Papers LC.
[23] The traffic was so profitable that some enterprising New Yorkers did not wait for farmers to bring in the produce, but went out to get it. See 1 GC 510.
[24] Isaac Beal to Adam Stephen, April 20, 1777, GW Papers LC.
[25] After the war the neutrals had a thousand reasons for their conduct. The story has often been repeated of Archibald Campbell, the Hackensack innkeeper, who asked Washington, as the army was retreating to the west, what he ought to do, considering his large family and his property. Washington, the innkeeper reported, pressed his hand and said, "Mr. Campbell, stay by your family and keep neutral." See HBP 192; Romeyn, Hackensack Church, 27. He could with equal plausibility have claimed that Washington had advised him to join the British army, and, in the particular case, the innkeeper sometimes acted as if that was indeed what Washington had said, for his inn became a center for British recruiting almost as soon as the Americans had left the town. 1 GC 573.
[26] HC Papers CL.   [27] LYT NYPL.

as did Van Horn in English Neighborhood and Stephen Terhune in Hackensack,[28] but there were others, too, who brought in produce: John Goetschius of Polifly, Jacob Bogert, Samuel Demarest, Hendrick Zabriskie, Cornelius Ackerman, Isaac Stagg, John Ackerman, Henry Bogert, Jacob Lozier, Peter Vreeland, Simeon Van Ripen, Benjamin Zabriskie, John Demott, Douah Vreeland, Hendrick Banta, and Jacob Outwater,[29] many of whom very probably had no reputation for any political views at all.

Even Hessians were shocked at the quick shifts in loyalty of many Jerseymen. One of their officers captured at Trenton said frankly to Henry Muhlenberg that he could not understand the American people. "When the Hessians entered Trenton and occupied the region, the inhabitants swore their allegiance to the King of Britain. But as soon as the American troops attacked on Christmas, the inhabitants shot at the Hessians from their houses. In fact, even a woman fired out of a window and mortally wounded a Captain." [30] If they had been able to reoccupy the town, the Hessians might have found some of the same inhabitants of Trenton selling them food and fuel. The times were indeed out of joint for simple country people.

If lukewarm Jersey Dutchmen had needed an excuse to trade with British New York, where hard money was waiting for any sort of country produce, Captain Johnston and men like him would have supplied it, but it was not the Captain Johnstons who were responsible for the trade, or anything other than that acquisitiveness which had always been the driving force for much of the conduct of American colonists.

Washington had hardly retreated from Hackensack when several Jersey Dutchmen, some of them Tories, others apparently patriotic enough, saw that, with Washington's seizure of most of Bergen County's horses and Howe's taking the rest, anyone who bought horses and brought them into Hackensack could make a very quick and handsome profit, particularly if he could get rid of worthless Continental bills at the same time.

Stephen Terhune, formerly of New York, now living near Hackensack, and Albert Van Voorhees, of Hackensack, got Van Voorhees's nephew, George Doremus, the son of John Doremus of Paramus, and two of his nephew's friends, Christian H. Zabriskie and Stephen Ryder, to agree to go up into New York State to buy horses, promising them a

28 MCSNJ 107, 170, 223, 228, 229, 278.
29 HC Papers CL.
30 2 Muhlenberg 772.

bonus of £300 if they succeeded.[31] When other friends heard of the scheme, Doremus, Zabriskie, and Ryder agreed to act for them as well, Pieter Demarest of Harrington adding $125 Continental currency to their funds and Samuel Brevoort adding £15 of New York currency. All of them except Terhune may have planned to buy the horses for their own use; Terhune planned to "sell and traffick them to farmers for such necessities as his family wanted"; he later gave Zabriskie additional funds to buy a Negro boy, if one could be had. Forage being in short supply in Hackensack, and very expensive, Van Voorhees and Terhune arranged with friends in the western part of the county to winter such horses as might be bought.

If they had ever doubted the wisdom of the speculation, the doubts disappeared when the British returned to Hackensack for winter quarters, this time with such a parade of force that all but the blindest Whigs could see that they would never leave; it was now hardly worth worrying about the possibility that patriots might think they were working for the British. Three or four days later Doremus, Zabriskie, and Ryder set off for the north, stopping first at General Clinton's headquarters.

"Doremus came to my lodgings at Ramapo and requested a pass to go to Esopus," Clinton later reported. ". . . I at first refused him, as it was suggested to me that sundry persons had been up in that quarter and purchased horses for the use of the enemy, and because his going there would create discontent while the militia of that part of the country were out to defend his neighborhood. He assured me his business was not to purchase horses, his only motive being to see his acquaintances while he could not follow his business or live at home on account of the enemy. . . . He said he had an aunt or an old neighbor woman who had lost all her horses but one by the army and if permitted he would

---

[31] 1 GC 606, 607. John Doremus had evidently been a zealous Whig. Even the captious Robert Morris, who was then at Paramus (1 GC 543), said of him that he had "in every instance so far as his conduct has come within my knowledge behaved in a friendly and spirited manner since the commencement of the disturbances which preceded this war . . . and in the distress which [the British occupation] threw [upon] some of the inhabitants, did every friendly office to those who applied to him or flew to his house that any man could do." He would have been named a Whig official, Morris added, "if the invasion of the county had not intimidated him from taking a part that would give his disaffected neighbors a handle against him." 1 GC 543, 715. Terhune was a Tory: "Terhune, who furnished them with cash to purchase horses, lives about a half mile out of Hackensack, has no farm of his own nor the keeping for horses. He lived among the enemy, had taken their protection." Colonel McClaghry, "who commanded at Closter . . . summoned Terhune to come in, give up his protection and swear allegiance to the states; he refused; the Colonel took and confined him with others. He still refused, alleging that he had taken protection from the enemy and could not be on both sides." 1 GC 609. See also MCSNY 425.

purchase one (he says two—be it so) for her to enable her to get fuel. I refused him a pass if to purchase one horse . . . whereupon he promised not to purchase a single horse." [32]

The story hardly could have deceived Clinton, but instead of refusing him out of hand he asked Doremus who the friends were. Young Doremus, in a particularly inspired falsehood, gave Clinton the names of two of his father's good friends, Domine Romeyn, who was then at New Paltz, and Domine Mauritius Goetschius, minister at Shawangunk, the brother of the late Domine John Henry Goetschius. Since Domine Romeyn was also a good friend of General Clinton's and Domine Goetschius was known throughout Ulster County as a violent patriot, this story turned the trick for Doremus: General Clinton said he would let him go, and after lecturing him that he was not to buy a single horse, that he would get nothing but high-priced horses and that they would inevitably fall into the hands of the enemy if he brought them back, he gave Doremus a pass to go to Domine Romeyn's and no farther. When Doremus vouched for the good character of Ryder and Zabriskie, Clinton added their names.

This ordeal over, the three rode off to the north, congratulating themselves on the innocence of General Clinton and on their own shrewdness. They passed Domine Romeyn's house at New Paltz without stopping, either going or returning, and went on to Esopus and Marbletown and bought thirteen horses at exorbitant prices, giving £60 for a pair that had been offered for £40 the previous fall. They assured the sellers that the horses were for Continental service, bought by General Clinton's order, and produced Clinton's pass as evidence. On their return they circled Ramapo widely and came down by way of Warwick and Pompton, where they were apprehended after a wild ride by an American officer who had been sent to intercept them.

Clinton, annoyed at himself for trusting the young rascals, could not but believe that the horses were bought to sell to the British or, at very least, to get rid of Continental bills which were virtually without credit at Hackensack at the time, and he strongly urged the Committee of Safety to take strong action to make examples of them. He scoffed at the prisoners' story of a speculation, pointing out that the winter's forage would cost more than the horses were worth. "No one in his senses," he observed, "could hope to make a penny in that way."

By the time the case came to trial Van Voorhees and Doremus' father were able to show evidence of their patriotic characters and that the venture was of a purely commercial nature, and the prisoners were ac-

[32] 1 GC 606, 607.

cordingly acquitted, but the seized horses and cash were never returned, though Van Voorhees tried for years to get them back.[33]

Domine Romeyn returned to Schraalenburgh on February 2, 1777, two months after he had been driven out by the British invasion. It was a dreary, foggy day. The snow was thawing, but the cold was piercing and unpleasant.[34] There he found a shattered and empty parsonage and a congregation in which almost everyone had been plundered and many had been carried away to British prisons in New York.[35]

His churches at Hackensack and Schraalenburgh, which had furnished the main support of Whig principles in the eastern part of the county when the war was a matter of philosophy, now supplied the hard core of the armed patriot forces fighting there. John Mauritius Goetschius, Samuel Demarest, John Huyler, James Christie, Garret Leydecker, Abraham Brouwer, and Joost Zabriskie were but a few of his people who were busy night and day with militia duty; Peter Zabriskie, John Varick, Peter Wilson, Roelif Westervelt, William Christie, Isaac Demarest, Hendrick Kuyper, Henry Bogert, and a dozen more of the older men were the mainstays of patriot leadership in the county; none of them the less zealous because their old conferentie enemies were either Tories or pretended neutrals. The time was to come, in point of fact, when Romeyn's people felt that he himself had too much concern with the grand strategy of the war and too little with the outrages of their conferentie enemies, a fault which would have been soon remedied if Romeyn had been forced to stay in Hackensack or Schraalenburgh fighting Tories day in and day out. For the moment no such thoughts crossed their minds; their anxiety lay in the danger of his capture.

[33] The details of the whole seriocomic affair of the horse traders are spread throughout the papers of General George Clinton, who never was persuaded that the participants were anything but rank Tories, and throughout the Minutes of the New York Committee for Detecting Conspiracies. The latter took a less serious view of the incident. 1 GC 543, 544, 563, 606–609, 627–630, 714–716; 4 GC 317, 318; MCSNY 130–131, 154, 157, 165–167, 422–425, 428–430. Major Goetschius was convinced that Ryder, at least, who had refused to march with the militia, was a Tory. 2 CHM 90. He certainly became one. He was later made a corporal in Lieutenant Colonel Van Buskirk's Company, though apparently on detached service as an irregular much of the time. Muster Rolls, Lieutenant Colonel Abraham Van Buskirk's Company, July 5, 1778, July 14, 1780, and Nov. 27, 1781, Public Archives of Canada, Muster Rolls, Vols. 1851–1866. See also 3 NJA (2) 358, 359.
[34] Serle Diary 182.
[35] Romeyn Papers UCL.

House of Captain Samuel Demarest, River Road, near Old Bridge.
After J. Spencer Newman.

After the war his congregations were to be accused of intemperate and unchristian hatred for their old Tory and conferentie enemies; [36] great patriot that he was, Dirck Romeyn himself came to be far more willing than they to forgive and forget Toryism. Romeyn was doubtless right in his tolerant attitude, but it is easy to see how patriots in the neutral ground came to feel differently. They had watched deceitful men turn the patriot government of Bergen County into a mockery; they had seen the same men plot with the British against them; they had seen their old neighbors burn their homes and strip their farms; they had been im-

[36] The distinguished Rev. Henry Ostrander, whose views may have crystallized after the coetus group at Hackensack and Schraalenburgh seceded from the Dutch Reformed Church, remembered and condemned the hatred for former Tories and their conferentie church which he found at Schraalenburgh in 1799, while he was studying theology under Romeyn's successor. "It seemed to me," he wrote, "that these [men] were really taught of God, and renewed by the grace of the Spirit. I admired their zeal, piety and devotion; and yet on many occasions they appeared malignant and extremely uncharitable and unforgiving. . . . Indeed, in order to win the approbation of the praying brethren, it seemed imperatively necessary not only to condemn indiscriminately every advocate of the opposite church [the North Schraalenburgh church], but also to speak in the strongest terms of reproach and condemnation against Toryism, from which their forefathers, as they alleged, suffered much cruelty and damage." Ostrander 27, et seq. Since the war had been over less than twenty years when Ostrander lived at Schraalenburgh, and he knew the victims and had seen some of the damage, the words "their forefathers, as they alleged" were hardly candid. It is possible that the biographer, and not Henry Ostrander, added them.

prisoned and driven into hiding by men who had once pretended to be patriots; for years they could not safely go into a plowed field alone or sleep in their own beds.

"As this revolutionary struggle was going on," a church historian of strong conferentie sympathies wrote after the war, "it proved an occasion of increased trouble [between the coetus and conferentie] congregations of Hackensack and Schraalenburgh.. 'Some few were traitorous—some indifferent; others entered not as warmly into the cause as might have been expected; others again, with enlightened patriotism, urged on the cause of their country, as the cause of God. A few, no doubt, were excessive in profession of patriotism, and used it to cloak their love of plunder, and their individual resentments. . . . All, or nearly all, who belonged to one communion, were of one political creed, and all, or nearly all, who were of the other communion, were on the opposite side in politics.' " [37] In February, 1777, Domine Romeyn's congregation would have cheerfully agreed that if any were excessive in their profession of patriotism, they and not their conferentie neighbors were guilty; they would have agreed too that Jacobus Peek and others of the conferentie were entering not as warmly into the patriot cause as might have been hoped.

There were exceptions, of course. John Zabriskie, Jr., who, like his father and his brother Peter, belonged to the coetus side of the church wars, once lieutenant colonel of the Bergen County militia, hardly bothered to conceal his Toryism in recent months. On February 18, 1777, Admiral Lord Howe's secretary noted in his journal that Mr. [John] Zabriskie, of Hackensack, "came into town this morning with the news that six battalions of New England Rebels had quitted Washington, that Washington was so much displeased at their leaving him that he disarmed them, and that the greater part of them were returning home

[37] Taylor, Bergen Classis, 187. It is interesting to observe, in the biographical sketches in Clayton's History of Bergen and Passaic Counties (published in 1882, a hundred years after the war, but while Bergen County was still largely Dutch), the remarkable unanimity with which the members of the (coetus) True Reformed Dutch Church stressed the patriotism of their forebears; and the number of times that members of the other Dutch Reformed churches avoided the subject, a fact that doubtless did not go unobserved by the True Reformed. See Brinkerhoff Genealogy 28. No one active in the conferentie church of Hackensack, Schraalenburgh or Tappan has been found who was a patriot during the war. Colonel Isaac Nicoll, of Orange County, bought the confiscated property of the Tory conferentie adherent, Abraham Zabriskie, in Schraalenburgh and attended the conferentie church after the war, being buried in the North Schraalenburgh Church cemetery, but he is not regarded as an exception. Doubtless specific research on the point would disclose pre-war conferentie adherents who took the patriot side, but they were certainly few and far between.

without provisions, or shoes and stockings." [38] The secretary, though often disappointed in such reports, cheerfully wrote down each new one.

Zabriskie was one of the Tories who, for the time at least, had stayed in the county. Many others had joined the Tory refugee colony in New York. The Rev. Garret Leydecker and Michael Moore of the English Neighborhood were two of them.[39] Moore, who had been a farmer before the war, was now baking bread in New York to earn his keep, if the word that came out of the city could be believed.[40] Patriots, who remembered him best as an elder of the conferentie church at English Neighborhood, bore the news of his troubles with equanimity [41] and would have been equally resigned to hear that Garret Leydecker also was in trouble, but for the moment Leydecker had few troubles indeed,

[38] Serle Diary 190. John Gesner and Famichas (Brower) Gesner also were coetus adherents who took the Tory side. Schraalenburgh Church Records, 175, 181. Gesner wished, his son wrote sixty years later, "to remain neutral in the war of the Revolution, refused to sign an association dreading the consequences, was called a Tory, but truly he was a peaceable man." He sent four sons in to New York who joined the Tory Orange County Rangers. Nicholas Gesner Diary, July 19, 1834, Palisades (N.Y.) Library. Cornelius Banta, father of Wiert Banta, was another adherent of the coetus church before the war who became a Tory.

The situation at the Paramus and Ponds churches was somewhat more complicated. Though Domine Vanderlinde opposed John Henry Goetschius and leaned to the conferentie side of the church war, his congregation seems to have included both coetus-minded and conferentie-minded members, and both patriots and Tories. Cf. Paramus Church History, 24. When the True Reformed Dutch Church was established in 1822 by the old coetus party at Hackensack and Schraalenburgh, a large group withdrew from the Paramus church and established a True Reformed Dutch Church, which is now the First Presbyterian Church of Ridgewood. Ridgewood Church History, 7.

[39] 1 GC 611, 634: LYT NYPL. An American raid in February captured a number of horses abandoned by Tories, now refugees in New York: "Two young horses of Michael Moore; 1 horse of Capt. Lawrence Van Buskirk; 1 horse the Owner went in New York for a commission; 2 horses of Jost Erl, gone to New York; 1 horse of Domine Leydecker; 1 box sled and 1 wood sled." 1 GC 634.

[40] 1 GC 611.

[41] ERNY 4211. The men listed as "Members of Consistory at Hackensack," at page 22 of the Schraalenburgh Church Records, are in fact the elders and deacons of the separated conferentie church at Hackensack for the years 1760 through 1766, ten years before the war. Of the forty or fifty names listed, almost all appear to have been Tories. Many are definitely identifiable: Roelif Vanderlinde, Stephen Terhune, Johannes Peek, Nicausie Kip, Martin Roelefson, Peter De Groot, Hendrick Kip, Abraham Dey, Johannes Demarest, Lawrence Ackerman, Seba Brinkerhoff and Jacob DeMott, for example. Substantially all of the others bear Tory names, but cannot be positively identified.

Though Domine Kuypers, the conferentie minister at Hacksensack, had made little outward show of zeal for the British cause, his seventeen-year old son Elias had gone off to the enemy and was working in his Majesty's Naval Office in New York. Few of the Romeyn congregation had any difficulty in concluding (as Elias wrote after the war) that he had gone to the city "by the advice of his father to avoid taking up arms against the King's government." 4 Carleton Papers 102 (7772).

having found a place for himself as the only Dutch Reformed minister in the city, and he was preaching regularly to those Dutchmen who were not offended by his politics, though all of the Dutch Reformed church buildings in New York had long since been seized as schools of rebellion and turned into hospitals or prisons or stables.[42]

Patriots in the Hackensack valley soon discovered that they were dangerously exposed to Tory and British military action.

It was not unusual for large parties of armed Tories, hiding by day and moving under cover of darkness, to make their way almost to the New York line, to break in on some sleeping patriot, bind him and carry him back to Van Buskirk's headquarters at Bergen Point, and the country between the city and the Highlands held all too many who were anxious to do everything they could to help the raiders. No patriot could be certain when he went to bed at night that his neighbor's barns and woods did not hide a party of Tories waiting only for nightfall to fall upon his home and carry him off to Sugar House Prison; or that his neutral neighbor was not secretly supplying as much intelligence to the British as he was openly supplying them with country produce.[43]

Colonel Joseph Barton, the one-time patriot leader of Sussex County,[44] who had joined the British at Hackensack in November, 1776, led some of his troops into English Neighborhood on March 20, 1777, a very rainy day, and carried off four American prisoners.[45] A month later, on April 21, Captain Van Allen, recently of Hackensack, raided Closter with about fifty of the Royal Bergen Volunteers, "in quest," as Rivington put it, "of a party of rebels that infested [the place]." The rebels, he went on, "on hearing of their approach made off, but in pursuing them smartly some miles, they took three rebel suttlers, with their stores

[42] MRC; LYT NYPL; Historical Magazine of the Protestant Episcopal Church, December, 1944; 1 Jones, New York During the Revolution, 423; Wertenbaker, Father Knickerbocker, 106.
[43] "Residing in the midst of enemies, the Refugees and Tories on every side . . . there was no safety for any male person competent to bear arms to stay at home in the night, and they were obliged, when not on actual duty, to collect together for . . . common safety or to sleep in the woods or some other place of safety." Affidavit of Henrietta Blanch, Pension Records, W23632. See Isaac Beal to Adam Stephen, April 20, 1777, GW Papers LC.
[44] 1951 NJHSP 287.
[45] 1 NJA (2) 322, 326; Serle Diary 200. Colonel Levi Pawling confirmed the loss. "I had [four] men taken the night before last at the entrance of the English Neighborhood. . . . The four men, when taken, was in a house some distance lower down than the guard (and for what I know asleep), by which means they were surprised and taken without even firing a gun." 1 GC 677.

of rum, sugar, coffee, chocolate, &c., to the amount of seven wagon loads, without losing a man." [46] On April 26 "a party of new levies under Colonel Barton, Lieutenant Colonel Drummond and Major Timpany, said to consist of about two hundred, a little after sunrise . . . surprised and carried off Captain Wynant Van Zandt and three others from Garret Hopper's neighborhood, [with] twelve guns, five or six horses, a wagon and a chest and cask of goods from Hopper's . . . said to belong to Peter Curtenius." Others in the neighborhood, he went on, "either run off or concealed themselves in the neighborhood and escaped." [47] Van Zandt was a resident of New York City.[48]

On May 12 Colonel Barton attacked again, this time with a force of upwards of three hundred men. His original objective was General Heard's post at Pompton, but, being delayed, turned off and attacked the picket under Peter Fell at Paramus church, "driving the rebels from their strongholds and [obliging] them to retreat to the woods" during the foggy morning operation.[49]

At the same time a smaller detachment under Colonel Dongan attacked the militia post at Slotterdam, on the east bank of the Passaic, capturing two American officers, Captain David Marinus and Lieutenant David Van Busson, and three enlisted men, John Van Busson, Andrew Cadmus, and one other.[50] Heard claimed that in their confusion Barton's men inflicted more casualties on themselves than on Peter Fell's detachment. Marinus and Van Busson were carried off to Sugar House as prisoners. After a year in prison they escaped. "While they were so kept as prisoners they had the privilege to go to market to purchase articles for themselves accompanied by the guard. [They] agreed that at a certain time when so accompanied by the guard that they would knock the guard down and make their escape." Their plan worked to perfection, and they escaped, but Marinus died from cold and exposure within two weeks after getting back to Slotterdam. Van Busson was subsequently named captain of Marinus' company and served with distinction throughout the war.[51]

Tories in the Hackensack valley found themselves almost equally vul-

[46]   1 NJA (2) 354.
[47]   The report was made by Lieutenant Colonel Gilbert Cooper of the Orange County militia, then commanding 259 men stationed from Nyack to Sidman's Clove, an officer who served with distinction throughout the war. 1 GC 740–741.
[48]   When he arrived in New York as a captive, Van Zandt was paraded through the streets "as a show and styled the great rebel." Boudinot Papers HSP.
[49]   1 NJA (2) 379; 8 GW 72; Heard to Washington, May 14, 1777, GW Papers LC.
[50]   Idem; Pension Records, W385 (David Marinus), passim.
[51]   Pension Records, W385 (David Marinus).

nerable to American counter action. On April 3, 1777, American troops were at Secaucus, almost within British lines.[52]

On April 20, 1777, Colonel Isaac Beal led an American expedition to Hackensack for intelligence, reporting to General Stephen that "Van Buskirk's, Barton's and Drummond's new recruits lay at and near Bergen, Paulus Hook and the Hoboken Ferry, with a picket guard two or three miles from Paulus Hook." "Scouting parties," he went on, "are kept constantly in English Neighborhood, detached from Bergen. About four hundred were there yesterday to guard the roads in order that provision wagons pass to Bergen and New York. Some new recruits took Hackensack inhabitants prisoners Thursday night last." He was "informed by P. Zabriskie," he went on, "that as soon as the [spring] campaign started, a group of Royalists would move upriver to Haverstraw to be joined by recruits to attack our forts." [53]

With all of this activity in the neutral ground and little elsewhere, Jersey Dutchmen could have been forgiven if they came to think during the spring of 1777 that most of the Revolutionary War was directed at them; that the celebrated General William Howe and twenty-five thousand of the finest troops of Europe had no purpose for being in New York City but to stand behind Van Buskirk, Barton, and Drummond while those Jersey Tories destroyed their old neighbors; and that the great George Washington and his four thousand Continentals, for their part, had decided to fight the Revolution by sending scouting parties into the Jersey Dutch country between the lines.

General Howe could be justly criticized for inaction that spring; General Washington of course had no alternative but to act cautiously.

Fearful that General Howe could depend on Tory support for perhaps fifty miles northward into the Jersey Highlands if he chose to move in that direction, Washington did what he could to strengthen the patriot forces in the neutral ground by moving a heavy contingent of Jersey militia into the country between Pompton and Hackensack on April 26, 1777, the troops which Barton had attacked. Washington's purpose, he said, was to "protect the well affected, awe the disaffected, and . . . to check the Tory regiments under Brown, Van Buskirk, &ca, who are kept at Bergen and incite many persons to join them, from the adjacent country and from Sussex." With a major British move expected at any hour, Washington was gravely concerned about disaffected Jersey Dutchmen: "I shall not be disappointed if a large number of the inhabitants . . . should openly appear in arms as soon as the enemy

[52] 1 NJA (2) 331. See also Serle Diary 198.
[53] Isaac Beal to Adam Stephen, April 20, 1777, GW Papers LC.

begin their operations," he wrote to Congress. Dozens from Bergen and Sussex counties continued to join the British army despite every measure in his power, he said, "and the spirit becomes more daring every day." [54]

Many patriots had been imprisoned at the time of the first British occupation. Six months later the capture and imprisonment of civilians in the neutral ground had come to be one of the accepted perils of war. Both sides were guilty, the British and Tories more than the Americans.

Colonel Beal had mentioned one such British seizure on the night of April 17 in his report to General Stephen. A few days later, on the 22nd, a Tory raiding party of twenty-five men captured the celebrated John Fell, who lived on the road to the Clove, in the northern part of Paramus, not far from the New York State line. Fell had been actively engaged in counteracting Tory activity; his was not a case, like so many others, of seizing a man for his opinions. "Last night," he wrote in his journal for April 23, 1777, "I was taken prisoner from my house by twenty-five armed men who brought me down to Colonel Buskirk's at Bergen Point, and from him I was sent to General Pigot at New York, who sent me with Captain Van Allen to the Provost Jail." Fell, who had been a wealthy shipowner and merchant in New York before he moved to Jersey, was fortunate in having a daughter married to a prominent loyalist, who arranged to have food and clothing sent in to him; he was fortunate to be treated as an officer and given a room with only nine other prisoners in Provost Jail, where an ordinary civilian or private soldier might have been thrown into an empty warehouse with hundreds; and he was more than fortunate to have a strong constitution, for dozens of his fellow prisoners died in his sight from British neglect as spring, summer, and fall went by and the terrible winter cold set in. After refusing several American offers of exchange (apparently in part as punishment for having received his daughter's help), in January, 1778, the British paroled him to the city and in May he was exchanged for Governor Skene and allowed to go home, carrying through the long years of the Revolution and an honorable service in the Continental Congress a memory of British cruelty which time could never erase.[55]

[54]   7 GW 476, 492.
[55]   1 NJA (2) 54 n., 456 n.; The New Jersey refugee Stephen Kemble noted in his journal: "April 23rd and 24th. Nothing extraordinary but the bringing in a great Tory hunter, John Fell, by some people from near Tappan." 1 Kemble 114. Two Tories who had been apprehended by Fell and Roelif Westervelt were brought before the New York Commission for Detecting Conspiracies at Fishkill on the very day that Fell was imprisoned in New York City. MCSNY 263; 1 GC 740; Fell Diary; Dandridge. See 2 NJA (2) 12; 1 Carleton Papers 186 (904).

The last time Fell had seen Van Buskirk, the Tory colonel was a prominent patriot official. "Times are altered since we last met," said Van Buskirk, to which Fell

Fell was the most prominent of Hackensack valley men to fall victim to Tory raiding parties in the spring of 1777. He was by no means the only one. Hardly a patriot family lived there who had not seen a son or father carried off in the dead of night by the Refugees. The Hackensack merchant John Varick had been dangerously wounded and taken prisoner, but had escaped, and was now away from Hackensack.[56]

At about the same time Major Blauvelt, of Tappan, probably Johannes Joseph Blauvelt, was seized at his home by a dozen Tories, led by David Peek, of Schraalenburgh. The Tory band included several of Blauvelt's relatives, Cornelius Johannes Blauvelt, Jacob Johannes Blauvelt and Garret Smith, his neighbors John Straat and Jacob Straat, and Abraham Parcels and Parcels' brother, of Schraalenburgh. John Straat, when arrested for the affair, testified that "he understood that . . . Peter T. Herring, as he was going down to the English Neighborhood with butter in order to procure some salt, was taken by a party of American troops near the *Tiene Fly,* and carried prisoner somewhere to the westward . . . Some time last spring . . . David Peek, who lives at Schraalenburgh, sent word to him . . . to come to the house of . . . [Herring] to assist to take Major Blauvelt in order to have him exchanged for Herring and by that means to effect Herring's releasement." Straat told the messenger, Isaac DePew, that "he would not come and assist, for that Major Blauvelt was a very clever man," but DePew threatened that Peek would come and take him and carry him off to Provost Jail in New York, and being intimidated by this he went to Herring's house unarmed but "kept at a distance without giving the party any assistance and as soon as he conveniently could went off privately to his own house." [57] Curiously enough, Captain Johannes Jacobus Blauvelt and others testified that they believed that Straat and some of the others were telling the truth when they said they had acted solely from fear of Peek, and they were released.[58]

coolly agreed. "Well, you are a prisoner now, and I am going to send you over to General Robertson, with whom I have the honor to be acquainted. I will give you a letter of introduction." Judge Fell thanked him and took the letter, saying nothing more, though he had been well acquainted with Robertson in the peninsular campaign of 1763. Fell later presented the letter to Robertson, who opened it, smiled and showed it to Fell. "You must be a greatly changed man and a great rascal indeed if you equal this Colonel Van Buskirk." The letter, of course, said that Fell was a rebel leader and notorious rascal and should be treated accordingly. HBP 50 n. The aged General Robertson himself was, unfortunately, not far behind Van Buskirk in rascality, and Fell's former friendship did nothing to spare him from the most severe treatment during the time that ensued before his exchange. Fell Diary; Boudinot Papers HSP. See MCSNJ 147.

[56] Varick Court of Inquiry 79.
[57] MCSNY 352, 353.
[58] MCSNY 359, 360.

Cornelius Blauvelt spent some time in an American prison for his part in the affair, and only his patriot uncle's testimony got him released. Major Blauvelt was exchanged after a time. He was fortunate indeed, for at the age of sixty-two he could not have borne a British prison long.[59]

Samuel and Bernardus Ver Bryck, sons of the Dutch minister at Tappan, had been taken prisoner while visiting their mother's people near Polifly.[60] The patriot views of their father, which were doubtless also their own, were reason enough to doom them to Sugar House.

William Christie's son John was carried off to New York, as was Lucas Brinkerhoff.[61] Abraham G. Haring,[62] John Cooper, Richard Cooper,[63] Isaac Blanch, Harmanus Tallman, Jacob Wortendyke, Peter Westervelt, Jacob Westervelt, John Westervelt, Henry Ver Valen, Jacob Ferdon, John Van Busson, Jacobus Blauvelt, William Heyer, Cornelius Haring and Jacob C. Zabriskie, and William Lawrence of Tappan and three of his relatives, were but a few of the others who learned early in the war what it meant to fall into the power of British prisonkeepers.[64] Another prisoner was Thomas Wiert Banta, who had been captured and sent in to Sugar House by three of his neighbors. He was exchanged May 30, 1778.[65] Another was 29-year-old Daniel J. Westervelt, the father of four young children, who would have escaped a Tory raiding party by hiding in the "wolf den" in a swamp near his Closter home if he had not been betrayed by a Tory neighbor, Samuel Cole. He died of jail fever in Sugar House on October 23, 1777, a few days after the birth of his fifth child. His young cousins, Cornelius P. Westervelt and Benjamin P. Westervelt, and Daniel Ver Valen were captured with him. Another cousin, John P. Westervelt, escaped. Benjamin was again captured at English Neighborhood later in the war by a party which included the same neighbor who had betrayed him in the wolf den, but the second time he had the good fortune to be retaken by American forces and escaped prison. Samuel Cole went to Halifax with other Tory refugees after the war, but returned to America seven years later,[66] probably not

59 MCSNY 350, 352, 353, 354, 359, 360; Blauvelt Genealogy Nos. 113, 586, 792.
60 Cole, Tappan Church, 64.
61 HBP 108.
62 Captain Haring died in prison. Affidavit of James Riker, Pension Records, W15877.
63 HBP, opposite page 326.
64 MCSNJ 159, 161, 169; Livingston to Boudinot, April 29, 1777, Boudinot Papers HSP; Fell Diary; Dandridge. William Lawrence died Sept. 6, 1777. Fell Diary.
65 Banta Genealogy No. 571; Livingston to Boudinot, April 29, 1777, Boudinot Papers HSP.
66 Westervelt Genealogy Nos. 45, 128, 152, 153. Cornelius, who had some skill as a tailor, helped to keep himself alive in prison by making clothes for others. HBP 276. Cole may have been hanged on his return. A. W. Sterling, The Book of Englewood (Englewood, 1922), p. 20.

at the solicitation of the Closter Westervelts. John Cadmus of Saddle River (on New Barbadoes Neck) survived his harsh treatment at British hands for only two weeks after his exchange. Cadmus had been taken by a band of Tories who had besieged his farmhouse for hours before he surrendered.[67]

The horrors of the British prisons and the even more horrible prison ships came to be, to the patriots of the neutral ground, the most terrifying single fact of the war, an ever-present threat, made worse by daily word of the death of some imprisoned friend or neighbor, and perhaps worst of all by the sight of the few emaciated, haggard survivors dragging themselves along the roads from the ferries after they had been exchanged. All too many were so weak that they did not survive a rough crossing of the Hudson; it was obvious to anyone on the highways that many of those who had lived through that ordeal would never reach their homes alive.[68]

The lot of the Tories who stayed in the neutral ground was little better than that of the Whigs.

As soon as a semblance of patriot government was re-established in the county, Whigs demanded that the state of New Jersey do something to punish those who were brazen enough to remain in New Jersey after their British friends withdrew. Some of the complaints were probably based on little more than disloyal talk; others were doubtless firmly grounded in patriot injuries. Adam Boyd, who had seen several of his friends carried off by Tory raiders a week before, could hardly be expected to ignore John Demarest's talk that "it was a pity that the British troops had not a field piece on the ferry stairs" during a recent skirmish with the Americans or that "the Americans would not fight but only meant to destroy the country"; [69] it was too easy, ten miles from the British lines, to move from words to action.

On July 11, 1777, the New Jersey Committee of Safety drew up a list of forty-eight men against whom complaints had been made, and directed Major Samuel Hayes of Newark to arrest them. All but three were Bergen County men, and many of them had been prominent before November, 1776, in the supposedly patriot government: Arent P. Schuyler and Henry Kingsland, of New Barbadoes Neck; John Demarest, Esq., Lawrence E. Ackerman, John Earl, Andrew Van Buskirk and Dr. James Van Buren of New Barbadoes; John Zabriskie, Esq., of New

---

[67] HBP 197. Cadmus may have been an American spy. William Nelson, History of Paterson (New York, 1920) 270.

[68] Wertenbaker, Father Knickerbocker, 163; Amerman, 1960 NJHSP 257.

[69] Affidavit of Adam Boyd, July 31, 1777, NJSL.

Bridge; Gabriel Van Norden of Steenrapie; Cornelius Banta of Sluckup; John Van Buskirk, Esq., and Daniel Van Buskirk, of Kinderkamack; Captain John Banta, Casparus Westervelt, Captain Garret Demarest of Pascack; Captain Cornelius Haring, Cornelius Haring, Esq., John Debaun, Peter J. (T.) Haring, Esq., "up Hackensack River"; John Durie (miller), of Old Tappan; Samuel Peek, Jacobus Peek (prisoner at Morris) and Daniel J. Durie, of Schraalenburgh; Derick Banta, Peter Bogert and Cornelius Banta, of Winkelman; Simon Simonson, Seba Brinkerhoff, John Paulison and Cornelius Bogert, of Old Hackensack; James Campbell, of Teaneck; Samuel Leydecker, Jacob Degroot, Jacob

I DO hereby Certify, That *Dirck Brinkerhoof* *of Bergen County* — has, in my Presence, voluntarily taken an OATH, to bear Faith and true Allegiance to His MAJESTY KING GEORGE the Third;—and to defend to the utmost of his Power, His sacred Person, Crown and Government, against all Persons whatsoever.

GIVEN under my Hand at NEW-YORK, this *15.* Day of *May* in the Seventeenth Year of His MAJESTY's Reign, Anno. Dom. 1777.

MAYOR of the City of NEW-YORK.

Certificate of Oath of Allegiance of Dirck Brinkerhoff, 1777.
Sir Henry Clinton Papers, Clements Library.

Demott, Lawrence Van Horn, Derick Vreeland, Abraham Dey, Jacob Dey (his son), Michael Smith, Captain John Brinkerhoff, Peter Degroot and John Degroot, of English Neighborhood; and Garret Van Giesen, Daniel Smith, Esq., and Job Smith, of Secaucus.[70]

Three days later, on July 14, 1777, Major Hayes and a small force of American troops set out from Newark, crossed the Hackensack on flatboats, landed at Snake Hill, back of Secaucus, and marched north, picking up as many as they could as they went. They arrested two at Secaucus, six at English Neighborhood, and six on New Barbadoes Neck

[70] MCS NJ 83. The Captain Garret Demarest listed was probably Garret J. Demarest, No. 89, Demarest Genealogy, the son-in-law of Theunis Helm, another Tory. He lived until 1819 and is buried in the (conferentie) North Schraalenburgh church burying ground. Blauvelt Genealogy Nos. 66, 378.

and at Hackensack and New Bridge.[71] A number of the others were presumably seized by local militia.[72] The Council of Safety spent months in gathering evidence against the prisoners. Of the forty-eight, there are records of the disposition of twenty-eight cases: fifteen, or about half, were acquitted: John Earl, Derick Banta, John De Groot, Seba Brinkerhoff, Lawrence Ackerman, Michael Smith, Cornelius Abraham Haring, Cornelius Haring, John Debaun, John Durie, Samuel Leydecker, James Campbell, Simon Simonson, Jacob Demott and Dr. James Van Buren.[73] One of the acquitted Tories, Derick Banta, who took the patriot oath and went off free, had taken an oath of allegiance to King George III only a few weeks before,[74] and at least two, Cornelius Abraham Haring and Dr. Van Buren, were probably dangerous to the American cause. Five of the twenty-eight were placed under bail to appear for trial by local courts: John Banta, Arent Schuyler, John Demarest, Casparus Westervelt, and Cornelius Banta;[75] and nine—Garret Van Giesen, Andrew Van Buskirk, Garret Demarest, Cornelius Bogert, John Paulison, Peter T. Haring, John Van Buskirk, Gabriel Van Norden, and Jacobus Peek—were judged guilty by the Committee of Safety and held at Morristown under jail limits of one mile, with a view to exchanging them for Americans held in prison in New York.[76]

---

[71] Major Samuel Hayes to Governor Livingston, July 16, 1777, William Livingston Papers, MHSL. The prisoners were Job Smyth, Garret Van Giesen, John De Groot, son of Peter De Groot, Michael Smyth, Abraham Dey and Jacob Dey, his son, Jacob DeMott, Samuel Leydecker and John Zabriskie, and, on New Barbadoes Neck, Arent Schuyler, Henry Kingsland, John Earl, Dr. James Van Buren and Andreas Van Buskirk.

[72] John Garlick, who lived about a mile below Bourdet's Ferry, and one Stephenson —probably the Francis Stephenson who took David Baulding for a Tory at the Three Pidgeons—were arrested and lodged in Tappan jail early in 1777. Stephenson "has been guilty of plundering our friends (to wit) eight bushels of grain from Joost Zabriskie, several things from Mr. Romeyn. When he went out to plunder he blackened his face in order to disguise himself; he owns he has been employed in cutting of wood for the enemy." He and Garlick were armed when taken. 1 GC 639. Others, arrested later in the year, were Simeon Van Riper, Benjamin Zabriskie, Stephen Terhune, John DeMott, Douah Vreeland, Hendrick Banta and Jacob Outwater. MCSNJ 228, 278. At the end of August, 1777, the American authorities agreed to send in to New York Gabriel Van Norden, John Van Buskirk, Garret Van Giesen, Garret Demarest, Peter T. Haring, John Paulison, Cornelius Bogert and Abraham Van Giesen, in exchange for the following American prisoners in British hands: Thomas Banta, Bernardus Ver Bryck, Isaac Blanch, Jacob Wortendyke, Harmanus Tallman, John Van Busson, Jacobus Blauvelt and William Heyer. Livington to Boudinot, Aug. 29, 1777, Boudinot Papers LC. See also MCSNJ 159. Jacobus Blauvelt had died in prison on the morning of Aug. 14 and was buried at noon, before the proposal for exchange reached New York. Fell Diary. A proposal to exchange John Fell was also made and refused. Idem.

[73] MCSNJ 107, 110, 112, 116; LYT NYPL "Van Buren."

[74] HC Papers CL.

[75] MCSNJ 110, 112, 116.   [76] MCSNJ 147.

Doubtless a few were convicted who were not Tories at all. Some zealous Whig had Isaac and Cornelius Van Saun arrested for selling Captain Campbell of the British army four bags of flour, five bushels of rye, and ten bushels of wheat, for which, the Van Sauns said, they were never paid. They had evidently also assured a man they believed to be a British officer of their loyalty to King George. They were brought before the Council of Safety at Morristown "and nothing appearing against them, they were discharged." Discharged, that is, until "Mr. Chief Justice Morris, happening to come into the Council of Safety, gave them such information . . . as induced the Council to remand them to prison." Despite petitions on their behalf by Peter Zabriskie, Peter Wilson, Abraham Brouwer, William Prevost, and six other leading Whigs of the county, who knew the Van Sauns far better than Morris, they were sent into the British lines as if they were Tories.[77]

Despite their mistakes, patriots tried to be guided by principles of law in judging disloyalty; no captive of the Tories ever saw a court or dreamed of an acquittal: he was condemned when he fell into their hands. It would, however, have been too much to expect Tories to see any difference. Indeed, as between trying men in court for loyalty to their king and jailing them without trial for rebellion against him, Tories had no difficulty whatever in choosing the latter. The result was that the neutral ground soon became a seething caldron of hatred, where each capture called for a reprisal and each reprisal called for a counterreprisal, a war of neighbors which went on side by side with the military war during the whole Revolution.

The country between the lines also sheltered spies. Every Hackensack valley Dutchman who brought his produce to the British was questioned closely about the latest changes in American positions and strength,[78] and on the patriot side every Whig in the neutral ground passed on to the Americans whatever news he had of British activity in New York—

77 MCSNJ 66, 67, 80; Petition of Sundry Inhabitants of the County of Bergen in Behalf of the Two Van Sauns, NJSL.

78 HC Papers CL include many notes of such intelligence. There were also British recruiting agents. An American prisoner, who pretended to join the British in order to desert, reported that "he left New York yesterday morning about ten o'clock, came to Hackensack on a pretence of recruiting [for the British], met Captain Campbell and his ensign, two new officers there on recruiting service; there was no guard but a corporal's at Hoboken, nor any from [there] to Hackensack. That he left them at Campbell's tavern about eleven o'clock last night. There were no soldiers in Hackensack town that he heard; there was a small guard at the [New] Bridge and to the north and some troops at Acquackanonk. 1 GC 573.

often a surprising amount of news, for passage into New York was almost completely open from Hackensack and the country nearby. There were also spies in the more usual sense among the men who moved in and out of the country between the armies.

One of Washington's agents, Nathaniel Sackett, of New Windsor, New York, reported to him from Suffern's Tavern that on the night of March 7, 1777, he had put a man through the American lines at the English Neighborhood to go into the city, where he was "to hire a room and get a license to carry on a secret trade for poultry to enable him to convey our intelligence once or twice a week." Unfortunately, he added, this man had not yet reported back, but he had high hopes for another prospective agent if the first failed him. The second man, he said, was "now counted among the principal Tories near the enemy's lines," one who would be able to go into New York with an express invitation from William Bayard, and highly recommended to Colonel Buskirk and Major Timpany. "I have given him," he went on, "liberty to enlist eight or ten men to take with him as evidence of his sincerity." [79] The particular spies may well have been double-dealers, anxious only to get safely through the American lines to join their Tory friends in New York City, but there were many such men who served their country well, many who sent a great deal of valuable intelligence out of New York. Needless to say, a great deal of British intelligence went into New York by the same route. Sackett, who had many spies working for him, and was one of the few agents who reported directly to Washington, was less likely to be deceived than most men who were new to the trade of espionage. He once took advantage of the anger of a Tory lady who had suffered from the American army, by giving her a pass to go through the lines to demand protection from Lord Howe. Howe's aides, she reported angrily, had put her off with the explanation that the first business of the 1777 campaign had to be a drive against Philadelphia, an explanation which, it turned out, was remarkably candid.[80]

★

[79] Sackett Papers. See 4 Freeman, App. IV–2. Col. John Bakeless identified Sackett as the agent. Bakeless 171–174.

[80] Sackett Papers. See 4 Freeman, App. IV–4. That many of the spies were double-dealers cannot be doubted. "The person I employed," Colonel Hay wrote from Acquackanonk of one of them, "has been down three days but brings no intelligence that can be depended upon. I suspect him to have business in New York and that he has got connected with a party of Tory villains, notwithstanding this very fellow has given me good intelligence sundry times." Hay to Wayne, Jan. 23, 1780, Wayne Papers HSP. During the spring of 1777, the American agent "W" was also active between the lines. See Chap. 8.

Though distracted Bergen County patriots probably saw little improvement, they had done much to adjust themselves to their unhappy situation in the few months since the Battle of Trenton. The militia had flown apart before it could fire a shot in November, 1776. By the late spring of 1777 it had become an effective American fighting force. Gone were the footless drills and the fifes and drums, gone from its ranks were the secret friends of Britain and the halfhearted friends of liberty; the new Bergen County militiaman was an earnest patriot who had seen the face of war at close hand and meant, if he could, to keep its terrors from his home.[81]

Colonel Theunis Dey of Totowa was head of the Bergen County militia.[82] He had become too important in the patriot government of New Jersey to be in day-to-day service, if indeed he had ever been suited for the hard task of leading troops against the British. When the time came to rally the militia, after the British withdrawal, it was Major John Mauritius Goetschius who took the lead in the country east of the Hackensack, and as the war went on he became the active head of patriot forces there.

Goetschius was the son of the late Domine John Henry Goetschius and the nephew of Domine John Mauritius Goetschius of Shawangunk, Ulster County, New York.[83] A large, handsome man, according to family tradition, he had once aspired to be a Dutch Reformed minister himself, had graduated from Peter Wilson's Academy and received, as a result of his studies under Dr. Wilson, a degree from the College of New Jersey.[84] When he applied to the church authorities for ordination, however, he was urged to apply himself more earnestly to the study of theology and to present himself later for a further examination.[85]

He never did so. He was named an officer of the Bergen County militia early in 1775,[86] at the very height of patriot enthusiasm in the county, and proved to be a far better military man than he would have made a clergyman, if one can judge from some of his spelling and grammar.[87]

---

[81] When the militia companies were better organized, the fifes and drums returned. Abraham I. Brouwer, the blacksmith, was a fifer in Captain Elias Romeyn's company "stationed at the New Bridge, Brouwer's Hill, the Liberty Pole, marching with said company from place to place as necessity required doing duty as a musissioner." Affidavit of Abraham I. Brouwer, Pension Records, W23707.

[82] HBP 71, 72; MPC 394.

[83] It is possible that he may have been a son of John *Mauritius* and a nephew of John *Henry*.

[84] 29 NJA 53.

[85] MRDC 37, 41; MRC 492.

[86] MPC 484, 565.

[87] See, e.g., letter to Dirck Romeyn, HSP; Livingston Papers, NYPL.

Few indeed of his fellow officers were to prove as useful to the patriot cause; in fact, as the war progressed it would have been hard to find any more active and spirited officer on the continent.

In the western part of the county, Major Peter Fell and Major Richard Dey were equally active. Crynes Bertholf, Thomas Blanch, Joseph Board, James Christie, Samuel P. Demarest,[88] Abraham Haring, Cornelius Haring, Abraham A. P. Haring, John Hopper, Jonathan Hopper, Adam Huyler, John Huyler, Jacobus Joraloman, Hendrick Kuyper, David Marinus, Henry Obest, John Outwater, Elias Romeyn, Jacob Terhune, Nicausa Terhune, David Van Bussom, Corines Van Houten, John Vreeland, Peter Ward, John Willis, Henry Berdan, Thomas Blair, David Duffe, William Denniston, David Doremus, John D. Haring, David Van Busson, Peter S. Van Norden, Cornelius D. Blauvelt, George Brinkerhoff, Peter Sandford, Gilliam Bogert, and John Uriancy were among the officers who served under Goetschius, Fell, and Dey. Adam Boyd, Abraham Allen, Abraham Huysman, Abraham T. Blauvelt, John D. Vanderbilt, Ryer Ryerson, Garret Post, Joseph Catterline, Abraham Hoagland, David Demarest, and Jacobus Bogert were others who served as captains or lieutenants at one time or another in the patriot militia.[89] The names of many non-commissioned officers and private soldiers have been lost in the confusion of the times.

To organize any military force between the lines presented great difficulties. Many able-bodied men claimed to be neutral, others insisted that the only safety for their families lay in their constant presence at home, others found they could not do their planting and harvesting and serve

[88] Samuel Demarest, the 23-year-old son of Peter Demarest, who lived on a large farm on the River Road at the old French burying ground, received a lieutenant's commission from Governor Livingston in January, 1777. He was subsequently promoted. Demarest had already seen some action when commissioned. He had been pressed into service with his wagon and horses when Washington retreated from Manhattan Island, removing "a load of sick" from New York and serving "at White Plains at the time of the battle in the capacity of a teamster."

"He was unable to attend to his business or even to remain at home except by stealth on account of his exposure to capture by the enemy . . . they having made repeated attempts to effect his capture from his own house." Demarest, whose farm yielded nothing to support his family because of his militia duties, "was compelled by necessity to sell his patrimonial estate . . . within a few years after the close of the war" for the payment of debts contracted to maintain his family. Affidavit of Samuel Demarest, Pension Records, S15081.

[89] HBP 71, 72; Pension Records, passim. Jacobus Bogert . . . "was a very active officer in the militia . . . a brave man and a violent Whig," to quote one of his neighbors. Affidavit of William Van Voorhees, Pension Records, W17890.

An effort has been made to exclude men who were on the rolls only before the British invasion, among them Cornelius Van Vorst, John Zabriskie, Jr., Jacob Van Saun and Abraham Van Buskirk.

in the militia too.[90] In one way or another Major Goetschius, Major Fell and Major Dey surmounted these obstacles, and before long Van Buskirk's Greencoats discovered that an attack on a patriot Dutchman's farm was likely to be met, not by a single terrified farmer, but by a determined force of farmer-soldiers who were quite prepared to trade point-blank musket fire with Tories.

"It was necessary," Cornelius D. Board wrote, "to keep up a constant guard each night in order to protect our families and ourselves from the depredations of the Cow Boys." His company "would assemble according to orders . . . just after sundown upon the heights and keeping themselves and their station concealed as much as possible would remain under arms through the night, those not engaged on sentry or on patrols sleeping on their arms until it came their turn to relieve those on guard and keeping out sentinels and patrols through the night, then returning to our ordinary business in the morning." [91]

Militia duty was a hard service, as a defensive operation is always hard; the Tories struck from bases at Paulus Hook and Hoboken so close to the main British army that they were virtually immune from counterattack, while patriots had to be prepared to defend every patriot farmhouse within a radius of twenty-five miles. The Tories drew British provisions, British pay, and British arms; the Bergen County militia fed and armed themselves and were paid seldom if at all. Their operations were never dramatic: the Tories were the men who were always falling upon some Dutch settlement to the loud applause of Rivington's *Royal Gazette*; the patriot militia had the unglamorous task of trying to drive them off.

Patriots in lower Orange County saw the same service; indeed the militia of the two states took little notice of state boundaries. "The

[90] Captain Turnure's company and others "were divided into classes of four men in a class, and an arrangement was made that one man in a class should guard one week and be relieved by another, and so continue until each had served his week, that a continued guard might be kept and their necessary labor at home might be done in which manner the militia served until the end of the war from early in the spring until winter and often in the winter." Affidavits of Cornelius Blauvelt, Pension Records, S22653; John I. Blauvelt, Pension Records, S22649 and passim. Turnure served in Orange County, New York. In New Jersey the classes served for one month in four. See e.g. Affidavit of Mary Hopper, Pension Records, W251.

[91] Affidavit of Cornelius D. Board, Pension Records, R974. Board was describing the procedures near Smith's Clove, but they were much the same on the lines to the south. "The inhabitants [of our neighborhood] were much in the British interest . . . which made it necessary for us to be extremely vigilant," Board added, explaining that he and his neighbors could muster only "twenty-eight individuals, among whom there were some blacks." Idem.

British, aided by disaffected Americans, Refugees and Tories, were very troublesome to the friends of liberty and independence, taking their property, stealing their horses, cattle and everything they could lay their hands on that was worth carrying away, burning, plundering and destroying by fire and otherwise killing the friends of their country and taking them prisoners to New York," John G. Blauvelt of Orangetown wrote sixty years after the war.[92] His cousin, John I. Blauvelt, recalled how "they had to guard along the river to prevent as far as possible the enemy from landing to plunder, burn and destroy, and ascouting through the different parts of the now County of Rockland and the County of Bergen, in the State of New Jersey. . . . He was ordered to hold himself in readiness to march at a minute's warning whenever there was an alarm, which was very often for whenever the enemy came out in large bodies the guard that did first discover them would give the alarm by firing guns, which was repeated by the next and so continued, by which means the intelligence was given many miles in a few minutes and all that were at home had to march to assist in driving them off. They then joined the first company they met with, under different officers at different alarms, and some of their excursions would last for eight and sometimes ten days, before they got home again." "We were obliged," he added, "to take our arms and equipments with us to our daily labor, to be ready to pursue the enemy immediately." [93]

[92] Affidavit of John G. Blauvelt, Pension Records, W20728.
[93] Affidavit of John I. Blauvelt, Pension Records, S22649.

8

★

A T T H E end of 1776 General Howe had all but crushed Washington's army. During the spring and early summer of 1777, to the dismay of Tory New York, he gave no evidence at all of any plan to do more, making one modest foray into middle Jersey which accomplished nothing but to burn and sack a few New Jersey towns, an attack which finally ended with the abandonment of the local Tories who had helped him, leaving Washington's armies unharmed and still deployed at the edge of the mountains.

All during the summer General Burgoyne had been moving down the Champlain valley, and express after express from the north brought new word of his triumphs. On July 15 Ticonderoga fell; upstate New York was in panic. Here was Howe's great chance. If he could but force the American strong points at Fort Montgomery and Fort Clinton from the south and cut the iron chain across the Hudson, he would have clear sailing to Albany, where he could join Burgoyne and sever New England from the rest of the Union, a stroke which might well be the deathblow of the American cause. Convinced that this must be the British plan, as soon as his spies brought word that Howe was about to leave New York, General Washington moved his troops eastward, to Smith's Clove, where they could be quickly interposed between Howe and Burgoyne. "The complexion of things to the north and the preparations lately made by General Howe," he wrote to Governor Livingston on July 12, 1777, "leave little room for doubt that their intentions are to form a juncture up the North River." [1]

[1]   8 GW 389, 390.

At the same time, Washington ordered Lieutenant Colonel Daniel Morgan and his newly formed corps of riflemen into forward positions at Hackensack "to observe every motion of the enemy about New York by land or water; two or three light dragoons should be with them to convey any necessary intelligence, in order that I may be apprized as early as possible."

"While you are lying at Hackensack," he told Morgan a few days later, "you may be subject to a surprise by a party of the enemy from Fort Washington except you keep your guards advanced to Hackensack Ferry and the Bridge above, [though] patrolling parties may safely lay by day at Fort Lee . . . Hold your corps in readiness to march in an hour after you receive notice either by night or day." Morgan was given the name of Washington's principal intelligence agent in Hackensack; indeed the movement into Hackensack was probably calculated as much to support the work of "W" and to speed his dispatches to headquarters as to reconnoiter the British positions and shipping from the heights of the Palisades. Evidently acting upon W's suggestions, Morgan reported on July 24th, "I have taken a man whom I believe to be a great villain, but it appears to me through him some intelligence may be had, as he has free access in New York. W says he has made use of him in that way. I have therefore let him make his escape, he is to go to New York this morning and tell them he has been taken and made his escape and is afraid to be seen at home in the day, and is to collect what news he can in the day and deliver it to W at night. If he will be faithful he may be of great use to us, as the enemy has an entire confidence in him, and if he should play the double game he can't hurt us much. W returned from Bergen last night and says most of the fleet sailed out of the Hook three days ago, but whether intended for a feint or not he can't find out." [2]

Howe's move was not a feint. Instead of going to the support of Burgoyne, he had confounded both his friends and his enemies by moving toward Philadelphia. A few days later Washington amazed almost as many by following with the Continental army.

Howe's own first officer, Sir Henry Clinton, was utterly amazed. Despite "many unequivocal demonstrations" that Howe meant what he said, Clinton believed that Howe's move was a "feint intended to deceive us all," that he was not going to sea when he sailed down the

[2] 8 GW 359, 455; Morgan to Washington, July 24, 1777, GW Papers LC. The six-foot colonel and his mountain men were already famous; a few weeks later the defeated General Burgoyne was to tell him that he "commanded the finest regiment in the world." Callahan, Daniel Morgan (New York 1962), 149. The "W" in the Morgan letter may have been "W^r" or even "Mr. . ." The agent, who has not been identified, had evidently been acting for some time.

bay but would run up the North River on the first southerly breeze.[3]

Britons were later to say that Howe had lost the war by failing to go to the direct aid of Burgoyne. In point of fact, his strategy involved only one major error: Howe evidently believed that the ragged New England militia who made up most of the American forces in the Champlain valley would, like the disorganized army he had driven before him a year earlier, melt away at the first sight of British and Hessian troops. General Washington, on the other hand, being unwilling to let Howe take Philadelphia without a fight, felt obliged to gamble that, contrary to his own experience, the New England militia, with some stiffening by regular troops, could deal with Burgoyne.

On August 23, 1777, the American forces left in the New York area made an attack on Staten Island, which was heavily garrisoned at the time by Tory troops, many of them from Bergen County. About thirty or forty prisoners were taken, among them the celebrated Colonel Joseph Barton, and, even more important to Hackensack valley Dutchmen, Lieutenant Edward Earl of Hackensack and Lieutenant Jacob Van Buskirk, son of the Greencoat lieutenant colonel.[4] Some Americans thought they ought to be tried for treason. Van Buskirk had taken part in patriotic activities before he joined the British, and both he and Earl, it was claimed, had enlisted after that action was declared high treason by the legislature. The New Jersey Committee of Safety, under the chairmanship of Governor William Livingston, was quite prepared to try them, along with a third officer, John Hammell, not from Bergen County, who had actually been in the American army until the Battle of Long Island,[5] but General Washington insisted that all of them be treated as prisoners of war.[6] The British treated American prisoners outrageously, but they did not try them for treason, and Washington saved the New Jersey authorities from a grave mistake when he stopped the trials.

As the summer of 1777 wore on, the American situation became desperate. There was every reason to think that Burgoyne would capture the Hudson valley without Howe's help, that Howe would simultaneously seize the Continental capital, and that the British forces in New York City would occupy all of east Jersey. By September America was

---

3 "I own I could not to the very last bring myself to believe it. . . . If Washington is not a blockhead, he will leave Howe where he is and exert his whole strength against Burgoyne or me." Clinton, American Rebellion, 62, 64, 69, 69 n. See 8 GW 499.
4 1 NJA (2) 457, 459, 461, 508.
5 2 NJA (2) 11, 12, 13; MPC.
6 10 GW 233.

in its greatest crisis since the disastrous days at the end of 1776, a greater crisis than it was to see again for almost a century. Howe had landed at the head of the Chesapeake and was driving the American troops before him almost at will; even where the patriots stood and fought, they were outgeneraled and routed. Philadelphia was almost in Howe's grasp. To the north Burgoyne, with all the strong points of the century-old invasion route from Canada in his hands, stood at the head-waters of the Hudson with nothing between him and Albany but a few untried Continentals and a gathering horde of farmer-soldiers from New England.

Nearer at hand Sir Henry Clinton, as celebrated a commander as either Howe or Burgoyne, lay across the Hudson River with a force already far greater than any American command that could be mustered to meet him, a force soon to be augmented by new troopships from Europe.

Every word from New York City told of hurried British preparations for a new attack; [7] many in the city were saying openly that New Jersey was to be seized at once. The news could not be called surprising; Howe would scarcely have left an officer of Sir Henry's rank and reputation at New York merely to hold the post. It was obvious that Sir Henry's part in the grand British strategy, now coming to a swift climax, was either to strike at General Israel Putnam's small force in the Highlands or to invade New Jersey.

On September 7, 1777, Governor William Livingston, having finally got clear intelligence of the British plans, told Congress that New Jersey was definitely the objective,[8] and Congress took enough time from its own problems in panic-stricken Philadelphia to order General Putnam to hold a part of his Highland forces ready to move there if the attack came.[9]

On Friday, September 12, 1777, the day after Howe's crushing defeat of Washington at Brandywine, Clinton's invasion of New Jersey started.[10]

Two thousand British and provincial troops poured into the state

[7] McDougall Papers NYHS.
[8] 4 Freeman App. IV–4.
[9] 4 Freeman App. IV–4.
[10] 9 GW 218; 1 NJA (2) 473; HBP 53. On Sept. 3, 1777, General Clinton had laid his plans before the naval officers who were to arrange for the necessary transports: "The east side of Jersey is at present by everything I can learn in so unguarded a state, that I think that an incursion without *risque* may be made there." 1,250 men were to land at Staten Island; 320 men and 100 horses near Paulus Hook, 1,440 with three pieces of cannon at or near Fort Lee and 200 Provincials at or near Tappan. HC Papers CL. The Tory troops had been encamped at the Elizabethtown ferry on Staten Island and at Paulus Hook. Baurmeister 92.

from three landing points: Brigadier General Campbell, with the 7th, 26th, and 52nd Regiments, the Anspach and Waldeck Grenadiers and three hundred provincials, principally Colonel Van Buskirk's 4th New Jersey Volunteers, landed at Elizabethtown and moved north; Major General Vaughan with a company of Chasseurs, five companies of Grenadiers and Light Infantry, the 57th and 63rd and Prince Charles's Regiments, with five pieces of light artillery, landed at Fort Lee; and two hundred Tory troops and forty marines landed up the river toward Tappan and marched south. Vaughan's force from Fort Lee moved rapidly by way of New Bridge and Hackensack toward the heights over the Passaic at Slotterdam to the southwest, leaving a post at Hackensack and "a full battalion at New Bridge, to cover that important pass." After a daylong exchange of fire on the Passaic, Vaughan withdrew to occupy New Bridge in force, sending outposts up the Schraalenburgh Road toward Tappan against any possible American attack from the north.[11]

Van Buskirk's 4th New Jersey Volunteers won a citation for the action on the Passaic. At a time when all too many Tory refugees were content to sit at the Faithful Irishman or at Ashley's, drinking their ale and complaining of the government, Sir Henry was understandably delighted with his Bergen County Dutch loyalist troops in their green uniforms, white trousers and brown leggings. They made up a larger number of his provincial soldiers than many a whole colony had supplied, and even in their first maneuver with the Regulars they looked and acted like veterans. "To give [an] opportunity to the provincials," Clinton reported, "I ordered Buskirk's battalion to march through a corn field, with the intention of taking in flank a body of the rebels posted behind a stone wall, and which it would have been difficult to have removed by a front attack." They marched, he added, with such spirit that the Americans quit their positions without a shot.[12]

Latter-day partisans to the contrary, many Tories were neither rich,

11   HC Papers CL; 1 Kemble 132; 2 NJA (2) 42, 43, 44. "On Friday," wrote a young girl near Mountain Meeting House, in Essex County, "there was an alarm, our militia was called; the Regulars came over into Elizabethtown where they had a brush with a small party of our people; then marched quietly up to Newark; and took all the cattle they could. There was five of the militia at Newark. They killed [one and took three] prisoners. One out of five run and escaped. They went directly up to Second River and on Saturday morning marched up towards Wadsesson. Our people attacked them there, where they had a smart skirmish. Some of our people got wounded there; but I do not learn that any was killed. There was several killed of the Regulars, but the number is yet uncertain." Jemima Condict, Her Book. A transcript of the diary of an Essex County maid . . . , (Newark 1930) 66, 67. Watsessing is approximately modern Bloomfield.
12   2 NJA (2) 42, 43.

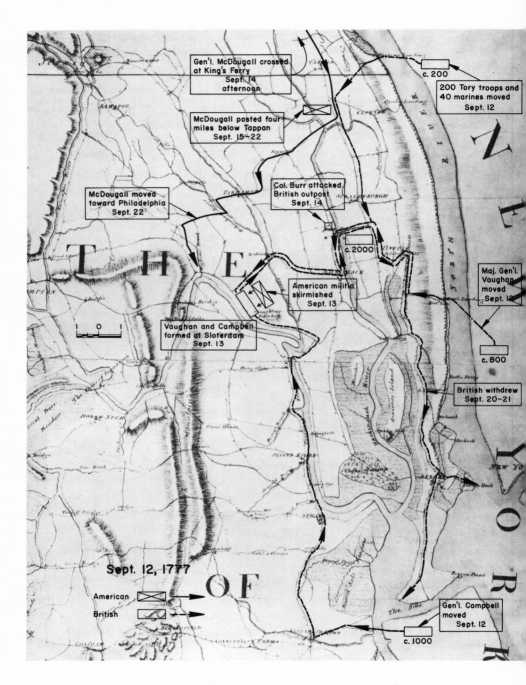

Operations of September 12–21, 1777.

Drawn on contemporary map. E. Tone, 1962.

wellborn nor able; indeed, many of the 4th Volunteers had been men, like the Ramapo Germans and the workers at the iron mines, out of step with Jersey Dutch society—New Jersey patriots delighted in making contemptuous comments on Van Buskirk's "two hundred banditti, collected in Bergen County, who eat King George's beef and pork to very little purpose" [13]--but aristocrats or not, and whatever may be said of their kidnapping and arson, King George had no more daring soldiers than these Jersey Tories and no better regimental officer than Dr. Van Buskirk, a man as deserving of fame as any de Lancey or Rogers. Van Buskirk led a well-equipped force raiding a country where every other house held a friend of the raiders, and patriots did themselves no honor to deny that Tories were first-rate fighters, whatever they might think of their principles.

As soon as word of the British entry into New Jersey reached General Putnam at Peekskill he sent off Brigadier General Alexander McDougall, with a force estimated at twelve hundred men, and two field pieces.[14] McDougall crossed the Hudson at King's Ferry on Sunday afternoon, September 14, 1777. Putnam had overestimated his numbers, which amounted to no more than about seven hundred Continentals and about two hundred New England militia. On Monday afternoon, McDougall proceeded to a point four miles below Tappan, halfway between that village and the British positions to the south, where he found that, "by the lowest accounts that can be relied on," the enemy probably numbered 2,000; "others as credible as high as 3,000, though many have represented them as high as 4,000 and 5,000." [15] The local militia, he complained, would not venture near Sir Henry's posts, and he was unable to get accurate intelligence, but his own discovering parties came back to camp with reports that "the main body of the enemy were strongly posted between Schraalenburgh Church and the New Bridge, with their plunder on their right flanks and somewhat in the rear." [16] He was also unable to learn the whereabouts of the other American troops in the area, which was not surprising, since Colonel Aaron Burr, in command of patriot forces at Paramus, was obliged to report at the same time that he found it "impossible to secure himself at any fixed post, acting merely as a party of observation." [17]

13 1 NJA (2) 508, 509.
14 General Putnam to Washington, Sept. 13, 1777, GW Papers LC.
15 McDougall to Washington, Sept. 17, 1777, GW Papers LC.
16 McDougall to Washington, Sept. 17, 1777, GW Papers LC.
17 Burr to Putnam, Sept. 14, 1777, GW Papers LC.

Colonel Burr had made a most successful sortie against the British on the previous Sunday night, about two miles out of the village of Hackensack. Leading "his men between [two sentinels] at the moment when they were farthest apart . . . he was almost upon the sleeping picket before a man of it began to stir. When at a distance of ten yards, Burr was challenged by a sentinel, whom he immediately shot dead, and then gave the word of attack. One officer, a sergeant, a corporal and twenty-seven privates, fell into their hands on this occasion. Only one of the pickets besides the sentinel made any resistance and he was over-powered after he had received two bayonet wounds." The last words of the dying soldier were that "it grieved him sore to the heart that he had served his king upward of twenty years, and at length must die with a charged musket in his hand." [18]

Burr's action somewhat disappointed the local militia, who had also marked the men for attack. Burr had hardly retired before a detach-ment of eighteen militiamen under Lieutenant Adam Boyd arrived to surprise the same post. "When we came into the guard house (Tim-pany's schoolhouse) we found it empty. Colonel Burr had taken the pickets without firing and carried them away and the enemy seemed then not to know their pickets was taken." [19]

After taking counsel with his staff, General McDougall decided against making any attempt upon the British, particularly after Burr's attack had alerted them, "doubting not," he added, "that they knew the position of our different parties better than I did, that part of the country being very unfriendly to us." [20] Lieutenant Boyd's party had evidently not thought it necessary to report their exploit to the general; some at least of that part of the country were friendly enough to the American cause to risk their lives against twice their own number, within earshot of the main British position.

Both Burr and McDougall fell easily into the line officer's contempt for the undisciplined farmer-soldier, though neither of them had any real reason to regard himself as a professional military man. Burr com-plained that "not a man of the militia are with me. Some joined us last night but are gone." [21] McDougall, for his part, was entirely unem-barrassed by the thought that the militia could hardly be expected to do what his nine hundred troops could not do, seeing no irony what-ever in complaining that the untrained Jersey Dutch militia, less than

[18] Romeyn, Hackensack Church, 30, 31.
[19] Affidavit of David R. Bogert, Pension Records, W3502.
[20] McDougall to Washington, Sept. 17,1777, GW Papers LC.
[21] Burr to Putnam, Sept. 14, 1777, GW Papers LC.

one hundred in number, would not venture near the Regulars, at the same time that he reported that he could not even attack Clinton's pickets because, as he put it, it was "too hazardous an experiment, considering our strength and theirs, by the lowest computation." [22]

Since it was the Continental officer and not the militiaman who left his journals and letters for the historian, over the years the militiaman's faults have been multiplied and his virtues forgotten. There are few Jersey Dutch militiamen's writings to tell how seldom any Continentals ventured down into the really dangerous part of the neutral ground when the British were near; none to note that, while the Bergen County militia daily risked brushes with Sir Henry's raiders from New York, all too many Continentals did not hear a gun fired in battle from one year to the next.

General McDougall was a sincere patriot and an able officer, a self-made New York merchant and a prewar leader of the Sons of Liberty, much given to cheerful self-ridicule about the early trials and mistakes of "Sawny McDougall, the milk-mon's son," [23] but in his immediate frame of mind there would have been little use in trying to tell him about the hundreds of zealous Whigs of Tappan, Schraalenburgh, and Hackensack; frustrated in any plans to attack the enemy himself, fearful that Putnam and Washington would think him timid for not making at least one desperate throw at the British, McDougall vented his feelings against the Jersey militiamen. It would have been too much to expect more; Washington himself often yielded to the same temptation.

Both Burr's raid and McDougall's discovering parties had made one thing reasonably clear: contrary to American fears, Sir Henry's three-pronged drive into New Jersey was no move to seize the state. Washington had overestimated the British general's planning when he told Congress that if the British had four thousand men in the Jerseys, "it is probable they have something more serious in view than a mere diversion." [24] As he was often to do again, Clinton had manned an invasion and produced a forage party, and a few days after his descent upon Bergen County he reassembled his whole force at New Bridge and moved them back to New York. "Having collected our cattle, the sol-

---

[22]   McDougall to Washington, Sept. 17, 1777, GW Papers LC. Daniel (Albert) Banta was one of the local Dutchmen who tried to do what he could to help the Continentals while they were in the county, a hardy patriot who was captured and carried to New York the next year, where he was assaulted for resenting aspersions on his patriot father. He was exchanged within a week. Banta Genealogy No. 512.

[23]   Thacher 325.

[24]   9 GW 231.

diers without tents and blankets and the weather threatening," he wrote, "I thought it advisable to fall back." [25]

On the next day General McDougall sent a company of Continentals down as far as Bergen Woods without finding a redcoat. Sir Henry, McDougall reported, had carried off "two hundred horne cattle, some of which were very poor." He had also carried off two hundred sheep and a good deal of other Jersey Dutch provisions and property,[26] and several Hackensack valley Whigs, Captain John Varick, William Prevost and Mr. Brouwer among them. Varick spent thirteen months in Sugar House or Bridewell; Prevost probably was released earlier.[27] Americans away from the neutral ground, who were sometimes quick to believe that the Jersey Dutchmen who lived there profited by British invasions, would have been enlightened to know that Sir Henry, for

[25] 2 NJA (2) 44. The 1777 invasion is discussed by Sir Henry Clinton in The American Rebellion, 71, etc., in a deprecatory manner which would have done him credit if the raid had not been so plainly footless: "I thought I could not employ the intermediate time better than by a desultory move into East Jersey, which [besides producing forage] might at so critical a moment possibly operate in favor of either Sir William Howe or General Burgoyne, or might at least draw off some part of the force that protected the Highlands, which were the destined object of my next move. I had moreover, some little hopes that an opportunity might offer of making a blow at two of the Jersey brigades which, I was told, were then on their march to the northward, if they should in their route happen to pass by the neighborhood of New Bridge. . . . But I cannot presume to say it was really of service to either Sir William Howe's or General Burgoyne's operations. It is sufficient to know my intentions were good, and I had the satisfaction to see most of its other objects accomplished without affront or material loss."

The sharp-tongued Tory, Judge Thomas Jones, who had little use for Sir Henry Clinton or any other British commander, saw it in a different light: "General Clinton, conceiving it . . . a critical time for both the northern and southern army to make a diversion in favor of them both, projected an expedition into New Jersey. The army was landed in the night at three different places and formed a junction according to the settled plan, somewhere near Colonel Schuyler's upon the Passaic. . . . Two of the detachments made large circuitous marches before they joined the main body at Schuyler's and, according to orders, drove in all the cattle, hogs, horses and sheep that fell in their way, whether the property of Whigs or Tories, royalists or rebels, and indiscriminately robbed the inhabitants of whatever they found in their houses. This desultory expedition took up about three days, a few guns were fired, but not a man killed or wounded on either side. The expedition had not the least effect as to the operations either to the southward or the northward." Jones went on to complain that the commissaries charged the crown 1s. 6d. for every pound of meat delivered by the army. 1 Jones, New York During the Revolution, 197, 198.

[26] McDougall Papers, NYHS. Clinton's figures were exactly double those of McDougall: "about four hundred cattle and the same quantity of sheep." Clinton, American Rebellion, 71.

[27] Fell Diary, Sept. 16, 1777. Captain Varick's title was probably honorary; he was not a militia officer. Damages by British, NJSL, New Barbadoes Precinct, 16, 40.

one, considered the Hackensack valley to be enemy territory and paid no one anything for what he carried off.[28]

With Sir Henry gone, General McDougall moved on to Paramus to forage for the supplies he would need on his march to Philadelphia, where he had been ordered to move in support of Washington.[29]

The country people who were the victims of Clinton's foraging, seeing their goods going off to feed their enemies in New York without leave and without pay, could hardly be blamed if they remembered for years the story of the time the tables were turned on the marauders, particularly when it was done by a youngster in his teens.

John Demarest lived on the New Bridge Road just east of the River Road with his father and mother and seven brothers and sisters. One of his uncles, who lived near the old French burying ground a mile or so to the north, on the River Road, was Captain Samuel Demarest of the patriot militia, and his other uncle, John, was a private in Captain Outwater's militia company.[30]

John's two older brothers, Peter and Philip, eighteen and sixteen years old in 1777, were in their uncle's military company. "He belonged," one of his neighbors wrote after the war, "to one of the Whig families who continued to dwell on the lines during the war by alternate flight and return to their homes." [31]

On one of the British foraging parties John was carried off by a Hessian trooper. The Hessian was drunk and he probably seized the boy for some real or fancied insult; even Hessians were not given to kidnapping children. Forced to mount the trooper's horse behind him, John waited until he was fording a stream, slid from the horse, pulled the unsteady trooper's foot and unhorsed him, and while his captor was floundering in the shallow creek John seized the reins, turned the horse about and galloped home. "As the Hessian never appeared to claim his property," John's biographer adds, "the horse remained in the boy's possession. In the saddle bags was found a goodly supply of King George's gold, which helped the boy secure an education in the prepa-

28 The booty, Clinton boasted, "afforded a seasonable refreshment to the squadron and to the army (amongst whom they were all distributed) without costing either them or the government a shilling." Clinton, American Rebellion, 71.
29 See 4 Freeman App. IV–4.
30 His aunt Elizabeth, however, was married to Lawrence Van Buskirk, an officer in Abraham Van Buskirk's Greencoat regiment, and two other uncles by marriage were also Tories. Demarest Genealogy Nos. 42, 43, 176.
31 Affidavits of Philip Demarest, Pension Records, S29114; Benjamin Romeyn, Pension Records, W16952; John Demarest, Pension Records, R2860; BHSP 1915–1916; Demarest Genealogy No. 176. Philip, who was called "swart Philip," because he was so dark, had enlisted when he was only fifteen so that his father could stay at home and look out for his mother and five young children.

ration for the ministry of the Reformed Church." [32] His father had lost all of his hay and "14 sheep, 3 heffers, 5 hogs, 2 pigs" on the first British incursion into Jersey, for which he received a receipt: "Taken from Jacobus Demoray by order of Colonel Monckton 4 waggon loads of hay." It is doubtful whether the Jacobus Demarests ever considered inserting a notice in Rivington's *Gazette* advising the Hessian that the horse had been taken up by John. John lived until 1837, an uncompromising Calvinist and a thorough Whig to his dying day.[33]

Sir Henry's leisurely Bergen County raid over, he finally started to move up the Hudson to the assistance of Burgoyne. Two thousand troops under General Vaughan first attacked Fort Montgomery and Fort Clinton, the two strong points by which the Americans had controlled the Hudson River in the Highlands since the outbreak of war. Feinting in one direction and attacking from the rear, Vaughan quickly disposed of the garrison of six hundred soldiers, mostly militia, and seized the supposedly impregnable forts,[34] a loss which had once been universally assumed to be fatal to the American cause. As it was, Burgoyne's surrender at Saratoga on the next day robbed the victory of any importance whatever, and General Vaughan, who had every reason to hope that he had made his name famous in British military annals by

[32] Demarest Genealogy No. 177. John "was in actual service . . . during the greater part of the Revolutionary War, by day and by night, even before he attained the age of sixteen . . . sometimes spending whole nights in the guard houses and on sentinel . . . and sometimes in remote places of retreat, when too much fatigued to watch through the night for fear of being carried off or slain by the enemy . . . whilst the Tories remained unmolested at home, in the same neighborhood, enjoying all the comforts and even the luxuries of life." Affidavit of John Demarest, Pension Records, R2860. He, like his cousin John (Demarest Genealogy No. 169), was "a Whig of the old stamp," and a leader in the "seceder" church. He lived at one time in Tappan, the André grave being on his property.

[33] Demarest Genealogy Nos. 42, 43.

One day late in the war, about April 10, 1781, John's brother, Philip Demarest, went out from his home near New Bridge with his young cousin Guiliam Demarest and another neighbor "to pilot a party of regular [American] troops under command of a lieutenant that was sent from Paramus to discover the movements of the enemy." Young Guiliam's father was David G. Demarest, a Tory refugee in New York, who had formerly lived at Schraalenburgh.

"They went into the vicinity of Fort Lee and returned in the evening to the house of . . . John Zabriskie, near Hackensack New Bridge." There the three militiamen and most of the rest of the party were surprised by the enemy and carried to Captain Ward's quarters at Pemrepough, below Paulus Hook. After a time Philip's uncle, Captain Samuel Demarest, went down under a flag of truce and arranged their parole. The captain did not know it, but Ward was negotiating with Captain Lawrence of the New York militia to defect to the American side at the same time. Affidavits of Philip Demarest, Pension Records, S29115; Benjamin Romeyn, Pension Records, W16952; John Demarest, Pension Records, S15081. Demarest Genealogy Nos. 68, 176, 177, 220, 593.

[34] See 2 GC 387.

his exploit, has gone down in history instead as the man who wantonly burned Kingston, the only fruit of Clinton's belated campaign.

One Bergen County patriot had more than the usual reason to cheer the great victory at Saratoga. John Fell still lay in Provost Jail under the most severe treatment. By some device—it has been suggested that a message must have been hidden in a loaf of bread—the American prisoners heard of the patriot victory before Tory New York learned of it, and they set up a cheering that left no doubt in the minds of their captors of the purport of the message. "Glorious news from the Northward," Fell wrote in his journal, adding on the next day: "Confirmation strong as Holy Writ. Beef, loaf bread and butter drawn today." [35]

The great victory at Saratoga saved the American campaign of 1777 as the Battle of Trenton had saved the campaign of 1776: after Saratoga, Washington's defeat at Philadelphia, the failure of the boom and chain across the Hudson, and the loss of the Highland forts all faded into insignificance.[36]

Some Jersey Dutchmen may even have been amused in December, 1777, when Governor William Livingston wrote to the papers, under his well-known pen name Hortentius, at their expense:

Sir, I am afraid that while we are employed in furnishing our battalions with clothing we forget the County of Bergen, which alone is sufficient amply to provide them with winter waistcoats and breeches from the redundance and superfluity of certain woolen habits which are at present applied to no kind of use whatsoever. It is well known that the rural ladies in that part of our state pride themselves in an incredible number of petticoats which like house furniture are displayed by way of ostentation for many years before they are decreed to invest the fair bodies of the proprietors. Until that period they are never worn, but neatly piled up on each side of an immense escritoire, the top of which is decorated with a most capacious brass-clasped Bible, seldom read. What I would therefore humbly propose to our superiors is to make prize of those future female habiliments and after proper transformation immediately apply them to screen from the inclemencies of the weather those gallant males who are now fighting for the liberties of their country, and to clear this measure from every imputation of injustice I have only to observe that the generality of the women of that county having for above a century worn

35 Fell Diary.
36 During November or December of 1777 a detachment of Orange County militia under Captain Johnston had a small engagement with the British or Tories near Weehawken, in which Garret C. Oblenis was "wounded by a shot of the enemy through the left arm, which broke two of my ribs." Affidavits of Garret C. Oblenis and Harmanus Blauvelt, Pension Records, S22653.

the breeches it is highly reasonable that the men should now and especially upon so important an occasion, make booty of the petticoats.[37]

As the winter of 1777–78 set in, it must have been hard for Jersey Dutchmen to realize that but a single year had passed since the dread days of the British occupation; a year since Washington and his whole army seemed ready to collapse at Hackensack; a year since Bergen County had been a conquered land, helpless in the hands of its enemies. The improvement in patriots' affairs during the past twelve months was little short of miraculous, a reproach indeed to men of little faith. A year earlier patriotic Jerseymen had been the hapless victims of a cruel invader; in the fall and winter of 1777, though by no means beyond the reach of British power, they were again actors in the war, not mere sufferers of its cruelties.

Abraham Brouwer and John Lozier were two soldiers in Major Goetschius' Bergen County Rangers, not particularly to be distinguished from the other Jersey Dutchmen who tried to work their farms in the neutral ground and to carry on as soldiers at the same time, men with no expectation or desire of bringing themselves to public notice. Like almost all of Major Goetschius' men, Brouwer and Lozier seem to have been of the coetus branch of the Dutch Reformed church, Brouwer evidently having been an elder of Domine Romeyn's congregation at Schraalenburgh. Brouwer came from New Bridge, to judge by his name, and Lozier seems to have come from Harrington,[38] solid Jersey Dutchmen of the kind that made up the backbone of the patriot forces of the neutral ground. Willing to do their tour of duty if they had to but far happier to think back to the days when they could sit before their huge Dutch fireplaces and smoke their pipes when their work was done; they were farmers first and soldiers second, with none of the pride of arms that had already begun to mark the troops of the Continental Line. Major Goetschius was later to call Brouwer and Lozier brave soldiers. He must have regarded them as somewhat more daring than most mi-

---

[37] 1 NJA (2) 532.

[38] There were several Abraham Brouwers of military age in Hackensack and Schraalenburgh, all apparently of the coetus churches. Hackensack Church Records 211, 214, 300, 301 and passim; Schraalenburgh Church Records, passim; Romeyn Papers UCL. An Abraham J. (or I.) Brouwer, not the particular Abraham Brouwer, sought and obtained a land grant as a Revolutionary War soldier. Pension Records, BLW 26331–160–55; W23707. Lozier was, if correctly identified, born near Hackensack, March 14, 1740, and died Aug. 4, 1805. GHHB 604. There was also a John Lozier, of Pompton, who served in the militia throughout the war, but he was not the celebrated John Lozier. Pension Records, W20525. A third John Lozier, of Paramus, was a Tory. Affidavit of Abraham D. Banta, Pension Records, S6575.

litiamen when he sent them off on the task that nearly brought their destruction.

On January 29, 1778, Goetschius ordered Brouwer and Lozier down to intercept Tory commerce between New Jersey and New York and to reconnoiter the enemy picket at Paulus Hook,[39] twenty miles from headquarters, in a country where few patriots indeed would have willingly exposed themselves in the dead of winter. The only travelers one was likely to see in that country were men busy with illicit trade with New York, who had no intention of letting patriot militiamen interfere with their affairs; often enough men who would not have needed the excuse of trade to shoot a ranting Whig if they could.

Finding themselves in this situation, well below the Three Pidgeons Tavern and thus virtually within enemy lines,[40] Brouwer and Lozier could hardly have been expected to be judicial in dealing with Tories who happened along the highroad. As it turned out, they were not judicial about one of them. While they were posted beside the road, John Richards, a loyalist refugee from New York, came up to them. Richards, who had formerly lived on New Barbadoes Neck and whose family still lived there, had heard that his family was sick at home with the smallpox, had got himself a British pass to go through the lines and had gone out to visit them. An active Tory, he had been warned by his New York friends not to risk travel in the neutral ground but had insisted that none of his old neighbors would injure him.[41] He was on his way back to New York with a wagon and two Negroes [42] when he came up to Brouwer and Lozier. It is hard to say whether they regarded him or his baggage or the two Negroes as contraband or whether they simply feared that if they passed him he would alert the nearby British forces against them; in any case they ordered him to return to militia headquarters for examination. They may have been overzealous in taking him up; on the other hand, Richards was far more liable to seizure than most men seized by the British. Whatever the facts, the reason for their decision was soon lost in the trouble that followed.

Lozier climbed aboard the wagon with Richards and one of the Negroes and Brouwer rode at their rear, and all five set off toward militia headquarters, Richards fuming at the outrage. They had not gone far before Richards seemingly thought he saw a chance to escape,

---

[39] 2 NJA (2) 47.
[40] The American report was that they were "in ambush at Prior's Mill, within sight of the enemy sentry," about six miles below the Three Pidgeons. 2 NJA (2) 47.
[41] 2 NJA (2) 32.
[42] One of his own slaves and one of Cornelius Van Vorst's. 2 NJA (2) 47. One of Van Vorst's slaves was notorious for his work with Tory raiders. Winfield, Hudson County, 434, 435.

and with the help of the Negro in the wagon tried to seize Lozier's gun, whereupon Brouwer galloped up and shot and killed him. The wagon and the two Negroes were taken to headquarters.[43]

Prior's Mills, near Bergen (*New York Magazine*, November 1794).
Courtesy New-York Historical Society.

New York City was soon in an uproar. Bergen County loyalists in New York, who knew that Richards had gone out to see his sick family, were infuriated. Always prepared to assume the worst of patriot actions, when word came from the Three Pidgeons that Richards had been killed, they were sure it was a simple highway robbery, with Brouwer and Lozier cast in the part of the despicable thieves.[44] Other Tories, not so intimately connected with Bergen County's past wars, hearing that the affair had occurred near the Three Pidgeons, spread the report that "Richards, on his way, stopped at a pub, where he was robbed and shot," a somewhat less praiseworthy end for the unfortunate Richards, but equally reprehensible for the two rangers.[45]

[43]   2 NJA (2) 47.
[44]   Richards, according to this story, "was shot dead by one of them as he was preventing the other from robbing him of his watch." 2 NJA (2) 32.
[45]   Judge Thomas Jones told a different story when he came to write his "history" of the revolution after the war. Though Jones's tale was designed more to injure Sir Henry Clinton in Britain than to slander patriot militiamen, there may have been some Englishmen, who did not know Jones, who believed it.
   "In the summer of 1778, Mr. John Richards, a native of Barbadoes [possibly reflecting confusion with New Barbadoes], but a long resident in New Jersey, where he inherited a genteel estate, situated upon the banks of the Passaic, was foully murdered. He was a steady, noted Loyalist, spoke his mind freely in favor of Great

All of Tory New York agreed that Richards was blameless in the affair. Rivington called him "a man universally known, and as universally loved, warmly attached to his friends, humane and candid to his enemies, benevolent and hospitable to all men," and all agreed also that quick retaliation against the "monsters who perpetrated the horrid tragedy" was in order.[46] There is no reason to think that Richards was otherwise than Rivington painted him;[47] indeed there is none to suggest that Brouwer and Lozier were not equally exemplary; the times were out of joint, not Jersey Dutchmen.

A large Tory purse was subscribed to reward anyone who would bring in Brouwer and Lozier. Within a week after the shooting, on February 5, 1778, Brouwer was captured and brought to New York.[48] One of the four men who accomplished the speedy capture was Wiert Banta, born and raised within a stone's throw of Brouwer's Hill in New Bridge, a Tory who had more than once put the New York refugees in his debt. It was a daring exploit, made more difficult by two successive heavy snowstorms, and Banta and his party deserved great credit for it.[49] Dutch patriots had taken too long to learn that unguarded farms were distinctly unsafe quarters for militiamen.

New York was overjoyed at the brilliant stroke, and Banta was the hero of the day; Brouwer, for his part, was thrown into the dungeon to await the hangman. The celebration was short-lived. To the disgust of

---

Britain, but never was in arms, or served in any civil capacity. This gentleman . . . removed to New York but left his family at home. Hearing that the small-pox had appeared in his family, he determined to pay them a visit. Upon his way he stopped at a public house. Here were a number of rebels, to one of whom he was well known. This fellow abused him, called him a tory, a villain, a British scoundrel, and demanded his watch. This Richards refused to deliver, upon which the rebel drew a pistol from his pocket, and with great composure shot Richards through the head. He instantly died. The rebels then took his watch, his money, what things he had with him, stripped the body of its clothes and deliberately marched off. This horrid, cruel, malicious murder was approved of by Governor Livingston. He recommended the murderer to Congress. Congress rewarded him with a Captain's commission."

The story bears little relation to the known facts. It is a piece with the rest of Jones's history, in which King George, the British commanders, the British civil government, other Tories, the patriot Congress, Whigs, Presbyterians and the Continental army were equal objects of his venom. 1 Jones, New York During the Revolution, 280.

[46] 2 NJA (2) 32. See 1 Jones, New York During the Revolution, 280.
[47] He had often held county office before the war and seems to have been highly regarded. MJFBC. Richards had given his parole at Trenton on July 13, 1776, that he would remain within a circle of two miles of his farm in New Barbadoes "and that I will not carry on any political correspondence whatever on the subject of the dispute between Great Britain and the United colonies, neither will I furnish any provisions or give any intelligence to the enemies of the colony." Parole of John Richards, NJSL.
[48] 2 NJA (2) 47.
[49] LYT NYPL "Wiert Banta"; Smith Journal NYPL.

every Tory in the city, Brouwer was left in jail, and many, doubting that he was going to be hanged at all, blamed Sir Henry Clinton.[50]

On March 27 Lozier too was captured, at De Groot's house in English Neighborhood,[51] and a new clamor was raised, made the louder by Rivington's report that Richards' watch had been found on the prisoner when he was captured. Nonetheless, he too was jailed and not hanged forthwith.

Tories who deplored Sir Henry's supposed softheartedness despaired too soon. Sir Henry's rule of New York ended at the doors of his prisons. Sir Henry's jailers were far more willing allies of Tories than the general, indeed they needed no Tory help to give Whigs full punishment for rebelling against their king, certainly not two such celebrated rebels as Brouwer and Lozier, and they wanted no interference from officers and gentlemen. Tories who had hoped to see the rangers hanged could now congratulate themselves on their own mistake. Every traveler from New York brought new word of the cruel treatment of the two prisoners. Major Goetschius wrote to Elisha Boudinot, the American commissary of prisoners, that Major Hammond, an exchanged American prisoner, had come to him on April 22, 1778, "with this account: that Abraham Brouwer, John Lozier and Peter Vanton are now still in the dungeon in New York and John Lozier and Brouwer are handcuffed. . . . A woman from Bergentown who I have appointed to provide for them sends me the same account. They are only allowed one *hutsput* a day and a pint of water. This you may depend upon is the real truth. Said woman further informs me that we must send provisions for them and clothing or they will certainly die. This I beg: that there be sent in a flag to have them removed out of that hole or else retaliated. . . . Said soldiers were regularly enlisted by the Governor's orders and taken in their duty and are very brave soldiers." [52]

Goetschius pleaded that he himself be sent in under a flag of truce to see what he could do, adding a postscript that he had just spoken to another woman from Bergentown "who can and will give affidavits that

[50] "An officer in Skinner's Corps, and formerly an intimate of the murdered man, got information where the murderer was, with a few men only, with Skinner's leave he passed to Jersey, surprised the rebel party, and in about twelve hours they were all safely lodged in the provost in New York. General Clinton had never complained of this barbarous and inhuman murder either to Governor Livington, Washington, or the Congress. He now had the villain in his power. Everybody supposed retaliation would take place. Nothing of the kind. In five days . . . he had the liberty of the city upon his parole; in about ten he was exchanged as a prisoner of war." 1 Jones, New York During the Revolution, 280. Jones's report doubtless reflected Tory sentiment at the time; Brouwer's actual treatment was far different.
[51] 2 NJA (2) 134.
[52] Goetschius to Boudinot, April 28, 1778, Boudinot Papers HSP.

Abraham Brouwer and John Lozier are certainly in the dungeon and pinned down on the floor and they have been there since the time they have been taken," British reports that "Brouwer was declared a prisoner of war and used as such" to the contrary notwithstanding.[53]

On November 6, 1778, after six months had passed, the state authorities ordered retaliation. Colonel Christopher Billop, a Staten Island Loyalist, was the man selected. He had been held as an American prisoner of war, which probably meant that he had been kept at Morristown or elsewhere, free to move about within limits of one mile of the village. He was removed to the common jail of the County of Burlington. "You are to receive the body of . . . [Colonel Billop] . . . , herewith delivered to you," Elisha Boudinot, the Commissary of Prisoners, told the keeper of the jail, "and having put irons on his hands and feet, you are to chain him to the floor in a close room in the said jail, and there to detain him, giving him bread and water only for food, until you receive further orders . . ." Boudinot added, in a letter to Billop, "Sorry I am that I have been put under the disagreeable necessity . . . , but retaliation is directed, and it will, I most sincerely hope, be in your power to relieve yourself [by] relaxation of the sufferings of John Lozier. Nothing short of retaliation will teach Britons to act like men of humanity." [54]

Nine days later, General Pattison ordered Lozier's irons removed: "Notwithstanding the many crimes laid to the charge of John Lozier, and for which [the general] ordered him to be put in irons; as he has remained so long in that situation the general desires that he may now be released from them, and put upon the same footing as other prisoners under your charge." [55]

The New Jersey authorities had also put the case before General Washington, and on December 26, 1778, the general himself passed on to Sir Henry Clinton the commissary's complaint that "Brouwer and Lozier, two soldiers in the service of these states," were suffering "a confinement of peculiar severity, without a sufficient cause for so injurious a discrimination."

"I am persuaded," Washington added, "I need only call your attention to the situation of these men to induce you to order them relief, and to have them placed precisely on the same footing with other prisoners of war. This will lead to their immediate exchange." [56] A day or two later John Fell, of the Continental Congress, met General Wash-

[53]   Goetschius to Boudinot, April 28, 1778, Boudinot Papers HSP.
[54]   J. W. Lawrence, Foot-Prints; or, Incidents in Early History of New Brunswick (St. John, N. B., 1883), 64, 65.
[55]   Pattison 300.
[56]   13 GW 454, 455. 1 Carleton Papers 361, 365, 380 (1633, 1654, 1704, 9825).

ington on a Philadelphia street and he also urged him to do what he could to save the two. Washington explained what he had done and said that he could do nothing more.[57]

For once the eighteenth-century euphemisms of Washington's letter proved correct: it was in fact only necessary to call Clinton's attention to the situation of the men to get them relief. Clinton probably welcomed the protest. His faults were many, but they did not include so unmilitary a vice as holding prisoners of war in irons.

When Washington's letter arrived, Clinton seems to have acted decisively to end the matter once and for all; he ordered the two to be exchanged at once as prisoners of war, let the New York refugees think what they would. Though he did not directly answer Washington's accusation of inhuman treatment of Brouwer and Lozier, neither did he repeat the Tory slanders against them, observing only that it was his understanding of military custom in Europe that "infantry patrolling without a non-commissioned officer" could properly be treated as spies or marauders, and that "as Brouwer and Lozier stood in this predicament when they killed Mr. Richards, I should have been justified in any severities." He had not done so, he said, only to spare the country new turmoil. He closed his letter: "Since you have avowed Brouwer and Lozier, I have ordered them exchanged immediately." [58]

Tories vilified Sir Henry to his dying day for his action, and in truth he got little enough credit for it among patriots, who chose to remember the cruel treatment of the militiamen, not their release, but whatever Clinton's reward, his action spared the neutral ground one at least of the brutalities of civil war, the hanging of prisoners; spared it, that is, until the Tories themselves came into power late in the war in the dark days of William Franklin and his Associated Loyalists.

As for Brouwer and Lozier, they went back to fighting the war. Far from letting his experience in the dungeon keep him safely at home, Lozier was soon again patrolling the roads to the ferries, where, on July

[57] Fell Diary.

[58] Sir Henry Clinton to Washington, Jan. 23, 1779, GW Papers LC. Two enclosures were sent purporting to show that Lozier and Brouwer had not been mistreated. Jones and Pintard to Smith, Jan. 1, 1779, GW Papers LC. The truth was directly to the contrary. See Pattison 300. Brouwer and Lozier were in fact held as criminals, not prisoners of war, at the express direction of General Robertson. "Report of Prisoners Confined in Provost, New York, 1st Jany, 1779," HC Papers CL. The report to Clinton indicated that Brouwer had been confined only since Sept. 26, 1779, which possibly related to an earlier capture in September 1777. See Fell Diary, Sept. 16, 1777. Clements Library has a draft of a letter from Clinton to Washington, defending the treatment of prisoners and attacking American excesses during the war. He evidently changed his mind and sent the quoted letter, which is in the Washington Papers but not in the Clinton Papers. John Lozier may have been an ensign in the Bergen County militia. MPC 534.

23, 1779, he had the misfortune to be recaptured, along with David Ritzema Bogert. Rivington's *Gazette*, remembering the Richards affair, made much of the capture, calling Lozier and Bogert members of "a gang of rebels who paint themselves black and commit murders and thefts in Bergen County." [59] Since any patriot militiaman was a murderer and thief to Rivington, the news probably deceived no one, unless a few armchair Tories were taken in by the added touch about the black paint. Those few would have been enlightened to know that David Bogert was the grandson of the noted Dutch divine, John Ritzema, and the nephew of the celebrated Tory colonel, Rudolph Ritzema, and only sixteen years old.[60]

Indeed, young Bogert is almost as deserving of notice as Brouwer and Lozier themselves. The son of Nicholas Bogert and Alida Ritzema, he was born in New York City on February 3, 1763. He was thirteen or fourteen years old when Captain Outwater's company of state troops was formed at Hackensack, where he was then living, but he joined at once and "was with the company in all the services they performed at least two years before he was enrolled as one of the company." He was appointed corporal early in 1779, "taken prisoner in a skirmish at Bergen and after his exchange in December, and resuming his duties in the company, he continued so to act." Lieutenant Terhune commanded the party when Bogert and Lozier were taken. Bogert "was carried before Major General Pattison, the British commander in New York and in the street he was separated from his companion John Lozier (who was taken with him), he [Lozier] was sent to the Provost . . . and deponent to Sugar House." Bogert, "in 1779 drew rations of flour, pork and whiskey till he was taken prisoner and eight dollars as one month's pay and that was all the compensation he ever received, except that the State of New Jersey has since paid him for his *musquet* and accoutrements taken with him." Bogert did not exaggerate when he said in his pension application more than a half century later that there was little rest for the soldiers of that period.[61]

The winter of 1777–78 was a terrible one for Washington's army encamped at Valley Forge, but with Sir William Howe in Philadelphia

59 3 NJA (2) 514, 515.
60 Riker, History of Harlem (1904 ed.), 459. Bogert lived to be seventy-six despite his imprisonment. Idem.
61 Affidavits of Henry Berdan and David R. Bogert, Pension Records, W3502. Bogert's old lieutenant, Adam Boyd, then very sick, was unable to help. He "emphatically said, My dear sir, you and your family have suffered everything and if anything can be got you ought to have it, but how can you expect that I, 86 years old and nearly in the grave, should remember your services." Idem.

and the Continental army away from New York, and with the threat of Burgoyne removed, Jersey Dutchmen could turn their thoughts, for a few months at least, to the hard problems of food and fuel.[62]

During the latter part of February some of the people of Bergen and Paulus Hook who had taken advantage of the lull in the fighting and the snow-covered roads to go out into the county and bring back flour, grain, and household goods that had been removed under Washington's orders in the fall of 1776, were arrested by Newark militiamen, who congratulated themselves that the Tory supply route to New York had thus been uncovered. "We have frequent intelligence that the enemy received great part of their supplies of provisions from Bergen County, which induced us to use our utmost endeavor to discover the manner in which it was done," the militia officers wrote to the Governor and Council on February 25, 1778. "Accounts daily declared that the inhabitants near Paulus Hook had free egress and regress to the interior parts of the country to purchase provisions under protection of their private wants —and that this was done by the express consent of Colonel Dey. . . . A few days ago . . . the three men (now sent) . . . [were] . . . taken unlading their sleds of flour, grain, &c., at Hackensack River; they produced their papers from Colonel Dey." [63]

The writers had been deceived by appearances. Colonel Dey was a zealous patriot. Few indeed of New York's supplies came in under any pass of his, or through any of his friends at Bergen, some of whom were probably as good patriots as he was himself, or indeed as were the people of Newark. Tories needed no passes to go to New York; they simply

---

[62] The war did not stop for militiamen. Captain James Christie's militia company was stationed at Tenafly during most of March, 1778. One of his men, Daniel Banta, was "taken prisoner by the Tories and carried to New York, where in a few days he was exchanged and in about one week was again back at Tenafly with his company." Affidavit of Daniel Banta, Pension Records, S2090. On June 23, 1778, Captain Joost Zabriskie, active in patriot affairs from the earliest days of the war, "who commanded a company of Rangers . . . , having received orders to impress a number of wagons to carry some grain for the use of the army, was murdered by Tories. Two guns were discharged at him as he passed by a wood in a disaffected part of the county; one of the balls entered his body in the small of the back, and he lived only thirty-eight hours." 2 NJA (2) 265, 297. See MPC 115, 116, 164; Committee to Provincial Congress, NJHS "Provincial Congress." Patriot militiamen also continued their efforts to discourage traffic with New York over the Paulus Hook ferry. "A small party of the rebels were on the night of last Sunday week as far down as Prior's Mills, and carried away two negro men that were coming to market with a few eggs and a small quantity of butter," Rivington's *Gazette* reported on May 18. "They were also down at the same place last Friday and Saturday, and carried off some more negroes, but were pursued by a party from Paulus Hook, when they took to their heels." 2 NJA (2) 218.

[63] Boudinot, Burnet, Hayes, et al., to the Governor of New Jersey, Feb. 25, 1778, Lot 163, catalogue of J. Lawrence Boggs' sale, May 11, 1938. Parke-Bernet Galleries.

loaded their wagons and sleds, or their pettiaugers, and slipped through the patriot guards.

The summer of 1778 saw the British abandon Philadelphia, which they had been at such pains to take the year before, plain evidence of the small progress the British were making in subduing the American rebellion.[64]

One of the reasons, of course, was the dogged but undramatic resistance of civilian patriots. King George had sent thousands of his Regulars to America, hired thousands of Europe's most dreaded soldiers, and brought to his side thousands of Tory Americans anxious to show their military prowess, all for one purpose, to overawe and discourage Whigs and their revolutionary ideas. Yet even in the Hackensack valley, within easy reach of Britain's power, there were hundreds of men who had no thought of abandoning their Whiggish ideas, who instead spent all their waking hours plotting King George's destruction. Their neighbors by the dozen went off to Tory New York or made peace with the King's agents; all that they themselves had to do was to walk a few miles to find the same peace. No great patriot figures were there to deter them, and there were no Continental lines to pass, but they went on electing rebel legislatures and rebel judges as if they had been sovereign and independent since the time of William the Conqueror. More than self-interest moved these stubborn men; little wonder the frustrated British burned their courthouses and their homes.

[64] Captain James Christie, Lieutenant John Terhune and others were in action at the Battle of Monmouth during the British withdrawal, one of the few instances when Bergen County militiamen served outside the neutral ground. See Pension Records, W1010 (Cornelius P. Westervelt); W9849 (John Terhune); W16774 (Samuel Vervalen).

It may have been at this time that John Goelet of New Bridge was brought down by camp fever. (The family had moved to New Bridge from New York City "after the A.ia, Captain Parker, a British man-of-war, fired on the city," and he was drafted into the militia as a substitute for his father.) "There was another man from the same neighborhood," he wrote, "Hans [John or Johannes] Bogert, who was also sick. . . . There was also a man from the same neighborhood, who with his horse and cart had been pressed into service. . . . General Maxwell told this man that if he would take me and Bogert home, he would, on return of the cart, discharge the owner, horse and cart, and give him a certificate of impressment. . . . I started home, still sick, in the cart with the said Bogert. . . . In consequence of our having the camp fever we were not admitted into the houses, but at night the cart was rolled into a barn, and, a pitcher or can of water being set in the cart, we were left to sleep in the cart. . . . In the morning the driver of the cart remarked to me that Bogert was dead, which I found to be true, he having died some time during the night . . . I having been too sick to notice it." Goelet did not say so, but there is reason to think that he was so unnerved by his experience that he went into the British lines in the fall and never returned. Affidavit of John Goelet, Pension Records, R4084. (Goelet referred to himself in the third person in the original.)

"Good for nothing as these men may have been before the disturbances . . ." the Hessian Adjutant General Baurmeister wrote, "the Americans are bold, unyielding and fearless. . . . Though England has not lost the game so far, nevertheless she may lose everything." Baurmeister's estimate of patriots' standing before the war was based on Tory tales; his estimate of their fighting abilities was based on his own observations.

King George's representatives in America, had they been willing to listen, could have learned more about the rebellion from one John Fell, Peter Wilson, Hendrick Kuyper, Dirck Romeyn, Peter Zabriskie or Adam Boyd than from all the Tory refugees in New York. If London had fully understood any one of them, it might have saved itself millions of pounds sterling and two great armies. It might indeed have saved a continent.

Peter Wilson, to take one example, was a member of the New Jersey legislature throughout the war, an office he accepted at the bidding of men like himself who were willing to come to the polls at the risk of a rope around their necks or starvation in Sugar House. At one such election, with the British two miles away at New Bridge, seven Hackensack voters appeared, electing Wilson, John Outwater, and Isaac Blanch to the legislature, Peter Haring to the council, and Adam Boyd to the post of sheriff. Cynical friends may have inquired for the names of the other two voters.

Wilson, who had graduated from the University of Aberdeen with high honors, had turned down the flattering offers of civil employment that followed such a scholastic record and had come to America to become a schoolmaster, moved in good part by his contempt for the pretenses of Britain's aristocracy. He needed only to recall his home in Scotland, and his earnest old father standing in the cold rain, hat in hand, while the young laird of the manor carelessly amused himself with a light rattan cane, hat on and quite indifferent to the old man, to bring back all of his antipathy for the Old World and its ways.

Nor was his love of the old country renewed when by coincidence he came upon the young laird again during the war, though the particular meeting was more than fortunate for Wilson. Finding his home at Hackensack filled with marauding Scotch soldiers shouting their views of the damned rebels who owned it, he pleaded with them as Scotsmen to remember their upbringing and leave, particularly since they were endangering the life of his invalid wife. One of the officers, hearing the Scotch voice pleading so earnestly, came up and demanded Wilson's name.

Peter Wilson's Academy, Hackensack, built 1768.
Rus Anderson, 1962.

"What!" he said, "are ye Wilson's son, of Banff?" and identified himself as the laird. "I hope you are no rebel, but be that as it may, we'll make no more noise here," and he ordered the troops out of the house.

A leader in legislative affairs of no less stature than his compatriot John Witherspoon of Princeton, Wilson was one of the ablest scholars of the Revolutionary period. He is said to have refused the governorship of New Jersey on Livingston's retirement; he refused the presidency of Union College and some of the most distinguished pulpits in the Dutch Reformed church, and spent most of his years after the war as professor and sometime acting president of Columbia College. It has been said that the classical pre-eminence of that institution can be traced in some degree to Wilson's early work there. The Hackensack valley can be proud of the young schoolmaster from Banff, who deserves a place in history with the celebrated patriots of New England and Virginia.[65]

Wilson's great friend Adam Boyd, though less prominent, was another civilian patriot of Hackensack. Born in Mendham, New Jersey, on March 21, 1746, he moved to Hackensack a few years before the Revolution and built a substantial house on its main street, sometimes operating a stagecoach to the New York ferries. A zealous Whig, he was

65 HBP 183, etc.; Manuscript biography NJHS; Wilson Papers NJHS; Romeyn Papers UCL, NYPL; Matthews, History of Columbia University, New York (1904) 73, 81, 106; ERNY 4357, 4364, 4366, 4369.

elected sheriff of the county when it returned to patriot hands. It was he who ran the jail and fed the prisoners; it was he who hanged those whose offenses were capital. When American general officers needed spies to go down from Hackensack into the British lines, it was Sheriff Boyd who tried to supply them. He also found time to serve as an active officer of Captain Outwater's militia company.[66] We may be sure the British had no love for this plain six-foot Jerseyman who lived almost under their guns.

He went to his door late one night, to tell some noisy friends that they were disturbing his wife's sleep, only to find that the friends were Hessian troopers bent on breaking down his door. He escaped in his nightclothes through the top of the Dutch door at the rear of the house while the Hessians were vaulting the lower half of the similar door at the front. They proceeded to loot and burn the house, and for years after the war he kept in a prominent place in his rebuilt home the brass kettle which was the only possession the raiders left him. As time passed the story grew, until the trip in his nightgown extended to Paramus. Adam Boyd took a prominent part in politics during all of the early years of the republic; he too was a man of whom the Hackensack valley can be proud.[67]

Hendrick Kuyper was another stiff-necked Whig. He had large properties, and presumably his home, in the southern part of Bergen Township on the Hudson River.[68] He was a founder of Queens College.[69] He had often been a member of the Board of Freeholders before the war and he served throughout the war on the Board of Justices, probably then living at Hackensack. He lost two houses and thousands of pounds of property at the hands of the British; when the British carried off most of the able-bodied men of Hackensack in one raid, he was one of those who escaped and carried on its patriot government.[70] Kuyper would have been the first to say that there was nothing unusual about his losses. Dozens of patriot homes from New Barbadoes Neck to Closter were blackened shells, all testimonies to the patriot determination of the Hackensack valley.[71] Roelif Westervelt,[72] Joost Beam, Abraham

---

[66] Affidavit of David R. Bogert, Pension Records, W3502; affidavit of John Lozier, Pension Records, W20525. Congressional Biography, "Adam Boyd." MJFBC, passim.
[67] HBP 194; DAB; 31 NJA 181; MJFBC, passim; Wayne Papers HSP. His wife evidently escaped from the Hessians in a less spectacular way.
[68] Damages by the British NJSL, Hackensack Precinct.
[69] 25 NJA 343, 344, 345.
[70] MJFBC; HBP 79, 82; Kuyper to Stuart, March 22, 1780, GW Papers LC.
[71] HBP 108, 292 and passim; Damages by the British, NJSL passim.
[72] Roelif Westervelt, to take one of them, exemplified the Dutch Whig political leadership of the county, solid men, not rich in the sense that the Tory William Bayard or the Whig William Livingston was rich, but large landowners and leading

Ackerman, John Ryerson, Edo Marsellus, David Board, Lawrence Ackerman, Peter Haring, Garret Leydecker, Jacob Terhune, John Outwater, William Christie, David Banta, Jacob Zabriskie, David Terhune, Adrian Post, Daniel Haring, Isaac Blanch, Isaac Vanderbeek, David B. Demarest,[73] Martin Ryerson, William Nagel, John Dey, Harmanus Van Huysen, Andrew Hopper, Henry Meads, Garret Van Houten, Peter Demarest, Jacobus Demarest, John Kuyper, Albert Banta, John Benson, Garrabrant Van Houten, Thomas Blanch, Peter Bogert, John Terhune and Samuel Demarest were all men who risked their lives and property by openly serving as patriot officials in a no man's land between two armies.[74] It is hardly likely that they took the time to remark upon the irony of the fact that almost every one of their names had an exact counterpart among the Tories of the county. They had long since come to take it for granted that the Revolution in the Hackensack valley was a war of cousins when it was not a war of brothers.

---

men in the Dutch church and in politics for years before the Revolution, and descended from men who had been leaders in Jersey Dutch affairs for a century. Westervelt lived in Tenafly, a mile north of the Liberty Pole Tavern, on the road to Closter and Tappan, on a large farm, one-half of the tract patented by his father many years before (Bailey 326). He had been elected a member of the Board of Chosen Freeholders of Bergen County for many years before the war; at the outset of the war he and Abraham Van Buskirk had been named the two loan officers for the county (MJFBC 71, 75, 77, 79, 80, 82, 83, 91, 92, 98, 106, 108, 111, 112, 116, 120, 124) and for years during and after the war he continued to hold county office (idem, 126, 127, 128, 129, 132, 135, 143, 146, 151). He was often an officer of the Schraalenburgh (coetus) church, and when the war began he was an active patriot, he and John Fell being two of the men who seized Tories after the British withdrew from the county in the winter of 1776–77 (MCSNY 263). His son was the builder of the South Church in 1799. A grandson, the first child baptized in the new building, became mayor of New York City (Westervelt Genealogy).

73 Probably David Benjamin Demarest (Demarest Genealogy No. 117), a coetus adherent who owned a gristmill on Long Swamp Brook near the Schraalenburgh church.

74 HBP 82; MJFBC, passim. Theunis Dey was a member of the State Council from 1779 to and beyond 1781, Robert Morris having been a member of the Council before that. Peter Wilson, Isaac Blanch, Garret Leydecker, Joost Beam and John Outwater were among those who served in the Assembly. Votes and Proceedings of the General Assembly of New Jersey, passim.

O N C E the Philadelphia episode was closed, the British and American forces took up their old stations on either side of the Dutch neutral ground, the one on Manhattan and the other in the Highlands. For several days in early July, 1778, Washington made his headquarters at Paramus,[1] debating whether to hold his forces on the west side of the river, where the supply problem was easier, or to move over to Westchester, where he would be in better position to co-operate with his French allies in Rhode Island. He finally decided to cross the river and establish the American camp near White Plains. The decision gave little weight to the wishes of his staff, for the young officers had found Paramus an unusually suitable location for headquarters.

"After leaving the falls of the Passaic," wrote James McHenry, "we passed through a fertile country to a place called Paramus. We stopped at a Mrs. Watkins', whose house was marked for headquarters. But the General, receiving a note of invitation from a Mrs. Prevost to make her Hermitage, as it was called, the seat of his stay while at Paramus, we only dined with Mrs. Watkins and her two charming daughters, who sang us several pretty songs in a very agreeable manner." The wealthy Mrs. Prevost, wife of a British officer in the West Indies service, was hardly a zealous patriot, but she did not let politics keep her from entertaining distinguished guests who happened into the neighborhood, rebel or regular. She had many influential patriot friends, among them Colonel Aaron Burr (who, when she became a widow, made her his bride), and

[1]   12 GW 165–182.

General Arnold. Another was New Jersey's chief justice, Robert Morris, who had pleaded for leniency in applying the enemy property laws against her estate in light of Mrs. Prevost's help to patriots during the first British invasion.[2] "At Mrs. Prevost's we found some fair refugees from New York who were on a visit to the lady of the Hermitage. With them we talked and walked and laughed and danced and gallanted away the leisure hours of four days and four nights, and would have gallanted and danced and laughed and talked and walked with them till now had not the General given orders for our departure."[3]

On July 19, 1778, Washington ordered Colonel Van Schaick to move his regiment from the Clove to the neighborhood of Orangetown, keeping sufficiently to the west of the village to be sure that the enemy did not surprise him by coming suddenly upon him from the North River landings. At Orangetown he was to join with Captain Hopkins's fifty light horse stationed at Closter and patrol the country to the south in an effort to prevent supplies from going in to New York.[4] On the same day General Maxwell was ordered to the neighborhood of Hackensack, doubtless also in part to try to intercept traffic to New York, but in part to interpose his forces between the main army and a reported British move from Staten Island. Remembering his own concern when his army was in the same location, Washington's order warned Maxwell not to permit himself to be "hemmed in between the two rivers."[5]

A week or so later Colonel Moylan's American cavalry was in Hackensack, sending eighty horsemen as far south as Bergen and bringing back 300 cattle, 80 sheep, and other supplies. The people thereabouts, Moylan observed, "were taking every opportunity to supply the enemy."[6]

The British also came into the neutral ground in their turn. Domine Dirck Romeyn came down from New Paltz to be with his congregations for a time and to baptize children born since his last visit in May, but his ability to visit Schraalenburgh and Hackensack depended upon his lodging each night with a different militia guard,[7] where no Tory raiding party could find him and turn him in as a prisoner. Other patriots continued to sleep with muskets at their sides. Hardheaded Jersey Dutchmen understood clearly enough that the calm of summer and early fall did not mean that they had seen the last of the British army, that the

2   Draft letter Robert Morris to William Paterson, Sept. 4, 1777, RUL.
3   Steiner, Life and Correspondence of James McHenry, 21 etc. Headquarters were at Haverstraw from July 15 through July 18, 12 GW 182–191.
4   Tilghman to Van Schaik, July 19, 1778, GW Papers LC.
5   Tilghman to Maxwell, July 17, 1778, GW Papers LC. See 1 Kemble 155.
6   Moylan to Washington, July 29, 1778, GW Papers LC.
7   Romeyn Papers UCL.

British were only waiting, as they had waited in 1776 and 1777, to be sure that all the crops were harvested before they descended upon the farms along the Hackensack. There were undoubtedly all too many Dutchmen, of a pessimistic turn of mind, happy to warn their neighbors that when the British did invade the county they would, like the Midianites of old, come as grasshoppers for multitude and destroy the increase of the earth, leaving no sustenance for them, neither sheep, nor ox, nor ass, and the pessimists had only to wait for the end of September to see how right they were; indeed, the most pessimistic Dutchman in New Jersey could hardly have foreseen what a huge army was to descend upon Bergen County, an army as large as Burgoyne's, driving forward as if it intended to seize the entire Hudson valley, and at once. Patriots who had been resigned to another British foraging expedition now had every reason to believe that the long-awaited British offensive, the great final effort to cut off New England and end the war, had begun.

On the afternoon of September 22, 1778, British transports and flatboats began unloading thousands of troops at Paulus Hook. A regiment of dragoons immediately overran the American outpost at Liberty Pole, taking twenty-seven prisoners and killing several of the men. The outpost had been held by Captain Elias Romeyn's company of Bergen County militia and a detachment of southern troops under command of a Lieutenant Hayes. Warned by the attack on their picket, the main body of the Americans at New Bridge withdrew to Paramus.[8]

One full regiment of British troops pushed forward quickly almost as far as Liberty Pole. By nightfall of the 23rd, a cold rainy day, five thousand British Regulars encamped themselves along New Bridge Road, between Liberty Pole and the bridge.[9] Lord Cornwallis set up headquarters on Schraalenburgh Road at the junction of New Bridge Road, and Lord Rawdon's Volunteers of Ireland were on the lower ground to the west between the light infantry and the Long Swamp Brook. Other regiments were stationed to the east from Schraalenburgh Road to a point almost at the edge of the Palisades, and earthworks

[8] Affidavits of John House, Pension Records, S1022; John A. Haring, Pension Records, S6980; John G. Ryerson, S1099; Samuel Vervalen, W16774. The men had been "quartered on the inhabitants and fed as they could get it." Affidavit of John A. Haring, supra. "After fighting until many on both sides was killed and wounded, we were overpowered and I having received a severe cut with a saber on the head, being badly wounded, was taken prisoner and with others was taken to New York, where I remained a prisoner for nearly three months." Affidavit of Samuel Vervalen, supra. Robertson Diary 182.
[9] 2 André Journal 45, 46. The troops spent the rainy night without provisions, which were sent by mistake to Paulus Hook and not to Bourdet's Landing. Cornwallis to Clinton, 7 P.M., Sept. 23, 1778, HC Papers CL.

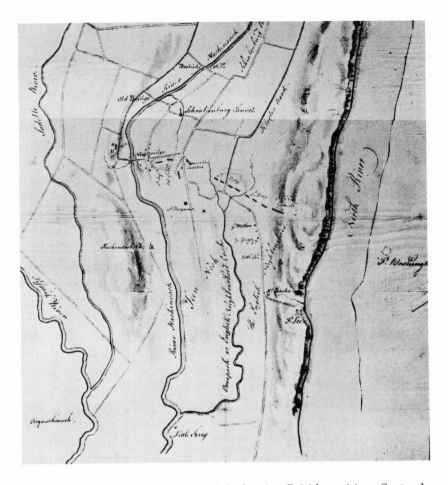

Portion of map drawn by John André, showing British positions September 23–27, 1778, in Schraalenburgh, Teaneck and the English Neighborhood.
André Journal.

were thrown up at Tenafly and on Brouwer's Hill at New Bridge.[10] "I have sent out people to inquire about militia, cattle, &c., and will do the best I can to get at one or the other," Cornwallis reported at 11 A.M. on September 25, adding that "there are certainly not above two hundred men of the Continental army in this part of the country." [11]

[10] 2 André Journal 45, 46, map opp. p. 46; See Baylor to Washington, Sept. 24, 1778, Sept. 26, 1778, GW Papers LC; Robertson Diary 182; Baurmeister 218. On the next day a comparable movement was made into lower Westchester. Baurmeister 217.
[11] Cornwallis to Clinton, Sept. 25, 1778, HC Papers CL.

Tory New York, which had been complaining bitterly about Sir Henry's inactivity, now saw his inaction as a piece of masterly strategy, hiding from the Americans, as he had hidden from his friends, his preparations for throwing his whole army into Jersey for a drive to the north. When he first put 5,000 men ashore at Paulus Hook, New York was elated; when, three days later, Sir Henry himself boarded a barge in the Hudson and was rowed off to the north, Tory hopes rose even higher. "The general opinion is now," Judge William Smith wrote in his journal, "that the colony is to be occupied to Albany." He too marveled that Sir Henry had been able to keep such important plans to himself, the force in the field being rumored at 16,000 men. "The campaign began," Smith observed, "with so little preparation that most people imagined till now that the object was merely to gain forage. . . . If Sir H. Clinton meant to press on to Albany it is what he had kept a profound secret from everybody. He rather discountenanced the affair by supposing the Highland forts more formidable than I thought them, and yet I recollect his mentioning the defile about Clove as a good pass." [12]

Judge Smith had more than a spectator's interest in Clinton's offensive: he had been working hopefully for weeks with three parliamentary commissioners on a manifesto offering Americans pardon for their rebellion and holding out the olive branch of an easy peace. "The present object," Smith was convinced, "is a union only of forces under one sovereign. America may have what else she pleases." [13] He had himself once been a zealous Whig, he could see no reason why other Americans would not accept such a peace. There was little point, however, in making any offer until Britain had gained some military advantage; an offer of peace after the unhappy withdrawal from Philadelphia and an idle summer would only make her contemptible. Seizure of the Hudson would be exactly what was needed to back up the manifesto and end the war.

General Washington, who was at Fredericksburgh in the Highlands on the east side of the Hudson, ordered troops shifted to meet the threat. "The design of these movements," he wrote to General Lord Stirling as soon as he received word of them, "is probably a forage and the gathering of stock, etc., [but]," he warned, "it may also be something else." [14] He urged Stirling to put his troops on the west side of the river in a firm posture of defense, emphasizing that the Highland forts

12 Smith Journal NYPL.
13 Smith Journal NYPL.
14 12 GW 493.

View of Hackensack, circa 1800.

New York from Hobuck Ferry House, New Jersey. Engraving after Alexander Robertson.

Captain John Hopper and his wife Mary. The British burned and destroyed "two dwelling houses, one store house and one grist mill" of Captain Hopper, who "lost all his private property contained in the buildings." He "escaped at the time with the loss of his hat." For years after the war he operated Hopper's Tavern, under the sign of Thomas Jefferson, in Hopperstown. Mrs. Hopper "attributed the loss" of her husband's property "mainly and altogether that the buildings destroyed were used and occupied by the American troops and arms."

Peter Wilson, LL.D.,
1746–1825

Peter Wilson, founder of a flourishing academy at Hackensack in 1767, became a patriot leader in the State Legislature during the war and was later for many years professor of Greek and Latin at Columbia College.

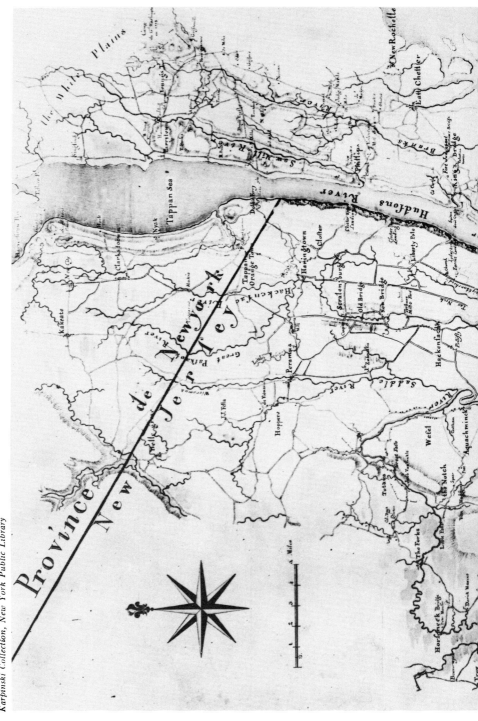

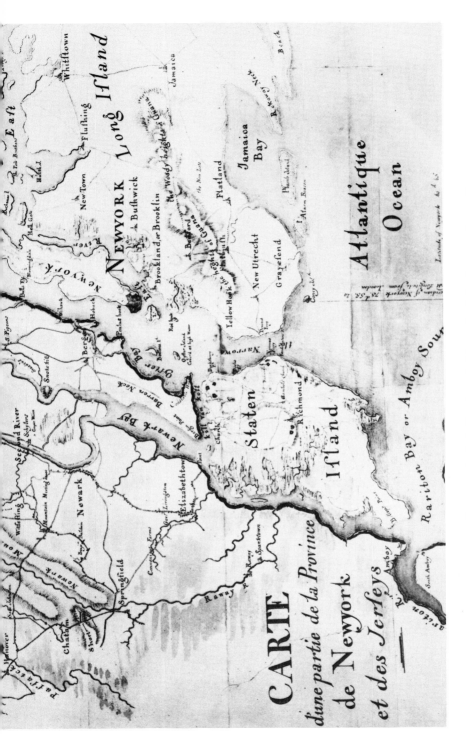

Carte d'une partie de la Province de Newyork et des Jerseys, circa 1781.

House of Captain John Terhune, built circa 1709–1729, Hackensack. Terhune served both as a militia officer and as a patriot official of the county.

With quaint gambrel roofs, wide overhanging eaves and broad flat walls of brown stone, the early architecture found in New Jersey, particularly on the banks of the Hackensack River, stands apart from all other early American domestic architecture.

The Dutch in northern New Jersey clung very closely to a set type of plan and design; the characteristic feature was the enormous overhang and sweep of the eaves. There was a faithful adherence to tradition as to lines and roof pitches: the steeper slope being slightly less than forty-five degrees and the top slope ranging from twenty to twenty-three degrees and usually quite short.

The stone, which was originally laid in ordinary clay taken from the surrounding fields and mixed with straw, is usually called brown stone, and is to be found in great profusion throughout New Jersey. *See Clifford C. Wendenhack, Early Dutch Houses of New Jersey. The White Pine Series of Architectural Monographs, Volume XI, Number 3.*

Van Dyke

Grave of Peter S. Van Orden in Christian Reformed Church cemetery at Monsey, New York. Van Orden, an orphan, became a soldier at fourteen and served in many engagements in the neutral ground. The stone reads ". . . He loved his country and adhered to her cause in the darkest days of her struggles against oppression from British tyranny."

J. Spencer Newman, *Courtesy of the Bergen County Historical Society*

House of John Zabriskie, New Bridge. Built by John Zabriskie, Sr., probably in the 1730's, as a residence and store, the site became an important shipping point for the New Jersey iron trade. The elder Zabriskie was a leading merchant of the time.

House of Frederick Blauvelt, Tappan. Built by Daniel de Clerck in 1700. Headquarters of General Washington on several occasions.

Van Dyke

"View of Tapan, or Orange Town taken 28th Septr. 1778 and finished 15th June 1780 on board the Littledale Transport on the Passage from Charles Town to New York. A. R."

which were menaced by the huge British force were of infinite importance to the American cause.

Washington, as often before, proved right, and Smith, as often before, wrong. Clinton's carefully planned maneuver was nothing but a general forage, enlivened by a plan to envelop the whole Hackensack valley and take up any troops caught in the pincers, and by the hope that if Washington was "tempted to quit his mountains to interrupt our foraging in the Jerseys, I had a good chance of having a fair stroke at him, the probability being great that by such a move he must have risked a general action." [15] It had the additional advantage, Clinton felt, of favoring the operations of a corps under Captain Patrick Ferguson "to destroy a nest of privateers at Egg Harbor, which had done us a great deal of mischief." [16]

Washington had been as much at a loss to guess what Sir Henry's earlier inactivity meant as had Tory New York, and he had been trying desperately for months to get enough authentic intelligence out of New York to anticipate the next British move. Like the Tories, he had had no hint that any large movement into Jersey was planned; in fact when the British marched in they almost overran his unsuspecting intelligence officer in the Hackensack valley,[17] a man who was to have a dramatic part in the happenings of the next few days.

All during the late summer Washington had kept Major Alexander Clough, his chief of intelligence on the west side of the Hudson, stationed at New Bridge, a place from which he could intercept and question every traveler who had been in New York City, and, even more important, a place from which he could send spies of his own into the city. As a cover for his espionage, Clough had with him a regiment of American light horse, the regiment of Colonel George Baylor, who was the wealthy son of an old friend of General Washington and a fellow Virginia planter.[18] Clough was in constant friction with the Bergen County militia and the civil authorities from the day he arrived in New

[15] Clinton to Germain, Oct. 8, 1778, HC Papers CL. Clinton knew that if Washington came into the neutral ground to oppose him, "he must for that purpose have met me in an angle between the mountains and the river, on terms replete with risk on his part and little or none on mine." Clinton, American Rebellion, 122, 123.

[16] Clinton to Germain, Oct. 8, 1778, HC Papers CL; Clinton, American Rebellion, 104, 105.

[17] The British passed New Bridge without taking "the smallest notice of us," Baylor reported. Baylor to Washington, Sept. 24, 1778, GW Papers LC.

[18] 12 GW 480. See 7 GW 413. He had been the officer honored with the task of carrying the dispatches from the Battle of Trenton to Congress, and his light horse had had a prominent part in all of Washington's maneuvers. See 4 Freeman 359, 391, 463, 489.

Bridge. Unable to explain his secret mission and making little effort to hide an amused contempt for Jersey Dutchmen, Clough wasted little time in listening to local patriots who demurred at the traffic with Tories. Washington himself understood clearly enough that intelligence officers were "often obliged to make use of ambiguous characters as the vehicles, and to permit them to carry on some traffic, both as an encouragement and a cover to their mission," but all that patriots knew was that Clough was consorting with their enemies and permitting an intercourse with the city which they had been trying for years to stop.

Clough was under Washington's specific orders to send intelligent local people into New York with a memorized list of questions and to forward the answers to headquarters where they could be evaluated in light of other reports. "If the person that goes in cannot make an excuse of business," Washington directed, "he must be allowed to carry a small matter of provisions, and bring something out by way of pretext." [19] Since no known patriot of the region could risk such a trip, Clough had to use men of dubious politics whose interest was money, men whom the militia guards would seize at once as double-dealers, and Washington himself finally had to direct the militia to stop,[20] probably leaving the local people to believe that Clough was twice guilty, first of deceiving Washington and second of trading with the enemy.

At another time Clough almost came to blows with Sheriff Boyd and two regiments of Bergen County militia.

"The major of Colonel Baylor's Regiment, named Clough, commanded in the absence of Colonel Baylor," a local militiaman wrote after the war. "The quartermaster of the regiment pressed a quantity of grain at the house of a farmer named Berry for the use of the regiment and Berry took out a writ for the quartermaster and Clough refused leave to the sheriff to execute the writ. The sheriff called out the posse, when the regiment of militia assembled and our company were also assembled to assist the sheriff. But good men in the place interfered and the major allowed the writ to be served." [21] It is most unlikely, considering the events of the next two weeks, that the case ever came to trial.

[19]   12 GW 355, 356. The British were not blind to the ruse, but could not stop all traffic to stop the intelligence. Pattison 228.
[20]   Washington's letter read: "To the officer commanding the militia at Hackensack New Bridge: Major Clough, who commands at Hackensack, is under the necessity of sometimes allowing persons to carry small matters into New York, and to bring a few goods out, that he may the better obtain intelligence. The persons employed in that way are sometimes stopped by your guards, under suspicion that they are carrying on a contraband trade. You will therefore be pleased to give orders to your officers not to detain or molest any person showing a pass from Major Clough." 12 GW 417. See Baylor to Washington, Sept. 22, 1780, GW Papers LC.
[21]   Affidavit of David R. Bogert, Pension Records, W3502.

Hackensack patriots must have breathed a small sigh of relief, then, when Clough and the Lady Washington's Guards mounted their horses and rode off to the north, though their relief was certainly tempered when they found that several thousand British Regulars had decided to encamp at the same place.

Dutch patriots may not have known that Alexander Clough was an intelligence officer, but it was not long before Dutch Tories learned that the British had brought with them General Grey's chief of intelligence. When they came to camp, whether they brought word of the location of American troops or of patriot barns, the officer who heard them was an urbane young man of twenty-six years, of slight build and medium height, who made it his business to be as charming to Dutch country-men as if he had met them in a London drawing room, as polite to Dutch Tories, in fact, as Clough had been rude to Dutch patriots, the brilliant, smiling young officer, Captain John André. Patiently listening to their reports, however long, carefully noting what they had to say in his books, never hinting by so much as a raised eyebrow whether word of the forts at Smith's Clove was more important to him than informa-tion about a barn full of grain, he would smile blandly at any Dutchman who was so forward as to say that he hoped Sir Henry would succeed in his drive on Albany.

Clough had hardly been able to conceal his smiles at the Dutch accents of patriot farmers; it is easy to imagine the amazement and delight of Dutch Tories when the young British captain interrupted their stories about Major Clough with the observation that Clough was "een verv-lockte schurick," and told them to go on in plain Dutch.[22] Major Clough could hardly have been expected to compete with John André as a linguist; it would have been well for him if he had at least come to recognize Dutch Tories and Dutch patriots while he was in the neutral ground. His blindness about Dutchmen may have cost him his life.

From the American lines at Paramus Colonel Baylor watched the British as best he could. Major Clough's light horsemen, sent back to the south to scout out Sir Henry's forces, found that entrenchments had been thrown across the road leading from Tappan to Liberty Pole and that there were other entrenchments "near the Schraalenburgh meeting house, two and one-half miles from New Bridge," adding the somewhat disturbing intelligence that "from all reports they are collect-ing no more provisions than they can use."[23]

22 Cf. Flexner 22.
23 Baylor to Washington, Sept. 26, 1778, GW Papers LC. "The enemy have seven-teen field pieces at Liberty Pole. They daily receive reinforcements from New York and have part of their army near the New Bridge. This intelligence . . . we have from

The British patrols, for their part, had met "many militia, both mounted and dismounted, who had been sent hither and yon to urge the country people to remove their cattle, grain and forage. . . . Contrary to expectations, General Cornwallis found an abundance of provisions." [24] It is hardly necessary to say that the country people whose provisions Cornwallis carried off were not as impersonal about them as the British general. Nicausie Brinkerhoff had "two rooms of his house much damaged, the glass windows broke and the wall at one end pulled down," Joost Zabriskie, of Hackensack Precinct, was severely wounded by the soldiers, doubtless in trying to protect his property, Matthew Bogert lost all his cattle; Aury Auryansen, Jacob Wortendyke, Effye Cole, Maritie Tallman, Garret Durie, David Campbell, Jacob Cole, Thomas Blanch, Thomas Campbell, Isaac Ver Valen, William Ellsworth, Philip Marra, Cornelius Hoghlan, Johannes Terhune, Albert Terhune, John Demarest, William Christie, Abraham Brouwer, and Samuel Ver Bryck, to mention but a few who left written records of the British depredations, lost property having a value, in modern terms, of hundreds of thousands of dollars in those few weeks.[25] "It gives me pain to report the distress the late movements of the enemy into Jersey have occasioned," Richard Varick wrote from Hackensack on October 30. "Numbers of families are left destitute of not only every comfort and convenience but every necessary of life." Though his own family, he said, had in some measure escaped the worst of their fury, their loss was not inconsiderable, including a slave, all of their poultry and their kitchen furniture.[26]

Early Sunday night, September 27, 1778, the British started to move to the north. Four regiments under General Charles Grey (the 2nd Light Infantry, the 2nd Grenadiers, the 33rd and 64th Regiments, and fifty

---

a creditable woman who has been among the enemy, she has seen the above number of field pieces." John Haring and Gilbert Cooper to Clinton, Sept. 25, 1778, 4 GC 86, 87. Rev. James Caldwell reported to General Greene that a small flotilla had passed through Newark Bay to supply them on the morning of the 27th. "They have in their power near one-half of Bergen County, that half which have traded with them and supplies them rather than sell to us. Their operations have something of the appearance of opening a campaign up the North River." Caldwell to an officer, Sept. 27, 1778, Greene Papers, American Philosophical Society Library.

[24] Baurmeister 218. The Americans evidently at one time made a threat against the British defenses on Brouwer's Hill, above New Bridge, but withdrew under artillery fire. Affidavit of Abraham D. Banta, Pension Records, S6575. See André Journal 45.

[25] Damages by British NJSL, passim.

[26] Varick to Van Rensselaer, Oct. 30, 1778, NYHS.

dragoons) formed near the New Bridge and marched up Kinderkamack Road, just west of the Hackensack River, toward Tappan.[27]

With the marching columns were a dozen or more local Tories, Wiert Banta, Dr. James Van Buren and Peter Ackerman among them.[28] Two hours later, the regiments under Lord Cornwallis, the 1st Grenadiers, the guards, and the 42nd and 37th, set off up Closter Road, two or three miles to the east, while by prearrangement with New York headquarters, the Rangers, Emerich's Corps, and the 71st Regiment were to be put ashore at Tappan Landing at daybreak on the next morning, to move toward Tappan from the Hudson River in a three-pronged assault of major proportions.[29] General Grey had a brilliant military record, he gloried in the name of No-flint Grey, which he had earned by descending on an encampment of Wayne's troops near Paoli, Pennsylvania, and destroying them without a shot.

Earlier in the same evening Colonel Baylor had set off to move the American light horse nearer Tappan, probably as a precaution against an attack from the south. At about twilight they came to the bridge at Old Tappan, where the road from Paramus crosses the Hackensack, a few miles southwest of Tappan village, and there Colonel Baylor decided to halt for the night.[30]

Just west of the river, on a little hill looking down over the bridge, stood the stone farmhouse of Cornelius Abraham Haring, with a Dutch barn, tan house, and other outbuildings nearby.[31] Plainly there could be no better place for miles around for Baylor to quarter his 12 officers and 140 dragoons. Haring's son Ralph, who opened the door—no more pleased than the necessities of the case required—told Baylor that he understood that the British were at New Bridge and might at any moment move to the north,[32] for which he got no more thanks than

[27]   2 André Journal 46; Robertson Diary 183.
[28]   LYT NYPL, "Banta," "Van Buren," "Ackerman."
[29]   André Journal 46, 47.
[30]   Stryker, Massacre near Old Tappan. HBP 56, etc. It has been suggested that Baylor halted to avoid putting himself under the command of General Wayne at Tappan. There were in fact no other Continentals within many miles of Tappan. Wayne appears to have been in Westchester or nearby Connecticut. Wayne Papers HSP. Lt. Col. Gilbert Cooper to Maj. Gen'l. Putnam, September 26, 1776, GW Papers LC. It seems possible that the mistake originated from the belief that a letter of General Washington to Wayne, written October 27, 1779, was misdated. The 1779 letter ordered Wayne, then at Haverstraw, to attach Baylor's corps to his own. 17 GW 34. See also Cornwallis to Clinton, September 25, 1778, HC Papers CL.
[31]   HBP 57. The Pascack Historical Society has a copy of the royal grant to the Harings.
[32]   HBP 57.

might have been expected from an officer who understood clearly enough that Haring would have preferred to see him quarter himself somewhere else. The Harings had cause to remember and tell of Ralph's warnings later, and to blame Colonel Baylor for ignoring them, but Baylor knew far more about the British positions than Ralph Haring and could hardly have been expected to be effusive in thanking the young Dutchman for urging him to move on. After seeing to the disposition of his men in the outbuildings and nearby farms, Baylor posted a sergeant's guard of twelve men at the bridge over the Hackensack, with strict orders to keep a patrol on each road a mile below the bridge. He ordered

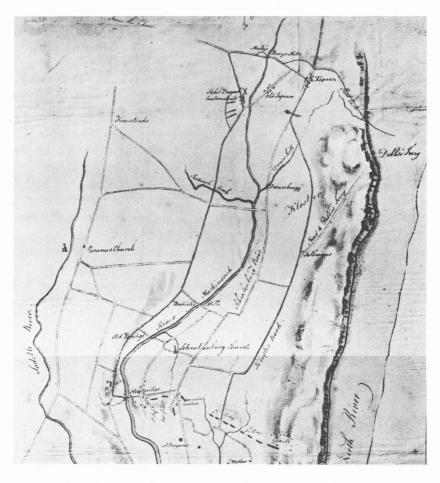

Portion of map drawn by John André showing British attack on "Rebel Dragoon's Cantonments" at Old Tappan, September 28, 1778.
André Journal.

the patrol to be relieved every hour and retired early in fancied security.[33] Situated as he was almost in the shadow of the Highlands, hardly more exposed than the many other American troops who had camped in and about Tappan, there seemed to be no reason for panic over the fact that the British forces were ten miles away.

Even the self-confident Colonel Baylor might have been considerably more concerned if he had known that his unwilling host was regarded in the neighborhood as a notorious Tory[34] and that another Tory had started off to the British lines with word of his arrival almost as soon as he knocked on the door of Haring's house. Tradition has it that an ingenious loyalist drove a herd of cows down the Overkill Road in front of Haring's, observing the American positions minutely as he trudged slowly behind the cattle, passing the picket guard as a simple cowherd and waiting only until he was out of sight to abandon the cattle in a nearby field and dash off madly toward British headquarters at New Bridge.[35] The difficulty of planning this maneuver between the time that Baylor arrived, almost at nightfall, and the hour when it would have been too dark to see the American positions or to drive the cattle without suspicion casts some doubt on the tradition; indeed one can hardly escape noticing the strong possibility that the Harings themselves may have had a hand in sending off the word to the British.

Abraham Mabie, a close family friend of the Harings, was an active British spy. There is no scrap of evidence today that the Harings or Mabie were ever accused of a guilty part in the massacre, but both apparently had the opportunity and the inclination.

In any case, whoever the enterprising Tory was, whether a messenger of Cornelius Haring or someone else in the neighborhood acting on his

---

[33] Stryker, Massacre near Old Tappan. HBP 57.

[34] MCSNJ 112. Haring had been arrested and imprisoned at the outset of the war as a dangerous Tory, although afterwards released. (MCSNJ 112.) Less than a year before, a party of militiamen under Lieutenant Resolvert Van Houten had pursued three Refugees who were stealing horses two miles west of Dwars Brook "as far as the dwelling house of one Cornelius Haring, when they all made their escape except one man who they found in the house of Haring under a bed." Though the thieves may have chosen Haring's place for a refuge by chance, it would have been hard to convince Van Houten that they had. (Affidavits of Abraham P. Blauvelt and Resolvert Van Houten, Pension Records, S22654.) Haring was a leader—one of the founders, in fact—of the conferentie schism in the Tappan Dutch Reformed church. Cole, Tappan Church 53. The son Ralph also was a conferentie adherent. See Blauvelt Genealogy No. 225.

[35] Haring acted as the witness to the baptism of a brother of Abraham P. Mabie, evidence among the Jersey Dutch of the closest family friendship. See Tappan Church Records, Cole, Rockland County. Mabie was a British agent. André, Intelligence, HC Papers CL.

own initiative, he must have been overjoyed when, instead of a hazardous ten-mile journey by night to New Bridge, he found that he had to go but a few miles below Haring's farm to meet General Grey's British forces marching north toward him, and with them the head of Grey's intelligence service.[36] The timing was, of course, an even greater stroke of luck for General Grey, and he moved decisively, marching the whole of his forces up to a point about a mile south of Haring's and detaching six companies of light infantry to spread around Haring's houses and barns, while the rest of his troops, after a little halt, marched directly up the road toward Baylor's pickets.[37]

Just before two o'clock in the morning, the main force drove in the pickets, while the light infantry fell on the house from the sides and rear.[38] Bursting in with shouts of "No quarter to rebels," they bayoneted and clubbed the defenseless inmates. Colonel Baylor and Major Clough tried to conceal themselves up the huge Dutch fireplace in the house, but were discovered and brought down severely wounded, Major Clough with bayonet wounds that were soon to prove fatal. The orders were to kill them all and take no prisoners, though many of the junior officers refused to carry out so bloodthirsty a command. Out of one hundred twenty, fifty were killed, the British reported.[39] Some of the defenseless troopers who had been sleeping under the buckwheat hay in the loft of Haring's barn tried to escape by hiding under the hay. They were bayoneted without mercy until blood flowed through the cracks in the floor to the ground below. The fifth troop, in another barn, were first offered quarters, and then ordered killed after they had surrendered themselves.

Some of the men who were left for dead survived, among them Thomas Talley and George Wyllis. When Talley found that the barn in which he was quartered was surrounded, "he got up and put on his clothes and went to the barn door and asked the enemy for quarter; upon which they told him to come on and he should not be hurt." When he came up to them, "they pulled off his breeches, and took from him his money, and silver stock and knee buckles . . . They then sent to one of their officers at a neighboring house to know what was to be done with the prisoners . . . In a few minutes thereafter, word was brought that the officer ordered all the prisoners to be killed; upon which. . . . [he] . . . was ordered into the . . . barn, and had no

---

[36] 2 André Journal 47, 48.
[37] 2 André Journal 47; Robertson Diary 183.
[38] 2 André Journal 47; Robertson Diary 183. André fixed the hour as three in the morning. Ibid.
[39] 1 Kemble 162, 163, which includes other details. See Stryker, Massacre near Old Tappan.

sooner entered the barn than they struck him with three bayonets about the breast, upon which he dropped on the ground, and afterwards found that he had received three more wounds in the back, of which he was then insensible . . . The enemy held a candle to his face to discover, as he believes, whether he was dead, and he supposes left him, taking him to be dead or expiring." Wyllis had surrendered at the same time. When "the man returned and hallowed at the barn door that the captain said they must kill them all, he immediately received two wounds with a bayonet in his breast, and on turning about to the other door, he received two more in his back, and they continued stabbing him until he received twelve wounds . . . After he had fallen with his wounds, they stripped him, and . . . left him for dead, with two more of the said troops who lay near him." Some of the troops, many of them wounded, escaped into the nearby woods in the confusion.[40]

A British detachment under General Charles Grey surprised and destroyed a regiment of Virginia Light Horse at Old Tappan, September 28, 1778.
E. Tone, 1961.

The melancholy aftermath fell to the lot of the local militia. John Haring, whose company had retreated to Paramus when the British drove them from New Bridge, recalled later that "one morning about daylight word was brought that the British had murdered the Light

[40] 7 Remembrancer 297; Thacher 150, 151. See NJA (2) 457, 458, 463, 484; Carrington 459.

Horse under the command of Colonel Baylor; that [he] was detailed among others to bury the murdered men." [41]

Their merciless work done at Haring's, the British took up Baylor's seventy horses, all of his arms and those Americans they had spared as prisoners, and marched on to the north to the Kakiat Road, where they turned to the right, crossing the Hackensack River at Perry's Mills, and thence to Tappan. [42]

The light infantry, on approaching the village, was again detached to the left, in the hope of surrounding any Americans who might be there, but, warned of the British movement by two deserters, Colonel Hay's militiamen had escaped an hour or two before into the Highlands. [43] Hay's men had marched down into New Jersey two or three miles on the first alarm, but soon found to their sorrow, as he wrote later, "that we had not one twentieth part of strength enough" to oppose the British. [44]

They were fortunate indeed to have withdrawn, for they were the targets of the water-borne troop movement which had been timed to coincide with the land attack. "The 71st Regiment under the command of Colonel Campbell, as well as Colonel Simcoe, embarked on twenty-five flatboats at Phillipse's house and let themselves be carried by the tide to the mouth of Tappan Creek on the Jersey shore. Colonel Campbell landed his troops on the left of the creek and marched by a short roundabout route as far as Harrington." Colonel Campbell was, however, discovered and most of the four hundred militia between Old Tappan and Harrington escaped. [45]

One party of militia, ordered out under Captain Crane to scout the neutral ground, was not so fortunate. It received no warning of the approach of the British and was cut off. This detachment, one of the men wrote, "after scouting some time at different places, marched on their return . . . as far as the barn of a person named Hogenkamp, when, worn out with fatigue, laid all night in the barn, which was but a few miles south of the place of the massacre. . . . The company slept quietly until morning when they were alarmed and informed that the British were above them. Captain Crane immediately paraded his men and marched upon an eminence, and . . . discovered that the British had surrounded them, and gave orders for every man to make his escape, when part of the company were killed or wounded . . . among those

---

[41] Affidavit of John A. Haring, Pension Records, S6980.
[42] 2 André Journal 48.
[43] 2 André Journal 48; Robertson Diary 183.
[44] 4 GC 158, 159.
[45] Clinton to Germain, Oct. 8, 1778, HC Papers CL; Baurmeister 220.

that were killed were . . . John Burges and Jacob Archer, and . . . Lieutenant Blauvelt was among the wounded." Blauvelt told American authorities later that when he found that he was surrounded by a vastly superior force, he had "offered to surrender himself, but that instead of quarters, he was instantly fired upon and wounded in the thigh, and afterwards stabbed in the breast with a bayonet, and left for dead . . . He heard the British officers and soldiers swear that they would give quarters to no militiaman." [46]

The British turned the little Dutch church on the Tappan green into a hospital and prison, and there Major Clough died.[47] If Captain André could have known what that church was to hold in store for him, he would have turned from it in horror; had he looked to the west with the power of prophecy, he would have seen on the little hill just south of the Kakiat Road a sight even more horrible.

[46] Affidavit of James Quackenbush, Pension Records, S15200; 7 Remembrancer 298.
[47] HBP 58.

10

THE Tappan raid over, Sir Henry Clinton left Grey and Cornwallis and the army and went back to headquarters, thoroughly pleased at the success of his night attack.[1] There were others with a longer view who were not impressed. "Last Sunday night," Judge Smith wrote after he had talked to Clinton, "General Grey cut off Washington's Guards near Orangetown. They were in barns and asleep. 90 were put to the bayonet, 40 wounded, 30 escaped—all the rest with their accoutrements taken." [2]

If this was less than enthusiastic, after his great hopes for a Hudson River offensive, a day or two later Smith's hopes had vanished entirely. "I am now convinced this campaign will produce nothing of consequence. . . . I hear the troops are retiring from New Jersey. . . . It will confirm the tale that they were only a foraging party, propagated by Washington to conceal his weakness. . . . Now malapropos the manifesto!" [3]

Unseasonable indeed, the manifesto! After its careful preparation, its publication in both Dutch and English,[4] the few copies that found their way into American hands were treated with derision. Lord Stirling

---

[1] "I had the satisfaction," Clinton wrote, "to find that the move had not proved altogether fruitless, Lord Cornwallis having . . . surprised and carried off almost an entire regiment of the enemy's light cavalry and a few militia." Clinton, American Rebellion, 105.
[2] Smith Journal NYPL.
[3] Smith Journal NYPL.
[4] Smith Journal NYPL.

called it "the last effort of the expiring tyranny of Great Britain"; it is doubtful if a single patriot in Jersey did more than glance at it. Smith expected little more: Clinton's footless strategy had ruined his plans, and the troops who, Smith noted, had "plundered as usual and made enemies of friends in Jersey," had only made matters worse.[5]

Judge Smith was right in expecting little from patriots in the circumstances, but he was profoundly wrong in thinking that Tories in Jersey were outraged at British plundering. They had not been won to the British cause by its justice; they were not to be lost to it by its excesses. In point of fact Smith soon found that the expedition into the Hackensack valley, however disappointing in other ways, had at least brought in large numbers of newly avowed Tories.

Grey and Cornwallis kept their troops at Tappan for a week or more, stripping the countryside of all the cattle and produce within reach, to the great distress of the feeble patriot militia, who could, of course, do nothing whatever to stop the depredations.[6]

Their urgent pleas for Continental troops had produced no results. On the day before the massacre, Lieutenant Colonel Gilbert Cooper, commanding the militia at Harrington, had written to General Putnam at Peekskill that "the men under my command begin to be much disheartened that no Continental troops come to their assistance," pointing out that the British force appeared to be about six thousand men, who were hourly expected to move to the north, "which can be prevented if your honour sends speedy relief." "As we make no doubt you must be sensible . . . three or four hundred militia cannot stop the progress of such an enemy. . . . If you have any regard for the sons of liberty in this quarter . . . send us relief as quick as possible to prevent this plentiful country from being despoiled." [7]

The militia of Bergen and southern Orange had been kept in continuous service since the first British entry into New Jersey. "Many of them," Colonel A. Hawkes Hay reported, "have not sown any winter grain this season, and none have cut their buckwheat, which is now spoiling." [8]

---

5 Smith Journal NYPL. Clinton, ignoring his own part in the failure, blamed it on "the strong appearances which our present [political] measures bore of imbecility on the side of Great Britain." Clinton, American Rebellion, 112.

6 4 GC 169, 171; 1 Kemble 163; 2 André Journal 48; Robertson Diary 183, 184.

7 Cooper to Putnam, Sept. 26, 1778, GW Papers LC; see also Cooper's letter to Smith (4 GC 86, 87). "Unless [the general officers] send us relief they will not have occasion to send or give any, as it is not worth while for us to think of maintaining our ground much longer."

A council of war was held on the subject, but no troops were sent across the river. 12 GW 522.

8 4 GC 158, 159.

After the British raid on Tappan more than a hundred local people sent off a petition to Governor George Clinton pleading for state assistance. "The enemy," they wrote, ". . . are now extending their ravages into this state, and on Monday the 29th ulto. made their appearance at Tappan with a large body commanded by Cornwallis in person, and after butchering in a most inhuman manner a number of Light Horse, they turned their cruelties to women and old men, whom they treated with every kind of brutality their perfidiousness could invent." [9] Surely the good people of Tappan had reason to petition for help; they suffered under almost every frustration that patriots could imagine: they had seen a Continental officer blindly quarter his men in the barns of a man they knew to be a British sympathizer; they had listened angrily to the groundless rumors, spread by Continentals, that the reason for Baylor's massacre was the failure of militia guards; they had themselves been called out in the night to resist another overwhelming force of British and Hessian troops coming up from the southeast under the command of Lord Cornwallis; they had seen the British encamp themselves in Tappan in utter contempt of the American army and proceed to strip the country of every trace of grain and forage that they had stored for the winter. "Knowing the small number of our whole force," they pleaded, "we have every reason to expect we must, unless immediately relieved, fall a sacrifice to the enemy. We have every reason to believe that no aid will be afforded from the Continental army." [10] One of the signers, Abraham Blauvelt, had particular reason to join in the petition. He had been shot through the thigh and bayoneted through the chest on September 29.[11]

However poorly the local Dutchmen thought of their plunderers, the British for their part were charmed by the rich countryside and the quaint little Dutch town in which they found themselves. Archibald Robertson, one of Sir Henry's engineers, climbed the road to the west of town and sketched his "View of Tapan or Orangetown taken the 28th day of September, 1778." [12] The one-story Dutch church, with its high peaked roof and steeple, stands out prominently, and if one looks closely he can see Casparus Mabie's tavern and the other houses along the Schraalenburgh Road as they appeared in that day. Two years later, almost to the day, the small eminence on which Robertson made his sketch, and the church and tavern too, were to find themselves identi-

[9]   4 GC 169, 171.
[10] 4 GC 170, 171.
[11] 1 Arch. N.Y. 326.
[12] Robertson Diary.

fied forever with the name of one of Robertson's close friends, the young British major who was to achieve a place in Westminster Abbey, three thousand miles away, in the little village of "Tapan or Orangetown."

Having thoroughly stripped Tappan, the soldiers returned to their camp below Schraalenburgh in two columns, one on the Closter Road and one on the Schraalenburgh Road, and the 71st Rangers and Emerich's division recrossed the North River at Dobbs Ferry and went back to New York.[18]

Patriotic Dutchmen who watched the British solemnly as they marched through Harrington, Closter and Schraalenburgh saw, to their disgust, at the rear of the British troops, all too many of their neighbors, taking their families and possessions in to New York with the invaders— fit companions, patriots said bitterly, for the bloody soldiers of General Grey. Few patriots could claim to be surprised at these defections, for every new American reverse saw more lukewarm patriots of the neutral ground fall away from the American cause, but none could fail to be disheartened at the sight. In the country between the contending armies, where every man had to stand and be counted, none but the firm patriot, the zealot, held to the rebellion; the self-styled moderate, the neutral, all too often proved to be a Tory without the courage to espouse his own cause.

Only a handful of the Bergen County Committee of Correspondence which had been elected in the heat of patriot fervor that followed Lexington had remained stanch patriots—steadfast men like Peter Zabriskie, Theunis Dey and John Fell, men who were confident that Providence meant to raise up a new Zion in America; the others had either openly gone over to the British or made their peace with them.

Neutrals could hardly be expected to do otherwise, confronted as they were by regiment after regiment of British troops, led by the greatest military figures of Europe.

Dr. James Van Buren of Hackensack had once been an ostensible neutral. Evidently a lukewarm adherent of the conferentie church,[14] he

---

13 2 André Journal 48. The withdrawal was treated with the utmost seriousness by Cornwallis, whose intelligence agents watched the King's Ferry crossing warily lest Washington move troops to the west of the Hudson to trap him on Bergen Neck. Cornwallis to Clinton, Oct. 6, 1778, HC Papers CL.

After Cornwallis withdrew, "Brigadier General Heard with some militia and an old iron 9-pounder came into . . . [Hackensack] in pursuit of part of Cornwallis' army." Affidavit of David R. Bogert, Pension Records, W3502.

14 See Romeyn, Hackensack Church, 76. Dr. James Van Buren was born Aug. 3, 1729. After the war he went to Nova Scotia but returned in the year 1790 to practice medicine in Totowa. He died in 1797. He and his brother Dr. Beekman Van Buren came from a distinguished line of physicians. His brother was evidently a patriot,

had once seemed moderately favorable to the American cause, and when the beaten American troops retreated from Fort Lee he was asked by Washington himself to treat the sick and wounded, which he did with every evidence of zeal. When the British seized Hackensack, he set up a hospital for the 26th Regiment stationed there,[15] an act which in itself was laudable enough. Where the British were concerned, however, he did not stop at medical care, he went along as a guide for British General Grant on some of his expeditions from Hackensack [16] and, as has been said, was imprisoned by the Americans for doing so.[17] He was, however, soon released and returned to Hackensack, apparently confident that he held the friendship of Whig and Tory alike. For the next two years he studiously avoided quarrels with his patriot neighbors, insisting that he had helped General Grant only as necessity required. This pretense ended once and for all in October, 1778. When Cornwallis and Grey returned to New York, James Van Buren went with them.[18]

Abraham Vanderbeek, whose son had been with the Greencoats from the dark days of November, 1776, went along too. Though he himself did not join the British when his son enlisted and though he said little about the issues of the war to anyone, he had prudently deeded his farm to his son early in the war, "thinking the British would get the better of it." [19] There were dozens of other Dutchmen, nominal patriots and neutrals, who, impressed more by the thousands of British Regulars under Grey and Cornwallis than by the zeal of patriots, finally cut off their ties with the American cause forever when the British left the Hackensack valley in that fall of 1778.

Abraham Lent was one of them. "A plain husbandman in easy circumstances, a man of fair character and small understanding," to quote the Tory William Bayard's estimate of him, Lent lived north of Tappan on the road to the Orangeburgh settlement. He possessed, Bayard thought, "enough to live comfortably on the produce of his farm and keep out of debt, without possessing money at interest or having any superfluities." [20] Bayard's uncharitable estimate of Lent's understanding may well have traced to Lent's early patriot activities, for at the outset

---

since he purchased a confiscated Tory estate. 63 NYG&B 27 (1932). James attended the conferentie church (Schraalenburgh Church Records 231, 255); Beekman the coetus church (Schraalenburgh Church Records 196, 197, 205, etc.).

15 LYT NYPL.
16 LYT NYPL.
17 MCSNJ 83, 113.
18 LYT NYPL.
19 LYT NYPL, "Abraham Vanderbeek."
20 LYT NYPL; "Abraham Lent"; see Bailey 198.

of the Revolution Lent was commissioned colonel of the foot militia of Orangetown and served in that capacity for some time before he finally became discouraged and resigned.[21]

For a man who was never too firm in his grasp of political principles, it was not a long step from a discouraged colonel of patriot militia to a neutral bystander in the war; and after the recent show of British military might, it was no great further step to the British side. When Cornwallis and Grey finished their forage at Tappan, Abraham Lent and his son, James, using the King's wagons to bring in their grain and other property, left Tappan and became open loyalists,[22] leaving John Haring, Domine Ver Bryck and their other neighbors who were blinded by Whig fanaticism to do as they pleased. For their part, the Lents were done with living in terror at the edge of the neutral ground. Henceforth their lives and fortunes were pledged to a British victory. With Lent and his son went Jacobus Bogert.[23] Within a year Abraham Lent himself was busy pillaging Whig farms in the Hackensack valley.[24]

Peter Ackerman, who had disappeared into the British lines in the spring of 1777, also was with the Tappan refugees, having come out with Grey's expedition to act as pilot and guide to the troops. He was now taking advantage of the situation to bring off his wife and four children and his few belongings.[25]

Theunis (Davidse) Blauvelt was another British guide who had been moving about among his old neighbors during the past few days, not in the least concerned about their hatred and anger. Several of his uncles were officers of the Orange County militia; he himself had gone off to join the British when they first overran New Jersey—as soon, his enemies said, as it seemed clear that the patriot cause was doomed. Twenty-nine years old in 1776, Theunis had been at odds with most of the Blauvelts because of his connection with the local conferentie church, and Tappan patriots who distrusted all conferentie people doubtless said that it was exactly what might have been expected from him. After a career as an

---

21   Chapter 3. See 1 Arch. N.Y. 290, 291.
22   LYT NYPL.
23   LYT NYPL. After a brief period of exile in Nova Scotia after the war, Lent and his son returned to take up life in Orangetown where they left it after Baylor's massacre. His late descendants assumed he had been captured by the British. Bailey 198.
24   "In the spring of 1780 . . . a notorious man by the name of Lent, called Colonel Lent, came from New York and landed at Closter . . . he was driven off by [Captain Blanch's] company." Affidavit of John A. Haring, Pension Records, S6980. Paulus Paulison lost "one milk cow and one calf to a party under Lent's command." Damages by the British, NJSL, Harrington Precinct No. 68. In the fall of 1779 Lent had reported himself to the British authorities as destitute. 2 Carleton Papers 52 (2379).
25   LYT NYPL. 2 Carleton Papers 51, 68 (2375, 2825).

irregular and a spy, he went to Canada in exile when the war was over.[26]

British officials were delighted to see these Americans fall away from the rebellion, and it would have been remarkable if they had not; yet in these men, in these Abraham Lents, Peter Ackermans and Dr. Van Burens, the British carried into New York a source of misinformation about American patriots which was as great a handicap to the British command as any false intelligence it received about Washington's army; men who could only deceive Britons, as they had deceived themselves, with the comforting assurance that American leaders were knaves and their followers fools.

Indeed, many refugees did not stop with misinforming the British military authorities in New York, who had some means of weighing their prejudiced views; the ministry in London lent a willing ear to every loyalist story of American weakness and discontent, to every promise that the people of this place or that were waiting anxiously for an attack to be made in their quarter. Even Sir Henry was obliged to lecture London sharply on the subject: "Why then, my Lord, without consulting me, will you admit the ill-digested or interested suggestions of people, who cannot be competent judges of the subject, and puzzle me by hinting wishes, with which I cannot agree, and yet am loath to disregard? . . . For God's sake, my Lord, if you wish that I should do anything . . . let me adopt my efforts to the hourly change of circumstance, and take the risk of want of success."

Puritanical and patriotic Jerseymen regarded Tory New York City as the very sink of iniquity, an evil place reflecting only too clearly the character of the men who wished to reduce Americans to slavery, and even many Tories agreed, at least in their judgment of the moral climate of the city. Officers who were not corrupt were too often hotheaded, vain, and weak. Good loyalists were ejected from their homes at the whim of some young girl who was a favorite for the moment of a British officer. Civilians were thrown in jail for complaining at the beating of some drunken hanger-on of the ruling clique. Tory merchants feared to press claims against friends of the military.

[26] 1 Sabine 232; Blauvelt Genealogy No. 222. Blauvelt had received a lieutenant's commission in the (apparently irregular) King's Militia Rangers, but like Wiert Banta and James Moody, his name does not appear in the official British army lists. If Blauvelt was in uniform, which may be doubtful, he now wore the new Tory red coat with blue lapels, with lace, which, under orders of June 17, 1778, had superseded the green uniform. C. M. Lefferts, Uniforms . . . in . . . the American Revolution . . . New York 1926. In Canada he married the daughter of the Steenrapie Tory Gabriel Van Norden. Another Theunis Blauvelt, across the state line in Harrington Precinct, lost property worth £283 (perhaps $25,000 in present value of money) to Tory pillaging. Damages by British, NJSL, Harrington Precinct No. 69.

But those who exercised military power over the city were almost saintly when compared with the evil men in charge of the prisons. Modern distrust of propaganda, a reluctance to believe that any man is truly wicked, the tendency to believe that there is much truth on both sides of every question, have led some to doubt patriot reports about the British prisons. The facts are beyond dispute: the men in charge of the British prisons carried to the extreme their view, colored by greed, that any British subject who rebelled against his king was a traitor and an outlaw who deserved hanging and thus should be thankful for anything less than capital punishment. Hundreds of the poor wretches were crowded into buildings which had been built for sugar warehouses, with nothing to protect them from the winter cold but the iron bars on the windows and neither fuel nor clothing to ward off the cruel New York winter. The little food that was set aside for the prisoners was in good part stolen by the commissaries through whom it passed, one of whom was the contemptible husband of Clinton's mistress. Prisoners were given, for three days' rations, what an ordinary man would eat at one meal, and often for days at a time they were given nothing. Bad as Sugar House Prison and Bridewell were, the prison ships at Wallabout Bay were worse. Yellow fever, smallpox, and other diseases were rampant.

The morning salutation of the guards at the prison doors was "Rebels, turn out your dead." Worse, the dead were often left lying alongside the prison walls for hours before being carted off.

Though not directly chargeable with these outrages, the military did nothing to stop them; indeed Sir William Howe was brazen enough to answer an American complaint by saying that the prisoners "were confined in the most airy buildings and on board the largest transports of the fleet." (Washington answered with the contemptuous observation that "whether this is an advantage, or not, in the winter season, I leave it to you to decide.") It has been said that Pine Street was never extended to the west of Broadway because the northern end of Trinity churchyard holds the bones of tens of thousands of Americans, buried in common graves, who died in the British prisons and prison ships during the Revolution.[27]

There were only two means of escape. A prisoner might by good fortune be exchanged for a Briton or Tory held by the patriots. Among officers and the more prominent prisoners there was a very considerable

---

[27] The evidence, from both patriot and Tory sources, is overwhelming. Amerman, 1960 NJHSP 257. Wertenbaker, Father Knickerbocker, 151–171, summarizes much of it and cites the authorities. The author concluded that "the corruption which was in such large measure responsible for the mistreatment of prisoners, was an important factor in the failure of the British to win the war."

commerce of this sort, though a year or more sometimes passed before an exchange could be effected, even for well-connected patriots. The men who were prominent enough to be exchanged, sickened by exposure and malnutrition, were often bundles of rags and bones, half alive, half dead, when they finally came through the lines; the fate of ordinary patriots can be imagined.

There was yet another way out of British prisons. Each prisoner constantly had before him the choice of continuing in his cold, disease-ridden prison or of ending his torture at once by enlisting in the British service. Some Americans simply could not resist the temptation; indeed those who did must have had more than human determination. Some perhaps who yielded were patriots of convenience, not too dismayed to let chance put them in the British forces as chance had hitherto put them in the American, but there must also have been many a conscience-stricken wretch who, however patriotic, simply could not stand the cold and starvation.

The names of most of these men are buried in the dust of two hundred years, the names of a few have gone down in infamy.

Samuel Geek and Major Hammell were two who became infamous. Geek, while a prisoner in New York, met Major Hammell, who had been captured at the fall of Fort Montgomery. Both Geek and Hammell yielded to British offers, forsook the American cause and joined the British army, but neither of them contented himself with merely bearing arms for King George. Under instructions from Sir Henry Clinton the two went back and set to work trying to enlist Irishmen out of the American army to form a new regiment in the British service, with Hammell as colonel and Geek as a lieutenant. Colonel Richard Varick, whose suspicions were aroused by Geek's conduct, was the means of uncovering the plot, and Geek made a full confession upon his trial by a general court-martial.[28]

The history of Geek and Hammell is, in fact, one small piece of the evidence that suggests the identity of the man whose last-minute intelligence cost the lives of Baylor's dragoons, for that man too may have been an American prisoner who joined the British.

Abraham Mabie was one of the twin sons of Peter Mabie, who had a farm and mill at Tappan, on Naurashan Creek, near the Hackensack River.[29] Abraham was a name somewhat favored by Mabies: there were three Abraham Mabies in and near the little town of Tappan at the time of the Revolution, one of them having been an active patriot who

---

[28]   4 GC 50, 51 n.
[29]   Cole, Rockland County, Baptisms at Tappan No. 1508.

lived at the Tappan Sloat long after the war and left numerous descendants there.[30]

Though the Mabie family was an old and respected one in lower Orange County, Abraham's father, Peter Mabie, was probably not one of its outstanding members. His farmhouse was small; his mill never seemed to grind enough grain to come up to his hopes; indeed, since the Dutch had no confidence in the honesty of millers,[31] it must often have served more to earn him his neighbors' distrust than to put an extra shilling into his pockets. Probably never on entirely easy terms with the good people of Tappan, he cut himself off from them sharply when he joined the small group of embittered Dutchmen who set up the conferentie church there.[32] At the outset of the war, whatever the doubts of his neighbors may have been, his son, Abraham, twenty-seven years old when the war began,[33] seems to have joined the Orange County Rangers [34] like any patriotic Orange County Dutchman and shared the rigors of the cold, rainy 1776 campaign, marching night after night when British raiders threatened lower Orange County; Abraham Mabie seems also, as part of his arduous service as a militiaman, to have found himself one of the several hundred militiamen captured and thrown into prison in New York City when General Vaughan made his surprise attack on Fort Montgomery in October, 1777.[35] Perhaps some old friend from Tappan, now a refugee in New York, intimated to his captors that Mabie was no ranting patriot and that he might be useful to the British; perhaps Mabie himself decided to join the British without any suggestion from the outside.

In any case, a year after his capture at Fort Montgomery, Mabie was out of prison. Henceforth the former private soldier in the Orange

[30] Cole, Rockland County, Baptisms at Tappan; Rockland County Surrogate Records. Eleven chests of armorers' tools, bellows and anvils were stored at Mabie's store by the Continental army in December, 1776. Cole, Rockland County, 51.
[31] Perhaps the most popular of Jersey Dutch nursery rhymes began, "De molenaar is a groote dief" (The miller is a great thief).
[32] Cole, Tappan Church, gives the unhappy details of the conferentie schism. Abraham's baptism appears in the conferentie church records, along with several other references to him. Cole, Rockland County, Baptisms at Tappan.
[33] Cole, Rockland County, Baptisms at Tappan, No. 1508.
[34] 1 Arch. N.Y. 419; 1 Cal. Hist. MSS 263.
[35] See 2 GC 74, 155, 404. That he was taken at Fort Montgomery is not certain. Eager's incomplete list of prisoners omits his name, but it also omits that of his celebrated fellow prisoner, Major Stephen Lush. The fort being manned largely by Orange County militia, it seems a fair guess that any Orange County militiaman in prison after the battle was captured there. The American commissary of prisoners reported to General Washington that "the troops taken at Fort Montgomery [were] put in a Sugar House and not permitted victuals or drink for two days and two nights, and sixty of them obliged to enlist to save their lives." Boudinot Papers LC.

County militia was to be a British irregular and spy, worth ten militia-men to the British, perhaps a hundred. The men who recruited Mabie seem to have sensed at once that Mabie was no ordinary turncoat of indifferent sympathies, but a first-rate addition to the espionage service, doubly welcome because his home was in the very center of the usual American campsite south of the Highlands, and they set about at once to get him back within the American lines.

To the somewhat naïve Governor George Clinton, Sir Henry offered a cartel of three American prisoners in exchange for three not very distin-guished Tories. He baited the offer with a prisoner Clinton could hardly refuse, Major Stephen Lush, who had been the Governor's aide before the fall of Fort Montgomery, and Clinton, no more suspicious of Sir Henry than he had been of the young horse traders, hardly waited for the British messenger to dismount before sending off a letter to General Washing-ton asking him to approve the exchange:

Dear Sir, By the last flag which arrived from N. York I received Certifi-cates from the Commiss'y Genl. of Prisoners there with Proposals for ex-changing Stephen Lush (late my Brigade Major & taken at Fort Mont-gomerie) for Henry Cuyler—Corn's Van Tassel for Alex'r White & James Dole for Ab'm Maybie. As I conceive the Exchanges advantageous, I mean to agree to the Proposals.[36]

He hastily added a postscript, that he had forgotten to mention that any flag of truce would have to go by land, unless previous notice was given that they were to go by water.

The postscript was a trouble which he could have spared himself, for if "Ab'm Maybie" was Abraham P. Mabie there is every reason to believe that Sir Henry was waiting for his flag and would have accepted it by water, land or air: some of Sir Henry's intelligence officers were most anxious to return at least one American prisoner to his hearth and home at the edge of the Hudson Highlands as quickly as possible. Im-portant plans depended upon it.

Governor Clinton's acceptance of the proposed exchange went in to New York on September 19, 1778; three days later Cornwallis and Grey moved into New Jersey on the invasion that culminated in the massacre at Haring's. Six more days ensued before the massacre itself, in total nine unfortunate days which may well have enabled Mabie to get back to his home, survey the American positions in and around Tappan, and

[36] 4 GC 50. Despite the reversal of Tory and patriot names, Dole was clearly the prisoner in American hands and Mabie the prisoner in the hands of the British. 4 GC 112, 113, 149.

carry the details to the British for their night attack. Not even the most brilliant intelligence officer could have planned to have Colonel Baylor walk into a trap at the home of a close family friend of the Mabies on the very road leading from Mabie's house to the British camp; if Abraham Mabie was responsible for the intelligence, it was fate, not a British officer or Abraham Mabie, that made it possible to bring the word of Baylor's exposed position to the oncoming British army, and to do so after the march had started; but fate and zealous men have often joined forces. Mabie need never have apologized for that.

Few British agents indeed earned their pay with the lives of half an American brigade; perhaps Mabie did not, but no one knowing Abraham Mabie's later history can see the marvelously detailed map that Captain André drew of that Sunday-night expedition without observing that he did not fail to note a point a little north of Perry's Mills which he marked "Mabie's." [37]

One thing is sure, no Virginian who died at Haring's had the slightest notion that the Dutch sandstone farmhouses, so unlike the white mansions and log cabins of his native Virginia, held men as ruthless and determined as any Virginia frontiersman, men who were fighting a revolution and a war of neighbors at the same time; none suspected that Virginians were in mortal danger in the barns of Cornelius Abraham Haring because men like Haring and Abraham Mabie had been fighting a religious war long before the Revolution. The minds and passions of these seemingly stolid Dutchmen were by no means as quaint as their stone houses.

[37] 2 André Journal, Map opp. 46. Mabie left the neutral ground after the raid and went in to New York City and the Highlands. Major Goetschius, at Schraalenburgh, asked General Wayne for a pass to send Mabie's wife Gerritie and her two children into New York a year later. Goetschius to Wayne, Dec. 6, 1779, Wayne Papers HSP. Mabie reported to André, later, presumably from the Highlands, on his unsuccessful attempts to bring three of Butler's men through the Highlands, and he was one of the spies sent out in January, 1781, to try to estimate the seriousness of the mutiny of the Jersey Line. Intelligence reports, June 22, 1779, January, 1781, HC Papers CL.

11

Wꜱ I T H I N six weeks after the massacre at Haring's one of the Jersey Dutchmen who acted as pilot and guide to General Grey's troops was the hero of a Tory coup which reflected far more credit on him than his efforts for General Grey.

Wiert Banta was born in 1743 at the family homestead a mile or so west of the Hackensack River and a few miles north of the town of Hackensack, in the section which the Dutch people of the countryside somewhat curiously called Sluckup.[1] After living for a time at Acquacka-nonk, the Bantas moved back to the family homestead at Sluckup and Wiert was raised there. His family seems to have sided with the coetus faction in the Dutch Reformed church,[2] but Wiert at twenty-three moved to New York to become a carpenter, married a Lutheran girl, Elizabeth Mildeburger,[3] and thereafter had little connection with either the coetus or the conferentie faction in his own church. It has been said that most of the more recent German immigrants in New York were in

1 Banta Genealogy Nos. 51, 259. Wiert was a name as common among Bantas as David among Demarests, Johannes among Blauvelts, Abraham among Zabriskies and Guilliam among Bertholfs. Besides Wiert [Cornelius] Banta, the celebrated Tory, there were two Wiert W. Bantas, one Wiert Hendrick Banta, and probably many others. Some were active patriots. Banta Genealogy Nos. 225, 236, 259, 569. See Damages by British, NJSL, Hackensack Precinct.

2 His family baptismal records are in the Goetschius, rather than the Kuypers, records. Cf. Schraalenburgh Church Records, 93, 134, 144, 145, 163, 167. His father appears to have been one of the few Tories in the coetus church, quite possibly because of his celebrated son.

3 Banta Genealogy. New York Lutheran Church Records, Holland Society Library. An older Wiert Banta had also been a carpenter in New York. 1885 NYHS 164, 509, 510.

the camp of the Tory politicians,[4] and if that was so, Wiert Banta most certainly adopted the views of his wife's family without reservations, for no native Jersey Dutchman, not even Abraham Van Buskirk himself, was so consistently the supporter of the London ministry, and none was more daring in his support. As early as 1774 he and one of the city aldermen saved a Mr. Moore, a prominent friend of government, from some of the violent liberty boys at a time when (as Banta later described it) the mob "were using Moore very rough."

Even violent patriots had to admit that Wiert Banta had more than usual courage. Obliged to quit the city to avoid tar and feathers for his help to the unfortunate Moore, Banta was put in jail at the outset of the Revolution as a dangerous Tory and spent ten months in an Albany prison. When the British came into possession of New York City in 1776 he managed his escape to New York and made it his base for vengeance. His first work was to go back to Hackensack and recruit for Colonel Van Buskirk at risk of his life. Successful in this, he was next used by the British to procure intelligence, acting as pilot and guide on a number of expeditions into the Hackensack valley.

He first really distinguished himself in January, 1778, when New York's Tory refugees were seeking a man to avenge the death of Captain John Richards at the hands of Brouwer and Lozier. An old friend of Brouwer, raised within a mile or two of Abraham Brouwer's home and fearing neither liberty mobs nor the American militia, Wiert Banta was the ideal man for the job, and within a week after Richards' death Banta had gone into the neutral ground, captured Brouwer and brought him safely into a British prison. Wiert Banta was the toast of New York City; thereafter he never wanted for opportunities to exhibit his daring. He was one of the first of the Refugees to extend the British operations beyond the lower Hackensack valley and into the Highlands themselves, harrying American postriders and travelers under the very guns of the Continental army. Banta was one of the men who reconnoitered Fort Montgomery and gave General Vaughan the pattern of back-country roads which enabled the British to feint at a direct attack while falling upon it in force from the rear; he was with Cornwallis and Grey when they moved into Schraalenburgh and New Bridge; he was, as has been said, with the light infantry when they were cut out from the advancing columns to move through the fields back of Haring's, the night they fell upon and destroyed Baylor's dragoons.[5]

4 Cf. Wertenbaker, Father Knickerbocker, 22.
5 LYT NYPL. Patriot sources fully support his own reports of his activities. See e.g. Examination of William Cole, March 23, 1779, McDougall Papers NYHS; Eager, Orange County, 559.

Of course, not all of his efforts were heroic. John Nelson, of the township of Hackensack, who had never made a name for himself as a zealous patriot, probably remembered Banta best as the man who took one or two hogs and some bedding from his pillaged home, not as the daring captor of Abraham Brouwer; Isaac Naugle, the widow Tallman, and the widow Cole, of Closter, remembered him best as the man who carried off their furniture and grain, not as the pilot of the British in their attack on Fort Montgomery.[6] But even his enemies would not call Banta a mere Tory plunderer.

A few weeks after the Baylor attack, Banta proved his mettle in a brazen affront to the Continental army itself. A high British officer said that nothing like it had been done since the beginning of the war. Banta and five other men went out from New York to Kakiat, almost in the center of an American encampment in Orange County, disarmed a sergeant and twelve men and carried off two high American officers and the muster roll of the American army. The only detailed record of the daring action is a report of one of the other men, Thomas Ward. Ward, who was no man to underestimate his own help to the British, cast himself as the leader of the party. The actual leader was probably John Mason, who had led other Highland gangs.[7]

As Ward told the story, he had reported to British headquarters early in November "that there was a post that travelled the road from Washington to Congress and that he had learned where he put up, which was about twelve miles from Kings Ferry." The place—Harding's house at Kakiat—was not far from Ward's old home in the Clove. Lord Cathcart, at headquarters, Ward said, ordered him to take nine picked men, Banta among them, and go out and seize the mail.[8]

"So to the boat that was to take us to Bulls Ferry, where we was landed about nine o'clock, marched that night to Kakiat to within about five or six miles of Harding's. The whole of that night's march was forty-five miles. We was obliged to lie in the woods for eight days

[6] Damages by British, NJSL.
[7] Thomas Ward memorandum, undated papers, HC Papers CL. Ward was probably the son of a workman in the iron mines. No Jersey Dutchman, he could not spell and wrote with difficulty, but he had a considerable ability as a reporter. As to John Mason, see Examination of William Cole, March 23, 1779, McDougall Papers NYHS, and John Mason to John Stapleton, Dec. 21, 1780, HC Papers CL. See also 2 Carleton Papers 255 (3390).
[8] Idem. According to another Highland gang member, Richard and James Smith, sons of Claudius, and Nathaniel Biggs were among the others in the party. Examination of William Cole, March 23, 1779, McDougall Papers NYHS; Eager, Orange County, 560.

and had spies out so that we knew everything that transacted in the place, but was about perished from the cold." [9]

The route of the Continental mail through lower Orange County ran southwest from the Kings Ferry, back of the High Tor mountain for about five miles, then due south to Kakiat, where a road to the east led to New City and the post road turned west, passing the Kakiat Dutch Reformed church and going on to Suffern's Tavern and the south.[10] The little crossroads village of Kakiat boasted a small English Presbyterian church, an inn and a few houses, among them Harding's and Judge Coe's, the latter at the crossroads.[11]

After lying in hiding for the eight days Ward, Banta and the others "had word that [the postrider] was come into the neighborhood but could not find out whether he was gone to Harding's or the inn, but we were determined on making a trial on Harding's and if not there a try at the inn, not knowing that General [Sullivan?] had passed Kings Ferry and had marched to that same place, though hearing a great deal of noise we knew not what it was, but instead of finding the mail we found a guard and [twelve] and some grand officers in the house."

They sent one of their men to a Tory in the neighborhood. The man "came back in a great fright and said there was soldiers everywhere he went but said that the man would see me, though very fearful." The Tory reported to Ward that the postrider was not at Harding's, that "General [Sullivan] was come to Judge [Coe's] and he thought that he was gone there, but begged we would make no attempt as there was a guard of a sergeant and [twelve] at Harding's kitchen and there was some general officer there . . . that his house was full and the streets, so that it was impossible to walk without being discovered."

Four of the ten men in the party thought the risk of an attempt on Harding's too great, but Banta and five others said that they had come out to risk their lives and agreed to make the try:

Not discovering our plan to the others, we proceeded to put it into execution, which was done by creeping on our bellies along side of a fence. . . .

9   Thomas Ward memorandum, undated papers, HC Papers CL.
10   Erskine Map, NYHS, reproduced opposite p. 77, Cole, Rockland County.
11   Although there were many zealous patriots in Kakiat—Judge Coe among them —the man who had brought Ward the intelligence about the postrider was by no means the only Tory in the neighborhood. James Whitehill and John Ferguson, for example, came in from Kakiat to British headquarters with intelligence in November, 1780. British Intelligence Reports, Emmet Coll. NYPL. See also 2 GC 31; 4 GC 776; 7 GC 120. The wealthy New York City Tory, William Bayard, had owned a small farm two miles south of the village and had enlisted many of his Orange County Rangers there. LYT NYPL, "William Bayard"; I. Hills Map, No. 207 HC Papers CL.

The guard was making themselves merry, the sentry's eyes sometimes on the guard and sometimes on the general's horse and that gave us an opportunity of getting within three or four times the length of his musket, when I jumped and seized him by the gun and shoulders and crowded him . . . against the other guard and was between them and their arms. . . . They was all ordered down and two men put over them. Out of the other five men, two was placed as sentries and with the other three I went to the door of the house, which was only a few steps away.

I met the old lady at the door asking what was the noise, saying don't you know the general is here. [The general was the mustermaster general of the Continental army, Colonel Joseph Ward, not General Sullivan. He had with him Deputy Mustermaster General Colonel William Bradford.] Oh, yes, it is the general I want to see; please to conduct me to him. Oh, yes, sir, replied the old lady, follow me, taking a candle in her hand from the first room led us in where the two gentlemen sat, one on one side the table and the other on the other with their feet to the fire and leaning on the table, and on the table lay their swords and pistols. [I ordered them] to come with me to the guardhouse and have themselves dressed, otherwise they would be obliged to go as they was. The servant came to me unknown to his master, asked me what he should do with his master's papers, thinking he was going too. I told him to show me where they was and I would see they was taken care of. He took me to the carriage in the barn, where we was obliged to break several locks to come to them. We found the muster of the army.

I desired [name illegible] to mount the best horse he could find and push before there was any alarm. He was mounted and off in one minute. Desired him to inform the general that we should be in some time before day.

. . . We mounted our horses, and by this time the drums was beating, horns blowing and alarm guns firing in every part. We had not expended twenty minutes in the whole of what we had done. We mounted General Ward on his own horse and I rode behind him on the same horse for ten miles, when we discharged the horses and took to the woods, hearing the whole country alarmed before and behind.[12]

They reached Bull's Ferry at daybreak. Their boat, which had been hidden in a creek, was aground at low tide, so they hid themselves in the rocks to wait for the tide to change, knowing that the American patrols would soon follow. "Soon after sunup, we heard them coming, nothing between us but a few cedars and not to exceed thirty rod between the two parties." The patrol, made up of infantry and a troop of horsemen, halted a bare quarter of a mile from the raiders and proceeded, Ward wrote, to "put sentries all across the neck, thinking they had headed us."

When Ward and Banta found that their boat was afloat, they made

[12] Thomas Ward memorandum, undated papers, HC Papers CL.

a push for it and got out into the Hudson before the Americans were able to come up and fire upon them. "We received no shot of any kind and landed safe on York Island about 11 or 12 o'clock and took our prisoners to headquarters. . . . Lord Cathcart expressed his appreciation for what we had done and said there had been nothing equal to it since the war . . . and [made] us a present of one hundred guineas to divide equal among us, which I thanked him for." [13]

One hundred guineas was small enough pay for a stroke of such bravery and address.

The winter of 1778–79 was not particularly eventful in a military way in the New York-New Jersey theater. The Continental army from time to time sent troops into the neutral ground to forage and to try to discourage trade with the enemy,[14] and the British for their part made an impressive demonstration up the Hudson River in early December, a movement of fifty vessels which started Washington posthaste from his headquarters toward Paramus and led patriots to think that it might mean a winter campaign against the Highlands, but, like many of Sir Henry Clinton's ponderous efforts, it came to nothing.

The season itself was comparatively mild. Washington was at Middlebrook, near the Raritan, his troops "better clad and more healthy than they had been since the formation of the army."

Colonel Thomas Clark's 1st Carolina Regiment was at Paramus, guarding the Continental road and acting as an outpost for the Highland passes, on General Nathanael Greene's advice that "the line of communication to the eastward [would be] much endangered by leaving Paramus exposed." [15]

Though the winter, the fourth of the war for the Hackensack valley, was not eventful in a military way, it brought to a climax a menace to the Jersey Dutch country far worse than marching and countermarching soldiers, one which was of course implicit in the seizure of Muster-

---

13 Idem.
14 The Hackensack valley was not without military activity. On Nov. 1, 1778, an American party under Lieutenant Colonel Lindsley Eleazer went as far south as Bergen Point, killing a British guard and taking two prisoners and twenty horses. Eleazer to Stirling, Nov. 2, 1778, GW Papers LC. On Nov. 29, Colonel Christian Febiger reported from Hackensack that he had sent an American force of thirty-six men under a captain, down to Hoboken, Weehawken and Bergen the day before to intercept traffic to the ferries. Febiger to Washington, Nov. 29, 1778; GW Papers LC; Taliafero to Febiger, Nov. 29, 1778, GW Papers LC.
15 14 GW 93, 119, 168, 170. See Clinton, American Rebellion, 114, 115.

master Ward at Kakiat, the menace of plundering, kidnapping, and arson by outlaws and irregulars, who were bound by no military discipline and restrained by no officers.

Most British officials tried to stop private plundering and private vengeance. There were, however, enough highly placed Britons and Tories—Lord Cathcart, Governor Franklin, and Mayor David Matthews, to name three of them—who believed that the end justified the means and did everything in their power to encourage plundering, so long as rebels were the victims. Of a piece with the British use of Indians against the frontiers, outlaw gangs operated under British patronage along the shores of Connecticut, in upper Westchester County, in the pine barrens of south Jersey, and perhaps most actively, in the Highlands west of the Hudson.

The most celebrated of the Highland gangs was that led by Claudius Smith.[16] A member of a mountain family from the Clove north of Suffern's Tavern, he had a reputation for stealing before the war. "The first thing he ever stole was a pair of iron wedges, which had the initials of the owner's name stamped on them and in order to disguise them and escape detection his father assisted him to grind out the letters."[17] When the war came he turned the same talents to the use of King George. By 1777 he had been jailed for stealing oxen "belonging to the continent."[18] At the end of 1778 he had come to be the most notorious outlaw in the middle states, the terror of every patriot in lower Orange County and of every traveler on the Continental road. He also had gained some small reputation for robbing the rich and helping the poor, one report even crediting him with punishing "a man of means, but of a miserly disposition" for refusing to lend hard money to a woman whose husband was a patriot officer in a British prison.[19]

Although handicapped by family background, Smith was "a man whose abilities, if rightly directed, would have raised him to eminence and greatness,"[20] of impressive stature and quick wit, and considerable natural dignity. He and men like him stole horses, broke into houses and murdered the occupants in cold blood, in short, committed every imaginable crime of violence, confident that they were thus helping King George to bring his revolted colonies back to their sovereign. It is not hard to see how Smith came to believe that he was helping; it is harder

16 See 2 GC 634; 4 GC 145–149, 278, 498, 587, 588; 7 GC 347, 348; Eager, Orange County, 559 etc.; Map MacKenzie Papers CL.
17 Eager, Orange County, 552. His father was evidently David Smith. 7 GC 146.
18 Eager, Orange County, 552.
19 Eager, Orange County, 553, 554, 556.
20 Eager, Orange County, 556.

to excuse Britons of noble birth and self-proclaimed Tory aristocrats for aiding and abetting him in his pointless brutalities.

Smith died on the gallows at Goshen on January 22, 1779,[21] after having been taken on Long Island, where he was living at the time, by a daring party under Major John Brush,[22] who crossed the Sound and carried him off from his lodgings at midnight. Smith conducted himself with firmness and dignity during his trial, dressed himself with care for his execution, bowed graciously to several whom he knew in the crowd surrounding the gallows, and then, as if to show how hardened he was, "kicked off his shoes, with the observation that his mother had often told him that he would die like the trooper's horse, with his shoes on, but that he would make her a liar." [23]

During the fall of 1778 and the early winter of 1778–79 dozens of others made the Highlands their base for the same marauding.

On October 6, 1778, Major Nathaniel Strong had been murdered by one of the gangs. "When they came to his house, about twelve o'clock at night, he was in bed, and they broke and entered the outer door, broke a panel out of the door of the inner room. . . . He, being alarmed, entered the room armed with a pair of pistols and a gun. As soon as he entered the room, he was fired at through the window, but escaped unhurt. [They] called upon him to deliver up his arms and he should have quarter; on which, setting down his gun against the wall, he approached the door to open it, but as he advanced, they, through the broken panel, shot him with two balls, and he expired without speaking a word. Taking two bridles and a saddle they immediately left and retired to their old haunts." [24]

About the 10th of January, 1779, William Cole, a member of one of the gangs under the patronage of David Matthews, got a pass to go into the country from Peter DuBois, the police magistrate, and left New York in the company of five others, Thomas Welcher, D. Rutan, Henry Schultz, Jacob Brewer and John Tice. Peter Pue and Hank Blauvelt came out with them under a separate pass, to go home. "The first house they stopped at was in Schraalenburgh in possession of Cobus Peek, where they ate supper and went on. . . . Pue and Blauvelt were acquainted with Peek . . . they acquainted Peek that they came from New York. From Peek's they went to one [Theunis] Helm's in Werimus." Tice, Blauvelt and Pue left Cole at Helm's and went on. From

21 Cf. 4 GC 146. Smith was not tried for murder, but for burglaries at the homes of John Earl and Ebenezer Woodhull and robbery of William Bell. Nicoll Papers, No. 163, Washington Museum, Newburgh, N.Y.
22 Eager, Orange County, 557; 7 GC 347, 348. See 4 GC 278, 488.
23 Eager, Orange County, 554, 556.
24 Eager, Orange County, 554.

Helm's, Cole "went to Ezekiel Yeomans', in Kakiat." When he had finished in that neighborhood, he returned to Werimus, to a Mrs. Traphagen's, where he was to have met Welcher and Rutan, but missed them. He was captured the next night at Jacobus Peek's, in Schraalenburgh.[25]

Cole's history, as he told it to his captors, was hardly the story of a man of firm Tory convictions. He had enlisted in Colonel Bayard's regiment in 1777, but left it after the Battle of Fort Montgomery because, or so he said, he had become sick. When he recovered, however, he went with another former Tory soldier, not back to his regiment but to Sterling, near the ironworks, and then to Pompton Plains, where he lived for a time among patriots without being suspected of having been with the enemy. Tiring of Pompton, he went back to the Highlands to join some acquaintances. His acquaintances were evidently Highland marauders.

He came out from New York, he said, "in the latter end of last fall . . . in company with Thomas Ward, John Everet, Jacob Acker, James Cowen, George Harding, David Badcock, James Twaddle, Martinus Lawson, Peter Lawson and a certain John Mason, who was the head of the gang." [26] Though Cole disclaimed any part in it, he said that this was the gang which had broken in and robbed the Sidman and Erskine homes, that Harding had given Mrs. Erskine's watch to David Matthews and that Mason had given Mr. Erskine's rifle to Lord Cathcart. He identified the men who captured Mustermaster Ward as "the same party, together with Wiert C. Banta, and Richard and James Smith, sons of Claudius, and a certain Nathaniel Biggs." He said that "David Badcock, Richard Smith and Jonas Ward, with about ten of General Burgoyne's men, were the persons that fired upon Major Goetschius some time in last January," that "Henry McManus . . . , William Stagg and one or two of Burgoyne's men were the persons who robbed a certain Lightbody towards Wallkill," and that "David Badcock and Richard Smith brought two horses robbed from Nathaniel Seeley in Smith's Clove into New York . . . which they sold to John Dey, who formerly lived in Tenafly," that when he himself robbed Mr. Ackerman, the

---

[25] Examination of William Cole, March 23, 1779, McDougall Papers NYHS. Patriots put Captain Ryerson and Captain Outwater's companies over Cole and Jack Straw (Welcher) as a guard, at the log jail at Ponds Church, where they were confined, "being apprehensive of a rescue by the British parties in the vicinity." Affidavit of John S. Bertholf, Pension Records, W5810; Affidavit of David R. Bogert, Pension Records, W3502.

[26] Examination of William Cole, March 23, 1779, McDougall Papers NYHS. John Mason was called a "European." He was probably a British deserter. See "List of Offenders" April 26, 1779, McDougall Papers NYHS.

crime for which he was specifically charged and convicted, there were with him George Bull, Jacob Low, James Terwelling, all formerly of Wallkill, Archibald McCurdy, and Thomas Welcher. He confirmed that David Matthews had given fifty guineas for the capture of Abraham Brouwer and fifty for Jacob Zabriskie.[27]

A few weeks after Smith's execution one of the gangs murdered John Clark, who lived between Sterling and Warwick. "They came to the house of said Clark, knocked and were admitted. One pulled out a watch and said it is about twelve o'clock and by one, Clark, you shall be a dead man." When he pleaded that he had done nothing, they accused him of wounding a man during militia duty and having generally been very busy against Tories

and therefore they were determined to hang him . . . and to comfort his wife they told her that they intended to be the death of all the leading men of those parts. They drank very freely of sundry sorts of liquor . . . filled their bottles and stove the casks; took three bushels of salt and strewed it on the ground . . . filled bags with meat, bread, meal and many other things, took about £200 in cash and gave Mrs. Clark a paper written as follows . . . :

"A Warning to Rebels

"You are hereby forbid at your peril to hang no more friends to government as you did Claudius Smith. . . . We are determined to hang six for one, for the blood of the innocent cries aloud for vengeance. . . . There is particular companies of us that belongs to Col. Butler's army, Indians as well as white men and particularly numbers from New York that is resolved to be revenged on you for your cruelty and murders. . . . This is the first and we are determined to pursue it on your heads and leaders to the last till the whole of you is massacred." [28]

They then took Clark to one of his outbuildings. "Some said they would hang him, others said they had better shoot him and while they were disputing which they should do, Richard Smith shot him through the breast." They left him for dead. He lived only long enough to tell his wife what had happened. William Cole identified the murderers as

27 Examination of William Cole, March 23, 1779, McDougall Papers NYHS. They had originally also taken "a quantity of negroes, horses and plate, [at the Erskine and Sidman homes, but] . . . they were pursued by Captain Board's company . . . to the Ramapo mountains and the negroes and horses retaken." Affidavit of Cornelius P. Board, Pension Records, R974.
28 4 GC 587, 588, 589.

Thomas Ward, John Mason, David Badcock and Richard Smith.[29]

"They then went to Gideon Maces, drank some liquor, took some cash from one Hall, a traveller, which they again returned, threatening him. . . . After this they went in to the mountains." [30]

The principal theater of operations of the Highland gangs was the country to the north, around Goshen, not the neutral ground. The neutral ground supplied many of the Highland marauders—Wiert Banta, William Stagg, David Rutan, and Jacob Acker all bore good Bergen County names. It was principally important to the gangs because they had to have a safe and secret passageway through it to get to the Highlands and to bring their booty back to New York.[31] Unfortunately for patriots, there were all too many Dutch Tories in the Hackensack valley whose views of the war differed little if at all from those of the Highland gang leaders.

Cole had mentioned the old Schraalenburgh Tory "Cobus" Peek and the Werimus Tory Theunis Helm. Patriots in their neighborhoods may not have known that they were using their houses as underground depots for outlaws, but they would not have been surprised to hear it. Peek had already shown his Toryism in Schraalenburgh; Theunis Helm had been one of the most active leaders of the Schraalenburgh conferentie schism.[32] Benjamin Demarest, another of the harborers of outlaws, also was a conferentie adherent.[33] The others, "John Haring [obviously a namesake, not the distinguished patriot],[34] John Johnson, under Kakiat Mountain, William Concklin, Elisha Badcock, Elisha Badcock, Sr., John Dobbs, near Kakiat, Edward Roblins, in the Clove, Peter Nail, Benjamin Kelley, and Paulus Rutan, in the Clove, Ezekiel Yeomans and John Winter, in Kakiat, Petrus Acker and Arie Ackerman, in Pascack, and Isaac Mabie," were also well enough known for their Toryism.[35] It

---

[29] Examination of William Cole, March 23, 1779, McDougall Papers NYHS. James Smith (son of Claudius), James Flewelling, Jonas Rumsey, James McCormick and Daniel Keith, members of Smith's bands, were executed at Goshen, June 8, 1779. Nicoll Papers.

[30] 4 GC 587, 589.

[31] Cole described one route: "The house of one Garlick about a mile below Fort Lee [probably at the Bourdet's Ferry landing] is a common landing for them. . . . Large quantities of all sorts of provisions are transported from Garlick's to New York. . . . From Garlick's they cross the lots about a mile above the Liberty Pole, and cross Hackensack River on a log, near one Laubach's, on the west side of the river. . . . They often stop at Laubach's." Another route took them to Jacobus Peek's and Theunis Helm's. Confession of William Cole, March 29, 1779, McDougall Papers NYHS.

[32] See Schraalenburgh Church Records 31 and passim; Blauvelt Genealogy No. 66.

[33] Demarest Genealogy No. 326.

[34] Probably Johannes T. Haring, Blauvelt Genealogy No. 228.

[35] Examination of William Cole, March 23, 1779, McDougall Papers, NYHS.

may have surprised patriots to learn from William Cole "that there is a cave dug underground by the sons of Isaac Mabie, and on said Mabie's land, about a half mile from John Haring's, and another about a half a mile distant, dug by the same persons, and a third about three miles east from the house of Joseph Wessels, in the Clove, each of which contain about eight men, where the robbers generally resort," [36] but the names of the people who maintained the caves were no surprise. Patriots were already persuaded that their enemies were deceitful and wicked men.

Cole and Welcher were finally tried and hanged at Hackensack: [37]

At a Court of Oyer and Terminer held in Bergen County on the 12th ult., William Cole and Thomas Welcher alias Straw, were convicted of felony, and executed on Friday the ninth inst.

These are worthies by [the] Royal American Gazette of the 15th instant, called loyalists. They were famous all over the country for robbery, house-breaking, pocket-picking and horse-stealing, few so eminent in that vocation. Americans may perhaps wonder, but they will be pleased to know these are recommending qualifications in a loyalist.[38]

The Bergen County authorities sent Cole's confessions to Governor Livingston, and he in turn sent them to Governor Clinton of New York, who ordered patriot troops to seize the people named in them in simultaneous raids.[39] On May 26, 1779, Robert Harper, the New York commissioner on conspiracies, was able to report to Governor Livingston that he had Theunis Helm, Benjamin Demarest, Peter Mabie and Myndert Mabie in jail at Poughkeepsie, where the Jersey authorities could take them if they wished.[40]

Whatever punishment these accessories to murder and arson deserved, they seem to have got off lightly enough, for not long after his imprisonment at Poughkeepsie Peter Mabie was back in New York defending himself from a loyalist's horse-stealing charge [41] and Benjamin Demarest lived in Orange County until his death, long after the Revolution, prob-

36 Examination of William Cole, March 23, 1779, McDougall Papers, NYHS.
37 3 NJA (2) 291. Thomas Welcher had once been a private in Captain Samuel Hudnut's company, 3rd Battalion, New Jersey Volunteers. He was listed a year before as a "prisoner with the rebels." Muster Roll, Hudnut's Company, Aug. 31, 1778. Canadian Archives, Ottawa, Vols. 1854–1856, LC. See also MCSNJ 46, 110.
38 3 NJA (2) 291.
39 Livingston Papers MHS. George Washington, who also received a copy of the confession, ordered the Tories seized if any were found. 14 GW 396. See warrants and lists of offenders, April 26, 1779, McDougall Papers NYHS.
40 Livingston Papers, MHS.
41 See 4 Carleton Papers 132 (1922).

ably no more abashed by his war record than his neighbor, cousin and fellow conferentie adherent, Jacobus Demarest, who drew a will devising to a fugitive Tory son "the land I won in Upper Kennedy," land in upper Canada won beyond doubt for his aid to Smith, Banta, Ward, Mason, and the other gang leaders of the Highlands.[42] Hackensack valley patriots, after the war, found great difficulty, when they thought of the men who made up the Highland gangs and their patrons, in accepting the Tory view that they were really misguided aristocrats who happened to be on the losing side of the conflict.

John Mason, who was probably more important than either Thomas Ward or Wiert Banta—William Cole said that he was the leader of one of the gangs in which Ward was but a member—was a "European," according to Cole, possibly a British deserter, possibly one of Burgoyne's men.[43] Within a year he was jailed by the British authorities themselves for robbery, a robbery which he explained as "inadvertingly plundering some invetrite enemies to government." [44] The British could only blame themselves for letting men like Mason and Claudius Smith decide who were inveterate enemies to government and whether they ought to be inadvertently plundered. Mason put out a "Warning to Rebels" in New York City not long after Clark's murderers put out theirs; a warning which shows that Cole was probably right in placing him at the scene of the Clark murder. Designed to terrify rebels, it probably was better calculated to convince them of the utter depravity of their Tory enemies:

We loyalists do solemnly declare that we will hang six for one, which shall be inflicted on your head men and leaders. And wherever we loyal refugees finds militiamen in arms against us or against any of his Majesty's loyal subjects, we are fully determined to massacre them on the spot. We embody not with the British army but keeps by ourselves in full companies, chooses our own officers. . . . There is some thousand of us from all the provinces on the continent.[45]

Outlaws like Mason did indeed keep by themselves in full companies, embodying neither with the British army nor the Tory Greencoats, and as spring progressed and the weather improved these embodied refugees turned their activities more and more against Hackensack valley Dutchmen, apparently often with the help of Greencoats. They never made

[42] Demarest Genealogy Nos. 218, 326.
[43] Mason was, like Ward and Banta, active in espionage as well as Highland crime. Bakeless 255, 322–336.
[44] Van Doren, Secret History, 140.
[45] Van Doren, Secret History, 140.

the mistake of using Sir Henry Clinton's cumbersome tactics against farmers. Their strategy was the swift attack and quick retreat; their force was a small force—lately, as often as not, a force under the leadership of a man holding a British territorial commission. Defense against such attacks was almost impossible, for no one ever knew what isolated settlement was next marked for pillage, and patriot militiamen could not begin to protect them all. The regular American troops, of course, felt that they had far more important tasks than defending Jersey Dutch farmers.[46]

[46] McDougall to Washington, May 18, 1779, GW Papers LC.

12

★

T HERE were no military operations in the north during the early months of 1779. Washington spent several weeks in Philadelphia conferring with Congress, then returned to Middlebrook, seemingly more concerned with pacifying his general officers than fighting the British. Sir Henry Clinton, convinced as always that his numbers were insufficient for any but defensive operations, sat quietly in New York. Hackensack valley patriots seemed to be taking the whole brunt of British operations while the generals pondered grand strategy.

On March 28 thirty Refugees raided Closter. On April 12 a detachment under Captain Van Allen surprised and captured a Continental outpost at Little Ferry; on April 17 a small American patrol routed a party of Tories at Weehawken; on April 20 there was an engagement between Captain Ryerson's Tories and an advance guard of Continentals; on April 21 a small party of Refugees raided Paramus; on April 22 there was a skirmish at De Groot's in the lower English Neighborhood; on May 10 Closter was heavily attacked; later in May several hundred Regulars moved in and stripped the neutral ground from Little Ferry to the New York line.[1]

The militia could not have stopped the Regulars in any case, and they were seldom at hand when a Refugee raid was made; Tory spies knew too much of their movements. When Jacob Acker of Werimus was arrested, the principal charge was that he "had been engaged for

---

[1] See 3 NJA (2) 251, 265, 292, 293, 358, 369, 391.

some time in assisting the enemy, giving them all the information he was capable of to enable them to steal, plunder and destroy property of those that were true to their country's independence . . . informing them where they might have an opportunity with safety to plunder and steal." [2] Whether or not Jacob Acker was guilty, there were all too many others who were.

The March 28 raid, under the leadership of Captain David Peek and Lieutenant Wiert Banta, turned out well for patriots. "On Sunday night, the 28th ult.," the patriot *New Jersey Gazette* reported, "a party of about thirty men, belonging to Lieutenant Colonel Van Buskirk's corps of Tories and embodied Refugees stationed at Hoebuck in the County of Bergen, who came out as far as Closter, for the purpose of stealing horses and of robbing the inhabitants, were attacked and put to flight by nine of the militia, commanded by Lieutenant J. Huyler, leaving their plunder behind them, and one of their officers, the noted Peter Myer, Ensign in Captain David Peek's Company, dead on the field. Another of their officers was wounded in the arm, and the infamous Wiert Banta, so notoriously known for his complicated villainies, thefts and robberies, was shot through the knee, and it is supposed will, by the amputation of a limb, be disabled from kidnapping and plundering the loyal subjects of this state in future." [3]

In the distraught neutral ground no one thought it worth while to mention in the dispatch that Lieutenant John Huyler's mother and Wiert Banta's father were sister and brother.[4] Banta had received a lieutenant's commission only a short time before he was wounded. Patriots suspected with cause that the commission was designed more to protect him from the same hangman's noose that had cut off the life of Claudius Smith than to place him at the head of any territorial

---

[2] Affidavits of Harmanus Blauvelt and Cornelius Blauvelt, Pension Records, S22653.

[3] 3 NJA (2) 292. Affidavits of Abraham Blauvelt and John Powles, Pension Records, S2080, W15877.

[4] Banta Genealogy Nos. 51, 259, 269. The case of David G. Demarest and his eldest son, sixteen- or seventeen-year-old Guiliam, is an even more striking example of a divided family. "David Demarest," his neighbor Benjamin Romeyn wrote later, "deserted his country's cause and eloped to the enemy's service in the City of New York . . . and his farm was confiscated. He went to Nova Scotia. . . . The . . . father . . . repeatedly . . . demanded that . . . Guiliam join him in New York, but Guiliam held to his integrity . . ." Even after Guiliam's capture by Tories and imprisonment in New York, where his father again demanded that he join him, Guiliam "again went into military service, was severely wounded in . . . the hand in a personal contest with an enemy Refugee who sought to capture him." Affidavit of Benjamin Romeyn, Pension Records, W16952. Demarest Genealogy Nos. 220, 593. The Tory David's children were all baptized in the conferentie church (Schraalenburgh Church Records 235, etc.); when the war ended and Guiliam married, his children were baptized in the coetus church. (Idem 202, etc.).

troops. His leg was not amputated, but he walked with difficulty for the rest of his life.[5]

This may have been the engagement that began when Sergeant John Huyler (Captain Huyler's nephew) and three men fell in with a party of Refugees, "drew up near them . . . , fired, fell on the ground till their shot passed over us, then rose and retreated till we met a party of our company and a part of Captain Blanch's company, had a fight, killed two [and] took two prisoners," the engagement in which James I. Blauvelt's arm was shattered by a musket ball. Blauvelt's sister Catherine never forgot the next day, when their older brother Isaac brought James home with his shattered arm, in a gig.[6]

Ensign Myer, who met his death at the hands of Huyler's Rangers, was a member of an old Dutch family from in and around Tappan. By 1779 he had earned more of a reputation among patriots for horse-stealing than for his family connections or for his purely military merit. Indeed, even among the somewhat indifferent Americans within the British lines at Paulus Hook and Bergen, it was common talk that Myer had amassed a large hoard of gold from his efforts on behalf of King George, and obviously not from his ensign's pay.

Half a century after far more important things about the Revolution had been forgotten, Myer's gold was the subject of many a story in that part of New Jersey: Myer, it was said, was generally in the company of Half-Indian Jack, a runaway slave who used his sharp wits before the war to keep his fellow slaves at Cornelius Van Vorst's in subjection and was now applying the same wits to any Tory mischief that suggested a reward. "Both did their work for pay—Jack for whiskey, Myer for gold. Myer kept his money in a box, which he kept buried. Whenever he was in a position to add to the deposit, he and Jack would unearth the treasure. When uncovered, Jack would be dismissed, and Myer buried the money in a different place." As the slave told the story later, "as often as he had helped Myer dig up the box, he had never seen it buried, nor was it ever buried twice in the same place." When Myer failed to return from the Sunday-night raid, great efforts were made to discover the treasure. For years after the war "his widow, ever looking for the end of the rainbow where rests the pot of gold, every spring when the ground was soft, would go over the countryside prospecting with an iron rod, which she pushed into the ground, hoping to strike the box.

[5] LYT NYPL "Wiert Banta." See 2 Carleton Papers 98 (2619).
[6] Affidavits of Catherine Lozier, Pension Records, R936; James I. Blauvelt, Pension Records, W5828; and John Huyler, Pension Records, W1775. In another engagement at about the same time "Henry Cooper got wounded, taken prisoner and taken to New York, where his leg was taken off by a surgeon, recovered and returned home." Affidavit of Abraham Haring, Pension Records, W20728.

She never succeeded, though she worked and hoped while she lived." Half-Indian Jack lived to be 102 years old, but he never recalled anything that would help to find the treasure.[7]

Peter S. Van Orden was one of the militiamen who was with Huyler's company when Myer was killed. Born at Schraalenburgh in August, 1763, he was not quite sixteen years old in the spring of 1779, the eldest son of a recently widowed mother with four small children. Van Orden had served several times as a draft substitute for men who did not want to serve, the first time when he was only fourteen years old, probably enlisting to help support his needy mother. In point of fact he was serving as a substitute for Daniel Peek at the time of Huyler's skirmish. Substitute or not, few patriots could have acted with greater spirit than Peter Van Orden.

During the fall of 1778 he had been on duty with Captain Romeyn at Liberty Pole when the British dragoons attacked and overran the post. Just before the attack, a young cousin of Van Orden's recalled after the war, he had seen young Peter "alone take one prisoner and bring him back to headquarters." Within a few days after the Liberty Pole defeat, Peter had re-enlisted in Captain James Christie's company, then at Harrington, and narrowly escaped capture on the night of the Baylor massacre. "After the British returned to New York, Captain Christie and his company returned to Schraalenburgh. . . . [There he found] his mother, then a widow . . . robbed of all the necessaries of life, [and they] moved into the state of New York," where he "procured a small situation" for them near Kakiat. After a few months' service with the Orange County militia, he returned to New Jersey and enlisted in Huyler's company in time to be in the skirmish with Myer and Banta.

He continued in active service to the end of the war. He spent most of the year 1780 in Captain Jonathan Lawrence's company of Orange County state troops in the Mohawk valley, where he fought in several sharp engagements with the Regulars and Brant's Indians. He returned to Clarkstown in November, marching the last few miles through a deep fall of snow. He was with the militia in May, 1781, in the attack on the Fort Lee blockhouse, and a few weeks later, as a sergeant in Captain Christie's company, "Van Orden and Lieutenant David Demarest . . . attack[ed] in the night a party of British with some prisoners and horses, redeemed the prisoners although one mortally wounded

---

[7] Winfield, Hudson County, 434. Two weeks after Huyler's skirmish with Peek and Banta, a party of Greencoats, under Captain Van Allen, surprised a Continental guard post at Little Ferry and carried off a dozen Carolina dragoons and one militiaman. 3 NJA (2) 293, 359. The militiaman was Lucas Brinkerhoff, of Major Dey's troops. Return of Prisoners, April 13, 1779, HC Papers CL.

and some of the men wounded on both sides, but none killed, and a number of horses taken which they were taking to New York."

In the month of October, 1781, "Lieutenant Campbell with about thirty men under his command failed to attack a party of British Refugees who were then in the neighborhood of Schraalenburgh in a very dark night. . . . Van Orden with one soldier attack[ed] said party of British, retook one lieutenant and a private, one wounded, together with seven horses and brought them safe into headquarters, then under the command of . . . Captain James Christie."

"One night [in the latter part of June, 1782] Van Orden went on a patrolling party with two privates, one of them was killed before they returned . . . some time in August [he] took two deserters alone and delivered them to Major Goetschius, and a short time afterwards, with two men, brought in four deserters which he took near Fort Lee. . . . Van Orden, with a sergeant's command, was sent to the British outposts as near as practicable to intercept all trade and stop all communication with the enemy . . . he was taken prisoner and carried to New York and put in close confinement until cessation of arms . . . and afterwards returned home." He had then reached the age of nineteen.

He moved to lower Orange County (now Rockland) after the war, and became a major general during the War of 1812, in command of all militia in a large area of southern New York. He died at New Hempstead in 1846 with "an unblemished reputation," and is buried in the old True Reformed church cemetery at Monsey. His tombstone reads "Adhered to his Countrie's cause in the darkest hour of her struggle against British oppression." [8]

On April 21, 1779, Captain Jonathan Hopper of the Bergen County militia, born at Hopperstown in the northern part of the county, but living at Wagaraw (on the Passaic, opposite present-day Paterson) on a farm which he had bought from the commissioners for seized Tory

[8] The details of his Revolutionary War service are given in Pension Records, S11160, largely by his cousin, John Van Orden. He was the son of Stephen and Maria (Koning) Van Orden, of the branch of the Van Norden family that was active in the coetus church. Schraalenburgh Church Records 29, 50, 141 and passim. His later services are given in Blauvelt Genealogy Nos. 682, 973 and loc. cit. He was among the small group of Rockland County Dutchmen who joined the "seceder" True Reformed Church in 1822. Ibid. See Bailey 294. His second wife, Maria Blauvelt, "was the daughter of Theunis Blauvelt, the notorious Tory." Blauvelt Genealogy No. 973.

estates, was murdered by Tory raiders. Hopper found "a party of ruffians from New York . . . breaking open his stable door," the patriot
press reported, "and hailed them, upon which they fired and wounded
him; he returned to the house, they followed, burst open the door and
bayoneted him in upwards of twenty places." One of the party that
killed Hopper was Stephen Ryder, the old friend of George Doremus
and Christian Zabriskie, who had had some past experience with horses,
experience which had evidently convinced Ryder at least that it was
more profitable to steal horses from Whigs than to buy them and run
them through the American lines. Ryder had been a neighbor of Hopper's before the war.[9]

Though Captain Hopper probably could have escaped if he had not
tried to protect his horses, Rivington's *Gazette* of course saw his death
not as a warning against horse thieves but as a lesson to purchasers of
confiscated Tory property: "We are informed from Acquackanonk, in
Jersey, that the death of Mr. Hopper . . . had intimidated the pur-
chaser of Major Drummond's house, lately confiscated and publicly
sold, from taking possession of it, declaring that in the night he dreaded
his throat also would be cut, which happened to be the ghastly fate of
that poor devil Hopper." [10]

The confiscation of the property of Tories who had fled to the British
lines was at once the most obvious of the patriot actions and the one
most resented by the Tories, very probably the principal thing that Van
Buskirk had in mind when he spoke of "retaliating on the rebels (tho'
in a small degree) what they have long with impunity in a most cruel
and wanton manner inflicted on the friends of government." Even the
best of the Tories probably felt that Hopper deserved heavy punishment, though perhaps not death, for purchasing one of their properties
from the rebel government and moving into it. Few of them reflected
that the "R" which they saw cut with a broad ax on the door of every
Whig's property in New York City marked the forfeited home of a man
whose situation was exactly like their own.[11]

On October 4, 1776, at the outset of the war, the New Jersey legislature had passed a law directing commissioners to take possession of the
estates of those who had fled to the enemy, to sell the personal property, and to hold the proceeds for return to the fugitive if he returned
before August, 1777, otherwise to be paid over to the state. On April
18, 1778, the legislature passed another statute of somewhat the same
import; eight months later, on December 11, 1778, a stricter statute

9   3 NJA (2) 358.
10   3 NJA (2) 345.
11   Serle Diary 109; 2 Force (5) 1136.

was passed directing that conviction in absentia for high treason "should amount to a full and absolute forfeiture of such person's estate, both real and personal, whatsoever, within this state, to and for the use and benefit of the same," though not affecting the person of the accused.[12]

When the commissioners began their inquisitions and published lists of Tories, Bergen County names seemed to outnumber by far those in all the rest of New Jersey, and almost all of the names listed in Bergen County were those of men from the Hackensack valley.[13]

Bergen County patriots, who had long since given up hope of Continental aid in the neutral ground,[14] were often tempted in the spring

---

[12] 1 NJA (2) 152, 162, 163; HBP 67.

[13] (*Where the amount, sale price or location of the confiscated property is shown in the record, it is given in parentheses after the name. The sales prices are in grossly depreciated money.*) Lawrence A. Ackerman, David D. Ackerman (Franklin Township, 56 acres, £2,437), John Ackerson, Derick Ackerman (New Barbadoes), Theunis Blauvelt (Orangetown, New York), William Bayard (Bergen Township, £20,000 [the famous Castle Point property]), David Blauvelt, Christopher Benson, David Isaac Brown (New Barbadoes, 9 acres, £204), Peter P. Bogert (Harrington, 148 acres, £1,800), John Durie, John Demott, Aaron (Orey) Demarest, Jr. (Hackensack Township, 103 acres, £2,178), Hendrick Doremus (Saddle River, 304 acres, £6,575), Daniel S. Demarest (Hackensack Township, 25 acres, £1,125), Roelif Demarest, Nicholas DePuyster, Jacob Demarest (Hackensack Township, 12 acres), Edward Earl, Joost Earl, Peter Earl, Peter Goelet, Thomas Gardner, Peter T. Haring (Harrington Township), John C. and Abraham Haring (Harrington Township, 200 acres, £3,778), Nicausie Kipp, Garret Leydecker (English Neighborhood, 180 acres, £3,712), Hendrick and John Lutkins (New Barbadoes, 13 acres, £726), Nicholas Lozier (Hackensack Township, £153), Peter and Abraham Lent (Orangetown, New York), John Merselis (Schraalenburgh, 100 acres, £3,367), John Myer (New Barbadoes, 33 acres, £974), James McCullough, Michael Moore, Thomas Outwater (Harrington Township), Abraham Persel, John Persel, Samuel and Jacobus Peek (Harrington Township), David Peek (Schraalenburgh, 122 acres, £1,921), John Pell, Abraham A. Quackenbush (Hackensack Township, £1,320), John Richards (New Barbadoes, 100 acres), Henry Roome, John Francis Ryerson (Saddle River Township, 311 acres, £11,600), Martin Roelifse, Stephen Ryder, William Sorrell, Daniel Smith, John and Peter Tice, William Van Allen, Herman Van Blarcom (Paramus, 155 acres, £3,420), Peter J. Van Blarcom (Franklin Township), John J. Van Blarcom, Hendrick Van Blarcom, James Van Buren (New Barbadoes, £2,428), Abraham Van Buskirk, Andrew Van Buskirk (New Barbadoes), Cornelius Van Buskirk, David Van Buskirk (New Barbadoes), John Ja. Van Buskirk (Hackensack Township), John Van Buskirk, Peter Van Buskirk, Abraham and James Van Emburgh (New Barbadoes, 74 acres, £638), Lawrence Van Horn, Cornelius Van Horn, John H. Van Houten, Gabriel Van Norden, Cornelius Van Voorst, Jacob Van Winkle (Franklin Township), Albert Zabriskie (Schraalenburgh, 143 acres, £4,734) and Christian Zabriskie (Franklin Township). Governor Livingston was exaggerating when he called Bergen County "almost totally revolted," but the number of Bergen County names listed shows the great strength of loyalist sentiment there.

[14] General McDougall, in reporting the frequent attacks on Closter, explained the failure of Continentals to protect patriots there by saying that the troops at Paramus

of 1779 to think that the government of New Jersey also had abandoned them, but the mounting tempo of the Tory raids left them no choice but to renew their pleas for help, and Domine Dirck Romeyn sent off an express to his good friend Peter Wilson at Trenton, urging that the state authorities detach soldiers for the purpose at once.[15] Wilson agreed to do what he could, but, as he explained to Romeyn, a resolution had to be adopted by the Assembly, and before the necessary orders were put through almost a month passed. "I hired an express and paid twenty-five pounds to carry the orders to General Winds," Wilson wrote from Trenton on May 9, "but the forms in these things are so slow and the hands through which they must pass are so various, that Colonel Frelinghuysen did not set off from this place to take command until yesterday." [16]

Colonel Frelinghuysen left Trenton too late.[17]

On Sunday morning, May 9, 1779, Closter was violently attacked again, this time by a large party of Refugees who brought themselves up the Hudson by boat to the Closter Dock, from which they were able to move unobserved down the heavily wooded Closter Dock Road until they were almost upon the little settlement. The Tories particularly hated Closter, "a settlement," to quote Rivington, "abounding with many violent rebels, and persecutors of loyal subjects, and who are almost daily affording some fresh instance of barbarity," and when any

---

and Kings Ferry were "too remote to help" and that his own men "would be wasted in that territory." McDougall to Washington, May 18, 1779, GW Papers LC. Alexander Hamilton wrote the reply for the Commander in Chief. It would not have pleased Dutch patriots: "For the present I shall only say that I would not distress the posts under your command in order to cover that part of the country." 15 GW 132.

15 Romeyn Papers UCL. Indeed, later in the war, patriots of the county put it in the same terms: "Those of our county . . . are too weak and worn down with service and suffering to form an adequate defense, while those of the interior counties, in the fancied security of their own situation, indulge themselves with ease and plenty, and if we were to judge of their opinions by their practice would consider themselves as a sort of detached and independent republic unconnected with the well-being of the frontier counties." Bergen Petition for providing for the Defense of the Frontier, NJSL.

16 Wilson Papers NJHS. His resolution proposed that the Governor and Council "call forth and station by monthly relief [one class of militia of Morris and Sussex] provided they can be spared from the defense of the frontier in that quarter, to be joined by two classes of militia" of the County of Bergen already on duty. Votes of Assembly, April 24, 1779.

17 Indeed, he probably never reached Bergen County. "Some time since," John Fell wrote Robert Morris, "the Speaker of the Assembly wrote me Colonel Frelinghuysen was gone with a command of the militia to Bergen County, but I have since found it was a mistake (how happened it?). The measure would have given me great satisfaction as I have a high opinion of his military talents." Fell to Morris, June 13, 1779, Morris Papers RUL.

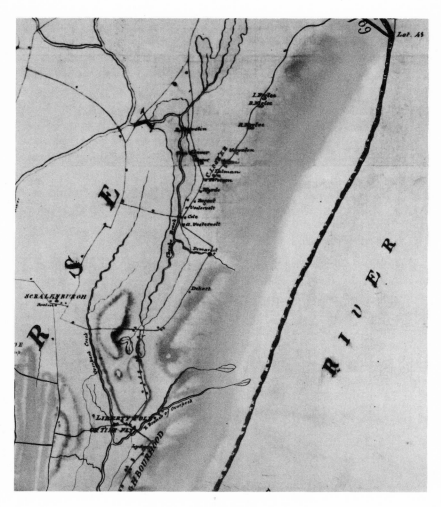

Closter and vicinity, 1779.
Sir Henry Clinton Papers, Clements Library. I. Hills.

scheme was afoot to attack it, there were always volunteers to go along.
The May 9 raid was no exception. Even the Hessians were a little sickened by the Tory urge to get at their old neighbors, and on this raid
they found an extra excuse in an atrocity story about Myer, the Refugees
claiming that Huyler had hung Myer's body as a warning to other
raiders, and also that they had found in many of the Closter homes
advertisements reading "No Quarters Shall be Given to Refugees." [18]
Samuel Demarest and his wife Margaritie Brinkerhoff Demarest lived

in a large house about a mile south of the Closter Dock Road on the old Closter Road, and Samuel operated a mill on the small brook that ran by the house on its way to the Tenakill. He had been an elder in Domine Romeyn's Schraalenburgh church (and now lies buried there). Afraid of no one, local people told for years how he stood in the doorway of his house and defied Van Buskirk's men as they came up the Closter Road. They seized him as a prisoner, applied the torch to his house, killed his son Cornelius and wounded his son Hendrick.[19]

The women buried Cornelius' body near the farmhouse and watched Samuel Demarest, Cornelius Tallman, Jacob Cole, George Van Buskirk, Jeremiah Westervelt, and others carried off to prison in New York.[20] Hendrick's life was saved only because one of the women of the household rushed to his rescue as he fell to the ground and boldly protected him from further injury.

Captain John Huyler's company was stationed a few miles to the west that morning. "The inhabitants turned out armed, gave us the alarm, we being in Schraalenburgh, we met them, had a fight, retook about ninety head of cattle which they had stolen," one of the militia men wrote after the war.[21] Huyler's men arrived too late to do anything but save the cattle. The Tories burned the dwelling houses of Peter S. Demarest, Matthias Bogert, and Cornelius Huyler. Though Samuel Demarest's house was partially saved, his barn was lost, and Cornelius Bogert's, John Westervelt's and John Banta's barns were also destroyed. The raiders, a local man wrote, "were some of our Closter and Tappan old neighbors, joined by a party of negroes. I should have mentioned the negroes first, in order to grace the British arms." [22]

19 Demarest Genealogy No. 145. See also Westervelt Genealogy. Baurmeister 275.
Samuel P. Demarest of Closter is not to be confused with Samuel P. Demarest, the militia captain, also active in the Romeyn church, who lived at the old Demarest home on the Hackensack. Demarest Genealogy No. 68.
20 Van Buskirk was "confined for upwards of five months, when he was exchanged." Affidavit of George Van Buskirk, Pension Records, S42601.
21 Affidavit of John Huyler, Pension Records, W1775.
22 3 NJA (2) 359, 370; Demarest Genealogy Nos. 145, 398; Baurmeister 275. Samuel Demarest's home was fifty feet across and twenty-one feet deep, the barn forty-five by forty-four. He also lost a "large wagon house [built] according to the Dutch construction," a corncrib and a large hay barrack. The Peter S. Demarest house was "a large dwelling fifty-six feet by twenty-one feet, with a cellar under the whole," with a wing of twenty-one feet finished off in three rooms, of a value of £220; the John Huyler home (not Cornelius Huyler's, as reported) was a "new dwelling genteely furnished . . . forty-five feet by twenty-one feet broad, half destroyed at a cost of £100"; Matthew Bogert, whose home, forty feet by thirty feet, was also burned, suffered a loss of £150. George Van Buskirk lost £35 of personal property; John C. Westervelt's barn of "four bents," worth £40, was also burned. All values are in hard money. The party was a part of the new corps under the command of

Four days after the raid John Haring reported to the Governor of the state of New York that "Mr. Douwe Tallman, who was stabbed by the Tories last Sunday morning, died of his wounds on Tuesday last; he wanted by a few weeks of being ninety years." [23]

A week and a day after the Tory raid Sir Henry mounted a full-scale military move through Closter, directed against the American troops at Paramus church. On Monday evening, May 18, the celebrated British rifleman Captain Patrick Ferguson, with three detachments from the 71st and 57th Regiments, moved to the northern end of Manhattan with orders to cross the river at night and make a swift drive on the American outpost. The 63rd Regiment crossed the river farther south, at Fort Lee, earlier in the evening, to cover Ferguson's flank, and Van Buskirk's corps was moved up from Paulus Hook in support of the 63rd.[24]

Ferguson's part of the expedition, to quote a British officer, was not "so successful as could be wished, owing to the delays and accidents attending the embarkation. It was daylight before he landed about a mile below the Closter landing place, having only seven boats with him in place of twelve, the other five being carried down the river, the men from [which] never joined him although he waited a considerable time. . . . Captain Ferguson, finding his force so much reduced, did not think it prudent to prosecute his intended plan, but marched two or three miles above Closter, where he got some cattle." [25]

The regiment which had landed at Fort Lee moved toward Hackensack and New Bridge. "When we appeared before New Bridge a party of about forty rebels attempted to take up the planks of the bridge, which they could not effect. Several shots were exchanged without damage I believe on either side." [26] Fifty of Van Buskirk's corps, with

the Tory Ryerson. Damages by the British NJSL, Harrington Precinct, Nos. 25, 28, 30, 39, 75.

Captain Blanch's militia did their best to harass the raiders with no great success. Among the militiamen who saw Cornelius Demarest killed was his brother-in-law, nineteen-year-old John A. Haring. Affidavit of John A. Haring, Pension Records, S6980. See also Pension Records, S6575.

[23] 4 GC 817. Local people believed that he was bayoneted because he would not tell where his money was hidden. See Demarest Genealogy No. 145.

Jacob Naugle, one of the prisoners, was allowed to return home. "He says Buskirk sent a verbal message by him that if Theunis Halling [Helm] could be released they would release John Naugle." 4 GC 840.

[24] 1 Kemble 177, 178. Ferguson was a most distinguished officer, who had come to America in 1777. L. C. Draper, Kings Mountain and Its Heroes (Cincinnati 1881) 52.

[25] Weymss to Lord Rawdon (undated letter), HC Papers CL.

[26] Idem.

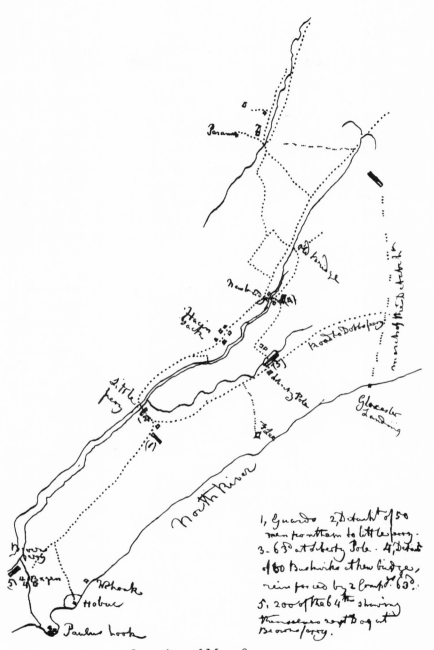

Operations of May 18–21, 1779.

Sir Henry Clinton Papers, Clements Library. Sketch by Patrick Ferguson.

two companies of the 63rd, were placed at New Bridge; two other companies were posted at Liberty Pole, and guards were placed at the Little Ferry and on the road to the Three Pidgeons.[27] On the next day the 64th Regiment was sent out from New York to guard the lower ferries over the Hackensack, and Ferguson's detachment and the 63rd joined at New Bridge and occupied the heights a quarter of a mile to the west;[28] on the following morning the whole force marched to Hoboken and recrossed the Hudson to New York. Sir Henry Clinton did nothing by halves. Three regiments of Regulars and one territorial regiment were involved in the carefully planned maneuver, yet, so far as Jersey Dutchmen could see, its only object was to plunder Jersey Dutch farms and destroy civilian homes. They naturally assumed that any such expedition would be under the command of Lieutenant Colonel Abraham Van Buskirk:

> The detachment of the enemy that landed in Bergen County on Monday . . . consisted of about 1,000 men, composed of several different corps, under the command of Col. Van Buskirk. Their path in this incursion was marked with desolation and unprovoked cruel murders. Not a house within their reach belonging to a Whig inhabitant escaped. Mr. Abraham Allen and George Campbell fell a prey to these more than savage men. Two negro women, who were endeavoring to drive off some cattle belonging to their masters, were also murdered. Mr. Joost Zabriskie was stabbed in thirteen different places.[29]

As a matter of fact, Clinton himself was probably thoroughly disappointed in the affair; it was not long before he put a stop to similar raids against Long Island civilians. "I could not but view with concern," he wrote, "the very afflicting damage [the raids] had already been productive of to private property, it never having been my intention to extend the destruction to homes of individuals, much less to those of public worship."[30] Pleased or not, he was never able to stop the equally

[27] Map No. 222, HC Papers CL. Reproduced in O'Dea, Washington's Army in Bergen County, where it is suggested that it may be the map used by the British in the November, 1776, invasion of the county. This appears to be a mistake. The map accurately describes the May, 1779, expedition of Major Patrick Ferguson, whose notes appear on it. See R. G. Adams, British Headquarters Maps and Sketches (Ann Arbor, 1928), 69. No other sources suggest such a troop placement at the time of the 1776 invasion. Van Buskirk's regiment came into being only upon completion of that invasion, and the 63rd and 64th Regiments do not appear to have participated in it.
[28] Weymss to Lord Rawdon, HC Papers CL.
[29] 3 NJA (2) 391. Joost Zabriskie paid the doctor £4 13s "for curing my body when wounded by the soldiers." Damages by British, NJSL, Hackensack Precinct No. 10.
[30] Clinton, American Rebellion, 131.

afflicting damage to property in the Dutch neutral ground west of the Hudson. By the end of spring John Fell wrote from the Continental Congress, half jokingly, to a friend in Monmouth County: "I really wonder that you venture to live in Monmouth as I have always thought that county was as bad as Bergen. For my part, I dare not go home while the enemy continues in that neighborhood; indeed I imagine I have little left to go to." [31]

In truth, even on the level of operations, many British officials and some Tories were gravely concerned about the moral aspects of a war that included the barbarities of the Highland marauders, the horse-stealing of men like Stephen Ryder and the arson and murder of the Closter raiders. Major General James Pattison, for instance, once ordered the commandant at Paulus Hook to have "the horses the Refugees stole . . . turned loose without the lines, and his disapprobation be made as publicly known to the country people as possible, and that they be also informed of his having taken this step in hopes of the horses again falling into the hands of their proper owners," adding that he "highly disapproved of these plundering parties." [32] Jersey Dutchmen must have been amazed, however, when the sharpest condemnation of all came from a Jersey Dutch Tory. Peter DuBois was a refugee from Second River high in loyalist councils, a member in fact of the police board of New York City and an active intelligence agent. [33] Shortly after the Closter raid, DuBois wrote a letter to his wife which fell into patriot hands and soon appeared in the Trenton paper. It could not have better described the Tory raiders and their patrons if it had been written by Samuel Demarest himself. DuBois described a recent raid into New Jersey as "a scene marked by circumstances of savage barbarity." Denying "any wish to plead the cause of those who were the props and supports of the present unnatural conflict," he saw "no reason to bring the horrors of war to the defenseless inhabitants of the neutral ground who were not engaged in warfare, merely because they differed in sentiment. . . . This, I must confess, is however an idea singular among those who are Jersey refugees,—they breathe nothing but fire and sword, and desolations—and those whom an ungovernable and rapacious soldiery have already plundered, they are for utterly destroying. . . . In this manner have they acted since they have been embodied and headed by their chief—everything that comes in their way is plunder, and its owner a damned rebel." [34] DuBois cited as a

31   Fell to Morris, July 10, 1779, Morris Papers RUL.
32   Pattison 334.
33   British Intelligence Reports, Emmet Coll. NYPL, Jan. 25, 1781; Bakeless 160.
34   3 NJA (2) 426, 428.

prime example "poor John Paulison, the companion of my sufferings," one of the men, who, like DuBois, had been taken up by Major Hayes in July, 1777,[35] and who, "for his invincible firmness and refusal to take the oath was a prisoner at Morristown eleven months, has been plundered for a rebel by these wretches, his horses have been publicly sold, and I yesterday met a fellow in the street with his negro, who, I understand from him, he was going to sell. I hope I shall be able to put a stop to it, if at the risk of grave looks from the Governor." For himself, DuBois placed the blame as much on William Franklin, who openly "patronizes the miscreants," as upon Abraham Van Buskirk, who was directly responsible.[36]

When the Trenton papers reached New York there was an uproar. Governor Franklin lost no time in gathering a few friends to call on DuBois and let him know that "the refugees and other loyalists were extremely offended at the letter" and that nothing short of its denunciation as a rebel forgery would satisfy them. The denial, when it was made, was far from satisfactory to Franklin and his friends; indeed it said little more than that the writer's sentiments "were not intended for the public eye," leaving the plain implication that he had not changed his opinion one iota about the acts of barbarity or their perpetrators. All that Franklin got from the public exchange of letters was a solemn assurance of Van Buskirk and the 4th New Jersey Volunteers that they wished to "take the earliest opportunity of showing our abhorrence to acts unbecoming British troops . . . [and their] resentment to any unmanly attacks on a character for which long acquaintance will justify our veneration and regard." [37] There is every evidence that many Britons and Tories, Sir Henry Clinton for one, did not share Van Buskirk's veneration and regard for the late Governor.

Patriots, we can be sure, dwelt much on the DuBois letter as proof of Tory wickedness and little on its evidence that there were high-minded men among their enemies. They had seen much of the one and little enough of the other.

The spring of 1779 loomed large in the minds of Bergen County Dutchmen long after the Revolution, long after their Tory neighbors had decided to forgive and forget the war, long after Tories had convinced themselves that there was no reason for undue remorse over

[35] MCSNJ 83, 147.
[36] 3 NJA (2) 426, 427.
[37] 3 NJA (2) 426, 427, 428, 471, 473.

their support of George III. To the prejudiced view of Samuel Demarest of Closter, or of Douwe Tallman's children, the war never ceased to be anything but a battle between the regenerate and the unregenerate, between right and wrong, and the Tories' arson, housebreaking and horse-stealing proved it so. To many Bergen County Dutchmen, Tories were simply cynical men who would have been at odds with their neighbors over something else if the Revolution had not brought them to the side of British oppression; indeed, so far as many of them were concerned, most of the Tories had given a sample of their mettle in the church wars before the Revolution.

Though the matter was by no means as simple as the country people considered it, their views were understandable. The Tories called themselves loyalists, and in a sense they were loyal: loyal to King George III and to the British government to which they owed allegiance. In another sense, they were profoundly disloyal, for they denied and fought the very principles on which America had been founded and built. To patriots, the Revolution was no mere nationalistic revolt against legitimate government, it was a rebellion against Toryism in politics, economics and religion, a Toryism that had bred poverty, ignorance, and despair in Europe and would, given a free hand, do the same in America. The Tories saw themselves as the very backbone of society, the wellborn, the able; earnest patriots saw them as the deadly enemies of the Western world, men who offered their lives and fortunes to divert America from that goal of a puritan Zion of high principles and bright optimism that seemed to them to offer the only hope of the future. To patriots far more than allegiance to Britain was at stake; Tory success would have meant a far different England and a far different world.

During the spring and summer of 1779 the people of Tappan and Haverstraw were almost as much exposed to enemy action as their neighbors at Closter and the English Neighborhood. British "war vessels . . . lay in the Haverstraw and Tappan Bays year after year during the Revolutionary War during the season of the year the ice would permit them to do so," and the British shipping in the river had been "more numerous and active" in 1779 than at any time during the war.[38]

38 Affidavit of John E. Smith, Pension Records, W1503. Smith had enlisted in 1777 in Captain Stagg's company "to break stone for the magazine built at West Point." Idem.

The wealthy Colonel Ann Hawkes Hay, of Haverstraw, was one who suffered greatly.

Born on the island of Jamaica in 1745, and named, probably to his great distress, after a wealthy lady, a benefactor of the family, 34-year-old Colonel Hay and his wife and children lived about a half mile inland from the river in the northern part of Haverstraw. Hay had come to New York to attend college and while there married the daughter of Judge William Smith, Sr. He and his wife lived first in Jamaica and then settled at Haverstraw, probably on a property inherited from her father, who had died ten years before. Mrs. Hay's oldest brother, William Smith, once a prominent Whig and a leading lawyer of the city of New York, had gone over to the British and was now the Tory Chief Justice of New York, and another brother, Joshua Hett Smith, nominally a patriot, but suspect by Whig and Tory alike, lived a stone's throw from the Hays' estate in the celebrated "Smith's White House" on the King's Highway. Hay, who had received large royal grants of land in Vermont and had been offered a commission in the British army, was as zealous a patriot as could be found in New York, and, despite his excellent connections with the royal government, as great a sufferer for his patriotism.[39]

Two years before, in the fall of 1777, a party of raiders under General William Tryon landed at Haverstraw and burned Hay's house, barn and stables, which were situated a considerable distance from the river. His family fled, stripped of everything but the apparel that covered them on their flight, and Hay was obliged to petition the state for bare subsistence. "My farm is now almost a wilderness, having no hands to work it. My negroes have all been taken away; and the whole of my little live stock has been for some time past expended." Though brought up to a state of affluence, Hay's losses reduced him to the point where "in the severity of last winter [he had] to fell, junk and draw fire wood" for his family.[40]

In the summer of 1779 another British raiding party took off all that remained of Hay's property. That summer a party also landed at Tappan Sloat, where the Sparkill empties into the Hudson, and set fire to the barns of Arie Smith and his brother John L. Smith, one-time captain and major, respectively, of patriot militia. By the time Lieutenant Theunis Tallman's detachment arrived the barns had burned to the ground.[41] The Smiths, despite their English-sounding name, were as

[39] Hay Genealogy 125, etc.
[40] 5 GC 877, etc.
[41] Affidavit of Theunis Tallman, Pension Records, S23017. Arie Smith resigned his commission and moved some miles back from the river. Idem; 3 GC 296. John L. Smith served through the war. 6 GC 903.

much Dutchmen as any Blauvelt or Haring, descendants of Adriaen Lambertse Smidt, one of the original patentees of Tappan.[42]

Many of the Orange County militiamen spent most of the time as river guards. Abraham P. Blauvelt, for example, was first called out for service along the river in 1776, when the *Phoenix* and the *Rose* anchored opposite the Short Clove and at Slaughter's Landing. He continued to serve "principally at Short Clove and at Haverstraw, but . . . occasionally marched down along the river at Slaughter's Landing, Nyack and a place called the Hook and the Tappan [Landing] and at Snedens' Landing, as the shipping moved up and down from Haverstraw Bay and from Tappan Bay." His company was quartered in houses—Philip Serven's at the Hook and Michael Cornelison's, among others—along the banks of the river. He remembered "in particular that he was at one time engaged in a skirmish with a British ship that was approaching the shore near Slaughter's Landing . . . in order to receive a deserter from the Americans who was making his way to them on a log and the barge succeeded in getting him on board, whether dead or alive [I] cannot say." [43]

His cousin, Harmanus Blauvelt, recalled another engagement "near the Hudson River, in the town of Haverstraw . . . with a company of British who landed from one of their ships laying anchored on the Hudson, their object in landing was to plunder and steal the cattle and whatever they could lay their hands on belonging to the inhabitants. Our company lay concealed in the woods until they had all landed from the barge, we rushed upon them and took them prisoners without any blood being shed, they fired at us from the ship, the cannon balls whistling about our ears and cutting the limbs, of which a splinter struck violently against my face." [44]

The people of Orangetown and Clarkstown who lived back from the river found themselves almost as much in the center of military activity as those on the river; indeed, at one time they were in the very center of the encampment of the grand army. That countryside, too, held many distinguished patriots, John Haring, the patriot official, Domine Samuel Ver Bryck, pastor of the Dutch Reformed church at Tappan, and Johannes Joseph Blauvelt, militia officer, to name but a few.

Haring had been at the forefront of patriot activity in the state long before the war. Domine Ver Bryck's zeal for the American cause was matched only by the hatred his church enemies bore for his patriot principles. Born at Raritan, Somerset County, New Jersey, in 1721, he had

42   Bailey 175, 215; Blauvelt Genealogy Nos. 916, 919.
43   Affidavit of Abraham P. Blauvelt, Pension Records, S22654.
44   Affidavit of Harmanus Blauvelt, Pension Records, S22653.

first decided to learn the wheelwright's trade, but like many another youth of his day he was brought to intense spiritual concern by the Great Awakening and entered the ministry, studying briefly under the great John Henry Goetschius. He took a prominent part in the founding of Queens College and in every progressive measure of his day. Two of his four sons were taken prisoner by the British and held for years despite every effort of patriot authorities to arrange their exchange; the domine himself once escaped capture only by the timely warning of a slave.[45]

Johannes Joseph Blauvelt, though sixty-two years old at the outset of the war, acted as a militia captain for years; indeed the whole Blauvelt family of Tappan, though not without Tories, had a record of patriotism hardly equaled in the colonies, with more than fifty Blauvelts from in and around Tappan in the patriot service.[46]

[45] Cole, Tappan Church 63; See also MCSNJ.
[46] Blauvelt Genealogy, No. 113 and passim; 1 Arch. N.Y. 326; HBP 71, 72.

13

T H E summer of 1779 saw two dramatic American successes in Orange and Bergen counties.

At the end of May, Sir Henry Clinton had sent a considerable expedition under General Vaughan up the Hudson to threaten the Highland posts. Putting ashore a thousand men a few miles south of the blockhouse which the Americans had built at Stony Point, Vaughan threatened the post with the same encirclement that had reduced Fort Montgomery two years before. Not to be twice outdone in that way, the Americans, with perhaps more prudence than valor, destroyed their blockhouse and withdrew into the Highlands without a battle. At the same time General Vaughan occupied and fortified Verplanck's Point, directly opposite.[1]

Four companies of the British 17th Regiment, a body of loyalist troops and a detachment of Royal Artillery were posted at Stony Point for a month and a half, a brazen affront to the Americans, part of whose main army lay within sight of the post, and a constant reminder of their inglorious abandonment of the position.

On the night of July 16, 1779, General Washington detached General Anthony Wayne with twelve hundred light infantry to avenge the earlier defeat. General Wayne, who had himself been the victim of General Grey's no-flint tactics, directed that any soldier who fired a shot was to be killed instantly, and the position was taken at his orders by the bayonet alone. The British, having cut down all of the woods and having made abatis at every point of practical approach that they could

1 Pattison 73–80.

imagine, felt safe from attack, and General Wayne quickly drove in the few pickets and surprised and captured the whole garrison. Though the Americans abandoned the position three days after its capture as not worth the risk of holding it (and the British, who reoccupied it, stayed only a few weeks thereafter), the success greatly buoyed up every American and made the name of Mad Anthony Wayne a household word throughout the States.[2]

Patriots in the lower Hackensack valley, heartened by the capture of Stony Point, must have hoped that some similar move was afoot when Captain Allen McLane of the Delaware Line and a company of the 4th Continental Dragoons moved down to Schraalenburgh from the main encampment in the Highlands soon after.[3] From Schraalenburgh he and his fellow officers first went over to the Palisades to observe the British positions across the river. On Saturday, July 31, he moved his camp a few miles, to a point near Liberty Pole, and sent out scouting parties as far south as the town of Bergen, to the east of which lay the strong British fort at Paulus Hook.

McLane and his troopers never spent two nights in the same spot, and at the end of ten days they had visited almost every farm and checked every road and pass in lower Bergen County, arranging to get Jersey Dutch scouts when they spent the night at Henry Banta's or John Bogert's; arranging to have Van Riper, a farmer at Bergen, carry produce into Paulus Hook by day and intelligence to the Americans by night. At Bergen Woods McLane's sentries were instructed "on no account to challenge on the approach of any person, the greatest secrecy to be observed, a seeming indifference to be put on." [4]

[2] See e.g. 2 Ward 596, etc.; Pattison 95–97; Wayne Papers HSP; 5 GC 152.
[3] Allan McLane Diary NYHS, partially reprinted in Paulus Hook Centennial 90. McLane listed the following as the names of the English Neighborhood farmers from the Liberty Pole toward Bergen, as far as the road leading down to Fort Lee: Thomas Harris, at Lozier's Mills; Elias Leydecker; Widow Benson on Domine Lydecker's place; John Benson on the right; Jacob Naugle and William Dey on the left; Peter DeGroot on the right; Widow Lemater on Covenhoven's place; Jacob DeMott on the left; John Moore at Van Horn's mill; Derick Vreeland and John Klase on the left, on Moore's place . . . Moore, on the left; widow [Maree], Samuel Moore, [P. Zame], Peter Bourdette. Below the road to the fort: John Moore, Daniel [Bralton] and Abraham Dey on the left; Michael Smith, . . . Anderson and . . . Montagna on the right; Stephen Bourdette, John Brinkerhoff, Widow Edsall, Jacob Edsall and Benjamin Westervelt on the left. Paulus Hook Centennial 91. Jacob DeMott, Abraham Dey and Michael Smith were no patriots (Hays to Livingston, July 16, 1779, Livingston Papers MHS), nor were several of the others. MCSNJ passim.
[4] Allan McLane Diary NYHS; Winfield, Hudson County, 154 etc. Another spy, whose name was suggested to Major Lee by Adam Boyd when he applied "for a person that could be intrusted to pass into the lines for better intelligence," was William Jackson, son of the patriot Dutch Reformed minister at Bergen. Boyd to Anthony Wayne, Nov. 8, 1779, Wayne Papers HSP.

King George had been much surprised and concerned to hear of the rebel success at Stony Point, the more so because of the aggravating circumstance of the loss of the whole garrison; Captain McLane and Light-Horse Harry Lee were to provide him with almost as aggravating a circumstance on the morning of August 19, 1779.

Two nights before, on the 17th, McLane posted troops in the Bergen Woods to cut off communication between the British and upper Bergen County. At half past ten on the morning of August 18 two companies of Continentals under Captain Levin Handy moved down from Paramus to New Bridge to join three hundred of Lee's Virginians. They took up their march toward Paulus Hook, about twenty miles away, at about five o'clock in the evening, passing Liberty Pole and English Neighborhood and reaching Bergen Woods late that night, where they were joined by McLane's dismounted dragoons. Through the confusion of incompetent guides they were delayed for several hours, arriving at the edge of the marsh which separated Paulus Hook from the mainland at four in the morning. They were able to cross the long causeway over the marsh without opposition because the guard thought they were Van Buskirk's men returning from a raid into the neutral ground. Just at dawn Lee's whole party rushed forward with bayonets and captured almost the whole British garrison in a short but desperate fight.[5] Not an American gun was primed during the entire attack.

Lee had expected to withdraw with his prisoners across the Hackensack River, due west of present-day Jersey City, and come up to New Bridge over the Polifly Road, putting the river between himself and his pursuers, but through some mischance the boats did not arrive on the Hackensack and the troops had to go back over the English Neighborhood Road within a mile or two of the Hudson, open to British attack at all times, a road which was so dangerous that Washington had once vetoed the plan until an alternative retreat was proposed. But McLane had scouted the route thoroughly, listing every farm on the road, checking the cowpaths through the marshes to the west and every bypass on the Palisades, and the weary troops, who by now had marched sixty miles and fought a battle between late afternoon of one day and dawn of the next, reached Liberty Pole, three miles from their starting point, without trouble.

There by coincidence Van Buskirk's Greencoats, on a raiding expedition from Paulus Hook, had lain concealed during the night, planning to attack patriots in the neighborhood of Liberty Pole at sunrise. The

5 Richardson, Paulus Hook; Paulus Hook Centennial; Winfield, Hudson County, 154, etc.; 3 NJA (2) 563, 567, 621, etc.; Captain Levin Handy to Handy, Aug. 22, 1779, quoted in 2 Commager and Morris 726 and 2 Reed, 125, 126; 2 Ward 604, etc.

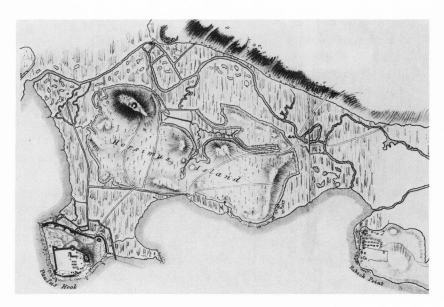

Map of Paulus Hook and Horsimus Island, circa 1779.
New York Public Library.

Greencoats, seeing Lee's troops returning to New Bridge and thinking that their own design had been discovered, moved into the main road and attacked the Americans, but Lee, after having the planks removed from the bridge over the English Neighborhood Creek, ordered a captain and a few men into the stone house which covered the bridge, and thus checked the Greencoats until his main force could be withdrawn.[6]

"Oppressed by every possible misfortune," Major Lee wrote to General Washington, "at the head of troops worn down by a rapid march of thirty miles, through mountains, swamps and deep morasses, without the least refreshment during the whole march, ammunition destroyed, encumbered with prisoners, and a retreat of fourteen miles to make good, on a route admissible of interception at several points by a march of two, three or four miles, one body moving in our rear and another . . . in all probability well advanced on our right, a retreat naturally impossible to our left. Under all these distressing circumstances, my sole dependence was in the persevering gallantry of the officers and obstinate courage of the troops." [7]

Though couched in the eloquent language of the times, Lee's report did not overstate his difficulties, and he and his officers and men de-

[6] Richardson, Paulus Hook; Paulus Hook Centennial; 3 NJA (2) 563, 567, 621, etc.
[7] 3 NJA (2) 621, 624.

served all the praise that was heaped on them for their daring exploit. All America was delighted: Washington called "the attempt critical, the success brilliant"; another called it one of the most daring and insolent assaults of history. True, the raid had one flaw to Jersey Dutchmen: though the hundred and fifty prisoners included a great many Dutch Tories from the neutral ground, patriots would have cheerfully exchanged the lot of them for their tormentor, Abraham Van Buskirk, and they loudly deplored their bad luck at finding him away from Paulus Hook on the morning of the raid. Despite Rivington's public references to the attack as "Lord Stirling's disappointment at Paulus Hook," other Britons did not hide their chagrin. "New York City," Judge William Smith declared, "is disgusted and dispirited." [8] Former Governor Tryon thought Sir Henry Clinton was playing into American hands; Sir Henry for his part complained that the London ministry had denied him enough troops to garrison his outlying posts; energetic Tories blamed indifferent English officials; English officials blamed the defeat on Tory provincial troops who could not be depended upon to fight.[9]

Clinton court-martialed the commander of the fort, and the court castigated the neglect and shameful behavior of the guards and the artillery, as well as the commander.[10]

Small as the actions were, Paulus Hook and Stony Point made the campaign of 1779 an American success, and Sir Henry himself conceded that the action at Stony Point had thrown his plans awry for the summer. Bergen County Dutchmen were soon to have tangible but unpleasant evidence that the wheel of fortune had turned: during the coming fall it was to be Continental troops, not redcoats, who emptied their barns and drove off their cattle.

After storming Stony Point, General Anthony Wayne and his Pennsylvania light infantry posted themselves just west of Haverstraw and south of the mountains, with General Woodford's Virginians at Kakiat and General Lord Stirling's New Jersey Line at Paramus, from which mounted patrols were kept constantly in the neutral ground.[11] Early on the morning of October 28, 1779, the three corps were sharply alerted by a report that a large invasion of New Jersey had started, with

8   Smith Journal NYPL. Major General Pattison reported to London that "the enterprise succeeded but too well, and little to the honor of the defendants." Pattison 99, etc.
9   Wertenbaker, Father Knickerbocker, 181.
10   Idem.
11   Wayne and his troops repeatedly foraged through Orange County south of the mountains. Wayne Papers HSP.

simultaneous landings at Fort Lee and in Monmouth County,[12] but the report about Fort Lee was false, and the whole business turned out to be no invasion at all but a party of one hundred of Simcoe's mounted raiders attacking Somerset Court House, a raid in which the celebrated Simcoe was made prisoner by a small company of Jersey militia.[13]

Five days later Wayne, having moved to Paramus, collected from sixty to a hundred wagons from the farmers in the vicinity, ordered a rendezvous with Colonel Washington's Virginia Light Horse "at either New Bridge or Schraalenburgh by eight o'clock" on the morning of November 2, 1779, and then moved his troops on a huge forage as far south as the "Overpeck Creek between Fort Lee and Paulus Hook," where he collected "upward of one hundred head of fat cattle and a considerable quantity of grain." [14]

The conduct of the American troops had been none too good before the forage; on the forage it was worse. "Our Brigade," one of Wayne's staff wrote, "has not been backward on their part in regard to divers irregularities and indecencies. They have indiscriminately stripped the neighbors of their corn, milk, ducks, fowls, &c, &c, and that too even in the sight and under the very noses of the owners." [15] When the forage was over even patriots must have wondered whether there was much to choose between Continentals and redcoats as plunderers.[16]

Sir Henry, uncertain whether more than a forage was planned, sent out a number of spies who idled about the camp for a time in the garb of countrymen and then went back to New York to report that "General Wayne, with about 1500 men and three or four field pieces, lay from New Bridge up along by Liberty Pole and Schraalenburgh Church to Closter. He has taken from the inhabitants all their grain, forage and stock, not leaving a milk cow to the people." [17]

One of Van Buskirk's agents in the neutral ground, who signed with a cipher, seemingly a well-connected and well-educated man from Paramus, reported that Stirling was about to attack Paulus Hook again and that "Washington was gathering a vast number of boats from the different parts of the Continent, and depositing them in such places as are most convenient to favor a descent upon New York and [that]

[12] Wayne Papers HSP.
[13] 17 GW 38.
[14] Wayne Papers HSP. On Nov. 9, 1779, he was reported on Polifly Lane, two miles south of New Bridge. Sullivan was at Paramus with 1,500 men and Stirling at Kakiat and on the road to Paramus with 1,800, all of the troops "in great order." Ferguson report, Nov. 9, 1779, HC Papers CL.
[15] Johnston to Wayne, Oct. 29, 1779, Wayne Papers HSP.
[16] In fact Americans were not as bad as the British and Tories. Compare Damages by the British NJSL and Damages by Americans NJSL.
[17] Intelligence Reports, Nov. 2, 1779, HC Papers CL.

the militia from the eastern and southern provinces are all ordered immediately to repair to Washington. . . . They say to act in concert with Compte de Estanges against New York." The agent had heard some tall talk from Continental officers; Wayne's huge forage expedition ended the campaign for 1779.[18]

Nonetheless, it was plain for anyone to see that it was Washington and not Sir Henry Clinton who dominated the neutral ground in 1779; the land that had filled the storehouses of the British during 1776, 1777, and 1778 now supplied the Continental magazines.

In early December the Hackensack valley saw an even more remarkable indication—or so it seemed—that the British cause had lost ground in the past three years, an incident for which there must be few parallels indeed in the history of war and revolution. When the British were in the full panoply of their power, at the end of 1776, dozens of young Jersey Dutchmen of families with Tory sympathies hurried to the side of Van Buskirk, Brown, Timpany and Barton to enlist in the Greencoat service for three years, seemingly far more time than needed to subdue the ragged American army then retreating across Jersey in disorder. These were the men who had stripped patriots' farms for British supplies, the men who had raided and burned Closter and Schraalenburgh, the men who had captured and killed their old neighbors without mercy in the years since the invasion.

When their enlistments expired, the same men returned to their homes in the neutral ground as if nothing had happened, quite obviously happy to be done with military discipline and to take up life where they had left off three years before. Patriots could hardly believe their eyes; Sheriff Adam Boyd seized eleven of them for high treason, and found to his amazement that they all insisted they were deserters from the British army.

"These persons," he informed General Anthony Wayne when he turned them over as prisoners on December 1, 1779, "joined the British some months after the Declaration of Independence. The time of their enlistments has expired." Before putting them to trial, he said he "thought it consistent to furnish the General with an opportunity of examining them." [19]

Wayne ordered the men released. "As it is the policy in one army to encourage deserters from the other, I think it highly improper to hold men under color of high treason (let the time of their enlistment be what it may), as a measure of this nature would inevitably deter all

18 Letter to Colonel Buskirk, Oct. 28, 1779, HC Papers CL.
19 Boyd to Wayne, Dec. 1, 1779, Wayne Papers HSP.

others under similar circumstances from coming over . . . and shutting the door of mercy against poor deluded wretches who wish to return to the bosom of their country." [20]

Wise as Wayne's order may have been on the level of high army policy, he might have spared Sheriff Boyd the literary flourish about Tories who wished to return to the bosom of their country. There were altogether too many Tories in the bosom of Boyd's country; to ask the victims of three years of Greencoat terror to welcome Greencoats back as neighbors, deluded or not, was a counsel of perfection, to say no more. Apparently, however, that was exactly what happened. That is, they returned to their farms. It is doubtful whether patriots welcomed them, then or later.

Indeed it might even have shaken the assurance of so distinguished a major general as Anthony Wayne to know that Sir Henry Clinton's adviser, Major Patrick Ferguson, after study of the problem of intelligence, had recommended just such desertions as a method of espionage less than a month before.

"Every effective soldier in America costs annually more than £100 sterling," the distinguished Scot observed. ". . . Your excellency would I am persuaded think fifty times the expense of one soldier well employed in providing frequent and factual intelligence, which might more influence the fate of the war than a reinforcement of ten thousand men. . . . There appears to me a very easy, safe and cheap method of gaining intelligence, by sending out Provincial soldiers as deserters, who after they were carried through the rebel army to headquarters might pass through the country to their friends, mix with the inhabitants without danger or difficulty and come in when any important intelligence offered. To manage this with success it would be necessary to have one person only in the secret, to correspond with the commanding officers of two or three provincial corps unacquainted with each others' proceedings." He recommended specifically that "two of Buskirk's late inhabitants of Tappan . . . go from Paulus Hook" for the purpose. Doubtless headquarters reasoned that if two would be useful, eleven would be better. Fortunately for Wayne, none of the deserters seem to have lived up to Ferguson's high expectations as spies.[21]

The continuous cold and snow of the winter of 1779–80 was the worst in recorded history.

Abraham Van Buskirk and the 4th New Jersey Volunteers were quartered on Staten Island, where they were attacked by Lord Stirling

[20] Wayne to Boyd, Dec. 2, 1779, Wayne Papers HSP.
[21] Ferguson to Clinton, Nov. 7, 1779, HC Papers CL.

with 2,700 men on January 14, 1780. Stirling took several Bergen County Tory notables as prisoners but his men were too nearly frozen to do anything more than carry off their prisoners and booty, and the raid could hardly be regarded as an outstanding American success.[22]

In retaliation for Stirling's action, Van Buskirk attacked Elizabeth-town in the dead of night on one of the coldest days of the winter, January 25, 1780.[23] It was a most successful expedition, but one which was again disgraced by private vengeance, the object of which showed only too clearly that the years of war had not erased from Tory minds the hatred for the Great Awakening that had been planted there long before the Revolution.

Van Buskirk and his men were able to enter Elizabethtown without any alarm, capturing about fifty American officers and men without the loss of a single man and with only a few scattering shot.

"It was impossible," Van Buskirk reported to headquarters, "to prevent the Refugees from burning the Presbyterian Meeting House and the Court House, against both of which (especially the former) the Refugees had particular Resentment—otherwise very little injury was done to the Inhabitants." [24]

The Jersey Refugees were not mistaken in seeing the Presbyterian church of central Jersey as the very root cause of their troubles. The roster of members of the church at Elizabethtown was a list of patriot leaders hardly paralleled in the colonies, and the membership of the other Presbyterian churches in the vicinity was not greatly different. The Rev. James Caldwell, at Springfield, constantly urged his congregation to act on Paul's words, "Let us not be weary in well doing: for in due season we shall reap, if we faint not"; nor did he end his efforts with exhortation, serving throughout the war as one of Washington's most trusted sources of military intelligence. No patriot of Union County was surprised when the British later singled out the Springfield church for one of their heavy raids, nor that the Rev. Mr. Caldwell's wife was killed during the attack.

It had been predicted long before the war that "those two weeds," the spirit of liberty and dissenting religion, would, if not uprooted, destroy British rule in the colonies, and subsequent events were to prove the shrewdness of these observations. One of Lord Dartmouth's representatives in America wrote him candidly after a few months of war: "When the war is over, there must be a great reform established,

---

22   4 NJA (2) 137, 143, 144, 145; 17 GW 370–390, 406; MCSNJ 167; 2 NJA (2) 12, 13; 10 GW 149, 233.
23   4 NJA (2) 151; Van Buskirk to Clinton, Jan. 26, 1780, HC Papers CL.
24   Van Buskirk to Clinton, Jan. 26, 1780, HC Papers CL.

ecclesiastical as well as civil; for, though it has not been much considered
at home, Presbyterianism is really at the bottom of this whole con-
spiracy, has supplied it with vigor, and will never rest till something is
decided upon it." 25 The Tory rector of Trinity Church had earlier reported to London angrily that he had not known one Presbyterian
minister, "nor have I been able, after strict inquiry, to hear of any, who
did not, by preaching and every effort in their power, promote all the
measures of the Congress, however extravagant." 26

In the Hackensack valley, of course, the promoters of rebellion were
not Presbyterians, but like-minded men among the Dutch Reformed,
those Dutchmen of the coetus party who, with others in New York and
New Jersey, had carried on a private rebellion against the religious rule
of Amsterdam for two decades before the war. Many of them acted as if
the Revolution was an extension of their own war.

It did not take British officialdom long to discover that the coetus
party of the Dutch Reformed were no less rebels than Presbyterians.
When he arrived in New York, Sir William Howe, who would have
blinked in astonishment at the very words "coetus" and "conferentie"
a few months before, soon found himself an authority on Dutch religious
quarrels and their political consequences; Dutch Tories saw to that.
"Finding," the Tory historian Jones reported, "the Presbyterian [coetus]
party was in possession [of New York's Dutch Reformed churches] and
that their leaders were nearly all on the American side, [Howe] took
possession of their edifices as rebel property." 27

The Dutch Tories had not misinformed the British command:
Ritzema, Rubel, Kern and Leydecker, all violent conferentie preachers,
had aligned themselves with Toryism; Kuypers, Van der Linde and
one or two other conferentie adherents were at best neutrals, generally
a euphemism for inactive Tory allegiance.28 The coetus ministers, for

25 Lundin 99, 100.
26 ERNY 4292 et seq.
27 1 Jones, New York During the Revolution, 423. The New York Dutch Reformed
church was returned to its Tory minister and the congregation on Feb. 25, 1780,
probably much the worse for its use. Pattison 373.
28 MRC 586, 693; Fraser 262. Rubel was removed by the church because "his behavior and spirit in regard to the three points of accusation against him . . . as a
wife beater, a drunkard and a tory . . . deserved the severest reprobation." Centennial Discourses 130. Muzelius, the Tappan Tory minister, was said to be addicted
to drinking, too, when he was removed before the war. ERNY 3057, 3087 and
passim. It was not suggested that he beat his wife.
So well had the British command been taught that most of the Dutch Reformed
were rebels, that Governor Tryon, when he sought a chaplaincy for Ritzema in a
Tory regiment as the father of the turncoat colonel, called him a "Dutch Lutheran,"
a falsehood for which the proud Reformed clergyman would not have thanked him.
See Tryon to Clinton, April 26, 1778, HC Papers CL. Ritzema did not return to

their part, were without exception patriots, many of them, like Romeyn, Ver Bryck, Hardenburgh, Laidlie, Livingston and Froeligh, great patriot leaders.[29]

"The Dutch paid dearly for their patriotism," one historian has pointed out. "Not only did the British occupation of New York City, Staten Island, western Long Island and other near-by points expose the Dutch inhabitants of those localities to severe repression, but innumerable raids up the Hackensack, Raritan, and Hudson brought fire and sword to the outlying settlements. So violent had the Dutch ministers been in their denunciations of the repressive measures of the British ministry, and so urgent in their advocacy of armed resistance, that they were hunted down as special objects of revenge. Many were compelled to flee before the invaders, happy to escape the horrors of the prison ships, while their church buildings and their homes went up in flames." [30]

The coetus party among the Dutch Reformed, like the Presbyterians, "each imbued with the stiff-neck spirit of Calvinism," had no reason to have any illusions as to the fate of their denominations if Toryism triumphed.

. . . The Jamaica church was used for a storage house, and its seats and floors as timber for huts and barracks, the Newtown church became a powder magazine. . . . In Staten Island the Port Richmond church was burned. With the occupation of New York City a floor was laid from gallery to gallery in the North Dutch Church and the building used as a prison. The pulpit was sent to England and set up in an Anglican church there. The Middle Dutch Church at first was also used as a prison . . . but later was converted into a riding school for dragoons. . . . The Raritan church . . . was burned to the ground, the Millstone church was plundered and the interior burned.[31]

That Van Buskirk's Greencoats did not put the torch to the Dutch churches at Hackensack and Schraalenburgh was not because they had less resentment against the Rev. Dirck Romeyn's congregations than against other Dutch churches; the contrary was the case, but the Hackensack and Schraalenburgh churches were used by the Tory conferentie

New York City to take up the commission. His Tory views and his age made it impossible for him to go back to his pulpit after the war. Cf. ERNY 4332.

Kuypers was in fact also a Tory. 4 Carleton Papers 102 (7772).

29 See MRC, Centennial Discourses, passim.

30 Wertenbaker, Middle Colonies, 99.

31 Wertenbaker, Middle Colonies, 99; 4 NJA (2) 422; Centennial Discourses 109, etc.; Wertenbaker, Father Knickerbocker, 107; Millstone Centennial 52; Onderdonk, Jamaica Church, 61; Riker, Newtown, 241.

congregations as well as by Romeyn's congregations, and Van Buskirk's Tories could not harm their enemies there without equally hurting their friends. They had ruined the Romeyn parsonage without scruple; their greatest joy would have been to seize Dirck Romeyn and the lot of his churchpeople and throw them all into Sugar House Prison.

Romeyn's friends away from the neutral ground knew this as well as he did, and he was often urged to move to a safer place. The domine's brother-in-law, Colonel John Cantine, had met General George Clinton on the street at Kingston early in the war, and, on being asked where Domine Romeyn was, said that he was with his congregations, presumably at the parsonage at Schraalenburgh, at which the General exclaimed that that was the most dangerous place on the continent and that if the domine had any concern for his family he would return to them at New Paltz. In passing this on to Romeyn, Colonel Cantine added that there were many churches in less exposed locations that would be happy to have him accept their calls.[32]

To a man of Dirck Romeyn's character the threats of the Greencoats and the pleading of friends had but one result: they fixed his determination to stay where Providence had placed him at the outset of the war. When the war was over he left almost at once to accept a better call from Schenectady.[33]

A firm enemy of the conferentie and an equally firm enemy of London tyranny, the young Princeton graduate was a marked man from his first arrival at the Schraalenburgh parsonage in the early days of the war. Driven from his pulpit by Tory violence, he had been forced to keep his family fifty miles to the north almost continuously after the outset of the war. Nevertheless, month after month he risked his life to pass through the Highlands under the muskets of criminal gangs in British pay to get to his congregations, and if he knew that there was a British price on his head, it changed his plans not one iota. A Bergen County Tory told a patriot captive of the British—one of Romeyn's elders, in fact—that the Tory and another Refugee had lain in ambush along the King's Highway to capture the domine and bring him in. "They were deterred from executing their designs," the domine wrote later, "by the formidable appearance of my companions, Major Goetschius and Captain Huyler. . . . We had five firearms between us, two muskets and

[32] Romeyn Papers UCL.
[33] Romeyn Papers UCL NYPL. MRC 683. He refused calls to even more prominent pulpits on the ground that he never felt entirely at ease preaching in English; a strange position for a graduate of Princeton whose English was flawless. Romeyn, who also refused a call to the presidency of Queens College (Rutgers), went on to found Union College at Schenectady and to become one of the most important men in the state of New York during the early days of the republic.

three pistols," the domine added, obviously a little sorry that he had been unable to use his own firearm on the skulking Tories.[34] Of course, he was naïve indeed if he thought that a Tory ambush would give him any chance to use the firearms he carried. Usually there would be a shot or two from the side of the road, a fallen traveler, a dash to seize his horse, saddlebags and purse, and an escape. The domine's good friend Captain Joost Zabriskie had met just such a death.

Perhaps Domine Romeyn was spared because he was wanted alive; perhaps the Tories knew they could not kill all three men and hesitated to risk shooting one or two and leaving a third to retaliate; in any case he was lucky to escape.

"Hackensack," a colleague wrote to the domine, "is often to me a subject of admiration; a village contiguous to the enemy's lines and accessible from all quarters, abounding with Whigs, warmly attached to their country's interest, and a larger number according to its dimensions than perhaps any town in the state could produce, to be preserved is indeed a striking instance of divine protection." No one on either side of the conflict had any doubt but that it was the stern Calvinism of Romeyn and his distinguished teacher and predecessor John Henry Goetschius that had put into the neutral ground a hard core of Dutch Whigs warmly attached to their country's interest, though both Goetschius and Romeyn would have added quickly enough that they had only been putting the spurs to a willing horse, that men like Peter Zabriskie, Abraham Brouwer, William Christie, and Peter Wilson needed no Calvinist preacher to make them patriots.[35]

34 Romeyn Papers UCL.
35 See Lundin 101; Froeligh to Romeyn, Feb. 6, 1781, Ford Mansion MSS, Morristown Historical National Park. A homely note from Major John Mauritius Goetschius indicates that the domine was also the agent for the New Jersey patriot paper. The major and some of his friends had subscribed for the paper, but he felt obliged to cancel the subscription, "his partners complaining it comes not at the proper time," a whole bundle of issues often arriving at once. Goetschius to Romeyn, June 20, 1779, HSP.

14

Hackensack's Whigs were to have a chance to prove their warm attachment to their country's interests before the spring of 1780 was over.

The worst drought in recent memory struck New York and New Jersey in the late fall of 1779. Never-failing streams, which the country people depended upon to grind their wheat, had gone completely dry, and, though Hackensack probably suffered less than the back country and the army, a drought of such severity meant a pinch even there for want of flour.

The winter began inauspiciously and became worse as the days passed. The first snow, which was soon gone, had fallen on November 17. Nine days later a heavy snow fell, the snowfall and a rainy gale continuing for eight days. December 4 was a fine day, but December 5 turned bitterly cold, and before the day ended two feet of snow had fallen.[1] The snow was still on the ground when the army passed through the northern part of the county a few days later, on December 9. The men reached Morristown on December 14.[2] On January 3, another storm struck. A New England officer called it one of the most tremendous snowstorms ever remembered. "No man," he said, "could endure its violence many minutes without danger of his life." When it ended, the countryside was covered to a depth of four to six feet,[3] and to make matters worse,

[1] Robertson Diary 205, Thacher 180.
[2] Thacher 180.
[3] Thacher 185.

intense cold followed the snow. The Hudson was covered with ice by early January, and the upper bay was soon frozen solid from shore to shore, thick enough—some reports said eleven feet—that cavalry battalions with heavy howitzers crossed over it safely.[4]

The British in New York suffered almost as much as the Americans, with fuel supplies so low that ships were broken up and burned and shade trees cut along the streets to keep people from freezing.[5] Sir Henry Clinton had gone to the south with the main British garrison, and the British command under Generals Pattison and Knyphausen, much concerned about a possible American attack across the ice, moved every available battalion from Long Island to Staten Island and Paulus Hook to meet the threat. They formed and armed a militia of five thousand civilians "for the defence and protection of their persons and properties and for the restoration of the old and happy Constitution which they are so loudly called upon by every laudable motive to assert and maintain," as Pattison put it, taking the risk of arming any Whigs among the five thousand who did not want to restore the old and happy Constitution.[6] As it turned out, however, both sides were unduly concerned. Stirling's abortive American move against Staten Island and countermoves like Van Buskirk's against Elizabethtown were the only military activity in the New York theater during the winter.

Not, of course, that the people in the neutral ground were permitted to forget the war. During the bitterly cold weather in the last week of January, Hackensack was stirred by the news that an American soldier from Paramus had been shot by a prowler at a Tory's house on New Barbadoes Neck.

A Continental officer and three soldiers, who had been collecting provisions a few miles south of town, were standing warming themselves at the fireside at Christian Jurianse's house when the door opened without warning and a boy looked in. When he saw the soldiers he slammed the door and ran. One of the soldiers ran after him, shouting "Who are you? Stand!"

A short man, in the garb of a farmer, stepped out from behind a fence, where he had evidently been sheltered by the bushes, and told the soldier not to hurt the boy, that he would tell him what he wanted. When the soldier came up, the man seized the soldier's musket and fired a cocked pistol concealed under his coat, wounding the soldier severely.

The assailant was tracked through the deep snow across New Barbadoes Neck, to the Passaic River and north along the edge of the woods

[4] Baurmeister 337.
[5] See Pattison 152, 342; Wertenbaker, Father Knickerbocker, 184, 186.
[6] Pattison 147, 152; 5 GC 448.

that bordered the river, to John Joralomen's farmyard at Acquackanonk. Joralomen insisted that he had seen no one and the tracks could not be traced farther. The Continentals brought Joralomen to Hackensack and showed him to the wounded soldier, but he said that Joralomen was not the man who shot him, being much taller than his assailant. Besides, the track was much too small for Joralomen's foot.[7]

John Joralomen was in fact not the man who had shot the soldier, but he was by no means innocent in the affair. The actual assailant was John the Regular, John Berry, as well known in and around Hackensack as Wiert Banta, James Mason, and Thomas Ward, and for much the same reasons.[8] Joralomen was a secret British agent.

Berry had been sent out from New York by the British to carry a letter from an intelligence officer to Joralomen, to be forwarded by Joralomen to a spy in Essex County. Berry had stopped in Secaucus to pick up the boy, Ned Deval, apparently the son of a Greencoat soldier. When the two arrived at Jurianse's house, Berry kept out of sight in the bushes and sent the boy ahead to see if the way was clear. When Berry discovered that he had run into an American patrol, he shot the soldier and went on through the heavy snow to complete his errand at Acquackanonk. There Joralomen put him on the beaten road to shake off his pursuers, and hid him for a time at the home of James Brown, a retired sergeant in the Royal Artillery. Berry finally returned to New York, but only after one of his feet and three of his fingers had been badly frozen while he slept overnight in a field at the edge of Secaucus, covered only with cornstalks.[9]

Berry's employer called his action cool intrepidity. Patriots would have found it hard to disagree, but when they learned who he was they put a price on his head nonetheless.[10] The next stranger they met on the highroad in the garb of a countryman might also be a British spy with a cocked pistol under his coat.

Whether Joralomen was ever suspected of his part in the affair is hard to say. He had evidently been named ensign of the New Barbadoes Neck company of patriot militia on February 28, 1776,[11] but, unless he was still active, no one in the neutral ground would have considered membership in the 1776 militia as evidence of patriotism four years later. Living, as he and his brother did, far below the American lines, they probably made no great pretense of support for the American cause, and probably they were thought of as Tories or, what was usually the same thing,

[7] AZ to Tryon, Jan. 28, 1780, British Transcripts LC.
[8] Cf. Affidavit of Cornelius D.Board, Pension Records, R974.
[9] AZ to Tryon, Jan. 28, 1780, British Transcripts LC.
[10] Romeyn Papers UCL; HBP 65.
[11] MPC 394. See Genealogical Magazine of New Jersey III, 157.

neutrals. Probably, but not certainly: even after the affair at Jurianse's, John Joralomen and his brother James were so little known as friends of the British that when they tried to bring important letters for British headquarters into the Paulus Hook post, the Tory garrison refused them admittance and they carried their letters back to Acquackanonk disgusted.[12] There must have been some among the many British agents in the neutral ground who passed for patriots with friend and foe. Perhaps the Joralomens were among them.

There was one actual alarm at Hackensack during the winter. On February 10 three hundred British light horse descended upon the town from New York, but finding the snow very deep and the roads not broken, they returned.[13] Evidently under orders not to molest the civilian population, they had plainly hoped to go beyond Hackensack before they discovered the state of the roads, in fact, General St. Clair believed their object was Washington's headquarters at Morristown. More probably it was the Continental post at Paramus Church.

By February 18 the ice in New York harbor had broken up, though it was still possible to bring wood over the Hudson by heavy sled from Hoboken.[14] As the days grew longer, the people of the Hackensack valley congratulated themselves on the end of the worst winter in a hundred years. The truth was that with the beginning of spring they were in worse danger from the British regular army than they had been since 1776.

The reason was not hard to see. Many of the Tory refugees who were living in comparative comfort as civilians in Manhattan were even less reconciled to rebellion than Greencoat soldiers, and many of them were certain that the only reason they were not taking their ease at home after five years of war was the tenderness of the British commanders toward rebels. One prominent Tory felt that the war would have ended in November, 1776, if Howe had publicly hanged the 2,400 American prisoners captured at Fort Washington; others believed that Howe and Clinton were both conspiring with the Americans to avoid a victory. With Sir Henry away on the Charleston campaign, these men hoped to see a change of policy.

Bergen County's late surrogate, Daniel Isaac Brown, the erstwhile major of the 4th New Jersey Volunteers, was now a seconded officer living in a confiscated house in New York.[15] Some of the Van Buskirks and other Bergen County notables were doing the same. The intelligence

12 AZ to Tryon, British Transcripts LC.
13 St. Clair 499; 18 GW 6, 7.
14 Pattison 371.
15 HC Papers CL. Major Timpany's family and one of the Van Buskirks were also in confiscated houses. Pattison 282, 338.

agent AZ, who had sent John the Regular to Joralomen's, may well have been another. AZ's identity remains hidden, but he knew Bergen County well. Any one of them would have been most happy to see some retaliation against Bergen County patriots.

AZ was in a particularly good position to urge such a move. He was serving not headquarters itself but William Tryon, the one-time royal governor of New York, now commissioned a major general and placed in command of all provincial troops.[16] In the days of the *Duchess of Gordon*, Tryon had been London's only link with New York and New Jersey, and he had put his Tory connections to good use in keeping up an intelligence system of his own. AZ, who had a wide acquaintance with young men of Tory families in the Hackensack valley, was one of his most useful correspondents.[17]

Tryon himself, who had suffered from Sir Henry's haughty attitude, sympathized with Tory demands for action, but when the Commander in Chief was in New York he got little encouragement for his views. At one time Sir Henry, feeling that one of Tryon's raids was destroying more churches than powder magazines, ordered him back to headquarters, where, Tryon's friends complained, he was received "with the utmost coolness." [18] The reception probably did not surprise Tryon, who had often made it clear that he and Sir Henry disagreed on the subject, boasting that if he were in more authority he would "burn every committeeman's house within my reach, as I deem those agents the wicked instruments of the continued calamities of this country." [19] In the early spring of 1780, with Clinton in Charleston and the command in the hands of General Knyphausen, Tryon found himself with the authority he had wanted, for Knyphausen was no man to stand in the way of polished, self-confident British men of affairs, particularly when their prescription for dealing with rebels accorded so well with his own.

On February 5, 1780, AZ had reported to Tryon "that the people sent out to Hackensack are returned and represent that there are neither Continental troops nor embodied militia anywhere in or about that town, or anywhere this side of Paramus, where by the best information they could procure there were between two hundred and two hundred

16 Wertenbaker, Father Knickerbocker, 223.
17 AZ knew the Jersey Dutch country intimately and was well connected in Hackensack and Paramus. It has been suggested that he was Albert Zabriskie, of Schraalenburgh, who had a farm on the Long Swamp Brook about a mile north of the Schraalenburgh church at the time of the war. His high-flown English is somewhat out of character for a Jersey Dutch farmer. William Bayard is another possibility.
18 1 Jones, New York During the Revolution 315.
19 Parsons to Tryon, Nov. 21, 1777; Tryon to Parsons, Nov. 23, 1777, 6 Remembrancer 84, 85.

fifty. I directed them to one John West, whose fidelity I have experienced, and he went several miles round the country for the purpose of making an enquiry from persons whose business had carried them abroad the day before yesterday, and whose information he could depend upon." [20]

On the next day AZ wrote Tryon that the wife of a British soldier who had come through Paramus and over the ice at Weehawken reported that "the regiment that has laid at Paramus for some time past was relieved a few days ago by another consisting of between two and three hundred men, that they have guards at Hendrick Zabriskie's and the widow Ackerman's, on the road from Paramus Church to New Bridge, also another guard at a fulling mill to the eastward of the church. This being the case, they are open and exposed on every side but their front." [21]

Tryon pressed AZ for his views as to the best route and the best guides for an attack on the American position, and on the evening of the same day—Sunday, February 6—AZ (observing that if time would admit, he "could have furnished a map with the houses laid down on it, for I know the country perfectly") described the roads through Hoboken, Secaucus, lower New Barbadoes Neck and along the Saddle River to Zabriskie's Mills and the church. He suggested two guides: "The best guide there can possibly be is Stephen Ryder, who may be depended upon. Theunis Blauvelt, a very enterprising, discreet and good young man, is perfectly acquainted from here to Wagaraw, but Ryder can find the most proper persons whenever they may be required."

AZ went on to suggest that Tryon consider "whether it might not be the most advisable to send out a couple of men tomorrow evening to get accurate information where and in what houses the officers and most of the men are quartered." "With your approbation," he went on, "I will send Ryder and Blauvelt, who may be depended upon, and they shall go by the shortest route and return the next day, and in the meanwhile I can furnish you with a map of the roads that lead to Paramus by the routes I have described." The man he actually sent out was Frederick De Voe, who brought back detailed intelligence of the American positions.[22]

Probably the only immediate result of these letters was the sortie of the light horse into Hackensack on February 10, but in the month and a half that followed the British did not forget the Continental post at

20 AZ to Tryon, Feb. 5, 1780, British Transcripts LC.
21 AZ to Tryon, Feb. 6, 1780, British Transcripts LC.
22 AZ to Tryon, Feb. 6, 7, 1780. British Transcripts LC.

Paramus, nor Hackensack.[23] Someone, possibly AZ, Ryder or Blauvelt, suggested that a two-pronged night attack would be better than an open cavalry assault, and suggested that one detachment move from the south through Little Ferry and Hackensack and the other from the north and east, through Closter and Harrington; someone, possibly the same man, also suggested that the attack could be used to advantage to even some Tory scores against patriot civilians at Hackensack, pointing out that the southern detachment could easily burn their homes on the way to Paramus Church. If anyone at headquarters was so naïve as to ask how the Regulars would know what homes were to be burned there was a ready answer: AZ would supply all the Refugees that could possibly be needed to point them out.

On March 22, 1780, word of these plans came to patriots at Hackensack. The town was to be attacked, the account said, and within five days.[24]

Though no one supposed that any major military move was planned against a small village like Hackensack, it was obvious that more than a Refugee raid was in prospect, and everyone agreed that the situation was serious enough to justify doing something which they had never done before, sending an appeal to the Continental army for help. Probably they were somewhat emboldened in this by the presence in town of a distinguished Continental officer, Lieutenant Colonel Richard Varick, who, by good fortune, was at his father's house at the time. The good fortune was Hackensack's, not young Varick's. Congress, in a pique over General Schuyler's haughty attitude, had not renewed Varick's commission as an officer on Schuyler's staff, and he had returned to Hackensack, disappointed at ending a promising military career, to try to improve his time at his legal studies.[25] "As I do not know of any other office in which I can with honor to myself offer to do service to my country," he explained to General Schuyler, "I shall as soon as I conveniently can, set myself down to books and attempt to recover the little law practice I professed to, which five years' avocations have almost erased from my memory." He closed his letter by asking Schuyler to keep him in mind if an opportunity arose. The request was one he may well have come

23   On Feb. 19 AZ reported that the Continentals were "in the same cantonments I last acquainted you with . . . but that a Captain Outwater of the militia, with about twenty men, were at Hackensack, from whence they send out small patrolling parties to Bergen." He also reported sending John West on "a jaunt to Morris County to take a circuit through General Washington's different posts." AZ to Tryon, Feb. 19, 1780, British Transcripts LC.
24   Hendrick Kuyper to Stuart, March 22, 1780, GW Papers LC.
25   Varick Court of Inquiry 24, 84; Varick to Schuyler, Feb. 10, 1780, Schuyler Papers NYPL.

to regret.[26] Varick and the local officials proceeded to draft a long application for help, and Colonel Varick himself set off as soon as it was finished to Major Stuart's headquarters to urge the case personally.

We, the subscribers, magistrates, sheriff and officers of militia . . . residing at Hackensack and its vicinity . . . make application to you for a detachment or party from your command to assist in protecting us and our neighbors, the well-affected inhabitants to the American cause against the incursions and depredations of small parties of the enemy and their vile abettors, the Refugees.

We are credibly informed that the enemy have in contemplation to make an attack and incursion on the inhabitants of Hackensack within five days. . . . The well-affected inhabitants, though willing to risk their persons in defense of their property, are too few in number . . . for the purpose of repelling the enemies' parties or keeping up continual guards and scouts for their security.

The application went on to point out that the security of the Continentals themselves depended in some measure on regular scouts and guards near the lines and urged the commanding officer, if his present orders were inadequate, to seek General Washington's approval for removing to or nearer Hackensack. For particulars it referred him to Lieutenant Colonel Varick. It was signed by Hendrick Kuyper and Peter Haring, justices; Jacob Terhune and Isaac Vanderbeek, freeholders; Adam Boyd, sheriff; Cornelius Haring, adjutant; and John Outwater, Samuel Demarest, Elias Romeyn, and David Demarest, militia captains.[27]

The plea was well reasoned and Richard Varick was an able advocate for it, but Varick reached Paramus too late to be of any help.

At seven o'clock in the evening of the same day, March 22, 1780, three hundred British Regulars under the command of Lieutenant Colonel Duncan MacPherson, of the 42nd Regiment, the celebrated Black Watch, embarked at the Hay Wharf on Manhattan Island for the attack. A little before ten they landed at Weehawken. MacPherson reported:

From thence we marched and got to the Little Ferry on Hackensack River by twelve o'clock, over which the detachment was transported in a small whale boat and one canoe by three o'clock in the morning. Here I made the disposition for surprising Hackensack, to effectuate which I ordered a subaltern and twenty-five men of the 43rd Regiment to push on briskly until they got to the end of the town, next to New Bridge, there to halt and inter-

26 Varick to Schuyler, Feb. 10, 1780, Schuyler Papers NYPL.
27 Hendrick Kuyper to Stuart, March 22, 1780, GW Papers LC.

cept every person who might make their escape; the remaining part of the detachment of the 43rd Regiment, with the fifty Anspachs, under the command of Captain Thorn of the 43rd, I ordered to follow and attack every house that should be pointed out to them by the guides and refugees, and to apprehend every man they found and bring them to Zabriskie's Mill, there to remain until the detachment returned from Paramus, and I have the pleasure to inform your excellency that the plan had the desired effect, the militia and the inhabitants being catched in their beds.[28]

Even in the perspective of two centuries the most that can be said in defense of the night's work at Hackensack was that it would not have happened if Britain's chief field officers had been in New York.

Lieutenant Colonel John Howard, of the British Guards, was to have moved from northern Manhattan at the same hour that MacPherson left the Hay Wharf, but he was delayed.

The boats from the obstructions met with at Kings Bridge, did not arrive [at Spuyten Duyvil] until half past ten o'clock, which occasioned our not reaching Closter Landing until twelve o'clock at night. The distance from thence to Paramus Church was at least seventeen miles from the detour we were obliged to make to come in the rear of the enemy's pickets, and to prevent our being discovered. As it was two hours after daybreak before we could possibly arrive at Paramus, and the surprise of the rebel posts could by no means be completed according to the plan first adopted, I took the liberty of ordering our men to load, and to make an alteration in the numbers detached under Lt. Cols. Stuart and Hall, as I had then learned the principal force was collected at Paramus Church.

I ordered Lt. Col. Stuart, with fifty men, to march on the road the east side of Saddle River, and Lt. Col. Hall, with sixty of the Light Infantry, to proceed to Hopper's house, taking with me one hundred ninety men on the road the west side of Saddle River, leading to their main body at Paramus, which I learned consisted of two hundred and fifty men. I have since learned from a deserter who came in on our retreat their numbers at the church were near three hundred.

I found them drawn up behind a stone wall before the church, afterwards they altered their position, with their left to a barn, part of them remaining behind the wall, and seemed determined to wait our coming up, but on ordering our men to form and attack, they immediately fled, and, as our soldiers had been greatly fatigued with a march of near eighteen miles, after

28 McPherson Report of the Surprise of Hackensack and Paramus, March 23, 1780, HC Papers CL; Baurmeister 345, 346; 4 NJA (2) 252, 253, 257; NJHC 82; 1882, NYHS 107; MJFBC 137; Klyberg, Action at Paramus, 1960 BHSP 1. The local militia made such resistance as they could. Affidavits of John Lozier, Pension Records, W20525; and Abraham Vanderbeek, Pension Records, S1130.

pursuing them a mile and a half and taking twenty prisoners, as I found nothing more could be effected, ordered the men back to Paramus Bridge, to join Lt. Cols. Stuart and Hall, who had directions to meet us there.

The former surprised a corporal and six men. Another picket, in a house adjoining, of an officer and twenty men, had just time to run off, leaving their arms, thirty stand of which Lt. Col. Stuart destroyed in the house. Lt. Col. Hall surprised a picket of nine men, one of which got off. The main body at Hopper's house having received information half an hour before, the main body made their escape.[29]

MacPherson's party had meanwhile moved up to Paramus from Hackensack. "At half after five o'clock," he reported, "I marched with the detachment from Hackensack, leaving Captain Thorn with one hundred men there for the purpose I have mentioned, and proceeded to Zabriskie's Mills, where I arrived a quarter of an hour after six o'clock, and from thence I continued marching toward Paramus without any opposition; and about a quarter after seven o'clock in the morning, we heard a scattering fire in our front. On this we pushed and got within a quarter of a mile of Paramus Church, when we observed the enemy run and Colonel Howard with the Guards in pursuit of them. Saddle River prevented my intercepting the fugitives. Here thirteen deserters joined us, and here I halted and sent to Col. Howard for orders, who sent me word that he with his detachment would join us immediately, which he accordingly did." [30] Zabriskie's Mills was about four miles from Hackensack; Paramus Church about five miles beyond Zabriskie's Mills.

The American report, though not so detailed about American retreats and losses, was not inconsistent with those of the British. Major Christopher Stuart wrote to General Washington:

I have the honor of informing your excellency that at six yesterday morning I received information of the enemy's being at Hackensack. In consequence . . . I gave the necessary orders for assembling the troops under my command (without the smallest expectation of their making my detachment their object at that hour), but the cantonments being so extensive prevented the troops collecting as soon as I could wish. Having detached small parties different ways, and riding around the cantonments myself to gain intelligence, I heard a firing up the road leading to Kings Ferry [the road to the north], upon which I readily concluded it must be an attack made upon a sergeant's picket posted there, and were chiefly taken. Immediately after this the small detached parties returned, being pressed close by the enemy to my quarters.

Previous to this I had given directions to the two left companies to take

29 Howard to Matthews, March 24, 1780, HC Papers CL.
30 McPherson Report, supra, HC Papers CL.

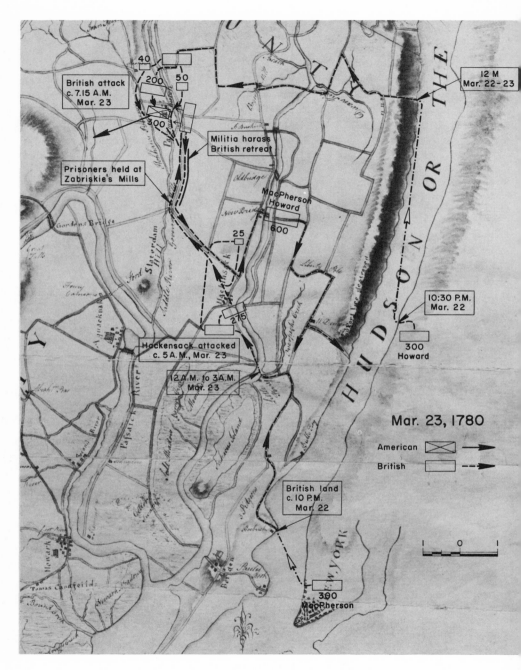

40

British attack
c. 7.15 A.M.
Mar. 23

200   50

300

12 M
Mar. 22-23

Militia harass
British retreat

Prisoners held at
Zabriskie's Mills

MacPherson
Howard

600

Gordens Bridge

25

10:30 P.M.
Mar. 22

275

Hackensack attacked
c. 5 A.M., Mar. 23

300
Howard

12 A.M. to 3 A.M.
Mar. 23

Mar. 23, 1780

American

British

British land
c. 10 P.M.
Mar. 22

NEW YORK

1   0   1

390
MacPherson

Operations of MacPherson and Howard, March 23, 1780.
Drawn on contemporary map. Courtesy New-York Historical Society. E. Tone, 1962.

post in an eminence opposite the church, to cover the retreat of the two companies cantoned on the right.

As soon as the enemy found their intentions were frustrated, they seemed more disposed to plunder than pursue us and immediately commenced their retreat from the church, down the Hackensack road, plundering indiscriminately.[31]

The Americans, who had not distinguished themselves in defense of their post,[32] took heart when they saw the Regulars in rapid retreat, and some of them—one hundred, Major Stuart reported—began a vigorous harassing action, in which they were joined by about thirty Bergen County militia, who had been aroused by the firing. The militia, who had seen nothing of the British but their retreating backs, behaved with great spirit, doubtless with greater spirit than some of the Continentals, who had been retreating themselves earlier in the morning.[33]

"During the enemy's retreat," Stuart went on, "they did not discover an inclination to halt. The subaltern's party [kept] a continual fire on their rear, which obliged them to run without intermission from a mile below the church to the New Bridge (the distance not less than eleven miles), at which place I was induced to believe the friendly inhabitants would have assembled and endeavored to obstruct their retreat by hoisting or cutting away the bridge, but on my arrival finding that the militia had not collected according to my expectations, and the enemy having taken up the bridge and posted themselves on an eminence on the other side, I thought it prudent to retire to my station, the men having received no refreshment during the day. The officers and men in general behaved with spirit and discovered a great disposition to chastise them. I beg leave to mention Mr. Peter Fell, from whom we received much benefit." [34] If it was Peter Fell who had assured the Pennsylvania major that the people of Hackensack would be at the bridge, he did not know what Hackensack had suffered in the past twenty-four hours.

Even the Hessians remembered their expedition as a frustrating one, in which they were obliged to abandon more of their booty than they carried off,[35] and the British themselves confirmed that they had "suf-

31 Stuart to Washington, March 25, 1780, GW Papers LC.
32 About one third of the Continental troops engaged in the battle were reported missing. Return of Wounded, March 25, 1780, GW Papers LC.
33 Stuart to Washington, March 25, 1780, GW Papers LC.
34 Idem.
35 BHSP (1908, 1909, 1910) 31.
Family tradition has it that one of the passing soldiers fired a musket over the heads of slave children swinging on the barn door of the Zabriskie–Wessells–Board house on Paramus Road, the musket ball resting in the beam of the barn until the present century. Bogert, Paramus 57.

fered some loss in our retreat, which the rebels, who had collected in force, harassed till we had passed the New Bridge." [36] Their casualty returns showed one rank and file killed, seventeen wounded and twelve missing, with one officer wounded. The Hessians reported nine killed, eighteen missing and a large number wounded.[37] The time was long past when the British could attack Bergen County as a refreshment for their troops.

When the day was over it was obvious that it was the village of Hackensack, not the Continental army, which was the chief sufferer. MacPherson's British and Hessians had set fire to the courthouse and proceeded systematically to try to burn every patriot's home in the village. Fortunately, with a favorable wind and good luck, only the courthouse and two homes were actually burned to the ground, but the marauders broke down the doors and windows of every Whig's house they could reach and took everything of value they could carry off.[38]

When daylight came the few patriots who were left discovered that the raiders had taken off virtually every grown man in town, fifty or sixty in all. Among them were Abraham Haring, John Bant, Abraham Storms, John Van Antwerp, John Bogert, William Prevost, Henry Van Winkle, G. Van Wagenen, Morris Earl, John Durie, Jacobus Brouwer, William Brouwer, John Van Giesen, David Baldwin, Isaac Ver Valen, Peter Zabriskie, John Demarest, John Romeyn, Guiliam Bertholf, Jonathan Doremus, Christian Demarest, and five Negro slaves, Will, Jack, John, Venter and Hector.[39] Some of them doubtless felt that the militia had been remiss in failing to have a patrol at Little Ferry through the night.

Two captives were not listed by the British. "In the course of the march," the Royal Gazette reported, "a clergyman with another in-

---

[36] Howard to Matthews, March 24, 1780, HC Papers CL.

[37] Return of Wounded, March 23, 1780, HC Papers CL; Baurmeister 246.

[38] 4 NJA (2) 252, 276. The burned houses belonged to Adam Boyd and Henry Chappel. Idem. See also affidavit of John Lozier, Pension Records, W20525.

[39] 4 NJA (2) 252; Wilson to Livingston, July 20, 1780, Livingston Papers, NYPL. The names of others, thought to be of the Pennsylvania Line, are omitted. John Bant had spent five months and five days in a British prison on an earlier raid. Damages of British, NJSL, New Barbadoes Precinct 17. Captain Outwater and Hendrick Van Giesen were wounded during the attack, the latter evidently being the "young man of the town who was wounded by a spent ball, which cut his upper lip, knocked out four teeth and was caught in his mouth. Captain Outwater received a ball below the knee which was never extracted. He carried it for many years and it was buried with him." 4 NJA (2) 252; NJHC 83. William Prevost, one of the wealthier men of Hackensack, had also been a prisoner for several months in 1777. Fell Diary.

offensive inhabitant (taken prisoners by mistake) were dismissed and are reported to have been accidentally shot by the rebels." [40] One may have been Mr. Periam, the Paramus schoolmaster, who was shot accidentally by the Americans while a prisoner in British hands, and released.[41] The clergyman was Warmoldus Kuypers, minister of the Tory conferentie church at Hackensack. His occupation did nothing to spare him until he was able to prove his standing as a Loyalist. ". . . He was obliged," his son Elias told British headquarters, "to march above twenty miles (in the hard wintry season) tho' excessive weak and in a bad state of health, and having his home plundered and himself beat and ill treated [until] (upon conviction of error) he was permitted to return home to a distressed family." "Amongst all these sufferings," the son went on, "he still persevered in his loyalty and remained with his congregation in hopes of doing good." [42]

Domine Dirck Romeyn, who had again left his wife and young daughter in the comparative safety of their refuge north of the Highlands to visit his congregations, was living at the home of Colonel Varick's father, John Varick, at the time of the raid. He and the others in the house were among the few who escaped. "I was providentially," he wrote, "the means of saving the men at Mr. Varick's, and escaped myself by secreting behind the chimney on the ceiling beams, a mercy for which I desire to be thankful to a kind Providence." His host was probably even more grateful than the domine; he had spent several months of the past year in a British prison, and was in no better state than Warmoldus Kuypers to be beaten and ill treated. The Varick house was set on fire, but the flames were put out before doing any considerable damage. "I was again plundered," Romeyn added, "of about £12 or £14 worth of clothing, etc." [43]

When the war was over, patriots of Hackensack tended to be cool to their old neighbors who had pointed out their homes to the Regulars; indeed, when the British put Hackensack to the torch on that cold spring night of 1780 they made many of the people of the town enemies of Toryism forever.

★

40   4 NJA (2) 254.
41   4 NJA (2) 280. Mr. Periam recovered and returned to his school at Elizabethtown that fall. 4 NJA (2) 647.
42   4 Carleton Papers 102 (7772).
43   Romeyn Papers UCL. Varick Court of Inquiry 79, 80. Another who escaped was the tavernkeeper Archibald Campbell. "This gentleman they forced from his bed, where he had been confined . . . with rheumatism, and obliged him to follow them. He is said to have escaped at New Bridge by hiding under the bridge and standing . . . in two feet of water." He is also said never to have suffered from rheumatism again. Romeyn, Hackensack Church, 35.

Peter Wilson set to work at once with the American commissary of prisoners to try to secure the exchange of the captives. On June 7 he wrote to Romeyn: "The prisoners I am in hopes will soon be enlarged. . . . The Commissary has promised me to propose the Van Boarsts for your brother and the other inhabitants from our county, Mr. Zabriskie and Doremus." [44] Wilson's hopes were disappointed, however, perhaps in part through the negligence of Governor Livingston, who had to be reminded by Wilson a month later that he had "forgotten to communicate to the Commissary the list I put into your hands, and as the families of some of those included therein are in a suffering condition, particularly a Jacob Brouwer and John Bant, the last of whom is also an armourer and a very necessary person here, I have taken the liberty of mentioning the matter to your Excellency, sensible that your Excellency's humanity and compassion for the unfortunate prisoners and their distressed families will induce you to give a spur to the activity and exertions of the Commissary for their relief." [45]

Thirteen weeks passed before all the prisoners were exchanged.[46]

When the main British army returned from Charleston later in the spring they found Knyphausen at Springfield, on another raid into the Jersey countryside. Clinton was furious, certain that the Hessian General had been gulled into the "ill-timed . . . malapropos" affair by "the ill-founded suggestions of a certain American governor and some other over-sanguine Refugees." "Sanguine enthusiasts," John André called them, who were "ever stimulating deep play" for their own purposes.[47] The Refugees' purposes at Hackensack had been simple enough, with very little connection with those of Sir Henry Clinton.

On Sunday, April 16, 1780, the British mounted another attack on Paramus Church. In this case, they moved with military precision, without wasting time on schemes of Tory vengeance.

At one o'clock on Sunday morning, under orders from New York headquarters, about a hundred cavalry from Staten Island—twenty drawn from the 17th Dragoons, forty-five from the mounted Queen's Rangers, and forty from the Hessian cavalry—joined forces at English Neighborhood with three hundred Hessian infantrymen, who had been ferried across the Hudson at Fort Lee earlier in the night. The whole force

---

[44] Wilson to Romeyn, June 7, 1780, Wilson Papers NJHS. Romeyn did not rest upon the hope that Wilson's efforts would secure the exchange of his brother and the other prisoners. He went directly to Continental headquarters and also wrote directly to the commissary of prisoners. Romeyn Papers UCL.

[45] Wilson to Livingston, July 10, 1780, Livingston Papers NYPL.

[46] Romeyn Papers UCL.

[47] Clinton, American Rebellion, 192; Flexner 310.

fell upon the Continental picket at New Bridge, an outpost held by a captain and thirty men, an hour later.[48]

There the Americans put up a spirited but futile opposition, after which the British pushed on to the north, leaving fifty men for the protection of the bridge and to facilitate the return to New York.

Two hundred fifty troops of the 3rd Pennsylvania Regiment, at Hopperstown, under Major Thomas Langhorne Byles,[49] were stationed along the road west of the Paramus church. Washington had continued the post there, even after it was shown to be vulnerable, "to restrain the traffic between that part of the country and New York, which from the disposition of the inhabitants has been very considerable. This consideration has induced me to station a party there, though at some hazard." [50] At the bridge over the Saddle River, where the road from New Bridge entered the town, a mile and a half east of the American headquarters and immediately below the church, a subaltern and twenty Continentals were posted as a second picket.[51] By daybreak on Sunday morning, Major Byles's mounted night patrols—he had earlier sent out two parties, each under a commissioned officer [52]—had been out and returned, and he had just finished morning drill and dismissed his men to their separate quarters in the farmhouses scattered along the road.

The British reached a point one mile below the American picket at sunrise.[53] There Colonel DuBuy halted his men and laid out his plan of attack on Hopperstown. Cornet George Spencer, of the Queen's Rangers, described the attack in detail:

I was ordered to push forward [with an advance party of Hussars and Queen's Rangers], without stopping at anything, to headquarters. At the bridge we received an ineffectual fire. I immediately galloped as fast as the horses would go through the town without taking notice of some few shots from the windows of those who had waked from the firing of the picket. On my arrival at headquarters, I found about five and twenty men drawn up opposite me on the road, with a brook between us, about twenty yards distant. Having but six men with me, no more being able to keep up on account of the fast gallop through the town, I halted and drew them up. The commanding officer whom I afterward found to be [Major Byles] talk-

48 4 NJA (2) 378, 379.
49 See 17 GW 321 n.
50 18 GW 271, 272.
51 George Spencer dispatch and map, April 15, 1780, HC Papers CL.
52 4 NJA (2) 378.
53 Stephen Lutkins remembered, long after the war, that a "valuable dog belonging to his father was shot by the British on their march up—about 1½ miles below said place." His mother "buried her silver spoons, finger rings, &c, to avoid them being taken by the enemy." Affidavit of Stephen Lutkins, Pension Records, W251.

Operations at Hopperstown, April 16, 1780.
Sir Henry Clinton Papers, Clements Library. Sketch by Cornet George Spencer.

ing to his men and asked his officers if they thought best to fire now or from the house. The latter was agreed to. The house was of stone, with three windows below and two above. At the moment of their going in I galloped across the ravine with about twelve men [the rest of the advance guard and two of the 17th Dragoons having joined] and got close to the wall of the house. From another house about twenty yards farther, nine men, mostly servants of the officers, fired on us. I ordered six or eight of the men, with Corporal Bart, to dismount and fire in the windows of the first house at random. Two were placed at the door. The rest of the men with Corporal Bart broke the second house open. The people in it then surrendered. I attempted to speak to the people in the first house to offer them quarter if they would surrender, but they had so many officers and were so well posted at the windows, and knowing the house to be stone, would not answer any other wise than with shot. Finding it impossible to break the door open, which was attempted and a man of mine shot through it, I ordered fire to be brought from the second house with which I set fire to the corner of the shingled roof. The house was in flame—I again and again offered them good usage if they would surrender. [Major Byles] now ordered his men to stop firing and asked me if I commanded. I told him I commanded the advance guard only, that Colonel DuBuy with five hundred infantry and one hundred cavalry were in the town, that the cavalry were galloping towards the house and it was in vain to attempt a further defense. By this time the quickest of the cavalry were up and Captain Wickham with Tucker and some few dragoons joined me, then DuBuy and Diemar. Seeing it impossible to escape he (on promise of good usage to his men) surrendered. It appeared he had posted an officer and six men to each of the lower windows and the rest above, he himself was at the door. Never was a house better defended. [Major Byles] was wounded in the chest, of which he died three days after.[54]

Americans claimed that he received the mortal wound in the act of surrender. The American loss in killed, wounded and taken was one major, two captains, four lieutenants, and about forty rank and file.[55]

The people of Hopperstown also suffered severely in all of this. "The enemy, agreeable to their usual mode of procedure," the Americans reported, "plundered and burnt the house and mill of Mr. John Hopper and that of his brother's. In the former the family of Mr. Abraham *Brasher* lived. . . . The commanding officer being requested by Mrs. Brasher on her knees to spare the house, he damn'd her, and bid her begone, declaring they all deserved to be bayoneted. They made their boast, that as Major Byles did not present the hilt of his sword in front when surrendering, they shot him." [56]

Mary Hopper, Captain. John Hopper's widow, recalled, almost sixty years later, that when the dragoons surprised the garrison at Hopperstown, they "burned and destroyed two dwelling houses, one store house and one grist mill . . . of her late husband, . . . [who] . . . lost all his private property contained in the buildings, consisting of household furniture, a large quantity of linen and various other goods, and also the sum of $7,000 in money, not a dollar of which was saved, . . . that her late husband escaped at the time with the loss of his hat." [57]

54 George Spencer dispatch and map, supra. The local people believed that the American army had a "general depot" of ammunition and provisions at Hopperstown, and assumed that the attack was directed at the depot. Affidavit of Peter Van Buskirk, Pension Records, R5219, and Pension Records, R5220, passim.
55 4 NJA (2) 379, 380.
56 Idem.
57 4 NJA (2) 350, 351. See 4 NJA (2) 306, 307, 324, 379. Mrs. Hopper "attributed the loss . . . of the money aforesaid," she said, "mainly and altogether that the buildings destroyed were used and occupied by the American troops and arms, ammunition and provisions kept and stored in the buildings . . ." Affidavit of Mary Hopper, Pension Records R5220. Though Hopper had been, as one of his neighbors described him, "an active and prominent officer and much feared by the Tories . . . ," the applications were denied, apparently because the pension clerks were pleased to think that Hopper was merely protecting his own property while he was a captain in the militia. Pension Records R5220.
Two years later, a traveler observed that the Hoppers kept no lock on the stable

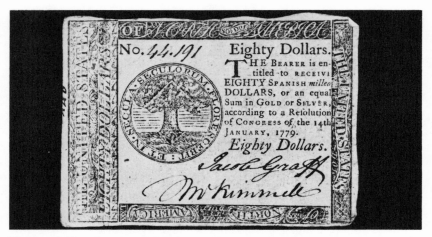

Eighty Dollar Continental Bill circulated in Bergen County, circa 1780.
Courtesy of Mr. and Mrs. Fred Bogert.

The Pennsylvanians blamed their surprise on "the situation of that part of the country, intersected with roads, and inhabited chiefly by disaffected people," [58] but disaffected local people had nothing to do with the American defeat. Actually, as soon as they received the alarm, large numbers of Bergen County militiamen again turned out like veterans, hanging on the flanks and rear of the withdrawing troops in the best tradition of the embattled farmer, firing from behind every stone fence and tree from Paramus to Fort Lee, inflicting heavy casualties on the British columns and finally forcing them to slow their march and throw out flanking parties to protect their main force from the galling fire, with the result that a great many prisoners escaped and a good deal of booty had to be abandoned. More often than not without officers or orders, the militia, stiffened by the remnants of the Continentals, continued to harass the withdrawing troops to the very water's edge, where they retook four wagons and sixteen horses.[59]

"The whole party of the enemy," Captain Peter Ward of the patriot militia reported, "consisted of about six hundred effective men, five hundred infantry and about one hundred cavalry composed of detachments from three different corps, Simcoe's, Hussars and the third dressed in red. The infantry was composed of Hessians and Buskirk's corps, commanded by Colonel Buskirk and Major Tappish, a Hessian officer. . . .

door, an item "which they said was here a superfluous article, as these banditti were guilty of every act of violence." Chastellux, Travels in North America, in the Years 1780, 1781, and 1782, Nov. 23, 1780, and note.
[58] 4 NJA (2) 378; 18 GW 271, 272.
[59] Hallett to Washington, April 16, 1780, GW Papers LC; 4 NJA (2) 379.

In the whole, the loss of the enemy . . . is reckoned in killed, wounded and prisoners, at upwards of thirty." In addition to the heavy Continental casualties, three militiamen were wounded. "Three or four of the well-affected inhabitants were taken in their beds and John Hopper received a desperate cut on the head from one of the Refugees, but is on a fair way to recovery." Ward closed with a plea for more troops, particularly light horsemen. Bergen County Dutchmen would have been flattered to read the last paragraph of his report, probably a far more just and accurate appraisal than the self-serving observations of the defeated Continentals: "The inhabitants on the frontiers of this County, already plundered, diffused and worn out with fatigue and watching, and who for their spirit of perseverance deserve a better fate, must unless speedily saved, soon fall a sacrifice to [enemy] violence." [60]

For the first time since the start of the war, in the spring of 1780, some of the Bergen County Tory soldiers were in action in another theater of war, fighting someone other than their old neighbors.

In the fall of 1779 Major Patrick Ferguson, the distinguished British officer who was principally remembered in Bergen County for his incursion into Paramus and New Bridge on May 18, 1779, received permission to enlist an elite force of Tory troops out of existing regiments to serve in the Carolinas, and many of Van Buskirk's men joined—a larger percentage than any other regiment, Van Buskirk claimed.[61] Major Robert Timpany, the Hackensack schoolmaster, was made second in command; Samuel Ryerson was made a captain.[62] Ferguson's men had sailed from New York on the day after Christmas, 1779. The early spring of 1780 saw them active in the siege and capture of Charleston; by late spring Ferguson and Timpany were engaged in partisan warfare in North and South Carolina, recruiting Tory militiamen as they proceeded and leaving hatred and desolation in their wake.[63] The end of their cam-

---

[60] Peter Ward to Livingston, April [20], 1780, Livingston Papers NYPL; John Fell started to propose Congressional action to reimburse John Hopper, but thought it would be a bad precedent. Fell to Livingston, May 7, 1780, Livingston Papers NYPL. See Petitions of John Hopper and John A. Hopper, Oct. 24, 1787, NJSL.

[61] Van Buskirk to MacKenzie, Aug. 19, 1780, MacKenzie Papers CL.

[62] Clinton, American Rebellion, 441; Samuel Ryerson [Ryerse] letter, May 19, 1781, RUL; 2 Sabine 250. Another brother, Joseph, received a commission as a lieutenant in the Regulars for carrying dispatches two hundred miles into the interior of North Carolina. Samuel's nephew died at Savannah during the southern expedition.

[63] Clinton, American Rebellion, 175, 221, 441, etc.; see Ferguson to Timpany. Oct. 6, 1780, HC Papers CL. L. G. Draper, Kings Mountain and its Heroes (Cincinnati 1881), passim.

paign was that most sanguinary of British defeats, the Battle of King's Mountain, where Ferguson was killed and Timpany and Ryerson were among the few who escaped with their lives, a battle in which, as Ryerson later described it in a letter to his brother, "after an action of one hour and five minutes we were all either killed, wounded or taken. I lost the ring finger and in a great measure the use of my (left) hand, though it did not hinder me from keeping the field. . . . Out of seventy in our [company] there was only nineteen that was not hurt." [64]

[64] Samuel Ryerson letter, May 19, 1781, Ryerson Papers RUL. Despite his experience at King's Mountain, Ryerson had every hope five months before Yorktown that another campaign would "drive the Rebels out of the country or make them own George their master." Idem.

15

L ATE in May, 1780, reports began to come to Bergen County militia headquarters that a number of the New York Refugees had "taken post and erected some works of defense" in the upper part of the township of Bergen, near Bull's Ferry. "The accounts being so imperfect that neither their number or strength could be ascertained with any degree of certainty," Captain John Huyler and Captain Thomas Blanch reported to Governor Livingston on May 27, "we . . . determined to go down with as many of the militia as we could hastily collect and obtain as satisfactory an account as the nature of the case would admit."

On the night of May 27, 1780, Huyler, Blanch and Ensign Banta set off from Closter with thirty militiamen to do so. Ensign Terhune marched with nineteen militiamen from Hackensack. "The two parties joined at the Liberty Pole, and at about two o'clock in the morning marched down under cover of the river mountain to within one-half mile from the Refugee post, a defenceable log house (so-called) erected in the highest part of the mountain about one-half mile below Bull's Ferry road." [1]

1 Huyler and Blanch to Livingston, May 27, 1780, Livingston Papers NYPL, Thomas Blanch lived in a one-story Dutch house about 200 yards west of the present-day railroad tracks in Closter, about half a mile north of the Closter station on the road to Tappan. He was a large powerful man, who, like other militiamen, spent most of his nights in hiding to avoid capture during the war. Nicholas Gilman, The Story of the Ferry, Palisades (N.Y.) Library; Erskine Map 113, NYHS. The blockhouse had been established April 30, 1780. Pattison 391.

When the militiamen reached the heights over Bull's Ferry and saw the strength of the Refugees' fort, they quickly laid aside any thoughts of trying to dislodge them, and set off to return by the main road. "The left flank," they reported, "soon fell in with a party of six of the enemy, of whom one was killed on the spot, one mortally wounded, dying in a little while after, and two taken prisoners. . . . The person killed appeared to be a certain Josiah Banks . . . the person mortally wounded proved to be the noted murderer and robber John Berry (alias) John the Regular. As appears from the enclosed pass, he appeared to be actuated by the most absolute despair, declining to surrender he received his death wound, and thus at last met justice which his complicated villainy fully deserved." [2] Cornelius D. Board, who was with Blanch's party, understood that Berry "boasted that he had killed forty-eight persons." One of the militiamen was wounded.[3]

The people in the neighborhood reported, and the prisoners confirmed, that there were two pieces of artillery, six-pounders, mounted at the blockhouse, that there were usually one or two hundred men on the ground, that they employed twelve or fourteen horsemen every night as a patrol to scout the English Neighborhood, and that the post was commanded by Lieutenant Colonel Abraham Cuyler.[4]

The militiamen, who saw quickly that the blockhouse was too formidable for them to assault—within a month it was to defy a thousand Continentals—wasted no time in self-examination and apologies: they would have attacked the blockhouse cheerfully enough if there had been any chance of success; as it was, killing two Refugees and capturing two others was reward enough for their night's work. They did not discover until later that they had earned a standing reward of $1,000 from the state of New Jersey for killing John the Regular.[5]

During the next two months, with the new blockhouse as a base, the Refugees ranged through the countryside in large parties and in small, plundering farmers and burning their homes; and, as if Refugees were not plague enough, in one case patriots found and captured a party of sailors from a British man-of-war, anchored off Closter Dock, out on the same business.

The first Tory foray was not particularly troublesome. On May 30, 1780, two detachments made a night raid on New Bridge, where, if patriot reports were to be credited, they "met at the house of J. Zabriskie at about one o'clock A.M. and, mistaking each other for the rebel guard

---

[2] Idem. Berry's body was taken to Hackensack and buried there. HBP.
[3] Affidavit of Cornelius D. Board, Pension Records, R974.
[4] Pattison 391. Cuyler had no military command there. Idem.
[5] Romeyn Papers UCL.

(as they call it), fell upon each other in a most furious manner. . . .
They appear to have made a dreadful slaughter, the ground round the
house being in a measure covered with blood." [6]

Nine days later, on June 8, 1780, at about half past four in the morning, a party of thirty to fifty of the Refugees appeared at Isaac Naugle's
house at Closter "and began to collect the horses, cows and sheep that
could be found from there to downwards, as they returned to their post
at Bull's Ferry." [7] The Isaac Naugle house was about two miles south
of the New York-New Jersey line, on the road to Sneden's Landing.[8]
Blanch and Huyler collected the local militia and attacked the marauders, killing one of them, wounding several, and driving the others
off "in such confusion that they dropped several of their greatcoats
and many other articles." They had apparently believed, Blanch said,
that the militia had been called on another expedition "and therefore
thought to take advantage of the neighborhood and strip us of all that's
left." [9]

Two days later, on June 10, Blanch reported the capture of the foraging sailors. "With pleasure I can acquaint you," he wrote to Governor
Livingston, "that . . . the Vulture of sixteen guns came up [the Hud-
son] as high as Closter where it landed [thirty] men," that, although he
had that very morning taken command of a number of new Bergen
County militiamen, he had been able to take "a mate shipman" and
eleven sailors prisoners.[10] He made it clear, however, that he could not
hope to continue to fight off the raiders.

"The Vulture," he went on, "commanded by Captain Sutherland [re-
mains] opposite the dock. The miserable situation we are in I cannot
express. We have no assistance in this quarter, only . . . our too small
company." All the rest, he said, had been ordered out of the county,
except Captain Logan of the Somerset militia, who was posted near
Hackensack, where he could not "do near the service" he could do at
some other place, presumably Closter.[11]

The day before, on June 9, Blanch's fellow officers, Van Busson,
Huyler and Logan, had written to Governor Livingston from Hackensack in even more detail about the need for help:

[6]   4 NJA (2) 433.
[7]   Blanch to Livingston, June 8, 1780, Livingston Papers NYPL.
[8]   I. Hills Map (Map No. 207), HC Papers CL.
[9]   Blanch to Livingston, June 8, 1780, Livingston Papers NYPL.
[10]   Blanch to Livingston, June 10, 1780, Livingston Papers NYPL.; see affidavit of
James Riker, Pension Records, W15877. Captain Blanch was evidently wounded
shortly thereafter. See affidavit of Peter S. Van Orden. Idem.
[11]   Blanch to Livingston, June 10, 1780, Livingston Papers NYPL.

In consequence of the enemy taking post in Bergen County and part of their shipping moving up the Hackensack River, one-half of the militia of Bergen County were ordered into active service for the term of one month unless sooner relieved, to be commanded by Captain Van Busson and Captain Huyler. . . . The former can at no time command upon the parade above thirty and the latter not above twenty-five men. . . . In addition to this Captain Logan of the Somerset militia arrived at this place on the 4th inst. with twenty men under his command. These, sir, compose the total of the defense in this part of the lines, which at a moderate computation extends east and west at least to the distance of eighteen miles.

The assistance we receive from the well-affected inhabitants exceeds our most sanguine wishes, especially if it be considered that they are perfectly worn down with a long series of incessant watchings and fatigues. . . .

We beg leave to recall your excellency's attention for a moment to the importance of this place. We find to our great satisfaction a chain of well-affected inhabitants extended all along the lines, from whom every assistance can be derived which may be expected from their abilities and their determined bravery, but the moment this chain is broke we humbly conceive that Bergen County will not afford a place of security to an active friend of this country even in its most distant parts, and that some of the inhabitants upon the lines will seek security elsewhere. . . . Whether any part of the distance between Morristown and Kings Ferry will be safe for any but an armed force, time only will discover.[12]

Governor Livingston himself could hardly have written a more eloquent plea, but, if anything, Van Busson, Huyler and Logan had understated the peril and the bravery of Hackensack valley Whigs. On June 24, 1780, Major John Mauritius Goetschius lost his house and barn and all his effects by Tory arson. The same Tories had recently burned the large stone house, barn and cowhouse of William J. Christie; the large Dutch house of Jacob Ferdon; the somewhat smaller farmhouse of David Banta; the house of David Samuel Demarest, with its outbuildings and all its furnishings; the home of David B. Demarest, with its huge barn and its cowhouse; the Derick Banta homestead and farm buildings and the John H. Banta farmhouse, barn, cowhouse, windmill and hay barracks.[13] Abraham Vanderbeek's family were "robbed

12 Van Busson, Huyler and Logan to Livingston, June 9, 1780. Livingston Papers NYPL.
13 Damages of British NJSL, Hackensack Precinct, 81, 84, 86, 89, 90, 91, 111, 112; HBP 108; Banta Genealogy No. 237. The Albert D. Banta homestead and the Oldis home had also been put to the torch by Tories. Banta Genealogy No. 580; HBP 322. Several houses were burned at Schraalenburgh on the same day that Major Goetschius' house and barn were lost. See affidavit of James I. Blauvelt, Pension Records, W5828; affidavit of Abraham Blauvelt, Pension Records, S2080. "The same year, he thinks before the harvest, the Refugees came up and burned Schraalenburgh, about

and plundered of all they had; they then removed for safety to . . . the County of Somerset." [14] New Jersey and the continent owed more to these men than to leave them unprotected from the cruelty and hatred of Tory Refugees.

The blockhouse from which their tormentors operated stood on the very edge of the Palisades, on a high point above a ravine running back from the Hudson at Bull's Ferry, protected on two sides by the perpendicular cliffs of the Palisades and in the front by abatis and stockades and a ditch and parapet; a daring location indeed, for the defenders left themselves no retreat once they had retired to it. Its only entrance was a covered way large enough to admit a single person.[15]

In the middle of June the Continental army decided to do something about the blockhouse, doubtless more to harass New York's wood supply than to protect the pillaged patriots of the Hackensack valley. On July 20, 1780, Brigadier General Anthony Wayne laid before Washington, at his headquarters in Preakness, a detailed plan for a full-scale Continental attack, and Washington immediately approved it, suggesting only one alteration, "that of detaching a few horse this afternoon to patrol all night, and to see that the enemy do not, in the course of the night, throw over any troops to form an ambuscade." "They need not go so low down, nor in such numbers," Washington went on to explain, "as to cause any alarm. . . . The enemy have so many emissaries among us, that scarce a move or an order passes unnoticed." [16]

As soon as he received Washington's approval Wayne set off with the 1st and 2nd Pennsylvania Brigades and Colonel Moylan's regiment of dragoons, arriving at New Bridge about nine o'clock at night. There he was joined by the local militia, which had recently been reinforced by four officers and ninety militiamen from Morris, Essex and Sussex counties. After resting four or five hours, he moved forward, nearing Bull's Ferry by daybreak without causing any alarm.[17]

General Irvine, with his brigade, moved along the top of the ridge;

two miles from English Neighborhood; that under the same Captain [Blanch], he went in pursuit of them, but they went off so quickly that it was ineffectual." Affidavit of John A. Haring, Pension Records, S6980.

14   Affidavit of Abraham Vanderbeek, Pension Records, S1130.

15   Winfield, Hudson County, 167; HBP 59, 60. General Pattison complained that it had become a nuisance in attracting runaway slaves, whose women and children merely added hungry mouths to New York. Pattison 391.

16   Wayne to Washington, July 20, 1780, GW Papers LC; 19 GW 216.

17   Huyler to Livingston, July 29, 1780, Livingston Papers NYPL. Winfield, Hudson County, 167. Major Goetschius' militia were with the Continentals. Goetschius to Livingston, Aug. (misdated July) 2, 1780. Livingston Papers NYPL. See e.g. affidavit of John G. Ryerson, Pension Records, S1099.

the 1st Brigade, with Moylan's dragoons and the artillery, by the direct road; the dragoons and a detachment of infantry remaining at the fork of the road leading to Paulus Hook and Bergen to prevent any surprise from that quarter. General Irvine was ordered to take a position north of the blockhouse, where he could intercept any of the enemy that might attempt to land near Fort Lee, the ravine at that place being occupied by two regiments of infantry under orders in case of any landing to hold the pass until supported by General Irvine.[18] At about ten o'clock in the morning of July 21, Wayne's remaining force surrounded the blockhouse, seized the landings on the Hudson below the Palisades and the woodboats and sloops tied up there, and began the attack.[19] Eighty-four Tories were inside, with Thomas Ward in charge.[20]

Sir Henry Clinton was embellishing the truth when he described them as "these poor people . . . only seventy in number (commanded by a Mr. Ward), who, being usually employed in cutting firewood for the inhabitants of New York for the support of their families, had erected this trifling work to protect them against such straggling parties of militia as might be disposed to molest them, not imagining they could ever become an object to a more formidable enemy." [21] Far more Highland gang members than deserving poor were working at the dangerous wood-cutting trade; nonetheless, even if all eighty-four had been hardened Highland marauders, they were no match for a thousand Continentals.

The American infantry surrounded the blockhouse on three sides and began a heavy musket fire, while the field pieces were brought up within sixty yards of the entrance. At this point-blank range a cannonade began at eleven o'clock which lasted for an hour.[22]

Neither the artillery nor the muskets, seemingly, made the slightest impression on the fort or on its defenders, and several attempts to force an entrance by infantry attack were driven back with heavy casualties. Three American officers and fifteen men were killed and forty-six wounded.[23]

Major Goetschius "had the misfortune," he reported to Governor Livingston, "of having two of his men wounded at the blockhouse en-

[18] Wayne to Washington, July 26, 1780, GW Papers LC; 19 GW 260.
[19] Winfield, Hudson County, 167; 4 NJA (2) 538, 546, 553, 556, 577, 581.
[20] The Tory press originally reported that it was "held only by eighty-four." The British later used the round figure seventy. 4 NJA (2) 546; Clinton, American Rebellion, 200.
[21] Clinton, American Rebellion, 200.
[22] Wayne to Washington, July 26, 1780, GW Papers LC; 19 GW 261.
[23] Winfield, Hudson County, 169; cf. 4 NJA (2) 546. Actually the blockhouse was severely damaged and many of its defenders killed or wounded. Clinton, American Rebellion, 200.

gagement . . . not mortal but very bad." [24] At length Wayne was forced to withdraw, fearing English reinforcements from across the Hudson.[25] The Tories claimed that they had but one round of ammunition left when the American decision was made, but that they pursued the chagrined attackers for a good distance back toward New Bridge as boldly as if they had hundreds.[26]

Some years earlier Wayne had been much given to cheerful ridicule of Dutchmen, telling one of his friends that if Dutch troops were ordered to be silent, "they one and all begin to gabble Dutch," and if ordered "to march, they make off in full speed to their respective huts." [27] There may well have been a few patriot farmers along his inglorious retreat who remarked to their wives that it was not always the Dutchmen who did things backwards.

In truth Wayne himself was more than downcast by the affair. Fearful that the story would shock his friends at Philadelphia, he wrote a number of letters defending the action, explaining to Colonel Joseph Reed, for example, that the grand object "was to draw the army which Sir Henry Clinton brought home from Charleston into an action in the defiles of the mountains in the vicinity of Fort Lee, where we expected them to land to succor the refugee post," an explanation which was hardly candid, since the minutes of a council of war of the eight line officers on the scene make it clear that it was the very risk of such a British move that induced the Americans "to withdraw in time to secure our passage over New Bridge and to drive off the cattle, after burning the boats at the [Bull's Ferry] landing." Reed thanked Wayne for the letter, said that it had "wiped off all doubts, [though] in some respects it tended to make the affair of the blockhouse a more important business than it really was." [28]

Sir Henry Clinton's aide and chief intelligence officer, Major John André, was so pleased by the Refugees' defense that he took pen in hand and wrote a mock-heroic poem, of three cantos and seventy-two verses, and sent them for publication to his good friend James Rivington,

24 Goetschius to Livingston, Aug. (misdated July) 2, 1780, Livingston Papers NYPL.
25 Wayne to Washington, July 26, 1780, GW Papers LC; 19 GW 261.
26 See Clinton, American Rebellion, 200; Winfield, Hudson County, 168 n. Ward himself sought and received £531 sterling (£944 New York currency) for "sundry wagons, horses, wood and clothing which were taken and destroyed by the rebels in the action at Bull's Ferry the 21st of July 1780." Undated memorandum, nom. "Great Britain," HC Papers LC.
27 Wayne to Wood, March 2, 1777, NYPL.
28 Wayne to Reed, July 26, 1780; Reed to Wayne, Aug. 4, 1780, Wayne Papers, HSP; Zebulon Pike to Wayne, July 21, 1780; Minutes of Council of War, July 21, 1780; Wayne to Delany and Johnston, July 26, 1780, American Art Association Catalog, Dec. 5 and 6, 1934. pp. 189 etc.

ridiculing the "warrior-drover" Wayne and the unfortunate cow-chase, mocking the "many heroes brave and bold from New Bridge and Tappan," and "the chief whom we beheld of late, near Schraalenburgh haranguing." [29] André knew the quaint Dutch settlements beyond the Palisades well, with their low stone houses and taverns, their one-story churches and large red barns with doors at the gable ends.

To the British the eighty-four brave defenders of the Bull's Ferry blockhouse had erased the disgrace of Paulus Hook and vindicated Tory arms. "This gallant band," Sir Henry Clinton wrote, "defended themselves with activity and spirit; and, after sustaining the enemy's fire for some hours (by which one face of their little blockhouse was perforated by at least fifty cannon shot and twenty-one of their number killed and wounded) and repulsing an assault on their works, they sallied out and pursued their assailants to some distance, picking up stragglers and rescuing from them part of the cattle they were driving off. Such rare and exalted bravery merited every encouragement in my power, and I did not fail to distinguish it at the time by suitable commendations and rewards." His Britannic Majesty, George III himself, sent a congratulatory message to "the survivors of the brave Seventy"; [30] Thomas Ward, the man who had led the defense, was, for a few weeks at least, the hero of every coffeehouse in Tory New York and the toast of London.

Ward had been well known to the good people of Bergen County long before he distinguished himself at Bull's Ferry, and was not likely to be toasted by patriots at Morris Earl's tavern at Hackensack, or indeed by anyone else in the neutral ground. He had been born and reared in the Clove, above Suffern's Tavern, probably the son of a workman in the iron trade.[31] He was enlisted into the Continental Line as a sergeant by Captain John Sandford on April 3, 1777.[32] He claimed to the British that he deserted from the American army and joined the British in New York City on June 16, 1777; [33] the American records indicate that he deserted almost a year later, on April 26, 1778.[34] Whatever the date, like many other deserters, he did not join the organized loyalist troops, but set out upon a career as an irregular, as a Highland gang member,[35] as an espionage agent, as a Tory woodcutter, and as a raider of patriot

---

[29] 4 NJA (2) 585, 610, 668; Winfield, Hudson County, 171 et seq., HBP 60, 61.
[30] Clinton, American Rebellion, 200; 5 NJA (2) 144; Winfield, Hudson County, 170.
[31] Thomas Ward memorandum, undated papers, HC Papers CL; Winfield, Hudson County, 166 n.
[32] 1 Arch. N.Y. 241.
[33] Thomas Ward memorandum, undated papers, HC Papers CL.
[34] 1 Arch. N.Y. 241.
[35] Eager, History of Orange County, 560.

farms in the neutral ground.[36] After the war Matthias Bogert and the widows Effye Cole and Maritie Tallman had particular reason to remember him for his raid into Closter on March 11 and 12, 1781.[37] If he had done nothing else for the British during the war, he deserved of course to be remembered as a member of the daring party who captured the American General Ward.[38] He had many narrow escapes. Pressed by headquarters to write a brief résumé of his work for King George after the defense of the blockhouse, and less adept at spelling than military affairs, he told of being attacked once by a whole troop of American cavalry. He had gone out, he wrote, "with a small partry with a vue of gitten hay and fuel for the troops but being continaly interpupted by the rebels maid but little hand of it and at a time when we had the grat quantey of hay on the ground the rebel hors was sent to burn the hay and drive us from the ground. The first nots of the comming was by the fire of a musket of our sentotre that about one quarter of a mile from us when fird hid himself in the roks as the was no other way of escape. Our bots was all at ground and no way to mak our ecape from them. We had ondly 10 armd men and new not there nombre but amedly apeard 25 lite hors men well mounted and rushed on towarde us. I desird the pepel that had no arms to hide them selves in the reads eceptn such as had hay forks and for the others to wash if any of us fell and if so to tate the place." The American light horsemen came up within one hundred fifty yards of Ward's small party, exchanged a round of fire in which an American was killed and another wounded, along with one of the mounts, and two of Ward's men wounded, after which the Americans retreated.

At another time on one of his forays into the Highlands, he added, "wee fell in with a large party of the rebels who being fetig'd on their march had taken lodgings on the rout to New England, eight or ten in a hows as they found conveanant, when wee was joined by three Loyalists, who with me incountered all dangers and in one night disarmed near 70 rebles and gave them their peroals sundry of which afterwards served to exchange for the same number of unfortunate Loyalists who had fallen in their hands." He was once taken prisoner.[39] He had been very active as an intelligence agent for Major André and had twice accepted the dangerous task of passing through the American lines to make

36 AZ to William Tryon, Feb. 1, 1780, British Transcripts LC; 2 Moore, Diary of American Revolution, 348; Damages by British NJSL.
37 Damages by British NJSL, Harrington Precinct Nos. 39, 47, 48. He had raised a company and received a commission under the Associated Loyalists by this date. Wertenbaker, Father Knickerbocker, 229.
38 Thomas Ward memorandum, undated papers, HC Papers CL.
39 Idem.

contact with Butler and his Indian raiders in the Mohawk valley, once meeting an emissary from Butler at Poughkeepsie, once going to the Mohawk itself, from which he brought back detailed and circumstantial reports of the Cherry Valley Massacre and other work of Britain's Indian allies.[40] He had been sent out in the fall of 1779 to loiter about Anthony Wayne's encampment at Schraalenburgh and Liberty Pole in the garb of a countryman, counting artillery pieces and gossiping with the troops, at the constant risk of recognition by local people.[41] The blockhouse defense was but the latest example of his daring.

During the spring of 1780 he had come to be as well known in and around the town of Bergen as Abraham Van Buskirk himself, though less favorably, for his woodchopping activities in the country south of English Neighborhood.[42]

With fuel as important to New York as powder and shot, the British barrackmasters made the supply of firewood for the British troops perhaps the most lucrative of their many peculations. These cheats, who were hated by the Regulars no less than by patriots, had obtained a monopoly of the fuel supply for the beleaguered city, sending out the worst of the Refugees, white and black, to strip the woodlands of Westchester, Long Island and nearby New Jersey for their greedy trade. The lower peninsula between the Hudson and the Hackensack marshes was one of their favorite sources because of the easy water transportation to the city, the Bull's Ferry blockhouse having been built specifically to cover woodcutting operations. The owners of the wood, whether loyalist or patriot, were paid nothing while the army was charged full price for every stick they delivered, and many a cord they did not.[43] Little wonder, then, that Ward found the prosaic work of protecting woodcutters more

[40] André, Intelligence, misc. undated papers, HC Papers CL. Bakeless 267.

[41] Ward to Clinton, Nov. 2, 1779, HC Papers CL. A few days later, Captain Patrick Ferguson, who had probably sent out Ward, and was reflecting his complaints, told Sir Henry that "the men employed in this important hazardous confidential service are generally disgusted with the very little encouragement they have met with, and complain that it is with the utmost difficulty they can procure at their return as much money as will barely defray the expense of a painful journey during which they are often obliged to live in the woods, avoid all human comfort and society and are under the constant apprehensions of being dragged from their skulking holes to an ignominious death." Ferguson to Clinton, Nov. 7, 1779, HC Papers CL. Any lack of monetary encouragement would certainly have disgusted Ward; it is hard to picture him as apprehensive.

[42] One patriot had reason to be grateful to him; he passed Domine Romeyn's niece through the British lines to visit her imprisoned father in New York on July 20, 1780, for which he was duly reprimanded. Pattison 413.

[43] Memorial from Inhabitants of Bergen Neck, nom. "Loyalists," undated papers, HC Papers CL. See 1 Jones, New York During the Revolution, 341, where an even more vehement attack is made on the woodcutters.

attractive than highway robbery on the Continental road, even before he became an international celebrity by doing so.

One long-suffering loyalist of Bergen Neck who had had much of his property ruined by Ward's woodcutters finally obtained an order from Sir Henry Clinton forbidding the cutting of trees on his farm. When this was triumphantly handed to the woodcutter, he said, "Well, I guess we can't cut any more trees here," hesitated a minute, and then added, "We'll just girdle them and get them ready for next year," after which he and his woodchoppers proceeded to kill every living tree that the loyalist owned; similar destruction elsewhere soon left the well-wooded lower peninsula between the Hackensack and the Hudson a country of bare stumps.[44] The Van Buskirks of the town of Bergen claimed that the woodcutters had chopped down every tree on their farms without leave and without pay (they finally received half the stipulated compensation).[45] Another resident of Bergen, probably not particularly patriotic, had good reason to think that Ward had hired a party of Negroes to murder him to keep him from pressing a debt against Ward.[46]

For a time after the blockhouse attack Ward was able to forget his debts. He collected handsomely from the British Treasury for the wagons and cattle he lost at Bull's Ferry; he collected £1,880 in hard money, long before other Tories dreamed of the possibility of such an indemnity, for a home in the Clove that would have been a modest rival for the Sidman and Erskine mansions if it had existed.[47] Later he was one of those who formed a company to serve under the banner of the Associated Loyalists, when that organization was founded to carry on freebooting under a royal charter,[48] and, if his old friend and fellow worker, John Mason, was to be believed under somewhat trying circumstances (he was on the way to the gallows at the time), Ward had once completed plans to take thirty men out from New York to capture General Washington, a project which Sir Henry Clinton had vetoed because he could not see how they could bring Washington in alive.[49] Ward capped a long and profitable career in support of his Tory principles by offering to desert to the American side shortly after his raid on Closter in March, 1781;[50] an offer which General Washington ordered refused "except he

44 Winfield, Hudson County, 183, 166.
45 Loyalists to Carleton, May 24, 1782; Van Buskirk to Carleton, May 27, 1782, HC Papers CL.
46 Winfield, Hudson County, 166. The Negroes were hanged. Idem.
47 Undated memorandum "Great Britain," HC Papers CL. The other Refugees received free uniforms. Winfield, Hudson County, 169. Ward's wife and child had been drawing British provisions at an earlier date. 1 Carleton Papers 431, 478 (1991, 2133).
48 Wertenbaker, Father Knickerbocker, 229.
49 Van Doren, Mutiny in January, 155.
50 22 GW 96, 127.

will engage to render some exceptional piece of service or to bring off a body of his men. He himself is of no manner of consequence and I had rather he would remain with the enemy than come off alone." [51] Thus frustrated in his plan to aid his countrymen, he evidently decided not to desert, and the last word of him is the complaint of David Babcock, a fellow refugee from Orange County, in 1786, from Shelburne, Nova Scotia, that Ward had failed to present Babcock's claims for British compensation.[52]

Three things occupied General Washington in the early summer of 1780: first, he was desperately concerned about the straits of the army under the disorganized system of supply; second, he was planning to attack Manhattan Island; and, third, he feared that Sir Henry would again attempt to force the Hudson Highlands, a fear that made him suspect that every British move, whether Knyphausen's march on Springfield, New Jersey, or Clinton's own expedition toward Newport, Rhode Island, was a diversion covering an attack on West Point.

The arrival of the French fleet and a French army at Newport on July 10, 1780, greatly improved Washington's military prospects, and he set to work at once upon plans for a grand assault on New York City, with thirty to forty thousand men, aided by the French fleet. On August 8, 1780, Washington took up headquarters at Tappan, in the De Windt house,[53] a low brick and stone cottage built by the Huguenot Daniel de Clerck in 1700. With Washington were his chief officers and the main body of the Continental army, ready to move at once to defend the Highlands or attack New York if an opportunity arose.

The summer had been intensely hot and dry, but the drought was broken almost as soon as they established themselves at Tappan. "We are encamped," one Jerseyman wrote, "near a pleasant little village about two miles from the Hudson. The inhabitants are principally low Dutch, though there are some refugees from New York. I am told that there are some very good Whigs here. Silver and gold is the only established currency in the country as the Dutch have substantial wealth. We are in the heart of a delightful and plentiful country but for the want of specie cannot reap much advantage from it." [54]

[51]   22 GW 127, 128.
[52]   Fraser 147. See also 7 GC 333 and 4 Carleton Papers passim.
[53]   19 GW 338, et seq. The house was then in the possession of Major Frederick Blauvelt of the New York militia. Blauvelt Genealogy No. 116. Affidavit of Harman Blauvelt, Pension Records, S959.
[54]   Diary of William S. Pennington, 63 NJHSP 199, 210. "A most excellent country, inhabited chiefly by low Dutch," a Pennsylvanian wrote. 11 Penn. Arch. (2) 571, et seq.

There were, of course, all too many who did not let the lack of specie keep them from profiting by their location. Continental foraging parties stripped Tappan's barns bare, and straggling soldiers took what was left. The Continental magazines had been entirely empty for a month, the receipts of one day issued the next. Justice John Haring told General Washington, only three days after the army moved to Tappan, that his neighbors were filled with apprehension of "being brought to a starving condition. . . . Cornfields, buckwheat, orchards, meadows, &c. &c. are laid waste, and we know not where it will end." Though Washington assured him "that the most pointed orders have been issued on this subject since we came on this ground," Haring and Washington both knew that it was impossible to keep half-starved soldiers from plundering, orders or no orders.[55] Nonetheless, few could have failed to see the irony of Americans plundering the homes of Orange County Dutchmen, while large numbers of Orange County patriots were in the Mohawk Valley, a hundred and fifty miles away, defending Americans from the ravages of Brant's Indians, and in daily combat with the Tories and Regulars.[56]

Nor could the most dedicated patriot fail to see that the troops of the line were no longer farm boys with muskets. The Continentals at Tappan were campaign-hardened professional soldiers, a good number of them captives and deserters from the redcoats, men who knew very well how to live on the country when the commissaries failed them, and plundering was only part of the story.

When the British issued a proclamation of pardon to British deserters, large numbers of Continental soldiers at Tappan re-deserted, and the British intelligence files are filled with their reports. One Hart and his wife, doubtless Tory refugees temporarily and conveniently resident in Tappan, passed many deserters on to the British and a great deal of intelligence with them. One deserter told British headquarters that he had dropped out of camp "about gunfiring," and gone directly to Hart's house, where Mrs. Hart had hidden him for a time, meanwhile giving him a mass of information to memorize and carry to headquarters.[57]

Except for militia patrols a few miles south of camp, the roads from Tappan to the British lines lay open to them. Guided by British agents, deserters would disappear into the house of some Tory or spy, only to appear in lower English Neighborhood a night or two later, hiding by

[55]   19 GW 358 n.; 19 GW 358.
[56]   19 GW 391. See, e.g., Pension S11160 (Peter S. Van Orden); W7185 (Garret Smith); S15200 (James Quackenbush).
[57]   British Intelligence Reports, Emmet Coll., NYPL. The Harts may have been Jacob and his wife, refugees from the English Neighborhood. See 4 Carleton Papers 195 (8279).

day in the same Tory cellars and barns that sheltered Highland marauders on their way back and forth to New York. Now and then the traffic fell into American hands: one party was attacked near Liberty Pole "by the rebels, who took the lieutenant and three men; the party dispersed and skirmished all day," and many others reported that they had been pursued by the militia when they thought themselves well below the lines, but most of the deserters reached the ferries safely and passed over into New York.[58]

Though headquarters were at Tappan, Washington's army occupied the country for several miles on either side of the town.

General Lafayette and his newly formed light infantry took up advanced positions at Steenrapie, on the west bank of the Hackensack just above the head of tidewater. Poor's, Stark's, the 1st, 2nd, 3rd and 4th Massachusetts, the New York, Jersey, 2nd Pennsylvania and the 1st and 2nd Connecticut Regiments lay in a semicircle from Steenrapie to the Tappan Sloat, a mile or so east of Tappan village, under Generals Lafayette, Hand, Poor, McDougall, Howe, Greene, Lord Stirling, St. Clair, von Steuben, and Parsons.[59]

General Arnold had been removed from the order of battle by his new command at West Point. Colonel Elias Dayton reported to New Jersey's Governor Livingston on August 17, 1780, that the "grand camp is pitched in and about [Tappan], with the light infantry advanced about four miles in front towards Schraalenburgh. . . . Our army is, in comparison to what it has been, pretty formidable in point of number and I hope will soon be in point of discipline, for the greatest industry is practiced in training the recruits, who have joined in considerable number from the other states." [60]

Washington instructed the Bergen County militia operating from Closter to continue to act as pickets, to patrol the shores of the Hudson, and to forward such intelligence as could be got of Clinton's moves.[61] On August 9, 1780, Major Goetschius was ordered to serve with the Continental light infantry, taking his orders from the Marquis de Lafayette, whose corps, the orders noted, was then "extending its attention

---

[58] Idem.
[59] See French War Office map of Northern New Jersey, NYPL; 69 NJHSP 16, etc. British intelligence placed the light infantry "three miles on this side of Tappan." British Intelligence Reports, Emmet Coll., NYPL.
[60] Dayton to Livingston, Aug. 17, 1780, NYPL. Despite their industry in training recruits, at least two of the officers of the Pennsylvania Light Infantry in advance positions sometimes found time to go huckleberrying in the morning and to drink punch in the afternoon. 11 Penn. Arch. (2) 571.
[61] 19 GW 349. See Goetschius to Washington, Aug. 8, 1780, GW Papers LC.

to the Closter Landing, the roads leading from Fort Lee, &ca." [62] Nineteen-year-old Harman Blauvelt, of the Tappan militia, remembered for years after the war that he often drilled under the direction of Baron von Steuben that summer and that "he would sit on his horse and give his orders through the officers of the regiment in French or broken English." [63]

The eastern pivot of the Continental camp was a large wood and stone blockhouse which was being built on the heights of the Palisades about fifteen hundred feet north of the road leading down to the ferry at Sneden's Landing.[64] The Dobbs Ferry blockhouse, as it was generally called, was probably built under the supervision of the French engineer Colonel Jean Baptiste Gouvion, who had designed and constructed many of the works at West Point and Verplanck's Point.[65]

A sergeant in the corps of sappers and miners who was stationed there recalled that "most of the artillery belonging to the army was at the same place" during the summer of 1780. "Here we lay till the close of the campaign. We built a strong blockhouse near the ferry, in which we were assisted by detachments from the main army, and erected a battery near it, but that fiend, scarcity, followed us here; and when we chanced to get any meat we had no salt. For a long time we had to go three-fourths of a mile to the river to get water, which was somewhat salt, before we could cook our breakfasts,—this was trifling, however, compared with the trouble of having nothing to cook, which was too often the case with us. There was, indeed, a plenty of fruit to be had, and we being few in number, and so far from the main army, this resource was not soon or easily exhausted; but there were mosquitoes enough to take a pound of blood from us while we could make an ounce." [66]

Construction went on all summer. Early in August a soldier who deserted by swimming out to H.M.S. *Vulture* told the British that the Americans were building a blockhouse at Sneden's Landing, "about three hundred fifty men there, no guns there, they expect the latter end of the week two eighteen-pounders. . . . There is a place there for three guns by the waterside." Later British intelligence indicated that two thousand men under Baron von Steuben were making fascines and that the batteries included howitzers and three eighteen-pounders.[67]

62 19 GW 348, 349.
63 Affidavit of Harman Blauvelt, Pension Records, S959.
64 Gilman 123. He located it there on the evidence of common repute and the piles of stones brought there to fill the walls.
65 See 19 GW 58; Heath to McDougall, Sept. 22, 1781, McDougall Papers NYHS.
66 Martin Narrative 143.
67 British Intelligence Reports, Emmet Coll., NYPL.

A Bergen County militiaman remembered after the war that General Washington himself, with his Life Guards, once rode up to the post "on the brink of the river . . . and commanded them to be diligent and watchful on this station . . . [promising] . . . that he would send a company of his regular troops to reinforce them, which he performed." [68]

Palisades of the Hudson.
Courtesy New-York Historical Society. Portion of engraving by I. Hill.

Washington had intended to use the Dobbs Ferry blockhouse in connection with his planned attack on New York, and he sometimes made his headquarters there.[69] It protected the important ferry landing, it served as a base for parties of observation going down into the neutral ground, and to some extent it was intended to harass navigation on the river. When Captain Joseph McClellan, of the 9th Pennsylvania Regiment, visited the construction on August 15, 1780, he found "the artillery under the command of Colonel Crane . . . throwing shells out of an 8½ inch howitzer in order to gain the channel of the river, the artillery then at the post being two iron 18-pounders, one 8½ inch howitzer and one 5½ inch ditto." [70]

The blockhouse was completed late in September. Nathanael Greene reported on September 23 that "the blockhouse goes on very well and

[68] Affidavits of Benjamin P. Westervelt, Pension Records, S1148, and Cornelius P. Westervelt, Pension Records, W1010.

[69] See 19 GW 108, 109.

[70] 11 Penn. Arch. 571, etc.

will be complete in about five days, and I think it will be a very strong place." The French minister, he added, "was down to view it yesterday." [71]

British intelligence reports include a description of the completed fort, brought in by Theunis Blauvelt in February, 1781:

There are to a certainty no cannon in the blockhouse and twenty-six men (which is the whole detachment) are posted in it at night, under the command of an officer; he neither knows the name nor rank. There are five batteau hauled up upon the beach, about a short half-mile below the blockhouse, but no guard to take care of them. There is one sentry only at nights; he is posted upon the top of the blockhouse, which is not roofed, but the side wall rises four feet above the upper floor, and there is a communication with the lower story at the southeast corner. The door of the blockhouse fronts at the northward and is covered by a log [triangular barrier]; beyond which an abatis is laid, which surrounds the whole and which has likewise an opening to the northward.

The opening in the abatis is closed [at about] eight or nine at night and the inner door is shut at the same time. The blockhouse may be approached 'till within fifty yards without discovery.

All of this detailed intelligence came to Blauvelt by a trusted friend "who lives near the blockhouse and went into it on purpose last Thursday: he remained 'till after sun setting and saw the night sentry posted, as well as the five batteaus. The enclosed sketch of the post he took upon his return home." [72] The sketch shows a rude outline of a square, with a triangular barrier at the entrance and a circular abatis, with a line to represent the North River, nothing more.

There were still Tories in the neutral ground in February, 1781, after half a decade of war, who were sufficiently accepted as patriots or neutrals to loiter about an American fort for hours, counting its men and watching what passed for security procedures. It is not likely that the trusting soldiers were Jersey Dutchmen; the men who were garrisoning the blockhouse that winter were almost certainly Continentals, happy to receive the Dutchman's produce and to listen to the slow-witted country bumpkin's talk.

Blauvelt was right in believing the blockhouse vulnerable. It was not designed as a strong point in itself, the commanding officer having been under Washington's specific orders to withdraw if attacked, first setting fire to the fort, "for which previous provision is to be made." If surrounded and unable to withdraw, the orders were, however, "to main-

[71] Greene to Washington, Sept. 23, 1780, GW Papers LC.
[72] George Beckwith Intelligence, Feb. 25, 1781, HC Papers CL.

tain the post to the last extremity . . . and for this purpose you will endeavor always to have five or six days' provisions on hand." [73]

Washington never made his attack on New York, nor, for that matter, did Sir Henry Clinton make any move during the summer. General Washington was disappointed in the amount of French aid available for the attack; Clinton, for his part, was pursuing other plans for breaching the Highlands.

After two weeks, Washington moved his army a few miles to the south. The forage at Tappan was exhausted. At seven in the morning on August 22, 1780, the right wing (Sinclair's division, Stirling's division, the Connecticut division, the artillery, with a vanguard and rearguard of picked troops) marched down Schraalenburgh Road, and the left wing (Howe's division, McDougall's division and von Steuben's division) down the Closter Road, the two meeting near Liberty Pole a few hours later.[74] It was "a very fine cool morning." [75]

"Our march," one of the officers of artillery wrote, "was through the formerly delightful village of Schraalenburgh but was at the commencement of this Campaign reduced to a heap of rubbish by a party of Refugees and Runaway Negroes, the inhabitants being mostly friendly to their country." [76]

The troops were posted to the east of Teaneck Road, for a mile south of the road to Liberty Pole, and in a northeasterly direction from the Liberty Road, toward Tenafly, with Lafayette's headquarters on Teaneck Road, just below Liberty Road,[77] and Washington's, traditionally, opposite the Liberty Pole Tavern in northern English Neighborhood.[78] Lafayette's light forces were stationed in an advanced position south and east of the junction of the English Neighborhood road and the road to Fort Lee.[79] Lafayette was justly proud of his new command and they of him; a few days earlier each officer in the corps had "received an elegant feather, cockade and epaulets, a present from the Marquis de Lafayette. Each non-commissioned officer received an elegant sword, feather, two bob and as much silver lace as would lace the front of their caps, a present from the Marquis de Lafayette." [80]

[73] 20 GW 139. See also 20 GW 394, 426, 427.
[74] Orderly Book of the N.J. Brigade, July 30 to Oct. 8, 1780 (BHSP 1922), 25, 26, 27; 19 GW 425.
[75] 11 Penn. Arch. (2) 571, et seq.
[76] 62 NJHSP 199, 211.
[77] See French War Office map of Northern New Jersey NYPL.
[78] HBP 263.
[79] See French War Office map of Northern New Jersey NYPL.
[80] 11 Penn. Arch. (2) 571, et seq.

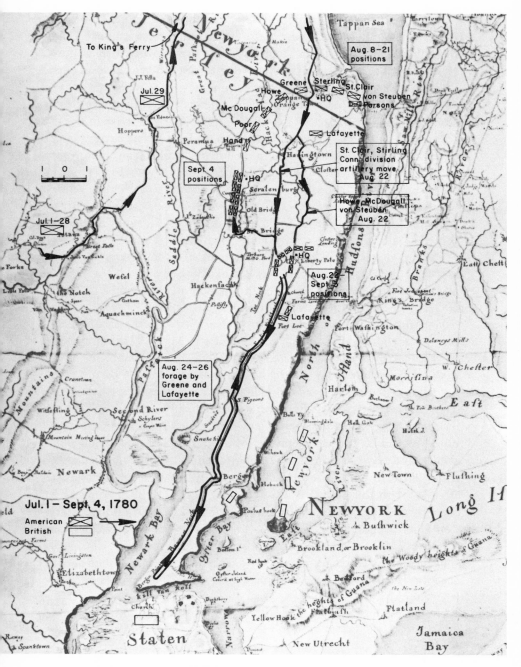

Movements of Continental Army July-September, 1780.
Drawn on contemporary map. Sir Henry Clinton Papers. Clements Library. E. Tone, 1962.

Three miles to the east of the main army's camp, looking as if the troops could almost reach over and touch them, were the hills forming the Palisades of the Hudson, and across the river was the British army. Never before in the years of campaigning for New York had the Americans so boldly placed themselves open to attack.

"The Army being now very near the Enemy," Washington declared, "the Gen'l flatters himself every Officer and Soldier will make it a point of Honor . . . to be at the shortest notice ready to Act as circumstances may require. He is at the same time persuaded, should an opportunity be afforded us, that every part of the Army will vie with each other in the display of that conduct, fortitude and bravery which ought to distinguish troops fighting for their Country, for their liberty, for everything dear to the Citizen, or to the Soldier. He also hopes to hear of no wanton depredation on the persons or property of the Inhabitants." [81]

Each man was supplied with forty rounds of ammunition, two days' supply of flour, and bayonets were ordered to be carried fixed.[82] Each brigade of light infantry had two three-pound artillery pieces and each of the other brigades had two six-pounders.[83]

Doubtless Washington remembered clearly enough the strategic reasons for withdrawing from the peninsula between the Hudson and the Hackensack four years before and was willing to face them, but there were many junior officers who had reservations: "We have been here in the vicinity of Fort Lee bidding defiance to Sir Henry for eight or ten days," Lieutenant Samuel Shaw wrote to General Lamb from Teaneck on August 31, "but he does not choose to take advantage of our position; which, with proper deference, I think a damnable one. Should the enemy land above us, they would have an amazing odds in their favor. If our left flank should be turned and a defeat ensue, a retreat must be attended with the utmost confusion, as we have two rivers directly in our rear, and the only passage across one of these is over a bridge which would not support two-thirds the weight of one of our heavy eighteen pounders." [84] The Hackensack was fordable a few miles to the north, and the young lieutenant probably overestimated his danger, but he was not wholly mistaken. The Continental army had often encamped on safer ground.

"I am very happy that the army has been in a situation to bully Sir

---

[81]   19 GW 429, 430. He added that the officers of police were to be "particularly careful to prevent the destruction of fences."

[82]   See 19 GW 435.

[83]   British Intelligence Reports, Emmet Coll., NYPL.

[84]   Shaw to Lamb, Aug. 31, 1780, Lamb Papers NYHS.

Harry with impunity," General John Lamb somewhat discreetly answered Shaw. "I say with impunity; had he plucked up courage, landed above you and turned your flank, I believe it would have been a very serious piece of business." [85]

Clinton had for years been trying to bring Washington into a general engagement in the neutral ground west of the Hudson, "in the angle between the mountains and the river," where, he felt, by reason of the British control of the river, a battle would be "on terms replete with risk on his part and little or none on mine." He had deliberately offered Washington battle there in 1777 and 1778 without success, but as he wrote later: "That wary officer saw the advantages my command of the river gave me over him in ground so critically circumstanced." [86] Now Washington's main army was encamped in the lower Hackensack valley, well within the angle between the mountains and the river, but Clinton made no move whatever.

Two days after the troops arrived at Teaneck, Washington sent off Major General Greene, with Lafayette's light infantry and four brigades of other troops, upon an even more brazen move, a forage extending from English Neighborhood down to Bergen Town. Greene doubtless remembered the English Neighborhood well; he had abandoned it most hurriedly four years before. Washington directed him to make the forage thorough: "Such are the necessities of the army, and such the situation of the inhabitants, being all within the power of the enemy, that you will make the forage as extensive as possible in the articles of hay and grain, as well as in cattle, hogs and sheep fit for slaughter; and horses fit for the use of the army." [87] That night Lafayette and his light camp

85   Lamb to Shaw, Sept. 10, 1780, Lamb Papers NYHS.
86   Clinton, American Rebellion, 122, 132. The Americans were in fact fully aware of the danger of a river landing on their flank and did their best to prevent one: "You are to detach a captain's guard to the bank of the river opposite a landing about one-half mile south of Spuyten Duyvil Creek, with orders to defend that pass at every hazard," General Anthony Wayne ordered on Aug. 23, 1780. "As your post is so situated that the enemy, after embarking at Spuyten Duyvil, may reach you in fifteen minutes," he went on, "you cannot be too attentive to their motions, and although it is not in your power to prevent a landing yet the defiles [behind you are] so difficult of access that your numbers will be sufficient to defend that pass for hours against thousands—which you are to do at every expense of blood until confined or drawn off—sending immediate intelligence to headquarters of any serious moves you may observe." Order dated Aug. 23, 1780, Wayne Papers HSP.
87   19 GW 431, 432.

posted themselves almost within musket range of Paulus Hook and insolently surveyed New York and the harbor from Bergen Heights, then went down Bergen Neck and foraged in sight of the Greencoats on Staten Island, who fired ineffectually upon the wagoners.[88] British intelligence officers were doubtless happy to learn from deserters that the Americans had brought 350 wagons with them, and only light artillery, and were planning nothing but a forage. They had heard earlier that "General Knox says if they get the heights of Bergen they can make our people quit Paulus Hook with shells. They have got a large mortar to the army lately and are hard at work in the country making shells."[89]

The raid was the boldest affront to the British that the suffering patriots of lower Bergen County could remember; unfortunately they were to remember the affair longer for other reasons. As one American officer wrote, "a business of this kind is seldom unattended by more or less of injury to the household property of the inhabitants. The soldiers will find occasions to pilfer, however watched by the officer. It is impossible to exclude every practice of this nature. All the officer can do in this case is to punish the offender when discovered and restore the goods. This was done in every instance; and one of the soldiers hanged on the spot."[90]

The Tory press in New York fumed that the Americans had insulted and robbed people going to the old Bergen church, "in one instance stripping off a man's breeches, leaving an old pair of trousers to cover his nakedness."[91] If the poor Tory went on to church in the old pair of trousers, he was probably subjected to the further indignity of having to listen to a good Whig sermon from Domine William Jackson, for the domine was no respecter of Tory feelings, having once pointedly preached to a Tory gathering on the text, "What will ye give me, and I will deliver him unto you? And they covenanted with him for thirty pieces of silver." Matt. 26:15.[92]

[88]   4 NJA (2) 601, 625–627.
[89]   British Intelligence Reports, Emmet Coll., NYPL.
[90]   4 NJA (2) 625; see Nathanael Greene to Washington, Aug. 26, 1780, GW Papers LC. Lieutenant Colonel Ebenezer Huntington wrote that "the rascality of our troops [on the Bergen forage] was equal to the British. They plundered the inhabitants villainously." Huntington to Samuel B. Webb, August 30, 1780. Webb Reminiscences 210.
[91]   4 NJA (2) 600, 601.
[92]   Winfield, Hudson County, 385, 386. MRC 539. He was taken before the British authorities for his boldness but quickly released, no new thing for the Jackson family. His father had once been jailed for holding Presbyterian services without a license. When one of the Tories in his congregation berated him for his Whig views, he is said to have replied, "If General Howe can forgive me, why can't you?" Jackson's son and namesake was evidently one of the spies who made the Paulus Hook expedition possible. Adam Boyd to Wayne, Nov. 8, 1779. Wayne Papers HSP.

Susannah Livingston, daughter of the Governor, took pen in hand to celebrate the Marquis's bold affront to Sir Henry:

> An army of rebels came down to'ther night,
> Expecting no doubt that the British would fight,
> Next morning we saw them parade at the Hook,
> And thought, to be sure, this was too much to brook,
> That soon would the river be crowded with boats,
> With Hessians and English to cut all their throats,
>
>   *   *   *
>
> The men who had wished for occasions for blows,
> Now suffered themselves to be pulled by the nose.[93]

Tories, who had little enough use for Clinton, privately agreed that the rebels had done just that, but Sir Henry was far too busy to worry about a mere foraging raid, even one on his doorstep. The Tory press made what propaganda it could from bad news, Rivington reporting that "after pilfering (in their old petit larceny way) all the honest and trusty inhabitants, the week was closed very tragically indeed to (one of the greatest sufferers in America) Col. William Bayard, for on Saturday (August 27) they visited his estate at Weehawk, destroyed the houses and burned his barns. They then repaired to Hoebuck, set fire to Col. Bayard's elegant house there, and one of the finest barns ever constructed; these, with several other improvements were burned to the ground; they proceeded still further, and set fire to the grass, parched by the late uncommon scorching weather, which continued two days in raging flames, when one of the most valuable orchards existing was utterly destroyed." [94] That the Americans had burned Bayard's house and barns was true enough; Rivington did not add (as Bayard himself found it advisable to point out when he sought British compensation) that "the reason it was burned was because it had been made a post of the British." [95] Nor did he explain what the Regulars were doing in New York that kept them from crossing the river to protect Bayard's property, or where the Tory troops were while their quarters were being burned.

The poorly fed and campaign-hardened soldiers encamped at Teaneck

---

[93] 4 NJA (2) 628.
[94] A year earlier the commanding general had been obliged to inform Colonel Van Buskirk "that great numbers of your regiment frequently go to Hobuck and there make great depredations on the house of Mr. William Bayard, as well as his goods and his lands." The Bayard house was one, however, they could not be accused of burning. Pattison 229, 231.
[95] LYT NYPL "William Bayard."

did not respect Teaneck and Schraalenburgh property any more than the Bergen Dutchman's breeches. At the request of the justices of the peace Major Goetschius pleaded with Washington to station a subaltern's command as a guard at Schraalenburgh. "The wicked and inconsiderate soldiery," he reported, were "entirely destroying the Schraalenburgh neighborhood." [96]

"They have within this three days robbed the inhabitants of Schraalenburgh neighborhood of five or six head of cattle, a number of sheep, hogs and fowl, and almost all their corn, potatoes and other vegetables, and in a violent manner abuse the well-affected in this place, running about with clubs and bayonets upon pikes by whole companies as bad as our enemies ever have done." [97] Moreover, Major Goetschius went on, as an additional reason for a guard, the soldiers were deserting through Schraalenburgh, six of the Pennsylvania Line going out that way on September 9, 1780. British agents were busy in the neighborhood urging desertions, Major Goetschius having taken up one deserter with his pilot, a Refugee's wife from New York, and turned them over to the Continental authorities.[98]

General Nathanael Greene was even more emphatic than Major Goetschius. "There has been committed some of the most horrid acts of plunder by some of the Pennsylvania Line that has disgraced the American army during the war. . . . Two soldiers were taken that were out upon the business, both of which fired upon the inhabitants to prevent their giving intelligence. A party plundered a house yesterday in sight of a number of officers, and even threatened the officers if they offered to interfere." [99] Greene had but one recommendation: hang several of the offenders without trial, as well as any deserters caught going in to Manhattan.

Washington found plundering as outrageous as did Greene and the people of Schraalenburgh, Teaneck and Liberty Pole. "Without a speedy change in circumstances," he wrote, ". . . either the army must disband,

[96] Goetschius to Washington, Sept. 30, 1780, GW Papers LC.
[97] Goetschius to Washington, Sept. 30, 1780, GW Papers LC. The plundering probably explains Captain Thomas Blanch's failure to move his company of Bergen County militia to the Closter landings, as he had been ordered to do by Continental headquarters. He apparently used the excuse that he had no tents and that he had no allotment of provisions, for which he received a sharp rebuke from Washington: "I cannot help expressing exceeding great surprise at your not obeying the order you received yesterday . . . nor do I see how you could have answered it to yourself or your country, if any disaster had happened in consequence of your neglect." 19 GW 433.
[98] Goetschius to Washington, Sept. 30, 1780, GW Papers LC.
[99] Nathanael Greene to Washington, Aug. 26, 1780, GW Papers LC. Washington fully approved Greene's recommendation of summary execution. 19 GW 446.

or what is if possible worse, subsist upon the plunder of the people." [100] The greater part of the army had been without meat for a week and now had but one day's supply in camp. The raid on Bergen Neck had been found to afford only two or three days' supply.[101]

"Military coercion is no longer of any avail," Washington wrote, "as nothing further can possibly be collected from the country in which we are obliged to take a position without depriving the inhabitants of the last morsel. This mode of subsisting, supposing the desired end could be answered by it, besides being in the highest degree distressing to individuals, is attended with ruin to the morals and discipline of the army; during the few days which we have been obliged to send out small parties to procure provisions for themselves, the most enormous excesses have been committed." [102]

Of course to the owner the loss was about the same whether things were taken officially or by plundering soldiers; indeed one of the Continental officers was obliged to use exactly that term to describe the conduct of the army: "The country between us and the enemy, and below him, has been pretty thoroughly gleaned by us of the little the enemy left there. We call this foraging, but it is only a gentle name for plundering." [103]

At nine in the morning on September 4, 1780, Washington's troops moved west across the Hackensack to somewhat safer ground at Steenrapie.[104] Here the troops were arrayed in two lines, one below and one upon the ridge that parallels the Kinderkamack Road on the west, the encampment extending about two miles north of the junction of the road over the Old Bridge. About thirty guns were brigaded in the artillery park in the center of camp, including five eighteen-pounders, two six-pounders and two howitzers.[105] The French War Office map of the campaign shows headquarters at the northern end of the camp, on the Kinderkamack Road. This was probably Lafayette's headquarters; Washington's were apparently first near the New Bridge and then at the farm of Aurt Cooper, at the southwest corner of the junction of the Kinderkamack Road and the road from Old Bridge to the Paramus

[100]   19 GW 449, 451; see 19 GW 468, 470.
[101]   19 GW 449, 450.
[102]   19 GW 449, 450. "One man was detected in robbing an inhabitant's house today and was hanged on a tree without a trial by order of his excellency George Washington." Dearborn Journal 202.
[103]   Shaw Journal 76.
[104]   19 GW 494, 498, 502. A Jersey Dutch variant of "Stone Arabia," the present River Edge, Oradell and Emerson, west of the Hackensack River.
[105]   British Intelligence Reports, Emmet Coll., NYPL.

church.[106] Again light forces were stationed as an outpost on the ridge south of the main encampment, back of New Bridge and between Old Bridge and New Bridge and west of Kinderkamack Road.[107] The artillery officer who had noted the wreckage of the formerly delightful village of Schraalenburgh was greatly pleased by Steenrapie: "It's a very Delightful Country, Milton's delineation of Paradise does not exceed the beauties of it." [108] (It must be confessed that the young captain had also noted, some days earlier, "I spent this afternoon very agreeable with a number of gentlemen of our battalion on the banks of the Hackensack River adrinking Milk Punch," and his observations of the low Dutch country may have been tinted by the punch. "We are," he wrote, "in the heart of a Delightful and plentiful country.") [109]

On September 13 six Indian chiefs, of tribes friendly to the patriot cause, favored the camp with a visit, and the army was paraded before them to be reviewed. Washington, on a bay charger, rode in front of the line and received its salute, thirteen pieces of cannon being fired as they passed the artillery park. "Six Indian chiefs followed in his train," an unimpressed officer noted in his journal for the day. "They appeared as the most disgusting and contemptible of the human race; their faces painted of various colors, their hair twisted into bunches on the top of their heads, and dressed in a miserable Indian habit, some with a dirty blanket over their shoulders, and others almost naked," adding that several of the chiefs were so full of rum during the review that they fell from their horses on the way back to headquarters. "It is," he added philosophically, "good policy to show them some attention." [110]

The residents of Steenrapie, who had watched the depredations across the river, soon saw them closer to home. Even at Washington's head-quarters the granaries and hen roosts were raided by hungry Continentals until the owner, elderly Aurt Cooper, complained directly to the General, who put a stop to the raids, as Mr. Cooper told his friends for years afterward.[111] General Greene, annoyed at the soldiers' use of fence rails for firewood, directed "police officers to visit them during cooking hours as well to see that the cooking is properly performed as that the fires were not made of fencing stuff." [112]

Deserters were probably not deceiving the British when they reported

106   French War Office map, NYPL; HBP 321; Bergen County Atlas 40, 41.
107   11 Penn. Arch. (2) 571, etc.
108   63 NJHSP 199, 213.
109   63 NJHSP 199, 212, 213.
110   Thacher 213, 214; 63 NJHSP 213.
111   HBP 321.
112   2 Greene Greene 217.

that Britain had many friends in the country occupied by Washington's army; some perhaps recently acquired.[113]

During the summer of 1780 there was a great deal of excitement in the Hackensack valley, and in the Continental camp as well, over the capture of James Moody, one of the most famous and successful Jersey loyalist raiders and spies. Moody was a Tory of Sussex County who had repeatedly defied the American militiamen and Continentals under their very noses and gone off scot free. Like Banta and other raiders, he held a commission as a territorial lieutenant without assignment.

"An artful and enterprising fellow employed by the British," one American officer called him, "[who has several times] succeeded in taking our mail from the post rider on the road, though he has had some very remarkable escapes." [114] By one daring raid Moody bore off all the dispatches to the Continental army and to Congress giving the details of the council of war between Washington and Count Rochambeau; at another time, with the aid of an inside accomplice, he almost succeeded in taking the very records of the Continental Congress. He once hid for two days, erect and without food or water, in a cornstack, surrounded by American soldiers; once, ambushed in the Highlands on three sides of a precipice, he and his party jumped off the high cliff and escaped.[115] Even patriots could not but respect and admire his daring, and when they had him in their hands they had no intention of letting him go.

He was captured at Liberty Pole on the day of the attack on Bull's Ferry blockhouse, by Captain Lawrence of the New York troops. He was first taken to militia headquarters at Tappan Sloat,[116] then to West Point, where he was imprisoned in irons, over the protests of General Arnold. General Lamb, who ordered the irons, hinted strongly to his friend Arnold that Washington concurred in the view that Moody was to be treated as a spy, not as an ordinary prisoner.[117] (After the war Moody blamed the traitor for his harsh treatment and praised Washington for easing it.[118])

Lamb, who knew only too well Moody's talent for escape, insisted that keeping him in irons was the only way to prevent his departure with

[113] British Intelligence Reports, Emmet Coll., NYPL.
[114] Thacher 263.
[115] 2 Sabine 90, etc.; Moody Narrative.
[116] See 4 NJA (2) 552; Affidavit of James Quackenbush, Pension Records, S15200. Thomas Richardson, of Colonel Barton's troops, "taken on the party with Lt. Moody the day of the blockhouse attack at the Liberty Pole," reported to British intelligence that they had been taken about the country, that he came in through Elizabethtown, where a Mr. Smith hid him in the hay, and that he had heard that Moody himself was in irons at headquarters. British Intelligence Reports, Emmet Coll., NYPL.
[117] Leake, Lamb, 248.
[118] Moody Narrative.

the entire plan of West Point and the numbers of its garrison. (Later, Americans who knew of Moody's record speculated that he had aided Arnold's treason by carrying Arnold's cipher to Sir Henry; actually, of course, no one in the Continental army was as anxious as Benedict Arnold to keep Moody from carrying the plans of the Highland forts to the British. Arnold intended to sell them for £20,000, not to give them away.)

Lamb finally suggested that Moody be sent down to the main army, and Arnold cheerfully complied, so that the Sussex County Greencoat found himself a prisoner of Washington while the Continentals were at Tappan, Teaneck, and Schraalenburgh.[119] Carried back across the New Bridge with the American troops as they moved to the west side of the Hackensack, he was lodged in a Dutchman's barn in the very center of the encampment at Steenrapie, with one guard inside the door, one outside, and four patrolling the grounds. He contrived, nevertheless, to break the bolt on his handcuffs under his greatcoat, to dash past the inside guard, and to overpower the outside guard and seize his musket. Once outside, he mingled with the searching troops in the darkness as one of them until he was able to slip off, taking the precaution to move first to the north, away from the British lines. Circling back after hours of near starvation, he made his way to the home of some Tory or ostensible neutral in the neighborhood, and thence to safety.[120]

"In every inhabited district he knew there were friends of government," he wrote later, "and he had now learned also where and how to find them out without endangering their safety." Having found one of these, "he received minute information how the pursuit after him was directed and where every guard was posted. Thus assisted he eluded the keenest vigilance . . . and at length arrived safe at Paulus Hook." [121]

Moody survived the war and exiled himself in England, printing his appeal to the crown for compensation as the celebrated "Narrative of the Exertions and Sufferings of Lieut. James Moody, in the Cause of Government since the Year 1776." [122]

On the 17th of September, Washington left the army at Steenrapie to go to Hartford to confer with the French military leaders who commanded the forces at Newport.[123] The conference was unable to pro-

119 Leake, Lamb, 254.
120 Moody Narrative.
121 Moody Narrative.
122 Moody Narrative.
123 20 GW 66.

pose any real action to counteract the recent British successes in the south, but its timing was providential; indeed, there were many who said later that it had saved the nation, that Washington's return from Hartford occurred on the very day, almost to the very hour, necessary to frustrate Arnold's treason and save West Point.

16

O N A U G U S T 5, 1780, Major General Benedict Arnold invited
Richard Varick to leave Hackensack and go to West Point to be his
secretary and aide.[1] The invitation seemed to Varick a rope let down
from heaven; it was of course to prove something less.

To a young officer who had tasted the excitement of battle at Saratoga, who had been in the highest councils of the Revolutionary army,
enforced idleness at Hackensack would have been tedious enough; the
life of a patriot militiaman in the neutral ground, hunted down by
Tories and irregulars without any real chance of reprisal, was intolerable. It meant sentry watches on alternate nights with country people
as companions; it meant hiding every other night in a barn or a hay
barrack, cold and fearful of Greencoat attack; it meant constant risk
of battle at odds of ten to one against the defenders. Hundreds of
patriotic Jersey Dutchmen had endured such duty for almost four years,
many of them were to tell their grandchildren after the war that they
never slept a night at home from 1776 to 1781, but it was a most unpleasant change for a young officer who had formerly spent his evenings
with the aristocratic General Philip Schuyler, sipping "juice" when they
could get it, and Quackenbush's shrub, when rum was in short supply.[2]

---

1   Varick Court of Inquiry, 82. See Varick to Schuyler, Feb. 10, 1780, Schuyler
Papers NYPL.
2   Varick to Philip Van Rensselaer, Oct. 30, 1779, NYHS; Varick Court of Inquiry
79, 86. See Romeyn Papers UCL; Kuyper to Major Stuart, March 22, 1780, GW
Papers LC; Schuyler to Varick, Jul. 17, 1776, private collection of Randall J. Le Boeuf.

Saratoga was no parade-ground victory, but Colonel Varick had seen nothing there to match the cruelty of the civil war in Bergen County. His father's case was but one example. While young Varick was with the army the old gentleman, whose only offense was that he was an outspoken patriot, had been twice seized at his home on Tory raids, carried off to Sugar House, and locked up like a common criminal. In one case he was held for thirteen months, and treated very badly, although dangerously ill.[3]

"I have cause to think," Varick wrote, "that my father is held up as a very obnoxious character and detained at the instance of some of his neighbors, probably of near connection to him, who are or have affected to show themselves friends and abettors to the enemies of their country." [4]

At the beginning of the war, Colonel Varick's family had had four middle-aged Negro slaves, three of whom were lost early in the war and the last taken off by an enemy raiding party while his father was in prison, along with a good deal of the Varick property. Colonel Varick had every good reason, as he said, "to wish for revenge against the adherents of their oppressors," and he welcomed an opportunity to return to active service.[5]

"No sooner had I sat down to my desk," Varick wrote to a friend, "when the invaders of our land disturbed my retreat and deprived me of a valuable share of the little property that remained my own after retiring from public service. Thus was I again reduced to the necessity of becoming a soldier in a more obscure, though not less honorable line —that of a volunteer militiaman—in which situation I continued till this day sennight, when wearied and almost worn out by alternate watches, I received a polite invitation from Major General Arnold to become a member of his military family." [6]

General Schuyler, who was at Tappan headquarters when Arnold passed through on his way to his new post at West Point, had recommended Varick to him. On its face there could hardly have been a happier suggestion. Varick had been so violent a partisan of Arnold in the bitter dispute between Arnold and Gates after the victory at Saratoga

---

3   Varick Court of Inquiry 79, 80.
4   Varick to Philip Van Rensselaer, Oct. 30, 1778, NYHS.
5   Idem.
6   Varick Court of Inquiry 86. He left Hackensack on Saturday Aug. 12 and arrived at West Point on the next day. "When operations are fairly begun against New York this post will no longer detain us," he wrote Domine Romeyn on the following Thursday. Varick to Romeyn, Aug. 17, 1780, Parke-Bernet Catalogue, March 2, 1960, No. 348.

that he finally found it prudent not to talk of the matter at all:[7] he and the other young officers had nothing but admiration for the dashing hero from Connecticut, and Arnold's friction with the civil authorities at Philadelphia had done nothing to lessen Varick's regard for him; many military men had had brushes with politicians.

West Point had been coming into great prominence in the last year or so. After the fall of Fort Clinton and Fort Montgomery, the patriots put more and more of their hopes on West Point, and a large body of Continentals was now kept constantly at work improving the fort. Though Sir Henry Clinton had forced the Highlands in 1777 without disaster to the Americans, both Clinton and Washington continued to regard the Highland passes as the keys to the continent.

Richard Varick.
Winfield, Hudson County.

Varick was doubly pleased to join Arnold: he was to be in the official family of the commander of the most important fort in America, and he was to be with friends who had shared the rigors of the northern campaign and the great victory of Saratoga. That Arnold had since taken a bride, the renowned Peggy Shippen of Philadelphia, toast of two armies, certainly did not make the post less attractive to the young

[7] Indeed, Varick has been accused of fomenting the trouble out of loyalty to the displaced General Schuyler. See Flexner 168, et seq. Arnold himself was most anxious to please and flatter the Albany aristocrat, partly from a desire to keep the friendship of one so highly placed, but also partly in the vain hope that once he deserted the American cause, Schuyler might follow. Pressure from Schuyler probably explains Arnold's appointment of Varick, who could only have been an encumbrance to Arnold's desperate scheme.

colonel; the wheel of fortune had seemingly come full turn for a man who had a few weeks ago been hiding in hay barracks in fear of his life.

Varick found a busy scene at West Point: Arnold himself described his own temperament as nervous, and Varick was soon in a constant flurry of activity. Arnold had taken over the secret service work of his predecessor at the fort and had added some of his own; his aide, Major David Franks, told Varick that a most important piece of secret service was being done under the cover of commercial correspondence with a spy who used the name of John Anderson. The John Anderson correspondence Arnold handled himself, though he sought Varick's advice as to the best method of getting it into New York without British detection, and doubtless found Varick's intimate knowledge of the neutral ground a help in that connection. Arnold's headquarters were at the Beverly Robinson house, east of the river, not at West Point itself.

Varick himself soon saw that Arnold had become friendly with Joshua Hett Smith, the one-time patriot Orange County committeeman, now of doubtful sympathies. Varick knew Joshua Smith's brother William well; the brother had been a close collaborator in every patriotic move before Lexington, but had early abandoned the American cause; as a turncoat he had been rewarded by the British with the highest judicial post in New York. Many patriots still considered William Smith to be an honest man; few were so charitable about Joshua. Varick once went so far as to insult Smith deliberately when he was a dinner guest of General and Peggy Arnold, an insult for which Arnold reprimanded him sharply. Varick also tried Arnold's patience by lecturing him about his loose dealings with government stores, but Arnold was so openly contemptuous of the penury of Congress that he seemed indifferent to such criticism. He did, however, promise to yield to Varick's advice and have nothing further to do with Smith.[8]

Varick had too recently been hunted down by Tory marauders to want to have anything to do with Tories. He was reminded only too sharply of his fever-ridden father and his months in prison when he heard Joshua Smith sneer at Continental currency; he suspected that Smith was carrying far more intelligence back to New York than he ever gave Arnold.

Varick, of course, had no means of knowing that Arnold's close friend, General John Lamb, had already told Arnold that Joshua Hett Smith was a rank Tory and a rascal to boot, flatly refusing Arnold's invitations to dine with him though Lamb's and Smith's wives were related;

8 See Varick Court of Inquiry 125, etc.; Van Doren, Secret History.

Varick had every reason to assume that until he had disillusioned him Arnold had been unaware of the Tory's local reputation.[9]

Actually what both Varick and Major Franks feared was that Arnold was involved in the same illegal commercial transactions in New York that he had been accused of in Philadelphia; worse, that he was now using his flags to bring in British contraband in partnership with the Tory Smith, and both Varick and Franks agreed on their honor to leave Arnold at once if their fears were confirmed.[10]

On September 25 Varick was ill at Arnold's headquarters. A militia officer arrived shortly after breakfast with a letter for Arnold, which Arnold took upstairs to Mrs. Arnold's room. We know now that the messenger brought word of André's arrest. A half hour later a servant arrived to announce that General Washington would soon reach head-quarters, at which Arnold came downstairs, ordered a horse, and asked Major Franks to tell Washington that he had gone to West Point and would return in an hour. As soon as Arnold left, Mrs. Arnold's hysteria brought the household into utter confusion; when Washington arrived, Franks and Varick were almost as agitated as Peggy Arnold, torn be-tween fear that Arnold had fled to the British and fear that they would be ruined forever if they voiced such suspicions and they proved to be wrong.

The disclosures of the next few hours are history: it was not long before Varick and Franks and all America knew that Arnold's guilt went far beyond trading with British New York; that only the most provi-dential circumstances had saved the American cause; that Sir Henry Clinton had come within a hair's breadth of carrying out his recent un-explained boast to Smith's brother that he would soon bring America down in one sudden crash.[11]

The sad finale of the Arnold tragedy, perhaps the most famous single incident of the Revolution in the Hackensack valley, was the trial and execution of the young British major who paid with his life for Arnold's

[9] Lamb Papers NYHS; Leake, Lamb, 256.
[10] Varick Court of Inquiry 127. See also Richard Varick letters, Parke-Bernet Cata-logue, March 2, 1960, Feb. 22, 1961.
[11] Smith Journal, NYPL. Patriots of course assumed that an immediate British attack was to be made on West Point. Wayne, at Tappan, got word of the treason at mid-night. He moved at once toward the north, leaving his tents standing, on a march of six-teen miles in four hours, "performed in the night without a single halt or a man falling behind." Wayne to Robinson, Oct. 1, 1780, Wayne Papers HSP. It was as well for Americans that no such attack was made, if General Irvine, who was put in charge, correctly described the state of the fort: "O, what a tribe was here to defend this post. Even yesterday . . . I would stake my salvation that I could have taken the place with three hundred men just in as much time as it would take to march round the redoubts." Irvine to Wayne, Sept. 29, 1780, Wayne Papers HSP.

mercenary scheme: André was tried before fourteen American general officers in the Dutch church at Tappan, the church which André had last entered when it held the prisoners from Baylor's regiment, a church which he now left under a verdict, signed by every member of the court, "that Major André, adjutant general of the British army, ought to be considered a spy from the enemy; and that agreeable to the law and usage of nations, it is their opinion he ought to suffer death." [12]

Major Benjamin Tallmadge, the young Connecticut dragoon officer who had brought André from the place of his capture in Westchester

Dutch Reformed Church, Tappan, circa 1780. Place of André Trial.
Cole, Tappan Church.

to his prison house in Casparus Mabie's tavern at Tappan, was Washington's chief of intelligence, as André had been Sir Henry Clinton's.[13] Under André's cheerful prodding, when Tallmadge could no longer evade his questions about the probable result of his capture, Tallmadge finally avoided a direct answer by telling the story of a beloved classmate at Yale College who had volunteered in 1776 to enter the British

[12] Even before the people of Tappan knew for certain that the officer who had been captured in Westchester was André, British spies were sending in word from Tappan that "they had a report that the captive was Adjutant General to the British Army and that he would hang unless Arnold was returned." Deserters (perhaps sent in for the purpose) were soon telling British headquarters the same thing. British Intelligence Reports, Emmet Coll., NYPL.
[13] 6 GC 256, et seq.

lines in New York for information, a young captain named Hale, whose end, Tallmadge said, he supposed André remembered.

Though André answered with a start that the cases were by no means the same, he dropped the subject at once, and Tallmadge regretted as long as he lived that it was he who had unwillingly brought the brilliant young officer the first hint of his fate.

"On the 2nd of October he was executed," Tallmadge wrote fifty years later. "I walked with him to the place of execution and parted with him under the gallows, entirely overwhelmed with grief, that so gallant an officer, and so accomplished a gentleman, should come to so ignominious an end." An old man when he wrote, Tallmadge added: "I believe I have never narrated the story . . . without shedding tears of sorrow over such blighted prospects. I hope and trust this will be the last trial of my feelings in this way." [14]

[14]   6 GC 264. See 5 Freeman 221. Thacher 227 and HBP 63 give detailed descriptions of the actual execution. The executioner appears to have been a man named Strickland (or Streckland), who was captured at Bergen Point about six months later. To Sir Henry's great credit, he ignored the pleas of the army to execute Strickland. 2 Mackenzie 481.

17

WASHINGTON'S troops did not stay long at Tappan after André's execution.

On Saturday, October 7, five days later, a good number were sent to the Highland posts around West Point, but the main body of the army moved westward through Paramus toward Preakness, a cold, wet and tedious march, the weather having turned very bad. As Washington explained, the forage about Tappan, Harrington, and Schraalenburgh was exhausted. Major Lee's light horse, which had been harassing the woodcutters in the upper Bergen Township, and some of the Pennsylvania light infantry, had been posted in and around Liberty Pole. They left their camp at three o'clock in the afternoon of October 7 and moved west over the New Bridge in the rain, the light infantry taking quarters in the barns between Hackensack and New Bridge that night, and going on toward Preakness in the morning.[1]

Washington ordered a captain's command from the Continental troops to remain at Sneden's Landing to guard the blockhouse, and directed Goetschius "to detach a subaltern and twenty men from your corps to join that garrison and be under orders of the commanding officer; the detachment to be relieved as often as you shall think necessary." "As the design of the post at Dobbs Ferry is to protect and cover the country below as far as possible," Washington went on, "the re-

---

1   20 GW 126, 129, 133. 11 Penn. Arch. (2) 571, et seq. A large forage party went in to Bergen on Oct. 30, and a field officer and sixty men, with ten wagons, were reported at Hackensack on Nov. 17. British Intelligence Reports, Emmet Coll., NYPL.

mainder of your corps . . . cannot be better employed than in patrolling and guarding the landing places and avenues leading to the
post, in order to obtain early intelligence of any movement of the
enemy, prevent a surprise and render every assistance in your power to
the garrison." [2]

Goetschius transferred the men reluctantly. "It makes a great uneasiness among the inhabitants at the lines of this county. My detachment
is particular enlisted for a guard at the frontiers of this county. To complete the number, the inhabitants at the lines paid a large sum of money
to the soldiery particular to have rest themselves and to follow their
lawful employ. . . . Garrisoning the blockhouse at Dobbs Ferry which
lays in York State is little or no guard to this county . . . [which] lays
now open [and] horse thieves and robbers slip through to the ruin of
the inhabitants . . ." [3]

Some of Washington's staff may have thought it narrow of Goetschius to complain about moving a mile across the state line into New
York; if they did they failed to observe that the ground of Goetschius'
complaint was not so much that he had to cross the state line as that the
move pulled back from the lines a good part of the only force that made
any effort to protect patriots who lived near the enemy. Goetschius did
not add, as he might have, that only a few months earlier, in the very
country he was ordered to leave, the Refugees had burned down his
house and barns and carried off everything else that he owned.

He did make it clear that there was another difficulty about serving at
the blockhouse, the matter of provisions. He had served during the last
few weeks "whilst the army laid here, [under] about fifteen different
commanders as a picket to the whole army," taking orders from all
and more often than not receiving rations from none. His problems
about provisions were not new. He had reported to Governor Livingston
earlier in the summer that the subject gave him "infinite trouble and
perplexity"; that he had been unable to get any allowance for himself
or his men, although he had many times "applied for provisions to his
Excellency General Washington, to the superintendent of the State, to
the county contractors of Bergen and Essex Counties and to the magistrates of this County."

"It is true I have had provisions from the Continental army when
they laid at the lines," he wrote to Governor Livingston on August 2,
1780. "I have also taken grain and cattle from the inhabitants by way

[2]   20 GW 124, 130, 139.
[3]   Goetschius to Washington, Oct. 8, 1780, GW Papers LC, reprinted with much
other material dealing with the Dobbs Ferry blockhouse in 3 Rockland Record,
George H. Budke (ed.), 3 vols., Nyack, N.Y. (1930–1940) 17.

of military power with the advice of his Excellency General Washington, [but I] am at present without any and know not where to apply for further support except to your honor.

"The grand army has left the inhabitants of this county a very scant support for their own consumption. There is some grain as yet but it must be taken by force of arms. The inhabitants will not sell any longer for certificates.

"Under all their fatigue," he went on, "[the men are] obliged to satisfy themselves with not above a pound of bread and [meat]; no vegetables or liquor. Sometimes not that." [4]

Goetschius, nevertheless, detached the men and he and they went on patrolling and guarding the landing places and avenues leading to the American lines.

They would have been more than human, however, if they had not observed the Continental's contempt for all militiamen and if they had not observed, even more clearly, how often Continentals marched and countermarched during a whole campaign without seeing a redcoat, how seldom any Continental ventured down as close to the British as the militia headquarters posts.[5]

After the war, when Goetschius' old militiamen stood outside the South Church at Schraalenburgh on Sunday mornings waiting for the service to begin and boasting quietly about their exploits in low Dutch, if some of them were a little scornful of Continental officers who never

---

4 Goetschius to Livingston, Aug. 2, 1780, Livingston Papers NYPL.

5 Militiamen saw action enough. Abraham Blauvelt, a militiaman of Harrington, for example, was in an "engagement at the [Bull's Ferry blockhouse] under Captain Blanch at which time he was one of the party who took a sentinel from one of the enemy's picket guards . . . he was in an engagement with the Refugees at Closter at which time he assisted in taking about sixty sheep and about fifty head of horned cattle and killed one of their party . . . he was also engaged with the Refugees in the English Neighborhood at which time he was one of a party which succeeded in retaking a Continental team driver and four horses from the enemy . . . he was also engaged with the Refugees at Schraalenburgh at which time they retook five horses and killed two Refugees . . . he was also one of the party that succeeded in taking John Berry, a Regular Refugee who had been advertised as an outlaw for the several murders and depredations he had committed . . . he was also engaged with the Refugee horse thieves near the New Bridge . . . at which time he received a wound from a musket ball passing through the fleshy part of his hip which confined him for three months . . . he was also in a battle with the Refugees at . . . the Liberty Pole at which time they succeeded in retaking about 150 head of horned cattle, his brother James I. Blauvelt was wounded at the same time." He was also in the Battle at Fort Lee in 1781, and in the attack on the blockhouse in June, 1780. Blauvelt was fifteen years old when he entered the service. (His brother Isaac and his twin brother, James, were in most of the same engagements.) Affidavit of Abraham Blauvelt, Pension Records, S2080.

The Blauvelts were but three of hundreds of militiamen who had seen similar service.

saw a British gun, it was perhaps natural jealousy over their own un-sung feats. No Continental need have troubled himself for a moment about their mild grumbling, there were none but Jersey Dutchmen to hear them, there was to be no Bancroft or Longfellow to tell of their deeds.

Despite the bold moves of the American army in the New York theater, the great losses in South Carolina in the Battle of Camden were a severe blow to Continental strategy, the French were slow in coming up to expected strength and, perhaps worse, five years of cam-paigning and hardship had changed the early patriot enthusiasm into mere sullen determination to push the British and Hessians from the American shores. Inflation meant that the pay of the officers and men was worthless, and many civilians had been wiped out by it.

Affairs in the south were in a distressing state. Congress had de-manded an inquiry into the conduct of General Gates at the Battle of Camden, enlistments were again expiring, and Washington greatly feared another blow in the Carolinas or Virginia. "Our accounts from New York respecting the intended embarkation continue vague and contradictory," he wrote from Preakness. First he received reports that the British were embarking, then that they were disembarking, and then that a plan entirely new was in agitation. "Unluckily the person in whom I have the greatest confidence is afraid to take any measure for communicating with me just at this time, as he is apprehensive that Arnold may possibly have some knowledge of the connexion, and may have him watched." Having assured the spy on this score, Washington hoped soon to hear from him as usual, but in this also he was disap-pointed. Washington wrote to Lafayette on October 30, "Arnold's flight seems to have frightened all my intelligencers out of their senses," ex-plaining that things were at a standstill and that all that could be done was "to endeavor to gain a more certain knowledge of the British situa-tion and act accordingly." [6]

In this endeavor he turned to Dirck Romeyn. On November 3, 1780, his aides sent an express to the domine at Hackensack with word of a rumored embarkation to the south: "It is more than probable that you will have heard something of it, as the communication between Hacken-sack and Bergen is frequent—you will be good enough to let me know by return of the Bearer whether anything of the kind has come to your

[6]   20 GW 190. See also 20 GW 26, 27, 104, 224. 20 GW 267. The British were being particularly vigilant at the time. Jacob Van Wagoner was arrested for spying on the Tory troops. Intelligence, Oct. 10, 1780, HC Papers CL.

knowledge, with any particulars you may have collected. Should you at any time in future gain any intelligence which you may think material, you will oblige His Excellency and render essential public service by communicating it to him." [7]

The domine had just returned from a two months' visit with his family at Marbletown, New York, and though he assured the Commander in Chief that "he would ever think it his duty and an honour to do his mite toward the important end of an American victory," he was unable to give the express an answer.[8] He said he hoped to have the fullest and most authentic information that he could wish for from New York when a lady who had been at Bergen returned the next day and he promised as soon as he was in possession of intelligence to send it by one of the militia horsemen. The lady arrived that evening and the next morning Romeyn sent word to General Washington that there were twelve warships drawn up in the East River and that the British were busy impressing every able-bodied man they could lay hands on for an apparent embarkation, which was thought in New York to be certain within a day or two. He added that his informant said that the British provision fleet was much overdue and food in short supply, despite the large quantities going in through New Barbadoes Neck and Long Island. "I am sorry," he wrote, "that I cannot answer my expectations and his Excellency's wishes on the principal subject," but expressed the hope that he might be able to do so within a day or so.[9]

This letter, evidently combined with other similar intelligence, convinced Washington that an embarkation was planned and he passed the word to the field officers. The embarkation in fact never occurred.[10]

[7] 20 GW 286.

[8] Romeyn to Washington, Nov. 3, 1780, Nov. 4, 1780, GW Papers LC; Romeyn Papers UCL, NYPL.

[9] Idem.

[10] Doubtless from a change of plan by Sir Henry; he had in the past been busily preparing to strengthen his southern forces. 20 GW 285, 289, 290, 292, 346, 364.

Domine Romeyn's colleague at Paramus, Benjamin Vanderlinde, joined Elizabeth Bartholf and Ensign Jacobus Bogert in marriage on October 13, 1780. A cousin of the bride recalled long after that she ". . . was present at the wedding and saw . . . Jacobus . . . Bogert and Elizabeth Bartholf married at the house of the father of said Elizabeth Bartholf . . . [in Yaughpaugh] . . . in the year 1780. . . ." William Van Voorhees, who served with Bogert, called him "a very active officer in the militia and a brave man and a violent Whig." Affidavits of Catherine Bartholf, Elizabeth Suffern and William Van Voorhees, Pension Records W17890.

Though Vanderlinde himself leaned to the conferentie, his churchpeople were by no means all Tories, as the conferentie people of Hackensack, Schraalenburgh and Tappan were, the existence of two separate congregations in the latter places making a sharp division possible and perhaps inevitable. Vanderlinde's successor William Eltinge found the Paramus church torn apart by dissension when he came there in 1799.

In late November, Washington, still intrigued with the possibility of a stroke at New York, had a trusted officer, a colonel of French engineers, go from New Bridge to Fort Lee and back along the river path below the Palisades to a point opposite Spuyten Duyvil and reconnoiter the British positions on Manhattan Island, from Fort Washington to the north, making every observation necessary for a plan to surprise those forts in a night assault.[11]

Detailed orders for the attack were sent out: Wayne's troops were to rendezvous at Acquackanonk, a scouting party under Colonel Moylan was to secure every crossing below Old Bridge on the Hackensack and to patrol from New Bridge toward Bergen Town, Bull's Ferry, Weehawken, and Hoboken.[12] Acting on his usual principle—which seems to have escaped the notice of Parson Weems—that if one did not deceive his own forces he could never deceive the enemy, he told Major Goetschius to have his local militia secure all the watercraft on the Hackensack from New Bridge downwards for a proposed raid which, he "disclosed in confidence," was to be made on Elizabethtown, adding that much depended on Goetschius' activity, secrecy and punctuality.[13] With the same dissimulation he ordered Heath's forces at West Point to move down the east side of the river ostensibly to forage, actually to attack Manhattan.

The great preparations went awry by the accidental intervention of British vessels on the Hudson, and the affair ended as nothing more than a successful forage party by Heath's troops. Having failed at his favorite project, Washington gave up the season's campaign and went into winter quarters at New Windsor. The Jersey troops were quartered at Pompton and the Pennsylvania Line at Morristown.

Washington openly doubted whether the army or the people in the active theaters of war could rub through another winter like the last. Like many of Washington's other predictions, this proved almost fatally correct. The winter of 1780–81 did not bring the record-breaking cold of its predecessor, but it saw the mutiny of the Pennsylvania Line, followed by the mutiny of the New Jersey Line at Pompton, both perhaps the best behaved and most justified mutinies of all time, but terribly discouraging to patriot leaders. They were directed at Congress, not at General Washington, and the first was put down by negotiation, but, fearing great danger to civil liberty from soldiers dictating to the country, if not an immediate collapse of American resistance, Washington demanded unconditional submission of the Jersey troops and ordered

[11] 20 GW 383.
[12] 20 GW 380–389.
[13] 20 GW 384. See also 20 GW 382.

the instant execution of a few of the most active and incendiary leaders.

Many Whigs who did not understand the delicacy of the situation were outraged at the compromise with the Pennsylvania troops. "I am pleased," wrote one of Domine Romeyn's ministerial brethren at Millstone, "with the mode in which the late Mutiny in the Jersey Line was Suppressed & Could wish the same Steps had been taken with the Pennsylvanians—The Soldiers in Our Army have Doubtless many causes of Complaint, but a Spirit of insurrection Should never be indulged in an Army." [14]

His concern was understandable, for the mutinies had offered infinite possibilities of harm. Even Sir Henry, for once, had got into a fever of activity at the prospect that the Revolution was now about to collapse: British Regulars were sent out, ready to cover any American troops that chose to join the mutiny; farmers like Benjamin Westerfield, Dowah Westerfield and Abraham Dye, who came in from English Neighborhood, Jasper Hart and John Eaton, of Hackensack, and "Jno. Gutches, of Pollifly near Hackensack," who had brought their produce in to the city in defiance of patriot patrols, found themselves taken up by Sir Henry's intelligence officers and questioned closely for any information they could add. Hart and Eaton said the country people felt the mutiny would end the rebellion, but that "rebel country people tell different stories about it and endeavor to make others believe things are not so bad as they are said to be." The militia, they reported, thought the men "were very right in going to Congress to demand what was due them." Linneas, a Negro belonging to Abraham Ackerman of Paramus, and Dougals, a Negro belonging to *Albus* Zabriskie of the same place, could only say that they had heard nothing of the revolt until they reached Paulus Hook, on January 7, 1781. Linneas added that the "inhabitants say the war must soon be over or it will be over for them, taxes are so high." Ezekiel Yeomans, Isaac Siscoe, William Badcock, and Abraham Mabie went out from New York to scour the countryside for the latest news of the revolt.[15]

John Mason, the Highland gang leader who had killed Major Clark in cold blood, the man who very probably had led the party that captured Mustermaster Ward at Kakiat, took a dramatic and indeed heroic part in the mutiny. Mason, who had recently found himself incarcerated by the British for plundering loyalists on Long Island, along with his wife (the recent house guest of the Arri Ackermans at Pascack), was recruited out of jail to go on an expedition to the West Indies, but as

14 Froeligh to Romeyn, Feb. 6, 1781, Ford House Manuscripts, Morristown Historical National Park.
15 British Intelligence Reports, Emmet Coll., NYPL.

soon as word of the mutiny came to New York he was shifted to the delicate and dangerous task of carrying Sir Henry's proposals to the mutineers, at Princeton. Taken up the Raritan on an armed galley and landed near South Amboy, carrying the message in lead foil, as if it were tea, Mason set off immediately with a lone guide to Princeton. There the leaders of the mutiny, possibly seeing Mason and his guide as valuable pawns in their negotiations, possibly actually insulted by British calls to treason, seized them and turned them over to an American court-martial to be hanged, after playing the most callous cat-and-mouse game with them. Whatever might be said of Mason's recent life, he behaved with great bravery at his death. He told the Americans he had but one favor to ask, "that General Clinton might be informed that he had done everything in his power to execute his trust, that he had been unfortunate and died like a brave man." [16] After the war the Tory David Matthews took credit for recruiting Mason for the mission.[17] He probably had nothing to do with it.[18]

The spring of 1781 saw no change for the better in the Hackensack valley. Lord Cornwallis and Arnold were in North Carolina and Virginia, but the broad pattern of the war was unchanged: the British continued to hold their small but powerful base in New York City, from which, with their superior forces and strong navy, they could lash out at any selected objective at will, while Washington held his troops in the shadow of the Highlands, ever hopeful that chance might permit him to drive in and destroy New York, if the garrison there was sufficiently weakened.

The neutral ground continued to be the stage for probing raids, espionage, and partisan warfare.[19]

On March 12 and 13, 1781, a large party of British and Tories—two hundred, with two field pieces, General Heath reported to Washington —came up to Closter on a plundering expedition under the command of Thomas Ward, of the Associated Loyalists. Heath reported that the local militia had driven them off before the Continentals arrived; not,

[16] Van Doren, Mutiny in January, 157.
[17] LYT NYPL "David Matthews."
[18] Van Doren, Mutiny in January, 92.
[19] If the complaints of some English Neighborhood people to British headquarters were to be believed, in January a party of Orange County militiamen came down from Kakiat and "seized Peter De Grow, who they hanged up immediately until he was near dead. They then cut him down." What real or fancied injury De Grow had done to the Orange County militiamen, they did not say. Benjamin Westervelt, Dowah Westervelt and Abraham Dey, British Intelligence, Jan. 9, 1781, Emmet Coll., NYPL. See also Isaac Siscoe, British Intelligence, Jan. 5, 1781, and Ezekiel Yeomans, British Intelligence, Jan. 11, 1781, ibid.

of course, before they had thoroughly stripped Closter of everything movable.[20]

Later in the spring a more important engagement took place a few miles south of the Hackensack courthouse. A British gunboat had come up the Hackensack to Moonachie Point, "plundered the inhabitants and carried off about twenty head of cattle." Captain Outwater collected his militia, "the cattle was retaken [and] the British routed with the loss of seven men killed and one prisoner." John Lozier, of Pompton, was an American casualty, shot through the thigh with a musket ball. "To stop the great effusion of blood from the wound [Abraham Vreeland] tore up his . . . shirt, with which the wound was dressed. . . . Lozier did not recover entirely from his wound till near a year later." [21] Vreeland carried him out of the salt marshes where the action occurred, first to the home of George Doremus, about eleven miles from Pompton, and after Lozier had somewhat improved, back to Pompton.[22]

The late spring of 1781 saw the whole force of the Bergen and Orange County militia in battle array for the only time during the war, in action against a Tory blockhouse at Fort Lee.[23]

About a hundred Refugees from New York City had occupied the old site of the fort and commenced to build a blockhouse there, moving back and forth across the Hudson in small boats under the protection of British warships. The move was a mistake. The time was long past when the patriot militia would sit idly by while Tories laid down a base for marauding at their very doors. Colonel Dey, with part of his forces, including Blanch's and Huyler's companies, tried to dislodge them by frontal attack on May 15, 1781, and failed. Three days later the colonel, with Major Goetschius, brought down upon the blockhouse the whole patriot military force of the Hackensack valley, several hundred men. John A. Haring recalled after the war that "it was the only occasion during the whole of his service that Colonel Dey or Major

20 Heath to Washington, March 14, 1781, GW Papers LC. Damages by British, NJSL, Harrington Precinct Nos. 39, 47, 48. "Two hundred soldiers of the standing forces came in to Tappan last Saturday and have one field piece with them. They lie four miles above the militia." Isaac Siscoe, British Intelligence, March 25, 1781, Emmet Coll., NYPL. About fifty militia were at New Bridge. Daniel Martin, idem.
21 Affidavit of John Lozier, Pension Records, W20525.
22 Affidavit of John Lozier, Pension Records, W20525; Abraham Vanderbeek, Pension Records, S1130. When the pension application was made, in 1832, Lozier was too feeble to go to Hackensack. William Colfax reported that a few days before the old soldier "was actually denied credit at the stores in our vicinity for a gallon of molasses and a few pounds of sugar," a fact which Colfax had himself confirmed at the stores. Idem.
23 Affidavits of local soldiers, Pension Records, passim.

Goetschius was in personal command of declarant. . . . There were several skirmishes . . . a considerable number wounded and taken prisoners on both sides till at last we dislodged them." [24] The British command was fortunate that the Bergen and Orange County militiamen were not being thrown against a more important objective.

On May 17 Washington, at New Windsor, unaware that the militia were poised to attack the blockhouse, ordered Colonel Scammell's battalion of Continentals to move against it. "I have received intelligence that a party of the enemy are establishing themselves at or near Fort Lee and building a blockhouse or some kind of work. If they are permitted to complete their plan they will not only be difficult to remove, but they will harass the country from thence and may be much in the way of some future operation." [25] He ordered Colonel Scammell to work closely with Captain Jonathan Lawrence, Jr., of the New York State troops, and "to take Captain Lawrence under your command with the Levies of New York and any Jersey militia that you may find embodied, but you will trust no officer among them nor any other but Lawrence with your design. His is sensible and appears discreet." [26] Colonel Tilghman, the secretary who prepared the order, may have been embarrassed to learn a few days later that, sensible and discreet or not, the Bergen County militia had reduced the fort to possession at some loss of men and blood while he was congratulating himself, in the comfort and safety of headquarters, on his fatuous directions to keep the object of the attack a secret from them.

At the end of May, 1781, Washington completed his plans for a massive attack on New York. He kept New York as an objective, he said, despite his inclination to move southward and attack Cornwallis in North Carolina and Virginia ("in defence of that country where all my property and connexions are") because he felt that the measures he had in train against New York would be more effectual to relieve Virginia than marching there, and New York was still Washington's first objective as late as July, 1781, three months before the Yorktown surrender.[27]

On July 18 he and several other general officers spent a good deal of

---

[24] Affidavit of John A. Haring, Pension Records, S6980, and most other pension records relating to local soldiers. Among the wounded were Daniel Banta, who received "a musket ball which passed through both his thighs. . . . He laid under the surgeon's hands from the 18th May, 1781, until some time in September following." Affidavit of Daniel Banta, Pension Records, S2090. John Van Allen also was wounded. Affidavit of Peter Van Allen, Pension Records, S6301.

[25] 22 GW 94.

[26] Idem.

[27] 22 GW 178, 179. 22 GW 295, et seq.

time along the Palisades reconnoitering as far south as Fort Lee,[28] covered by a party of Continental horsemen who "patrolled to the crossroad at the widow Demaries which leads to Fort Lee." Six days earlier four hundred men of the Jersey Brigade passed through Paramus on their way to Sneden's Landing, where they set up camp near the blockhouse. The Americans had thirty-six flatboats at the landing, poised for a move downriver.[29]

By the 1st of August, however, Washington was prepared to agree that if the French fleet should come into the Chesapeake, the enterprise against New York would be abandoned, and the army would move south against Cornwallis. In the middle of August the hoped-for word came: the French ships were off the Virginia capes. Washington instantly broke camp in the Highlands and moved over every bridge and by every boat across the Hackensack, the Passaic, the Raritan, and the Delaware, and was in Philadelphia while Sir Henry Clinton was still strengthening his garrison at Staten Island against a threatened attack. With Washington was the whole French army, which had been encamped in Westchester.[30]

General Heath and General Lord Stirling were left in charge of the Americans at Peekskill, protecting the Hudson River and anxiously awaiting word from Washington.

Once Washington and Rochambeau had reached the head of the Chesapeake, the next move was up to Sir Henry Clinton. Pursuit of Washington offered little hope for Cornwallis, but Tories urged Clinton to invade Jersey and Philadelphia, and to burn and destroy everything en route, in an effort to divert the huge allied army from its quarry at Yorktown.[31] Both patriot and Tory kept their eyes on New York Bay, fearful and hopeful that the expected men-of-war might yet tip the

---

28 See 22 GW 379. French officers continued the reconnaissance on July 22, 1781, sketching upper New York Island in detail from the heights opposite Spuyten Duyvil. French map, Karpinski Coll., No. 135, NYPL.

29 British Intelligence Reports, Emmet Coll., NYPL.

30 The French found the Jersey Dutch friendly and the Jersey Dutch countryside charming. A German nobleman with the French army wrote that "The Jerseys, where we are now (beautiful country!) abound in all kinds of produce. The inhabitants (who are of Dutch origin) have kept it neat and have retained their gentle and peaceful customs. . . . It is a land of milk and honey, with game, fish, poultry, etc. After leaving New York State, where misery is written on the brows of the inhabitants, the affluence in the State of the Jerseys seems to be much greater." The country between Suffern and Passaic Falls he found "superb and well cultivated . . . extremely beautiful." He saw "several large residences, many fine cattle, and an astonishing number of fruits of every description, which we tasted with pleasure." He added, mistakenly, that all the Dutch were "as attached to England as the Orange family." Von Closen Journal, 111, 112, 238.

31 Smith Journal, NYPL.

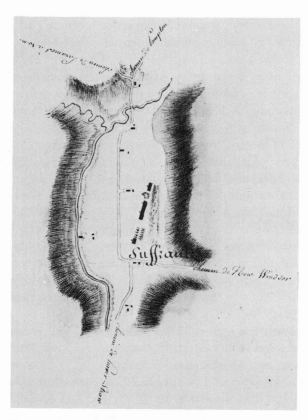

French Army Camp at Suffern, August 25, 1781.
Berthier Papers, Princeton University Library.

balance against the French. The British fleet could yet ruin Washington's plans.

As the allied armies moved closer to Yorktown the need for intelligence grew. Having victory almost in his grasp, Washington wanted no British surprise to tear it away. Benjamin Tallmadge pressed his two agents, the Culpers, for every scrap of news; Mercereau at Elizabethtown and Z in New York added what they could.[32] At Nyack Captain John Pray had the double task of picket for the patriot Highland posts and seeker of intelligence about the plans of British New York.

At the end of September, while Washington's forces were still aboard their transports in the Chesapeake, a Continental horseman dismounted at the home of William Prevost, in Hackensack, asked for Domine Dirck Romeyn, and, when he came down to the door, handed him a folded message. The domine had just moved to Prevost's; the messenger

[32] Bakeless, passim.

may very well have lost some time in seeking him at Hendrick Berdan's house, which the domine had left because he found the quarters "crowded and ineligible," not to mention the exorbitant price of 21s. a month "for a single room and the occasional use of the kitchen." [33]

The letter was from General Lord Stirling, the American commander of the Highland forces: "Your warm attachment to the cause we are engaged in, your good sense and prudence, induce me to ask the favour of you to collect every piece of intelligence you can of the situation of the enemy at New York."

"The moment being critical," he went on, he suggested that Romeyn reduce his information "to a daily journal which you will send twice or thrice a week" to General Heath, and particularly that he send along the New York papers. "For this conveyance of your letters a man will call on you as often, with a line from Captain Pray, to whom you may safely entrust your letters, which need not be signed but with the letters M 2." [34]

The officers on the lines had been instructed, Stirling assured the domine, to give him every assistance.

The messenger evidently took back one of the New York papers at once; Heath's diary for the next day speaks of Mr. Rivington's account of the French blow to the British fleet and of Clinton's debarking the troops which had been intended to succor Cornwallis, all quite probably part of the domine's intelligence.[35] However galling Americans found Rivington's abuse of patriots, his papers contained a great deal of valuable military information, and Heath and Stirling were not the only general officers who wished to have every issue of his *Royal Gazette* as quickly as possible. Neither General Heath nor the domine nor anyone else then knew that patriots had been able to make good use of Rivington's hatred. A century was to pass before anyone suspected that Washington's most effective spy in New York, Culper, Jr., was a partner in Rivington's Coffee House, a meeting place established to get news from British officers in tacit exchange for publicizing their exploits, where the spy was able to fill his secret dispatches to Washington with authentic intelligence from the same source.[36] Indeed there is good reason to think that by October, 1781, the cynical Rivington himself was sufficiently impressed by the chance of an American victory to be passing on important secret intelligence to the Americans.[37]

[33] Romeyn Papers UCL.
[34] Idem.
[35] Heath 287.
[36] Pennypacker, General Washington's Spies, 12.
[37] 1959 William and Mary Quarterly 61–72; Allan McLane Diary NYHS.

On October 23 Rivington, like the rest of New York, did not have to read his paper to learn the news from the Chesapeake.[38] The cannon firing on the Jersey shore made it clear that the siege of Yorktown was over, and that Cornwallis and his army were lost; patriots were not given to wasting powder to celebrate British victories. Nor were the Dutch Tories of Buskirk's brigade at Bergen Point heartened to learn, when the final word of surrender arrived, that Washington had winked at the departure of loyalist troops from Yorktown rather than admit that they were not punishable as traitors. Among those who thus made their escape were their good friends Major Robert Timpany, the Hackensack schoolmaster, Joseph and Samuel Ryerson of Saddle River, and Jacob Van Buskirk and a number of other Jersey Dutchmen who had been with the New Jersey Volunteers on Cornwallis' southern campaign.[39] Abraham Van Buskirk, for his part, had made no new friends among patriots when he joined Benedict Arnold in burning New London a month before.[40]

Van Buskirk's battalion had long since fallen to a fraction of its original strength.[41] Loyalists, like patriots, had their backsliders and summer soldiers. The majority of Tories now had lost their bright hopes of victory and had little more than a sullen wish to revenge themselves for their own woes, whatever the outcome of the war. In the Associated Loyalists they had found a fit vehicle for their feelings. In January, 1781, the London government, always deceived by Tory schemes, had been induced to charter an organization of American Tories to wage a private war-within-a-war, to take their own prisoners, and to treat military booty as their own; in a word, to wage war without let or hindrance from British headquarters.[42] A worse arrangement could hardly be imagined: in the Associated Loyalists, King George and Lord Germain had raised to a chartered enterprise the Highland gang warfare of Claudius Smith and John Mason. Patriots were not surprised to find

38   1882 NYHS 152.
39   Clinton, American Rebellion, 352, 353; 5 Freeman 383 n.; Wertenbaker, Father Knickerbocker, 244, 245. Timpany was evidently a paroled prisoner of the French naval forces. 2 Carleton Papers 473 (3943, 4506, 4507, 4933).
40   Van Buskirk had earned the particular hatred of New London for taking the proffered sword of its surrendered commander, Lieutenant Colonel William Ledyard, and plunging it into Ledyard's body; after which his subordinates finished the work with their bayonets. Ward, War of the Revolution, 626, 627.
41   See Pattison 272. Cf. Wertenbaker, Father Knickerbocker, 228; cf. Buskirk to MacKenzie, Aug. 19, 1780, MacKenzie Papers, CL; MSS Army List pp. 126, 127, shows only about 120 in service out of 260 of the 4th Battalion of New Jersey Volunteers. Many of these may however have then been serving with Ferguson in the south. Cf. 4 Carleton Papers 427 (9451).
42   See Wertenbaker, Father Knickerbocker, 229.

both the proud William Franklin and the lowly Thomas Ward active in its affairs. Partisan warfare, murder of prisoners, arson, kidnapping and robbery, once peculiar to the neutral ground, the Hudson Highlands and the Jersey pine barrens, now extended as far as Tory power could reach. The effect on the Hackensack valley was not great; there seems to have been no hanging of prisoners there, and arson, kidnapping and robbery had always been the order of things in the Jersey Dutch country, but the Associated Loyalists did their best to bring to other parts of the colonies the terrors that the neutral ground had known since 1776. Their outrages were ended only when General Washington marked a British Regular officer for execution in retaliation for their brutal killing of a Jersey prisoner.[43]

Sir Henry Clinton had futilely opposed their measures. When he was recalled and Sir Guy Carleton named as his successor, their charter was revoked. The Associated Loyalists served only to underscore the senseless brutality of the worst of the Tories; every discerning man in New York knew that the British cause was lost at Yorktown and that the British ministry, which had seen two whole armies fall into the hands of their enemies, was not going to send another to meet the same end, whatever embittered loyalists might think.

Indeed even many loyalists were reconciled to peace and to any peace terms that the ministry and King George might grant so long as they did not grant American independence.

The Rev. Garret Leydecker, the English Neighborhood Tory and former conferentie leader, drew and circulated a petition urging no independence for Americans, had it signed by every Tory minister, and sent it to London.[44] He would have been no Tory if he had been able to see that Yorktown, not Tory pleas, had decided that issue.

Men like Benedict Arnold were not so naïve as to waste time signing petitions. When Cornwallis sailed for London on parole, Arnold decided to put the Atlantic between himself and his countrymen, and many of the shrewder loyalists soon made arrangements to do the same.

There was little official fighting after Yorktown, and the severest means had to be taken to prevent desertions, for hundreds of British soldiers decided to stay under the new government, but Tory and refugee raids into the Hackensack valley continued, and the illicit trade through the lines became bolder and bolder. Single farmers no longer carried a few pounds of butter in to New York and a basket of salt back, commercial traders—both friend and foe now called them "London

[43] See 5 Freeman 412, 413, 414, 419, 420.
[44] LYT NYPL.

traders"—brought salt up the Hackensack by the boatload and country produce back in the same quantity.[45]

Where once a farmer would drive a fat ox into New York by night, hiding it in the woods by day, by 1782 "herds of cattle [were] driven to the enemy from all quarters of this and the neighboring state," local people told the state authorities. The militia, they said, were "too weak and too much worn down with service and suffering" to help stop either the raids or the London traders.[46] By the summer of 1782 it was clear enough that the war had been won so that local Tories and neutrals were busy fortifying themselves against an American victory. Unfortunately there were patriots willing to help. Captain Elias Romeyn of the Bergen County militia was tried and convicted by a court-martial for taking bribes from Tories along the Hackensack, after threatening that he would make Whigs sweat for complaining about him,[47] and even the most hard-shelled Jersey Dutchmen knew the war was won when Fort Delancey was torn down and the hated Van Buskirks and their friends took ship for Nova Scotia and New Brunswick.[48]

In March, 1783, word of the Treaty of Paris of January 20, 1783, reached America, and the war was officially ended.[49]

[45] Abraham Vanderbeek, "being ordered out on the bank of the Hackensack River to watch and detect London traders, at which place he discovered a boat in the said river of which he informed . . . [Captain Outwater] . . . when Vanderbeek, his captain and another of his comrades went with all speed to capture the same, on coming to it, the men had deserted and left the boat with twelve live sheep, which they took as a prize, which boat they towed up the said river and had the prize condemned." At another time Vanderbeek learned that a boat "on board of which was a quantity of salt" was coming up the Hackensack River ". . . in possession of London traders." Outwater, Vanderbeek and a few others went in pursuit of it, "but before they could come up with her they were informed that she had landed her salt at a private house in the neighborhood." They went to the house, seized the salt, and again took their prize before Justice Jacob Terhune to be condemned. Affidavit of Abraham Vanderbeek, Pension Records, S1130.

[46] Bergen Petition for providing for the Defense of the Frontier of the County, Nov. 8, 1782, NJSL.

[47] 5 NJA (2) 430. Romeyn's troops were at the time "doing guard duty, and also to prevent illicit trade carried on (by a party called London Traders) with the British in the City of New York." Affidavit of Abraham I. Brouwer, Pension Records, W23707.

[48] Almost two centuries later many of the most distinguished families of Canada proudly bear Hackensack valley Dutch names. See e.g. Wertenbaker, Father Knickerbocker, Chap. 11; Fraser, passim; LYT NYPL, passim; Blauvelt, Banta, Demarest, Ryerson, and other genealogies.

[49] Tory plundering parties were active almost to the day when the news arrived. "Near the close of the said war and but a short time before the news of peace arrived, a company consisting of thirty or forty men, under the command of Capt. John M. Hogenkamp composed of men of different companies, of whom the said John I. Blauvelt was one, marched into the state of New Jersey to a place called English Neighborhood, and not expecting to meet with an enemy, as peace was expected and it was thought that hostilities had ceased, was fired upon by a party of the British,

Washington was at Newburgh, behind the Highlands, and Tappan and Sneden's Landing were now the points of contact with British New York. Tappan was several times the scene of meetings with the defeated enemy; on September 27, 1782, there had been a conference at the De Windt house, which had hitherto seen little to cheer patriots, between General Campbell and Andrew Elliot, representing Sir Guy Carleton, and Generals Heath and Knox, representing Washington, to try to effect a general exchange of prisoners; [50] eight months later, on May 6, 1783, Washington and Sir Guy themselves held a cordial meeting there to arrange the evacuation of New York.[51] At that meeting, after an hour's chat in and before the door, the two commanders, with Governor George Clinton of New York, and Judge William Smith and others, retired to discuss the matter. "When all were seated Washington opened the business," Smith wrote later, "[talking] without animation, with great slowness and in a low tone of voice." [52] Seven years earlier the quick-tongued Smith would have taken this mannerism for dullness; he and Sir Guy could not now mistake the firmness that had humbled the British Empire.

The war over, reconciliation came fast in those places where there had been no fighting and where the Tories had not remained near patriots and striven to injure them.

It came so fast, in point of fact, that the Whigs of the Hackensack valley soon found themselves crotchety old men among their enlightened and tolerant friends elsewhere. As William Livingston had predicted years before, the neutrals, those political hypocrites who hoped by not espousing either side to secure a favorable reception with the prevailing party, whether the oppressing or the oppressed, now came from their lurking holes as if there had never been a war, and, though even Livingston would have never dared to predict it, the Tories did the same.[53]

Refugees and Tories, who lay in ambush, but fortunately all escaped unhurt but one man who was wounded in the knee and taken prisoner." Affidavit of John I. Blauvelt, Pension Records, W20721. The Americans, notably Cornelius Haring, a commissioner of seized estates, had been in considerable friction with the British over efforts to seize Tory property below the American lines. 3 Carleton Papers 345 (6485); See 4 Carleton Papers 73 (7647).

50 Heath 326, et seq.
51 Memorandum of conference Carleton and Washington, May 6, 1783, GW Papers LC; Smith Journal NYPL.
52 Smith Journal NYPL. See Richard Varick to Henry Glen, May 10, 1783, Parke-Bernet Catalogue, Feb. 22, 1961, No. 474.
53 Not, however, without some hesitation. Two months after the news of peace, Warmoldus Kuypers, the conferentie minister at Hackensack, a comparatively inof-

Governor Livingston, an unreconstructed Whig himself, put the feelings of many patriotic Jerseymen into words when he wrote of the public forgetfulness: "I have seen Tories members of Congress, Judges upon tribunals, Tories representatives in our Legislative councils, Tories members of our Assemblies . . . I have seen self-interest predominating and patriotism languishing."

There were all too many places on the continent where the former enemies of independence soon learned that a scornful attitude toward Whiggish zeal and open admission that they held patriot fanaticism in low esteem got them a far better reception than the twice-told tales of patriot valor. Patriots of the neutral ground had no answer but to withdraw themselves further from the company of those who had never suffered the terrors of an unequal civil war.

The age produced deeply religious men; the divisions peculiar to the Hackensack valley had brought to the side of America men who might have stepped directly out of the Old Testament. Captain James Christie was but one of hundreds of old soldiers of the Hackensack valley who was "very highly esteemed for his most excellent character"; Jacob Tallman but one "with principles of incorruptible integrity and . . . evenness of temperament . . . who spent his life as free from reproach as it is ever our privilege to record of our fellow men." [54]

Strangers to the Hackensack valley found patriots' hatred for Toryism irreconcilable with their deep piety. They themselves had no such difficulty: they could say, as the prophet Obadiah had said to Edom, ". . . thou shouldest not . . . have rejoiced over the children of Judah in the day of their destruction, . . . nor laid hands on their substance in the day of their calamity; . . . neither shouldest thou have delivered

---

fensive Tory, was described by his Tory son as "having no expectation of being further serviceable since the acknowledgement of American independence. His people fearing to suffer by adhering to him, are leaving his church (and several refusing already to pay their annual stipend), he finds himself necessitated to seek an asylum from that government whose cause he had endeavored to support to the utmost of his power." The son accordingly prayed "that his father may be admitted as a subject" and granted an allowance. 4 Carleton Papers 102 (7772). Elias Kuypers may have overdrawn the case in order to enlist British help—Dom. Kuypers' congregation were in far worse repute with the patriots than he was, and were not likely to leave the conferentie church because of its Toryism—; in any event, it was not long before Mr. Kuypers and most of his congregation were going about Hackensack and Schraalenburgh as if there had never been a neutral ground or a war.

[54] Banta Genealogy No. 616; Pension Records, W26511 (Jacob Tallman). David Pye, an official of Rockland County, was not exaggerating when he told pension officials after the war that "the greater part of them . . . are men of eminent piety . . . [who] . . . could not have been prevailed upon to swear falsely for the whole United States treasury." Pension Records, S22656.

up those of his that did remain in the day of distress"; they could pray that the house of Esau would be as stubble before the fire of the house of Jacob and the flame of the house of Joseph, that there should be none remaining of the house of Esau.

After seven years of war, Dutch patriots could not forget their neighbors' treacheries nor understand the indifference of those away from the neutral ground who never suffered from Tory violence. Untaught in the uses of publicity, they let their Tory and neutral neighbors paint themselves as they chose, content to tell their children and their children's children of the day when a nation came upon their land, strong and without number. For a century and a half after the Revolution the story was passed down in patriot Hackensack valley families; now the last of the generation that heard these things from their grandparents has almost passed away.

The patriot dead in the Dutch churchyards of the South Church at Schraalenburgh, the Church on the Green at Hackensack, the Paramus Church, and the Reformed Church at Tappan, men who sleep in their graves with the scars of Tory and British wounds, deserve better of Americans than that their story be forgotten. "A great people and a strong; there hath not been ever the like, neither shall be any more after it, even to the years of many generations."

KEY TO SHORT TITLES

Anburey — *Thomas Anburey, Travels Through the Interior Parts of America*. 2 vols., Boston, 1923.

André Journal — *Major André's Journal*. Yonkers, N.Y., 1930.

Arch. N.Y. — *Archives of the State of New York, New York in the Revolution*. Albany, 1887.

Bailey — *R. F. Bailey, Pre-Revolutionary Dutch Houses and Families*. New York, 1936.

Bakeless — *John Bakeless, Turncoats, Traitors and Heroes*. Philadelphia, 1959.

Banner of Truth — *Banner of Truth, a pub*. Hackensack, N.J., and Grand Rapids, Mich., 1866–.

Banta Genealogy — *Theodore N. Banta, The Banta Genealogy*, New York, 1893.

Baurmeister — *Adjutant General Baurmeister, Revolution in America, Letters and Journals of*. New Brunswick, 1957.

Bergen County Atlas — *Atlas of Bergen County, N.J. Reading, Pa.*, 1876.

BHSP — *Bergen County Historical Society Papers and Proceedings*.

Blauvelt Genealogy — *L. L. Blauvelt, The Blauvelt Family Genealogy*. East Orange, N.J., 1957.

Bogert, Paramus — *Frederick W. Bogert, Paramus, A Chronicle of Four Centuries*. Paramus, 1961.

Boudinot Papers HSP — *Papers of Elias Boudinot, Historical Society of Pennsylvania*.

Boudinot Papers LC — *Papers of Elias Boudinot, Library of Congress*.

Brinckerhoff Genealogy — *Family of Joris Dircksen Brinckerhoff, New York*, 1887.

Brinkerhoff — *Jacob Brinkerhoff, The History of the True Reformed Church in the United States of America. New York*, 1873.

CHM — *Calendar of Historical Manuscripts Relating to the War of the Revolution in the Office of the Secretary of State [of New York]. New York*, 1868.

Callahan, Knox — *North Callahan, Henry Knox, General Washington's General. New York*, 1958.

Carleton Papers — *Historical Manuscript Commission—Report on American Manuscripts in the Royal Institution of Great Britain*. 4 vols. London 1904. *Copies at Colonial Williamsburg Research Center*.

Carrington — *Henry B. Carrington, Battles of the American Revolution. New York, 1876.*

Centennial Discourses — *Centennial Discourses delivered in the year 1876 by the order of . . . The Reformed (Dutch) Church in America. New York, 1877.*

Christie Genealogy — *Walter Christie, Genealogy of the Christie Family. Bergenfield, N.J., 1919.*

Classis of Paramus — *A History of the Classis of Paramus 1800–1900. New York, 1902.*

Clinton, American Rebellion — *Sir Henry Clinton, The American Rebellion. New Haven, 1954.*

Cole Genealogy — *Rev. David Cole, Cole Genealogy. Yonkers, N.Y., 1864.*

Cole, Rockland — *Rev. David Cole, History of Rockland County. New York, 1884.*

Cole, Tappan Church — *Rev. David Cole, History of the Reformed Church of Tappan. New York, 1894.*

Commager and Morris — *Commager and Morris, The Spirit of Seventy-Six. 2 vols. New York, 1958.*

Congressional Biography — *Congressional Biography, Washington, D.C.*

Crevecoeur — *M. G. St. J. Crevecoeur, Letters from an American Farmer. Boston, 1904.*

DAB — *Dictionary of American Biography. New York, 1928, etc.*

Damages by Americans NJSL — *Damages by the Americans in New Jersey, New Jersey State Library.*

Damages by British NJSL — *Damages by the British in New Jersey, New Jersey State Library.*

Dandridge — *D. Dandridge, American Prisoners of the Revolution. Charlottesville, Va., 1911.*

Dearborn Journal — *Henry Dearborn Journal 1776–1783. Chicago, 1939.*

Demarest Genealogy — *W. H. S. Demarest, The Demarest Family. New Bruswick, 1938.*

Demarest, Lamentation over Solomon Froeligh — *Rev. Cornelius T. Demarest, A Lamentation over the Rev. Solomon Froeligh. New York, 1827.*

Demarest, Reformed Church in America — *David D. Demarest, D.D., The Reformed Church in America, Its Origin, Development and Characteristics. New York, 1889.*

Duer, Lord Stirling — *William A. Duer, LLD., The Life of William Alexander. New York, 1847.*

Eager, Orange County — *Samuel W. Eager, An Outline History of Orange County. Newburgh, 1846–1847.*

ERNY — *Hugh Hastings (ed.), Ecclesiastical Records, State of New York. 6 vols. Albany, 1905.*

Erskine Maps NYHS — *Maps of Robert Erskine, New York Historical Society.*

Erskine Papers NJHS — *Papers of Robert Erskine, New Jersey Historical Society.*

Fell Diary — *Diary Entries of John Fell in E. C. Burnett, Letters of Members of the Continental Congress. 8 vols. Washington, 1921–1936.*

Flexner — *James T. Flexner, The Traitor and the Spy. New York, 1953.*

Force — *Peter Force (ed.), American Archives, Fourth and Fifth Series. 6 vols. and 3 vols. Washington, 1837–1853.*

Fraser — *Alexander Fraser, Second Report of the Bureau of Archives for the Province of Ontario. Toronto, 1905.*

Freeman — *D. S. Freeman, George Washington. 6 vols. New York, 1948.*

French War Office Map — *Carte D'une partie de la Province de Newyork et des Jerseys. Karpinski Coll. No. 141, New York Public Library.*

GC — *Hugh Hastings (ed.), Public Papers of George Clinton. New York, 1899.*

GHHB — C. B. Harvey, *Genealogical History of Hudson and Bergen Counties*. New York, 1900.

Gilman — *Nicholas Gilman, The Story of the Ferry, Palisades, N.Y., Library*, 1903.

Glorious Cause — Herbert T. Wade and Robert A. Lively, *This Glorious Cause*. Princeton, 1958.

Glyn Journal PUL — *Journal and Orderly Book of Thomas Glyn, April, 1776–August, 1777*, Princeton University Library.

Gordon — W. R. Gordon, *A Manual of Information and Direction for the use of the Ref. Protestant Dutch Church of Schraalenburgh*. New York 1861.

Greene, Examination — G. W. Greene, *Nathanael Greene, An Examination of Some Statements concerning Major General Greene. . . .* Boston, 1866.

Greene, Greene — G. W. Greene, *Life of Nathanael Greene. 3 vols.* New York, 1867–1871.

GW Papers LC — *Papers of George Washington, Library of Congress.*

GW — J. C. Fitzpatrick (ed.), *The Writings of George Washington. 39 vols.* Washington, 1931, etc.

Hackensack Church Records — *Records of the Reformed Dutch Churches of Hackensack and Schraalenburgh, New Jersey. Part I.* Holland Society, 1891.

HBP — W. Woodford Clayton and William Nelson (eds.), *History of Bergen and Passaic Counties, New Jersey*. Philadelphia, 1882.

HC Papers CL — *Papers of Sir Henry Clinton, Clements Library, Ann Arbor, Mich.*

Hall, Fort Lee — E. H. Hall, *Fort Lee, New Jersey, Fourteenth Annual Report, American Scenic and Historical Society*. New York, 1909.

Hay Genealogy — Charles J. Colcock, *The Family of Hay*. New York, 1908; New Orleans, 1959.

Heath Papers MHS — *Papers of William Heath, Massachusetts Historical Society.*

Henderson, Shadow on the River — Peter L. Henderson, *The Shadow on the River*. Haworth, N.J., 1959.

Heusser, The Forgotten General — Albert H. Heusser, *The Forgotten General*. Paterson, N.J., 1925.

HSYB — *Year Book of the Holland Society*. New York, 1891, etc.

Huntington Papers HL — *Papers of Ebenezer Huntington, Huntington Library, San Marino, Calif.*

Johnston, Stony Point — H. P. Johnston, *The Storming of Stony Point*. New York, 1900.

Jones, Loyalists of New Jersey — E. A. Jones, *The Loyalists of New Jersey*. Newark, 1927.

Jones, New York During the Revolution — Thomas Jones, *A History of New York during the Revolutionary War. 2 vols.* New York, 1879.

Kemble — *Kemble's Journals, 1773–1789*, N.Y.H.S. Coll., 1883–1884.

Knox Papers MHS — *Papers of Henry Knox, Massachusetts Historical Society.*

Koehler, Three Hundred Years — Francis C. Koehler, *Three Hundred Years*. Chester, N.J., 1940.

Kull, New Jersey, a History — I. S. Kull, *New Jersey, a History. 4 vols.* New York, 1930.

Labaw, Preakness Church — Rev. G. W. Labaw, *Preakness and the Preakness Reformed Church*. New York, 1902.

Lamb Papers NYHS — *Papers of John Lamb, New York Historical Society.*

Leake, Lamb — I. Q. Leake, *Memoir of the Life and Times of General John Lamb*. Albany, 1857.

Livingston Papers MHS — *Papers of William Livingston, Massachusetts Historical Society.*

Livingston Papers NYPL — *Papers of William Livingston, New York Public Library.*

Lundin — Leonard Lundin, *Cockpit of the Revolution*. Princeton, 1940.

LYT NYPL — *Loyalist Transcripts, New York Public Library.*

Mackenzie Papers CL — *Papers of Frederick Mackenzie, Clements Library, Ann Arbor, Mich.*

Martin — *Martin, Joseph Plume, A Narrative of some of the Adventures, Dangers & Sufferings of a Revolutionary Soldier; Interspersed with Anecdotes of Incidents that Occurred within His Own Observation. Hallowell, Printed by Glazier, Masters & Co., No. 1, Kennebec, Row, 1830.*

Maxson — *C. H. Maxson, The Great Awakening in the Middle Colonies. Chicago, 1920.*

McCormick, Experiment in Independence — *Richard P. McCormick, Experiment in Independence. New Brunswick, 1950.*

McDougall Papers NYHS — *Papers of Maj. Gen'l. Alexander McDougall, New York Historical Society.*

MCSNJ — *Minutes of the Council of Safety of the State of New Jersey. Jersey City, 1872.*

Messler, Memorial Sermons — *Abraham Messler, D.D., Forty Years at Raritan, Eight Memorial Sermons. New York, 1873.*

Millstone Centennial — *E. T. Corwin, Historical Discourse on . . . the Centennial Anniversary of the Reformed Dutch Church of Millstone. New York, 1866.*

Mins. Genl. Synod — *Acts and Proceedings of the General Synod of the Reformed Protestant Dutch Church. New York, 1859.*

Mins. Board of Proprietors — *Minutes of the Board of Proprietors of the Eastern Division of New Jersey. 3 vols. Perth Amboy, 1949–1960.*

MJFBC — *Minutes of the Justices and Freeholders of Bergen County, Bergen County Historical Society publication.*

Moody, Narrative — *Lieut. James Moody, Exertions & Sufferings . . . New York, 1865.*

Moore — *Frank Moore, Diary of the American Revolution. New York, 1860*

Morris Papers RUL — *Papers of Robert Morris, Rutgers University Library.*

MPC — *Minutes of the Provincial Congress and Council of Safety of the State of New Jersey. Trenton, 1879.*

MRC — *E. T. Corwin, Manual of the Reformed Church in America. 4th ed. New York, 1902.*

MRDC — *Minutes of the Reformed Dutch Church.*

Muhlenberg — *H. M. Muhlenberg, The Journals of Henry Melchior Muhlenberg. 3 vols. Philadelphia, 1942.*

Nicoll Papers — *Papers of Isaac Nicoll, Washington Museum, Newburgh, N.Y.*

NJA — *Archives of the State of New Jersey. 1st and 2nd Series. Paterson, 1880–*

NJHC — *Barber and Howe, Historical Collections of the State of New Jersey. Newark, 1844.*

NJHSP — *Proceedings of the New Jersey Historical Society.*

NJRC — *Selections from the Correspondence of the Executive of New Jersey from 1776 to 1786. Newark, 1848.*

NYAR — *New York City during the American Revolution. New York, 1861.*

NYG&B — *New York Genealogical and Biographical Magazine.*

NYHS — *New York Historical Society Collections, 1868–*

Onderdonk, Jamaica Church — *Henry Onderdonk, History of the First Reformed Dutch Church of Jamaica, L.I. Jamaica, 1884.*

Ostrander — *W. R. Gordon, The Life of Henry Ostrander, D.D. New York, 1875.*

Paramus Church History — *Manual and Record of the Church of Paramus, 1859. New York, 1859.*

Paramus Classis History — *E. T. Corwin, A History of the Classis of Paramus. New York, 1902.*

Pattison — *Letters of Major General James Pattison, N.Y.H.S. Cols., 1875.*

Paulus Hook Centennial — *George H. Farrier (ed.), Memorial of the Centennial Celebration of the Battle of Paulus Hook. Jersey City, 1879.*

Penn. Arch. — *Pennsylvania Archives. Nine Series. Philadelphia, 1852.*

Pennypacker — *Morton Pennypacker, General Washington's Spies on Long Island and in New York. Brooklyn, 1939.*

Pension Records — *Revolutionary War Pension Records, National Archives, Washington.*

Reed — *W. B. Reed, Life and Correspondence of Joseph Reed. 2 vols. Philadelphia, 1847.*

Remembrancer — *J. Almon, The Remembrancer, or, Impartial Repository of Public Events. 17 vols. London, 1775–1784.*

Richardson, Paulus Hook — *William H. Richardson, Washington and "The Enterprise against Powles Hook." Jersey City, 1938.*

Ridgewood Church History — *First Presbyterian Church, Ridgewood, New Jersey. Ridgewood, 1956.*

Riker, Harlem — *James Riker, Harlem, Its Origin and Early Annals. New York, 1881, 1904.*

Riker, Newtown — *James Riker, The Annals of Newtown. New York, 1852.*

Robertson Diary — *Archibald Robertson, His Diary and Sketches, 1762–1780. New York, 1930.*

Romeyn, Hackensack Church — *Rev. T. B. Romeyn, Historical Discourse delivered on the occasion of the reopening and dedication of the First Reformed (Dutch) Church at Hackensack, N.J. New York, 1870.*

Romeyn Papers NYPL — *Papers of Rev. Dirck Romeyn, New York Public Library.*

Romeyn Papers UCL — *Papers of Rev. Dirck Romeyn, Union College Library.*

Ryerson Papers RUL — *Papers of the Ryerson Family, Rutgers University Library.*

Sabine — *Lorenzo Sabine, Loyalists of the American Revolution. 2 vols. Boston, 1864.*

Sackett Papers — *Papers of Nathaniel Sackett, Washington Museum, Newburgh, N.Y.*

Schoonmaker, History of Kingston — *Marinus Schoonmaker, History of Kingston, New York. Kingston, 1888.*

Schraalenburgh Church Records — *Records of the Reformed Dutch Churches of Hackensack and Schraalenburgh. Part II, Holland Society. New York, 1891.*

Schuyler Papers NYPL — *Papers of Philip Schuyler, New York Public Library.*

Serle Diary — *The American Journal of Ambrose Serle. San Marino, Calif., 1940.*

Shaw Journal — *Josiah Quincy, The Journals of Major Samuel Shaw. Boston, 1847.*

Smith Journal NYPL — *William Smith Journal, New York Public Library.*

St. Clair — *W. H. Smith (ed.), Life and Public Services of Arthur St. Clair. 2 vols.*

Stryker, Battles of Trenton and Princeton — *W. S. Stryker, Battles of Trenton and Princeton. Boston, 1898.*

Stryker, Massacre near Old Tappan — *William S. Stryker, The Massacre near Old Tappan. Trenton, 1882.*

Taylor, Bergen Classis — *B. C. Taylor, Annals of the Classis of Bergen of the Reformed Dutch Church. New York, 1857.*

Thacher — *James Thacher, M.D., The American Revolution. Hartford, 1861.*

Thayer, Greene — *Theodore Thayer, Nathanael Greene. New York, 1960.*

Van Doren, Mutiny in January — *Carl Van Doren, Mutiny in January. New York, 1943.*

Van Doren, Secret History — *Carl Van Doren, Secret History of the American Revolution. New York, 1941.*

Van Norden Genealogy — *T. L. Van Norden, The Van Norden Family. Lancaster, Pa., 1923.*

Varick Court of Inquiry — A. B. Hart (ed.), The Varick Court of Inquiry. Boston, 1907.
Von Closen Journal — E. M. Acomb (ed.), Revolutionary Journal of Baron Ludwig von Closen. Chapel Hill, 1958.
Ward — Christopher Ward, The War of the Revolution. New York, 1952.
Wayne Papers HSP — Papers of Maj. Gen. Anthony Wayne, Historical Society of Pennsylvania.
Webb — W. C. Ford (ed.), Correspondence and Journals of Samuel Blachley Webb. 3 vols. New York, 1893.
Wertenbaker, Father Knickerbocker — T. J. Wertenbaker, Father Knickerbocker Rebels. New York, 1948.
Wertenbaker, Middle Colonies — T. J. Wertenbaker, The Founding of American Civilization, The Middle Colonies. New York, 1938.
Westervelt, Bergen County — Frances A. Westervelt (ed.), History of Bergen County, New Jersey. 4 vols. New York, 1923.
Westervelt Genealogy — Walter T. Westervelt, Genealogy of the Westervelt Family. New York, 1905.
Wilson Papers NJHS — Papers of Peter Wilson, New Jersey Historical Society.
Winfield, Hudson County — C. H. Winfield, History of the County of Hudson, New Jersey. New York, 1874.
Zabriskie Genealogy — Herbert S. Ackerman, Descendants of Albert Zabriskie of 1662. Ridgewood, N.J., 1950.

Index